Pathways to Power

Readings in Contextual Social Work Practice

Edited by

Michael O'Melia

St. Ambrose University

Karla Krogsrud Miley

Black Hawk College

Allyn and Bacon

Boston • London • Toronto • Sydney • Tokyo • Singapore

Series Editor, Social Work and Family Therapy: *Patricia Quinlin*
Editor-in-Chief, Social Sciences: *Karen Hanson*
Series Editorial Assistant: *Annemarie Kennedy*
Marketing Manager: *Brad Parkins*
Editorial-Production Service: *Omegatype Typography, Inc.*
Composition and Prepress Buyer: *Linda Cox*
Manufacturing Buyer: *Suzanne Lareau*
Cover Administrator: *Kristina Mose-Libon*
Electronic Composition: *Omegatype Typography, Inc.*

Library of Congress Cataloging-in-Publication Data

Pathways to power : readings in contextual social work practice / edited by Michael
O'Melia, Karla Krogsrud Miley.
    p. cm.
    Includes bibliographical references and index.
    ISBN 0-205-32314-6 (alk. paper)
    1. Social service.   2. Social service—Citizen participation.   I. O'Melia, Michael   II.
Miley, Karla Krogsrud

  HV40 .P315 2002
  361.3—dc21

                                        2001035410

Printed in the United States of America

10 9 8 7 6 5 4 3 2 1   06 05 04 03 02 01

Contents

Preface

These readings offer critical perspectives and practice applications to define and illustrate an empowerment method of social work. The organizing theme, pathways to power, focuses on how people acquire and maintain power. Exploring these issues broadens our perspectives beyond traditional social work practice to include empowerment-based methods that emphasize social justice, environmental contexts, strengths, collaborative partnerships with clients and others, and the realization of affirming organizations and communities.

The authors of each chapter speak directly with us to present their concepts, reflections, and practice examples representing work in a multiplicity of settings and with diverse population groups. Their voices, whether telling personal stories or conveying professional experiences, are compelling; they draw us into the material and help us understand the context from which their view of social work practice evolves. The questions they pose in "Continuing the Conversation," a section concluding each chapter, engage us in a reflective dialogue and invite us to consider the implications of their work for our professional practices and our lives.

The opening chapter articulates an empowerment method of practice and traces how people gain power through various changes initiated on a continuum of micro- to macrolevel interventions. Other chapters address key theoretical perspectives, emphasizing contextual social work, social justice, multicultural competence, and social constructionism. Practice methods exemplifying the empowerment social work method include policy practice, community action research, self-directed group work, grassroots community change, organizational redevelopment, community collaboration, and strengths-based practice. Practice illustrations feature empowerment-based activities with people who are homeless and those with disabilities; in various fields of practice such as child welfare, aging, substance abuse, and mental health services; in community development; and by gays, lesbians, and their allies in creating an affirming community. Contributing authors represent a diverse group of practitioners in the United States and Canada.

Plan of the Book

Chapter 1, "From Person to Context: The Evolution of an Empowering Practice," traces the transformation of a clinical social worker from a person-centered practice to the more integrated approach that characterizes an empowerment method. Michael O'Melia's practice reflections illustrate his developing awareness as a family counselor who finds his best work stifled in an oppressive environment, and who subsequently shifts his attention and energy to intervening in larger systems. O'Melia concludes by discussing six key dimensions of an empowerment method, including collaboration, a strengths orientation, a focus on context in understanding problems and planning change, alliances among stakeholders, client activism in defining services, and the synchronization of simultaneous strategies at many system levels.

In keeping with this integrated focus, Chapter 2, "Contextual Social Work Practice," written by Susan Kemp, James Whittaker, and Elizabeth Tracy, examines the role of environmental contexts in empowerment. They indicate that "the empowerment paradigm emphasizes the importance of external circumstances and conditions in client concerns" (p. 71). For them, opportunities and constraints are imbedded within the multiple dimensions of our environmental contexts, including the physical, social/interactional, institutional/organizational, and cultural/sociopolitical environments, as well as within our individual and collective constructions of meaning. Kemp, Whittaker, and Tracy explore the implications for social work practice through their discussion of contextual assessment and contextual intervention. They challenge us to move beyond an individual perspective to join with others in creating environments that are more equitable and empowering.

Empowering environments for all are available only in a context of social justice—a condition that exists in the abstract, a dream that has proven elusive in our climate of modern life. But is social injustice a given, based on the competitive and divisive nature of human relations? David Gil says no, and in Chapter 3, "Challenging Injustice and Oppression," he clarifies the meanings of injustice and oppression, traces their sources and history, and examines their consequences for various social institutions. Gil draws on a history of human interactions in society to illustrate that social justice is an attainable ideal undermined only by choices over time, choices that we could make differently if we intend to create a just society. Gil asserts that critical consciousness is the key to fundamental social change, and he suggests strategies for expanding critical consciousness to transform conventional interest-group politics into, what he calls, the "politics of common human needs"—politics that change individual behaviors and lead to institutional and social change.

Social work practice is inherently political. Even micropractitioners make choices that reflect political influences and perpetuate political realities. In Chapter 4, "Ethical and Inescapable: Politicized Social Work," Pamela Long exposes the political nature of practice and traces a path to a practice stance that is openly political. Drawing on her experiences in the fields of mental health and school social work, Long illustrates issues of power and politics in direct practice. She asserts that "practicing ethical social work means attending to power and political issues at every system level and intervening in ways to promote social justice and to ensure full client self-determination" (p. 57). Finally, challenging us to politicize our practice, Long details strategies leading to organizational, policy, and social change.

In Chapter 5, "Community Action Research," Marge Reitsma-Street and Leslie Brown push the boundaries of political practice further into the arena of research. They describe methods and applications of community action research (CAR), an empowerment-based model that brings communities together to design and implement their own research agendas. In concert with community organizing and other social justice initiatives, they contend that CAR works "towards a more just distribution of the resources needed for adequate lifeworlds for all citizens in a community" (p. 77). Reitsma-Street and Brown draw upon their experiences in facilitating CAR with people at the margins of society—with an Aboriginal reserve community in British Columbia and with people living on low incomes in marginalized urban communities in northern Ontario—to illustrate the values and processes integral to CAR.

Nowhere is the constructionist notion that people experience varying social realities more evident than in the study of human culture. Each human being is a unique configuration and blend of cultural influences. The social worker–client encounter has multicultural features; actions taken should reflect respect for the various cultural perspectives. In Chapter 6, "Cultural Competence: A Requirement for Empowerment Practice," Salome Raheim asserts that multicultural competence is an essential requisite for empowerment practice with people who are vulnerable, stigmatized, and marginalized. She further contends that "without specific cultural knowledge, skills, and attitudes, empowerment practice in cross-cultural situations may be ineffective at best, and harmful, at worst" (pp. 95–96). In this chapter, Raheim strategically applies the principles of cultural competence to social work practice to explicate what she calls culturally competent empowerment practice.

Tania Alameda-Lawson and Michael Lawson underscore the power of communities acting in groups in Chapter 7, "Building Community Collaboratives." They draw on their practice experiences, contrasting those "that have failed to capture the imagination, attention, and aspirations of professionals, residents, and clients alike" with other community "collaboratives that have helped to transform the way that professionals, residents, and clients view themselves, each other, and their communities" (p. 111). Reminiscent of grassroots organizing efforts, they describe methods to build community collaboratives—groups of citizens acting on their own behalf to resolve challenges in ways that fit their own unique circumstances. Alameda-Lawson and Lawson assert that community collaboratives can be powerful catalysts for stimulating community-based change.

In Chapter 8, "Creating an Affirming Community," Steve Stickle and Kim Gibson tell the story of Quad Citians Affirming Diversity (QCAD), a group effort to create a community that celebrates human diversity and supports its gay, lesbian, bisexual, and transgender community members. Focused on institutional rather than individual change, QCAD exemplifies a philosophy that an affirming environment is the key element in sustaining personal well-being. In this chapter, Stickle and Gibson trace the development of QCAD from its inception as a coalition of volunteers to its current status as an influential community organization, describing its philosophy and programmatic elements to serve as a model for grassroots initiatives in other communities.

In Chapter 9, "Pushing the Boundaries in Empowerment-Oriented Social Work Practice," Marcia Cohen continues to build the case that a responsive context is essential for sustaining empowerment. She explores some of the critical issues faced by social workers integrating empowerment principles into their day-to-day practice and examines the structural limitations imposed by inequalities. Highlighting the voices of workers and clients, Cohen emphasizes that to implement an empowerment-based practice, workers need agency support and clients need a voice in agency practices. She explicates ways to create organizational change and to involve clients in self-directed group work.

By example, Kathy Weiman, Carolyn Dosland-Hasenmiller, and Jane O'Melia demonstrate the positive effect that amplifying the voices of clients and staff can have. In Chapter 10, "Shutting Off That Damn Bell: Raising the Voices Within," they show the value of empowering practices with clients facing obstacles created by developmental disabilities. Their commitment to honoring the voices of those with whom they work is evident, as is their facility for creativity and innovation. They describe their journey from fixing, to translating, to connecting with program participants and detail their training approach to organizational change. Although Weiman, Dosland-Hasenmiller, and O'Melia caution against replicating their model, the principle that underlies their work, creating "a learning community in which all members have voice and privilege" (p. 173), has broad applications to other organizations.

Constructing a new context is not only possible in the realm of human interaction, but, as the postmodern movement declares, it is the context of "meaning" that makes the difference. The ways we define our lives and the actions of others construct the reality of our worlds. Gil Greene and Mo-Yee Lee survey this postmodern vision through their discussion of social construction. Chapter 11, "The Social Construction of Empowerment," presents their postmodern view of social constructivism and explains its application to empowerment practice through solution-focused and narrative methods.

Rowena Fong continues the conversation in Chapter 12, "Empowering Multicultural Clients by Using Cultural Values and Biculturalization of Interventions." Fong draws on a wealth of multicultural examples of working with people from Asia, Southeast Asia, Hawaii, and Eastern Europe to illustrate empowerment-oriented bicultural interventions in such fields of practice as substance abuse and child welfare. She challenges us to assess our own work with people of color by applying a series of questions to evaluate the competence of our multicultural practice.

Even the most vulnerable people benefit from their genuine participation in social work processes. In Chapter 13, "Empowering Mental Health Consumers: Assessing the Efficacy of a Partnership Model of Case Management," Wes Shera articulates a Partnership Model of case management for collaborating with persons with mental illness. Shera presents findings from his research on this model and discusses the implications of this research for individualizing, personalizing, and contextualizing empowerment practice with this vulnerable population. He also highlights the primary importance of organizational structures that support working in partnerships with others.

Finally, in Chapter 14, "Unacknowledged Resources of Aging: Empowerment for Older Adults," Karla Miley reflects on practice with older adults within a conceptual framework that highlights such facets of empowerment as telling life stories, promoting expertise, and honoring self-determination. Drawing on her own family's experience, as well as her professional work in a variety of practice settings, Miley presents a series of vignettes that illustrate ways to promote resiliency in dealing with the physical and cognitive frailties experienced by some older adults and to discover the unacknowledged resources of aging.

As these authors' stories indicate, an empowerment-based practice is a versatile one. The empowerment method is rooted in the social justice mission of the social work profession, targeted at individuals and the institutions that confine them, and directed toward a vision of self-determination and promise. There are many pathways to power in social work practice, and the contributors to this volume articulate many of these routes. The result is a road map directing social work practitioners and clients toward a sustainable position of individual well-being, community participation, resource availability, and citizen rights.

Acknowledgments

We are thankful for the encouragement and support offered by our friends and families, especially Jane and David! We appreciate the research and technical assistance of Rita Baugh, whose expertise and attention to detail was incredibly helpful to us in preparing the manuscript. We are deeply indebted to our colleagues from the United States and Canada, whose contributions and commitment to this project exceeded our expectations. They have helped to make our plans for *Pathways to Power* a reality. Finally, we value the direction and support provided by the staff at Allyn and Bacon—Karen Hanson, Patricia Quinlin, Alyssa Pratt, and the many others who work behind the scenes on all of the production and marketing details.

About the Contributors

Tania Alameda-Lawson, M.S.W., is assistant professor in the Division of Social Work at California State University, Sacramento, and a doctoral candidate at Florida International University. Alameda-Lawson has more than a decade's worth of practice and research experience in low-income communities and is a leading expert on bottom-up, family-guided systems reform.

Leslie Brown, Ph.D., is an associate professor in the School of Social Work at the University of Victoria, Canada. She is also a core instructor in the Masters of Indigenous Governance Program. Her scholarly and practice interests include Aboriginal governance issues, research education, and anti-oppressive social work practice.

Marcia B. Cohen, Ph.D., is professor of social work at the University of New England in Biddeford, Maine. She has taught generalist practice, group work, and social welfare policy. Her practice background includes case management and group work with homeless and other very poor people. Cohen's publications emphasize issues of homelessness, client/worker relationships, and practice with groups.

Carolyn Dosland-Hasenmiller, B.S.W., is a licensed social worker for the state of Illinois. As Training Director for the ARC of Rock Island County, Dosland-Hasenmiller has developed and implemented specialized agency training curricula. She has held previous human service and management positions, accumulating more than twenty years of social work experience.

Rowena Fong, Ed.D., an associate professor of social work at the University of Hawaii, received her M.S.W. at the University of California, Berkeley, and Ed.D. at Harvard University. Coauthor of *Culturally Competent Practice: Skills, Interventions, and Evaluation* (Allyn & Bacon, 2001), Fong has written, consulted, and done research in the areas of child welfare, Chinese children and families, and culturally competent practice.

Kim Gibson, B.A. psychology at State University of New York at Oswego, began community organizing in the violence against women movement in 1983, turning her attention to creating a more affirming environment for GLBT people in 1991. As a member of the board of directors of Quad Citians Affirming Diversity, she works on program expansion, in-service and workshop training, and administrative development.

David Gil, Ph.D., a native of Vienna, Austria, is professor of social policy and director of the Center for Social Change, Heller School, Brandeis University. Before coming to Brandeis in 1964, he was involved in social work practice, research, and administration in the United States and Israel, and he worked on farms in Sweden and Israel, where he also lived in kibbutz settlements. His teaching, research, practice, and political activism are concerned with understanding and overcoming forces that obstruct human development, liberation, cooperation, and social quality. Gil has served as cochair of the Socialist Party, USA, from 1995 to 1999. His writings include: *Violence Against Children, Unravelling Social Policy, The Challenge of Social Equality, Beyond the Jungle,* and *Confronting Injustice and Oppression.*

Gilbert J. Greene, Ph.D., LISW, ACSW, is a professor and chair of the clinical concentration at The Ohio State University, College of Social Work, and a clinical member of the American Association for Marital and Family Therapy.

Susan P. Kemp, Ph.D., is associate professor of social work at the University of Washington, Seattle. A New Zealander, she had extensive experience in that country in community-based social work practice with vulnerable children and families. In doctoral work at the Columbia University School of Social Work, she explored the idea of the environment in American social work practice theory. She currently teaches social work practice with children, youth, and families, and doctoral-level courses in social work history and theory. In her research and writing, Kemp continues to work on the environmental dimensions of direct social work practice.

Michael Lawson, M.S., is assistant director of Communities in Schools of Sacramento, Inc. With a background in family studies, Lawson's work has focused on the development of family and collaborative engagement strategies in ethnically concentrated, disenfranchised communities.

Mo-Yee Lee, Ph.D., LCSW, is an associate professor at The Ohio State University, College of Social Work. She specializes in solution-focused brief therapy and multicultural social work in her clinical practice, research, and scholarly work.

Pamela Long, M.S.W., is assistant professor of social work at St. Ambrose University. She received her master's degree in social work from Syracuse University, Syracuse, New York. Prior to teaching, Long practiced and consulted in a variety of settings, including child welfare, mental health, health, and public school social work.

Karla Krogsrud Miley, A.M., ACSW, is a professor at Black Hawk College in Moline, Illinois, teaching life-span psychology, marriage and family, and introductory social work. A graduate of the University of Chicago, School of Social Service Administration, Miley has experience in a variety of fields of practice, including school social work and aging services. She is coauthor of *Social Work: An Empowering Profession* (4th ed.) with Brenda DuBois and *Generalist Social Work Practice: An Empowering Approach* (3rd ed.) with Michael O'Melia and Brenda DuBois.

Jane O'Melia, J.D., is the associate executive director at the ARC of Rock Island County. She is responsible for an array of habilitation services for individuals with mental retardation. O'Melia is the recipient of the 2000 NISH Assistive Technology award for her efforts to promote employment of persons with severe disabilities.

Michael O'Melia, M.S.W., is an associate professor of social work at St. Ambrose University in Davenport, Iowa. Specializing in teaching empowerment strategies for family-centered, group, and generalist practice, O'Melia is a licensed clinical social worker with 25 years of experience in family therapy, community consultation, and program development. He is coauthor of *Generalist Social Work Practice: An Empowering Approach* (3rd ed.), also published by Allyn and Bacon.

Salome Raheim, Ph.D., is director and associate professor at the University of Iowa School of Social Work. Her research focus is economic empowerment with low-income individuals, particularly women. Her graduate and undergraduate teaching focus is social work's response to oppression. She conducts individual and organizational cultural competence workshops for human service and educational institutions.

Marge Reitsma-Street, Ph.D., is a professor in the graduate program of Studies in Policy and Practice in the Health and Social Services at the University of Victoria, British Columbia. Research and practice interests center on action research, poverty, housing, juvenile justice, and community development. Her publications include *Changing Lives: Women in Northern Ontario, Poverty and Inequality in the Capital Region of BC,* and *Housing Policy Options for Women Living in Urban Poverty.*

Wes Shera, Ph.D., is the dean of the Faculty of Social Work, University of Toronto. Mental health, community development, social policy, evaluation research, and multicultural and international social work have been the major areas of Shera's research and publications. More recently his work has focused on operationalizing and testing concepts of empowerment with individuals and communities.

Steve Stickle, M.A., has a degree in sociology from Stanford University. He is currently the executive director of Quad Citians Affirming Diversity, responsible for administration, public relations, grant writing, and program development. He is a lifelong advocate for the full inclusion and affirmation of GLBT people in community life.

Elizabeth M. Tracy, Ph.D., is associate professor at the Mandel School of Applied Social Sciences, Case Western Reserve University, where she teaches courses in direct social work practice methods, home-based family intervention, school social work, and child welfare. Tracy is particularly interested in social work models that support families and strengthen natural helping networks.

Kathy Weiman, B.A., is the director of team services for the ARC of Rock Island County. She has spent the past fifteen years learning from individuals with developmental disabilities how to design services. Weiman actively promotes individualized services, most notably communication and assistive technology, throughout the ARC.

James K. Whittaker, Ph.D., is professor of social work at the University of Washington, Seattle, and cochair of the Center for Policy and Practice Development at Boysville of Michigan. He has a lifelong interest in the intersection of professional helping and informal support systems, and he has written widely on this issue. Whittaker teaches classes in child and family policy and direct social work practice.

1

From Person to Context: The Evolution of an Empowering Practice

Michael O'Melia

Experienced practitioners will tell you just how much they have learned from their clients—lessons about listening and respect, examples of resilience and survival. And when you question these workers further, they can likely identify key client "mentors" who stand out. I remember Jacob. From the first time he sat in my office and unloaded the entire contents of his squirt gun on me (it had a plastic hose connected to a gallon reserve!) until my last letter from him written while in placement at a residential facility for adjudicated delinquents, he tested and honed my ability to accept, to empathize, and to collaborate. It was very early in my career. I hadn't heard of empowerment, but I had experienced the progress of my adolescent clients when they began to feel good about themselves, and I had observed their families improve as they learned to listen and respect each other.

I had made the move to the system, recognizing that the behavior of clients in my delinquency prevention agency could only shift if space were created by complementary changes in the people and situations around them. I had redefined myself from youth counselor to family counselor and was beginning to work with school and law enforcement systems as an advocate for my young clients. It was a natural evolution that my clients had stimulated. Jacob arrived in my office as a result of my newly forged connection with his school guidance counselor. The referral conversation on the phone began with the counselor's words, "I have an interesting one for you."

Jacob was in serious trouble, headed for juvenile court. He had been seen by several helping professionals and there had been no progress. The list of referral reasons was extensive, including truancy, disruptive behaviors at school, violent outbursts at home, shoplifting, and vandalism. The last reason—probably sociopathic—reflected a popular label of that time and set an expectation and acceptance of the likely failure of the work we were to begin.

I worked with Jacob for nearly two years. During that time, Jacob's self-esteem improved. He especially began to recognize his academic strengths and creativity, a resource to him as he navigated the various educational placements that his continuing school difficulties precipitated. The functioning of his family became more harmonious, with only occasional conflicts like those that had marked the past. Over time, Jacob learned to be more in control and expressed confidence in himself. He was mainstreamed back to regular classes. His family had learned to listen to and negotiate more respectfully with him, and he reciprocated. We had accomplished our goals, so we wrapped up our work. It was only a couple of months later when the school break-in occurred that led to the court hearing and subsequent residential placement. Jacob had been adjudicated delinquent, categorized among the agency's "4 percent failures," clients we were unable to divert from the courts.

Since that time I've thought a lot about my work with Jacob. I now recognize things that I did right and places where my work fell short. I had guided Jacob to experience his personal and interpersonal power, but I had abandoned him in a broader context that was not ready for his change. I had done empowering work at the individual and family level, but I had neglected a context that inhibited, and ultimately overwhelmed, Jacob's positive changes. In thinking about Jacob, I began to formulate my ideas about a more contextualized or generalist practice involving work with larger systems.

How People Acquire Power

Jacob stretched the boundaries of my practice. He directed me beyond my defined practice specialty, revealed to me the limits of my practice theory, and led me to question the prescriptive practices within the agency setting. He helped me acknowledge the necessity for social and environmental change to accommodate and sustain the momentum he could achieve at the personal level. Jacob also taught me a lot about the various ways that people gain and lose power. I saw how even a carefully chosen word or the most incremental achievement can spark a spiraling improvement in a client's sense of value and feelings of control. I observed how mutual respect among family and friends reinforces and perpetuates individual well-being. Yet, Jacob also demonstrated to me how the experience of power is fleeting unless supported by changes in social and institutional contexts.

An empowerment-based practice is an integrated approach, building avenues for clients to access power resources within themselves, their families, and their social contexts. The worker's task is one of emancipation, creating opportunities for significant participation in community and thereby freeing clients to experience themselves differently and act in new ways.

Exploring and Reconstructing Perspectives

Experience is not set in stone. "The terms by which we understand our world and our self are neither required nor demanded by 'what there is' " (Gergen, 1999, p. 47). Rather, our understanding of the world flows from our own unique filtering of events. And, our personal belief systems are strongly influenced by the belief systems of others around us and by the social institutions that embed dominant social and political views. "Social institutions are human creations; personal identity may change from context to context; and all beliefs are just that—beliefs" (Franklin, 1998, p. 59). This fluidity of personal experience is fertile ground for social work intervention to generate new feelings of esteem, power, and influence.

These ideas about how we construct our understanding of the world are currently described in the postmodern views of constructivism and social constructionism. Constructivism emphasizes the psychological realm, focusing "on how people make meaning in their lives through their perceptions, the operation of their cognitive and affective processes, and the mechanics of memory storage and retrieval" (Brower, 1998, p. 205). Social constructionism looks within the social and cultural milieu toward understandings rooted in language, cultural beliefs, social interaction, and institutional behavior (Gergen, 1994). Together these theories emphasize that how we interpret, remember, and describe events sets parameters in our perceptions of ourselves and our situations. When we examine, reflect on, and re-language our experience, our perceptions shift. When we question assumed meanings imposed on us by others, we generate new possibilities for action.

I observed such perceptual shifts and subsequent behavioral changes occur gradually in Jacob. Initially, each conversation with Jacob was a debate. He challenged everything I said. He was curious about what I thought about things and why I thought them, and then he would tell me what was wrong with my thinking. His ability to disagree was phenomenal, and the strength of his arguments was impressive. I couldn't help but compliment him on his critical view and analytic ability. Drawing on his ability to analyze, Jacob and I carefully examined the events in his life and what they meant to him. Helping him see the positive possibilities in his interactions with others, we framed his argumentative stance as thought provoking and hailed his resistance to influence by others as rational caution that should certainly come in handy dealing with the intense peer pressure in adolescence. Simultaneously, we worked to broaden the perceptions of others around him, specifically his parents and school officials, to experience Jacob the way I did—to see genius in his resistance to the norm and to appreciate his creativity as he completed required tasks in his own way.

As go perceptions, so go behavior and interaction. Jacob's new appreciation of self and increasing acceptance by others led to other positive changes. I've seen such shifts occur in other clients. A person with a developmental disability who overheard her drawings described as "works of genius" experienced a revolution in self-concept. A survivor of sexual abuse began to see her own potential differently after hearing stories of triumph from other survivors. An adolescent who reflected in her diary that her parents' controlling behaviors were "probably just because they love her" began to reexperience her interactions with them. Change in meaning reorients the view and maps a new course for interaction.

Developing Skills and Abilities

Acquiring personal and political skills are concrete steps toward empowerment (Raheim, 1997; Ziefert & Brown, 1991). Social policy aimed toward self-sufficiency hatches programs focused on job training, decision-making, and other types of skill development (Fong, 1998; Maynard, 1995; Stoner, 1999). On the front lines, workers help clients develop capabilities in communication, conflict resolution, and social activism (Williams, Ward, & Davis, 1998). Increased abilities to meet one's own needs coupled with skills to influence others often lead to feelings of competence and sometimes stir actions to confront oppressive environments.

A strengths orientation is an essential backdrop for skill development. Jacob responded best when I collaborated with him to discover what worked and how it might be useful, rather than to identify what was wrong and needed to be changed. He was obviously talented. His analytic mind, quick wit, and challenging disposition—characteristics previously defined as problems by family members and people at school—were readily available resources in the search for a way out of his difficult situations. Jacob could incorporate new information quickly, reconstitute his view immediately, and change direction in an interaction at any moment. (Sounds like the makings of a good social worker, politician, or college professor to me!) I dared Jacob to expand the range of choices he made in dealing with people. I taught him conflict resolution as a way to stay on top of any situation. I focused his quick assessment skills on people and his problems with them, and we worked as colleagues to analyze and rearrange his world.

Bolstered by new skills, Jacob experienced an increase in his social comfort and feelings of control in most situations. I learned how a social worker's focus on developing client skills and abilities is an important aspect of a practice focused on increasing a client's experience of power.

Setting and Achieving Goals

The ability to define what we want and to organize our lives in a way to get it defines us as competent. Even when steps are small, each successful step builds momentum to master the next. The success of our actions shapes the beliefs that we hold about ourselves and our abilities to achieve. Our experience of success and validation leads us to construct beliefs that we are in control. Goal setting and achievement is a direct path toward the experience of confidence and power (Letendre, 1999).

The goals Jacob and I set were incremental. We took steps toward school attendance and academic success, family harmony, and personal development. When we hit obstacles on one path, we switched to another, discovering that progress in one area energized our attempts in others. Contemporary practice approaches focused on developing solutions emphasize the empowering impact of incremental success (de Shazer, 1985; DeJong & Berg, 1998; Furman & Aloha, 1992; Walter & Peller, 1992).

Visible, concrete accomplishments shift feelings of helplessness toward feelings of hope and cultivate confidence to take more steps.

Building Reciprocity in Relationships

In keeping with my "move" to the system, I also focused on how Jacob related to others. I felt that I did my best work with the family relationships in Jacob's case. I operated from a structural/strategic perspective, attending carefully to issues of power and closeness in the family (Haley, 1976; Minuchin & Fishman, 1981, Watzlawick, Weakland, & Fisch, 1974). I worked toward an ideal structure, one in which parents worked together as family leaders and allotted power and privilege to children at differential rates to fit their abilities and development. I believed a family worked best when each person experienced the love and support of other members, yet each had freedom to define an individual self with unique qualities and views.

In family meetings, we focused on giving each member a chance to talk and be heard. I encouraged participation, responded to clarify situations and options, and identified how each member could contribute to the well-being of the family. Our motto became "you have to give to get." To act on this creed, all family members learned to assert what they wanted and to recognize their roles as resources in working toward other family members' goals. In a structural/strategic family approach, the marital dyad is seen as the foundation of a healthily functioning family. Separate meetings with Jacob's parents worked to reinforce their bonds as a couple and to increase their ability to give and take within their own relationship. As the mutual-support systems within the family strengthened, things got better.

The family didn't always act harmoniously in response to our efforts. Yet all family members did learn the benefits of working together, and they developed skills to collaborate for mutual benefit. Reciprocity in relationships is central to sustaining a client's access to power. Even temporary setbacks in feelings of esteem and control at the personal level can by assuaged by continuing rewards in interpersonal interactions. Validation and voice in family relationships, equity in social relationships, and alliances with those perceived to be powerful act as power generators to refuel reserves at the personal level. Generative interpersonal interaction also creates energy to address larger issues within social and political environments.

Participating in Community

Beyond family relationships, Jacob functioned as a citizen in a larger community, and my work toward reciprocity in relationships extended into this realm. People "are empowered because the result of their interactions with the environment has been a gain in access and control of resources" (Rappaport, Reischl, & Zimmerman, 1992, p. 86). I did my best to link Jacob and his family with formal community supports, such as recreational and summer job opportunities. Jacob went to the YMCA and participated in swimming classes. He joined a swimming team and contributed to the team's success.

In empowerment practice, access to environmental resources (Kemp, Whittaker, & Tracy, 1997) and quality of participation in community (Le Bosse et al., 1999) are seen as keys to client power. This theme of community inclusion is exemplified in the disability movement (Mackelprang & Salsgiver, 1996) and legally articulated in the Americans with Disabilities Act of 1990. As citizens, we all merit access to community resources to exercise our rights and privileges. When we benefit from and contribute to the community resource pool, we experience our value and receive the recognition of others.

Allying with Others in Similar Situations

Ongoing validation by those who share our views may be essential to sustain an experience of power. On reflection, I believe it is here that the fabric of my work with Jacob began to unravel. Jacob intermittently complained that he was a member of an oppressed group: adopted children. I said "sure," as I pointed out the middle-class advantages that surrounded him at home. Consistent with my strategic theory base, I naively viewed his complaints as symptoms of the system and worked to make them go away. I believed the frequent mention of adoption gave Jacob opportunities to distance himself from the parents that he often described as "those people I live with." I guided the family away from these discussions. My theoretical orientation overrode my client centeredness. When Jacob broached the topic of adoption, I guided the focus another way.

Skirting the issue of adoption also stifled speculation about Jacob's heritage. His dark skin and black hair contrasted sharply with the blond hair and blue eyes of both his parents and his adopted sister. In my first meeting with Jacob, I wondered whether he was Native American, African American, Latino, or some blend. I was later surprised to see his race listed as White within the referral information.

Never did I fully explore how either of these self-definitions played out in Jacob's life. Not once did I look to the community to determine whether adoption support groups were available. Delinquency prevention, not adoption, was the focus of the agency's work, and family counseling, not group work, was our theory and method of choice—a "one size fits all" approach. It never occurred to me to talk with coworkers to see whether a wider need among agency clientele for adoption support existed. Only since then have I learned how helpful groups can be in coping with some of the ambiguities of adoption.

Likewise, I avoided exploring the unspoken concern about race. I rationalized that it was a matter of self-determination. Neither Jacob nor the family had ever brought it up, but it was likely a matter of my own discomfort. I wanted to believe that it didn't matter. They were one family; that was a fact. However, in a social context in which race matters, race likely matters in families too.

I see now the benefits that might have accrued for Jacob within the context of a group. Groups are primary vehicles for an empowerment method of practice (Breton, 1994; Gutiérrez, 1994; Lee, 2001; Mullender & Ward, 1991). Alliances with others in similar situations stimulate awareness and lead to a critical consciousness—the linking of personal experiences with social issues. Experiencing solidarity in a group of people with common concerns can "encourage critical appraisals of the world and give support for analysis of the relationship between a new worldview and new concepts of self" (Rees, 1991, p. 94). Talking with others who have lived your perspective frequently leads to "externalizing" or relocating the target problem. What was previously perceived as a personal issue is recast into the shared vision of an environmental constraint. The power of alliances with others gives voice to unspoken feelings and unites people in common struggles against privileged views and norms.

Initiating Social and Ideological Change

My narrow focus on Jacob's personal and interpersonal attributes obscured my views of Jacob as a member of the larger community. I failed to apply an anti-oppressive perspective. "From an anti-oppressive perspective, a concentration upon personality, emotions, and individual motivation can be dangerously misleading, with the risk of the 'real' issues of poverty, gender, and social inequality becoming neglected" (Millar, 1999, p. 26). I never acknowledged who Jacob was in a social-cultural sense. I saw Jacob as an individual in the role of my client, a child in a family, and a student at school. I didn't look to the social context and see the truth of what Jacob was telling me. He was oppressed—adopted, dark skinned in a color-coded culture, behaviorally disordered in a system of educational classification and exclusion. If I had listened to the "felt" experience of Jacob and recognized who he was on the outside in full view of the world, maybe I would have looked more outside of him and his family for ways to help. I tacitly accepted the biases that oppressed Jacob each day.

Achieving a just society would mean many changes from current social, economic, political, and environmental conditions. Gender and racial equality, multicultural acceptance, the celebration of alternative lifestyles, and appreciation for the contributions of old and young and the differentially abled—each would be required to actualize social justice. Imagine working in such a just context. New options emerge. The issue of Jacob's heritage would have been intriguing to explore, rather than a taboo subject too hot to address.

Changing Institutions

Accepting the social and cultural status quo was not the only way I simply maintained the system. Contrary to an empowerment perspective, I believed the institutions affecting Jacob were immovable objects to work around and irresistible forces that demanded adaptation. Without any critical awareness or analysis, I had simply accepted the way things were in education, social service delivery, and the wider society. I never confronted a special education system that had labeling, exclusion, and isolation as its core. I failed to challenge my own agency's perspectives and practices, overlooking the resources of my own power within the organization and an agency legacy of innovation and activism. I defined racism and intolerance as beyond the limits of my work, too large for me to address and therefore best to avoid.

Empowerment-oriented social workers cannot escape the reality that their practice is political. "Empowerment is an inherently political idea in which issues of power, the ownership of power, inequalities of power and the acquisition and redistribution of power are central" (Beresford, 1999, p. 259). Connecting personal issues with organizational and political policies and actions remains the distinguishing characteristic of social work (Schneider & Netting, 1999). Efforts toward institutional change define a social worker's practice as ethical. Workers need skills in organizational development, political activism, and action research to affect changes in resource allocation at the agency, state, and national policy levels. "The promise—or the threat—of empowerment lies in its socio-political dimension, its potential to generate collective thought, action and research" (Ramon, 1999, p. 43).

Empowerment as a Practice Method

The example of Jacob teaches much about power. It illustrates how changes accomplished only at the individual and family level, although sometimes necessary and frequently exhilarating, are not sufficient to sustain empowered functioning. Working solely on the aspects of a situation that are readily accessible (individual, family, a few contacts within the immediate environment, such as school in the example of Jacob) defines other larger influences as beyond the sphere of control. That part of the ecosystem deemed inaccessible by social workers is left to clients to handle. Any practice approach centered on power acquisition must recognize and act on the complex nature of power. "Empowerment is not an end product but a dynamic state of continuing acquisition in an atmosphere of reciprocity" (Gutierrez, Parsons, & Cox, 1998, p. 4). Community inclusion and participation, economic privilege, institutional support, social affirmation, and resource access are all required supplements to personal efficacy in creating an enduring experience of power.

Scholars continue to work to articulate an empowerment method of social work practice (Breton, 1994; Gutiérrez, Parsons, & Cox, 1998; Lee, 2001; Miley, O'Melia, & DuBois, 2001). As a method, empowerment directs intervention toward the interplay of individual lives, interpersonal interaction, and social forces. These efforts are not separate. Empowering initiatives at the individual level are supported and sustained only by opening pathways to power sources in social, economic, and institutional structures. Empowering initiatives at the societal level only have benefit when those individuals and groups previously disenfranchised rise up to meet them. "Empowering—the process of empowerment—means recognizing, facilitating, and promoting a system's capacity for competent functioning. Empowering also implies taking actions that respond to the linkages among the personal, interpersonal, and sociopolitical dimensions of empowerment" (Miley, O'Melia, & Dubois, 2001, p. 87).

Dimensions of Empowerment Practice

Key strategies define empowerment-based social work. Actions necessary to implement an empowerment practice method include

- reorienting the way we relate with clients: collaboration, validation, and reconstruction of client experience replace expert diagnosis and treatment

- assuming, locating, developing, and incorporating client strengths and environmental resources into all phases of the practice process from assessment and planning through intervention and evaluation

- widening the scope of our work: operating in partnership *with* clients to change their situations, rather than operating *on* clients to adapt to negative stereotypes and labels, confining policies and service delivery systems, and oppressive conditions

- helping clients to build alliances with others for affirmation, support, consciousness raising, and social activism

- privileging client participation in setting service priorities and designing systems of service delivery: educating clients to work for themselves, and opening pathways for client influence to effect contextual change in social, political, and physical environments

- synchronizing practice activities at multiple system levels to maximize client access to power resources: simultaneously pursuing organizational, community, and societal change, as well as personal and interpersonal growth, regardless of the worker's specialized practice role

The presence of these six elements frames an empowerment-based practice approach that can generate and sustain client power in a continually changing context.

Collaborating

Because the experience of power is supported or inhibited in the context of relationships, empowerment-based workers carefully construct professional relationships with clients. Affirmation and expansion of the client's experience replaces expert intervention or treatment by the worker. Neither worker nor client is expected to solve the situation alone; rather, they are each to contribute to a collaborative process. "Interdependency, rather than autonomy, is a central feature in both individual and collective empowerment" (Ramon, 1999, p. 41).

Madsen (1999) recommends that workers position themselves in the stance of "appreciative ally . . . standing in solidarity with clients as they resist the influence of the problems in their lives" (pp. 15–16). Cohen's (1998) research shows that clients prefer relationships with workers that are either partnerships or mentorships. Both structures assume the central position of the client in any effort. "Empowerment is a reflexive activity, a process capable of being initiated and sustained only by the agent or subject who seeks power or self-determination. Others can only aid and abet in this empowerment process" (Simon, 1990, p. 32).

In empowerment practice, the collaborative character extends beyond the worker–client relationship, also emphasizing professional teaming at other levels, including "worker-to-colleague, worker-to-agency, agency-to-agency, and worker/agency-to-community/society" (Graham & Barter, 1999, p. 6). The power generated through reciprocal alliances resonates through client and worker support systems. The organizational, institutional, and social changes necessary to provide an environment conducive to empowerment require the collaborative power of numbers of people acting in concert.

Incorporating Strengths

Empowerment practice refocuses workers from centering on what causes problems in clients' lives toward examining the constraints that block clients from realizing their goals. This shift in perspective directs workers and clients away from reversing causes per se, because "previous problems are significant only if they interfere with achieving a desired future" (Miley, O'Melia, & DuBois, 2001, p. 149). The emphasis on identifying and removing constraints logically leads clients and workers to muster strengths and resources to fuel the effort—the essence of a strengths orientation. Adopting a strengths-saturated view in practice means "everything you do as a social worker will be predicated, in some way, on helping to discover and embellish, explore and exploit client strengths and resources in the service of assisting them to achieve their goals" (Saleebey, 1997, p. 3).

The strengths orientation is a selective way to look at situations, shifting workers into an advocacy role and away from a detached, neutral stance. Strengths-oriented practitioners accentuate client resources and solutions, believing that what people are doing right is more useful to assess than what they are doing wrong. This emphasis on strengths does not mean that problems are unimportant; instead, it simply questions the utility of a deficit focus in helping people achieve their goals. Building on strengths is the natural path toward success. Simply, it is easier to build on what you have than to create something that you don't have. A strengths orientation is also an essential prelude to worker–client collaboration. Indeed, workers would be foolhardy to partner with clients who appear to have no resources to offer.

A Focus on Context

For decades, the banner of person:environment has defined the social work profession and framed a worker's options for change. The relative emphasis given in practice to the person or to the environment is a significant choice. Any approach centered primarily on individual change cannot escape the presumption that there is something wrong with the individual in the first place. On the other hand, a change targeted toward a person's environment presumes the equally valid explanation that it is the situation, not the person, that is both the source of the problem and the path toward improvement. "This more radical approach to social work seeks to locate the problems experienced by clients in the wider social context of structured inequalities, poverty, inadequate amenities, discrimination, and oppression" (Thompson, 1993, p. 32).

"People's problems can never be fully understood if they are seen as a result of personal inadequacy. Issues of oppression, social policy, the environment and the economy are, more often than not, . . . major contributory forces" (Mullender & Ward, 1991, p. 31). For example, a worker who simply diagnoses and treats a particular client's depression ignores the more pervasive "diagnosis" that poverty is the client's affliction and depression the likely consequence. Defining the problem as internal threatens to immobilize the client further, instead of rallying the client to address the poverty issue.

In contrast, an empowerment approach leads workers to support clients in their struggles to overcome problems, collaborating to change environmental conditions rather than operating within clients toward adaptation or submission.

Individually oriented solutions risk blaming clients for their problems rather than arousing client energy to assume responsibility for change. An empowerment orientation contextualizes the understanding of the problem, shifting attention to the problematic situation and away from individual faultfinding. The worker joins the client in a search through the environment to identify issues and constraints, including those in the economic, institutional, social, and cultural arenas. Problems are constructed as outside forces to struggle against. Locating the problem of focus in the environment is particularly important for working with clients mandated to receive services (Rooney, 1992). Collaboration requires workers and clients to be on the same side, working together to overcome the problem.

Building Alliances with Others

Alliances with others nurture individual feelings of control. Much of our self-esteem and sense of worth come through social affirmation and support. We feel that we have the ability to succeed when we are able to activate others on our behalf. Alliances in groups also address "the inseparability of private troubles and public issues," leading to "consciousness-raising, a crucial component of the process of empowerment and of transformation at the personal level" and to "collective action . . . effecting transformations at the structural/political level" (Breton, 1999, p. 224). Individual motivation is more likely to endure in a supportive atmosphere. "Self-directed action is grounded in the collective strength of people organised together" (Mullender & Ward, 1991, p. 11). Group work offers clients direct opportunities to affiliate with others and to gather tangible resources to initiate change.

Group consciousness lifts personal awareness, connecting individual experience with wider events. In groups, members naturally externalize problems through conversation, as members acknowledge their similar experiences and identify social forces that underlie their individual concerns. Groups provide the "it can't be just me if other people feel the same way" experience. As we share our stories, we learn that our situation is not isolated. We begin to recognize the impact of environmental obstacles that disenfranchise us and others as well. "The proposition is that in the telling of a story, people see themselves in a different light, and from having others listen to their account of their experiences, they build a political analysis and identity" (Rees, 1991, p. 179). Seeing one's personal situation in a sociopolitical context reduces self-blame, stirs energy and indignation, and identifies environmental targets for intervention efforts. The conscientization that occurs redirects attention from internal change to social and political action.

Client Participation in Service Delivery

An empowering organization elevates the participation of clients in defining service priorities and systems of service delivery. A worker's success in sharing power with clients is only achieved in an organizational context that values the client's voice in a very real way. "Empowerment insists on the primacy of the target population's participation in any intervention affecting its welfare" (Swift, 1984, p. xiv). We must tailor service delivery systems to fit the service to the client, rather than force client submission to the existing service structure and approach. An empowerment-based organization mentors client activism through action research methods and organizes agency governance to ensure client representation in all decisions, from individual case collaboration to service delivery planning to agency interaction within the larger community. Empowered clients have significant, ongoing participation in agency decisions, rather than simple expectations of compliance with expert service regimes. Workers take roles to activate and educate clients on how to work for themselves, and workers advocate for system change to create new channels for client influence, rather than simply operating the system on the client's behalf.

Social work practice is political. An empowering organization acknowledges the political nature of practice and develops a clear policy agenda to guide its functioning. An apolitical stance by an organization is no longer an option. Such a position leads not to neutrality but to a lack of coherence in addressing the larger issues affecting direct practice and agency functioning. Empowering agencies need to clearly articulate the social policy, political, and sociocultural dimensions of all issues affecting clients and position themselves to work for policy development and change (Schneider & Netting, 1999). The role of clients in this process is essential. The client-driven organization, already involving clients to frame service delivery, can also use this same structure to define and address wider social and political issues.

Synchronizing Efforts at Multiple System Levels

Power is constantly in flux, always increasing or decreasing. Empowerment is a dynamic "state in which one's perception of self-efficacy and essential value is mirrored in and accentuated by social relationships and the larger environment" (St. Ambrose Self Study, 1998, p. 11). A personal feeling of well-being is fleeting if not reinforced in the larger context. Complementary changes in social structures and relationships are necessary in order to perpetuate power generated at the individual level. An enduring increase in power requires that any power incrementally gained in one domain is quickly echoed and amplified in others. Empowerment is a confluence of the individual, the interpersonal, and the sociopolitical, in which the experience of power in each sphere continually replenishes the others.

To implement an empowerment method requires social workers to structure their activities to reflect the complex nature of power. Effective empowerment practice must use a generalist approach, synchronizing practice activities at multiple system levels for maximum client access to power resources. Individual power is not sustainable in a resource-depleted environment. Personal efforts are fruitful only in a social and political environment that offers inclusion, access, choice, and justice. An empowering approach requires worker role flexibility, active intervention in context, and core practice skills that apply across all levels of practice. It requires multileveled agency functioning that is responsive to evolving client needs and committed to improvement in organizational, community, and societal environments.

Continuing the Conversation

Empowerment practitioners integrate strategies ranging from individual and relationship improvement to resource reallocation accomplished through social and institutional change. Empowerment efforts targeted at the personal level are important, but successes achieved with individuals provide only brief respite if these achievements are not supported by complementary shifts within environmental contexts. Likewise, even broad-based social and political improvements wane if not protected by the continuing influence of empowered individuals, families, and groups. Collaboration with clients, a strengths perspective, a contextual focus in assessment and change, alliances among clients and stakeholders, client privilege to shape service delivery, an agenda of social change, and a generalist intervention strategy are all elements necessary to construct an empowering approach.

The path toward an empowering practice may be illuminated, but the reality of contemporary social work practice falls far short of this ideal vision. How can we move from the pervasive effects of personal stigma and social oppression that result from so many of the models that dominate current practice? What is an individual social worker's role in realizing this hope for a more just and affirming approach? What can you do in your own life and practice to create a society that nurtures rather than impedes, that empowers rather than oppresses, that invites rather than constrains? In the past, we have been taught to look within ourselves for answers to such questions. I suggest a more external focus. Talk with others—your colleagues, your clients, your family, and your friends, as well as the people from whom you are most different, those from whom you have the most to learn. In the spirit of empowerment, maybe we can find our way together.

References

Beresford, P. (1999). Towards an empowering social work practice: Learning from service users and their movements. In W. Shera & L. Wells (Eds.), *Empowerment practice in social work: Developing richer conceptual foundations* (pp. 258–277). Toronto, Canada: Canadian Scholars Press.

Breton, M. (1994). On the meaning of empowerment and empowerment-oriented social work practice. *Social Work with Groups, 17*(3), 23–37.

Breton, M. (1999). Empowerment practice in a postmodern era. In W. Shera & L. Wells (Eds.), *Empowerment practice in social work: Developing richer conceptual foundations* (pp. 222–233). Toronto, Canada: Canadian Scholars Press.

Brower, A. (1998). The constructivism of small groups. In C. Franklin & P. S. Nurius (Eds.), *Constructivism in practice: Methods and challenges* (pp. 203–214). Milwaukee, WI: Families International.

Cohen, M. (1998). Perceptions of power in client/worker relationships. *Families in Society, 79*(4), 433–442.

de Shazar, S. (1985). *Keys to solution in brief therapy.* New York: W. W. Norton.

DeJong, P., & Berg, I. K. (1998). Interviewing for solutions. Pacific Grove, CA: Brooks/Cole.

Fong, L. Y. (1998). Borderland poverty: The case of the Rio Grande Valley at the United States–Mexican border. *Social Development Issues, 20*(3), 107–115.

Franklin, C. (1998). Distinctions between social constructionism and cognitive constructivism. In C. Franklin & P. S. Nurius (Eds.), *Contructivism in practice: Methods and challenges* (pp. 57–94). Milwaukee, WI: Families International.

Furman, B., & Aloha, T. (1992). *Solution talk: Hosting therapeutic conversations.* New York: W. W. Norton.

Gergen, K. (1994). *Realities and relationships: Soundings in social construction.* Cambridge, MA: Harvard University Press.

Gergen, K. J. (1999). *An invitation to social construction.* London: Sage Publications.

Graham, J. R., & Barter, K. (1999). Collaboration: A social work practice method. *Families in Society, 80,* 6–13.

Gutiérrez, L. (1994). Beyond coping: An empowerment perspective on stressful life events. *Journal of Sociology and Social Welfare, 21*(3), 201–219.

Gutiérrez, L. M., Parsons, R. J., & Cox, E. O. (1998). *Empowerment in social work practice: A sourcebook.* Pacific Grove, CA: Brooks Cole.

Haley, J. (1976). *Problem solving therapy.* New York: Harper.

Kemp, S. P., Whittaker, J. K., & Tracy, E. M. (1997). *Person–environment practice: The social ecology of interpersonal helping.* New York: Aldine de Gruyter.

Le Bosse, Y., Lavallee, M., Lacerte, D., Dube, N., Nadeau, J., Porcher, E., & Vandette, L. (1999). Is community participation empirical evidence for psychological empowerment? A distinction between passive and active participation. *Social Work and Social Science Review, 8*(1), 59–82.

Lee, J. A. B. (2001). *The empowerment approach to social work practice* (2nd ed.). New York: Columbia University Press.

Letendre, J. A. (1999). A group empowerment model with alienated, middle class eighth grade boys. *Journal of Child and Adolescent Group Therapy, 9*(3), 113–127.

Mackelprang, R. W., & Salsgiver, R. O. (1996). People with disabilities and social work: Historical and contemporary issues. *Social Work, 41*(1), 7–14.

Madsen, W. C. (1999). *Collaborative therapy with multistressed families: From old problems to new futures.* New York: Guilford Press.

Maynard, R. (1995). Teenage childbearing and welfare reform: Lessons from a decade of demonstration and evaluation research. *Children and Youth Services Review, 17*(1/2), 309–332.

Miley, K. K., O'Melia, M., & DuBois, B. (2001). *Generalist social work practice: An empowering approach* (3rd ed.). Boston: Allyn & Bacon.

Millar, M. (1999). Psychology and anti-oppressive social work: Understanding the complexity of individual lives. *Social Work and Social Sciences Review, 8*(1), 25–41.

Minuchin, S., & Fishman, C. (1981). *Family therapy techniques.* Cambridge, MA: Harvard University Press.

Mullender, A., & Ward, D. (1991). *Self-directed groupwork: Users take action for empowerment.* London: Whiting & Birch.

Raheim, S. (1997). Problems and prospects of self-employment as an economic independence option for welfare recipients, *Social Work 42*(1), 44–53.

Ramon, S. (1999). Collective empowerment: Conceptual and practice issues. In W. Shera & L. Wells (Eds.), *Empowerment practice in social work: Developing richer conceptual foundations* (pp. 38–49). Toronto, Canada: Canadian Scholars Press.

Rappaport, J., Reischl, T. M., & Zimmerman, M. A. (1992). Mutual help mechanisms in the empowerment of former mental patients. In D. Saleebey (Ed.), *The strengths perspective in social work practice* (pp. 84–87). New York: Longman.

Rees, S. (1991). *Achieving power: Practice and policy in social welfare.* North Sydney, Australia: Allen & Unwen.

Rooney, R. H. (1992). *Strategies for work with involuntary clients.* New York: Columbia University Press.

Saleebey, D. (1997). Introduction: Power in the people. In D. Saleebey (Ed.), *The strengths perspective in social work practice* (2nd ed., pp. 3–19). New York: Longman.

Schneider, R. L., & Netting, F. E. (1999). Influencing social policy in a time of devolution: Upholding social work's great tradition. *Social Work, 44*(4), 349–357.

Simon, B. L., (1990). Rethinking empowerment. *Journal of Progressive Human Services, 1,* 27–39.

St. Ambrose University School of Social Work (1998, June). *Self study for council on social work education accreditation.* Davenport, IA: Author.

Stoner, M. R. (1999). Life after foster care: Services and policies for former foster youth. *Journal of Sociology and Social Welfare, 26*(4), 159–175.

Swift, C. (1984). Empowerment: An antidote for folly. *Journal of Prevention in Human Services, 3,* xi–xv.

Thompson, N. (1993). *Anti-discriminatory practice.* London: Macmillan Press.

Walter, J. L., & Peller, J. E. (1992). *Becoming solution-focused in brief therapy.* New York: Brunner/Mazel.

Watzlawick, P., Weakland, J., & Fisch, R. (1974). *Change: Principles of problem formation and problem resolution.* New York: W. W. Norton.

Williams, L. J., Ward, R., & Davis, A. (1998). Welfare "reform": Com'in' up on the rough side of the mountain. *Journal of Sociology and Social Welfare, 25*(1), 153–179.

Ziefert, M., & Brown, K. S. (1991). Skill building for effective intervention with homeless families. *Families in Society, 72,* 212–219.

2

Contextual Social Work Practice

Susan P. Kemp, James K. Whittaker, and Elizabeth M. Tracy

> *[Empowerment] suggests the study of people in context. . . . There is built into the term a quality of the relationship between a person and his or her community, environment, or something outside one's self.*
>
> —(Rappaport, 1987, pp. 121, 130)

I [Susan] am writing this in my home office, which looks out to evergreen trees and a glimpse of the lake. There is a park at the end of our street, with walking trails and wooded places where local kids build hideaways. In the other direction, my children can easily walk or bike to their schools, a complex of sports fields and community playgrounds, and a small shopping center where the cashiers in the supermarket know them by face if not by name. In this relatively safe and self-contained residential neighborhood in the Pacific Northwest, children and their various activities are a major focus of community life. The children my kids go to school with are also on their soccer and tennis and baseball teams, and we meet the same families over and over again in different community settings.

In their primary daily environments—home, school, and neighborhood—children receive countless, multiply reinforced, and enduring messages about themselves, others, and the world around them (Sutton, 1996). These messages—about safety or risk, predictability or randomness, coherence or fragmentation—contribute directly, scholars suggest, to one's sense of self-in-the-world (Antonovsky, 1979; Nurius & Markus, 1991; Proshansky, Fabian, & Kaminoff, 1983). What, then, do my children learn and internalize in the social and physical environments they inhabit every day? By many criteria, this neighborhood is an optimal context for raising children, filled with resources designed to support their development and aspirations, and rich in tangible examples of adult concern for children and their well-being. In this place, children receive clear messages that they are valued and important. Yet embedded in this affirming, nurturing, and asset-filled environment are other, more problematic lessons—about power and privilege, about material success and its preeminent value in American society, about diversity (or lack of it) and difference, about access and opportunity, and about the lines that separate groups and communities. It is telling, furthermore, that in this privileged community children themselves report that they feel attended to but not heard, that they lack voice and opportunities for civic participation and influence, that comfortable homes, leafy streets, and well-equipped schools are not in themselves sufficient foundations for their senses of themselves as full and valued members of the community (University of Washington School of Public Health, 2000).

I compare my own children's environmental experiences to those of the children I worked with in the 1980s in a dilapidated manufacturing city in the urban Northeast. In that city—nearly bankrupt and so lacking in civic amenities that there was no bookstore within the city borders—difficulty and danger shaped the primary environments of childhood. In the large, poorly maintained housing project that was the focus of my work, drug deals and drug-related violence were daily realities. The neighborhood was so dangerous that almost no service providers ventured into the housing project. To discourage suburbanites from making quick journeys off the interstate to buy drugs, many local streets were blocked off with huge concrete barriers. These slowed drug trafficking but further emphasized the sense that this was a community under siege.

In this neighborhood, as in other "urban war zones" (Garbarino, Kostelny, & Dubrow, 1991) in America's inner cities, childhoods are lived in the face of environments that are at best challenging, and at worst toxic, full of random and often dangerous events. With their rundown playgrounds, underfunded schools, and sparse recreational amenities, they are lacking the usual markers of community investment in children and their well-being (Coulton, Korbin, & Su, 1996; Sutton, 1996). On multiple levels, these community environments eloquently convey the social and structural isolation, if not abandonment, of their inhabitants. In such developmental contexts, children learn quickly that they, their families, and their reference community (often, though not always, a community of color) are distanced in myriad ways from the opportunities and rewards of mainstream American society (Coulton & Pandey, 1992; Stanton-Salazar, 1997).

Which is not to say that these neighborhoods are without hope or joy or loving human interactions. Nor that parents and families in these neighborhoods do not nurture their children. To parent well in neighborhoods such as the one I knew in Bridgeport, Connecticut, requires, however, constant vigilance and effort (Halpern, 1995a). Ironically, the diligent efforts of caring parents may themselves compound the threats to positive child development such environments present. Strategies such as keeping children inside, for example, or greatly restricting their environmental activities and range (Brodsky, 1996; Valentine & McKendrick, 1997) limit children's opportunities for experiences that are essential to the development of environmental competence, itself a fundamental building block of sense of self and efficacy (Matthews, 1992; Saegert & Hart, 1978).

My suburban children and their inner city counterparts occupy vastly different environmental niches. These in turn have multiple layers and dimensions, not all of which are self-evident. Sutton (1996) has described the environment as a text that can be read in many different ways and through many different lenses. The environmental experiences of the children in these two communities, for example, can be explored from multiple perspectives. A developmental lens prompts us to consider the extent to which the physical and social environments provide resources for optimal child and family development (Weinstein & David, 1987). A cultural perspective brings to the foreground the environment as a vehicle for cultural symbols, resources, and expectations. From the perspective of social connections, we might consider the ways in which a particular neighborhood functions to support or undermine social networks. Through the lens of social justice, we can consider the ways in which children's everyday environments both mirror and sustain larger patterns of social inequity and privilege.

For social work practitioners, the ability to fully read the environment is an essential component of effective practice. This is so across all practice domains, but it is particularly central to empowering practice.

Environment and Empowerment

Social life is essentially spatial and contextual. Both oppressive and empowering relationships take place within, are constrained or supported by, and indeed may fundamentally reflect the particularities of the environments in which they are situated. The environments of daily life are themselves bearers of social messages and social scripts; they mark the bodies of those who occupy them in particular and differential ways. Social beliefs about people, their rights and responsibilities, and their places in the world are translated into and expressed through spatial arrangements and structures. Relationships of power are thus made concrete and tangible in the material world.

Empowerment practice, therefore, is inherently contextualized (Rappaport, 1987). In contrast to practice models and theories that locate the sources of client issues primarily in clients' personal or interpersonal experiences, the empowerment paradigm emphasizes the importance of external circumstances and conditions in client concerns (Freire, 1973; Parsons, 1991; Riger, 1993; Zimmerman & Rappaport, 1988). Indeed, an explicit focus of empowerment practice is to reduce the focus on person-centered explanations and interventions that is embedded in many dominant helping paradigms.

Primary goals of empowerment practice are for oppressed and marginalized people and communities to have equitable access to resources and services and to be able to resist and change social and physical conditions that adversely affect their quality of life (Gutiérrez & Lewis, 1999). This is an environmental as well as a human agenda: Changes in people's personal and interpersonal resources and aspirations must be supported and reinforced in their external contexts. The environmental dimensions of empowering social work practice include, for example: critical analysis of the relationships between people and their environmental contexts; transformation of perspectives and beliefs about one's social and physical circumstances; and the ability to act differently within one's wider environments, including in relation to oppressive social and environmental conditions. Involvement in environmental action feeds into and supports personal and interpersonal empowerment, and vice versa. People's actions within their everyday environments thus are an important bridge between personal transformation and larger social/environmental change (Gutiérrez, 1990).

Despite the centrality of the environment to empowerment and social justice, the empowerment literature has on the whole been preoccupied with the transformation of perceptions, beliefs, and behaviors at the personal and interpersonal levels (Rappaport, 1987). Such efforts are vital to more socially just social work practice. They are not, however, sufficient in themselves. In empowerment practice, as in social work as a whole, attention should continue to be focused on building a theory of environment sufficient to the task of carrying forward a professional mission that is environmental at its very core.

With this in mind, we map out in this chapter a critical contextual approach that expands current thinking on the environmental dimensions of transformative and empowering social work practice. We begin with a brief overview of the profession's ambivalent history with the idea and reality of the environment, because we believe that a fully developed engagement with the issues of the present requires us also to understand past efforts and challenges. We then draw on a rich interdisciplinary literature to develop a conceptual framework for contextual social work practice grounded in a multidimensional approach to the environment. We close with comments on the implications of this approach for contextual assessment and intervention, and with some thoughts and questions about issues that remain unresolved.

Person-in-Environment: Social Work's Unrealized Commitment

Historically, the social work profession has distinguished itself from other human service professions by its commitment to people in transaction with their surrounding environments. Potentially at least, this dual concern provides the organizing framework for socially just social work practice. The question of how to practice effectively in the environment has long vexed social workers, however, and in reality, full realization of a balanced focus on "person-in-environment" has proved to be elusive. Histories of social work practice show that, in general, people's personal and interpersonal issues have been of primary interest to social work theorists and practitioners (Kemp, 1994; Specht & Courtney, 1994).

Many factors interweave to support this privileging of person over environment in social work theory and practice. Psychological theories and related practice frameworks have strongly influenced social work practice. Personal and interpersonal issues tend to be more compelling and to offer more apparent hope of resolution than larger environmental constraints, and the profession's aspirations have drawn it toward the personal domain (and toward psychology and psychiatry as companion professions). For these and related reasons, personal and interpersonal theories and interventions have dominated the professional landscape, a state of affairs that continues into the present.

Despite this lack of balance, social work has a rich history of environmental practice. The profession's focus on people in context dates from the earliest days of the profession, in the neighborhood-based practice of the late nineteenth-century charity organization societies and the urban settlement houses. In both settings, social workers had firsthand exposure to the everyday lives of their clients in poor urban neighborhoods. The settlement house workers lived in the communities they served, and the friendly visitors and charity agents provided services to families in their homes and neighborhoods. On a day-to-day basis, therefore, both the settlement workers and the caseworkers built up powerful contextual knowledge of the "lived experience" of urban families. Despite obvious differences in approach, both groups were environmentalist in their understanding of and approach to social conditions. In the social settlements, concern about the impact of social and environmental conditions on poor families was connected to a larger program of social activism and legislative advocacy, as well as to efforts at the local level. In the charity organization societies, environmental understandings were incorporated into direct services to needy children and families. In both streams of social work practice, as in the wider society, there was, however, clear awareness of the centrality of environmental and social conditions to personal and family troubles (Boyer, 1978).

In the years after World War I, theories and methods that focused professional attention on personal rather than environmental factors overtook this central focus on the environment, particularly in social casework (direct practice), which then, as now, represented the professional mainstream. In the newly emerging family agencies, mental health clinics, and child guidance agencies, social casework's homegrown expertise appeared simplistic and imprecise against developing knowledge in psychology and psychiatry and in contrast with any of the more prestigious human services professions. The experiences of servicemen and their families in World War I supported a growing interest in mental hygiene and in the psychological well-being of the general population. At the same time, the location of social work practice shifted toward centralized agencies, at a distance from local neighborhoods and the everyday, lived worlds of clients.

These and other factors contributed to the long dominance, throughout the middle years of the last century, of theories and methods in direct practice that were focused on the treatment of individual and family difficulties, using primarily psychological methods. For many years, psychodynamic theory provided the organizing core for theoretical and practice innovation in social work (Hamilton, 1958). The 1960s and 1970s, however, brought strong challenges to social casework's effectiveness (Briar & Miller, 1971). Efforts to promote practice grounded in research evidence and in standardized interventions of proven efficacy contributed to a growing interest in behavioral and cognitive theories and methods (a shift that broadened the profession's theoretical base but maintained the dominance of psychological theories and methods in direct social work practice).

In the 1980s, concerned that the profession was in danger of losing sight of its core commitment to people in context and that social work lacked a unifying theoretical framework, theorists began to incorporate an ecological systems perspective into social work practice theory (Gitterman & Germain, 1976; Meyer, 1983). This holistic perspective enabled social workers to envision the environment more robustly in their practice and research, and it has since informed large bodies of practice literature and research. Limitations in this approach, however, include its lack of specificity for practice (Wakefield, 1996), and its lack of attention to questions of power, diversity, and difference (Gould, 1987), which is of particular relevance to our focus here. More work remains to be done, therefore, to flesh out this generative conceptual framework to better reflect the priorities and perspectives that animate contemporary practice.

New Conceptual Directions: Contextual Social Work Practice

We propose a critical and contextual approach to social work practice that brings into sharper focus the rich and complicated relationships between clients and their surrounding environments, both social and physical. Of central interest in this model, which we have termed *person–environment practice* (Kemp, Whittaker, & Tracy, 1997), are the links between people's current issues and the mosaic of challenges and resources that exist in everyday life contexts. In keeping with social work's historical commitments, we assume that people's troubles and concerns typically have environmental as well as personal dimensions and that careful assessment of contextual as well as personal factors is essential to effective helping. We place renewed emphasis on interventions that actively connect with and mobilize key factors in clients' environmental contexts. This unique social work focus, as Ann Hartman (1978) has pointed out, provides the opportunity for practice that builds capacity in client systems at the same time that it attends to immediate needs and issues of concern. In particular, we see social networks, neighborhoods, and community contexts as critical mediating structures (Berger & Neuhaus, 1977) that can buffer the force of personal and interpersonal difficulties through support, mutual aid, resources, and connection.

A fundamental tenet of our approach is the understanding that the environment is more than simply a static and neutral backdrop for the drama of human life. Physical and social environments are deeply implicated in patterns of social opportunity and constraint, and it is essential that social workers be able to read them in this way. Urban planner Kevin Lynch (1979) has described children's lived environments as "society mapped out on the ground" (p. 105). Sutton (1996, p. 2) likewise points out that everyday environments are profoundly shaped by "the heritage of race and social class," a heritage that is then carried forward and replicated in contemporary environmental inequities and exclusions. Physical and social environments not only reflect the existing social order, but they also are actively involved in the creation and re-creation of social and structural arrangements. Dangerous and physically isolated public housing projects, for example, perpetuate and compound the social difficulties of poor families. Conversely, privileged residential neighborhoods, created and sustained at the expense of less-advantaged communities (Pulido, Sidawi, & Vos, 1996), provide children with ready access to social resources and opportunities (Stanton-Salazar, 1997). Understanding and attending to environments as dynamic social entities, which themselves are deeply implicated in networks of social relations, is an essential element of social work assessments and interventions.

Recent scholarship in the social sciences and humanities provides the basis for a more robust and detailed understanding of everyday environments and their implications for socially just social work practice. Across fields as diverse as architecture, geography, urban studies, anthropology, history, women's studies, and environmental and community psychology, researchers and scholars have begun to explore the diverse and complex relationships between person and place (for overviews of this literature, see Kemp, Whittaker, & Tracy, 1997; McDowell, 1999; Soja, 1989). This body of work adds significantly to our understanding of people's differential experiences within everyday environments, and it raises important questions that social workers would do well to consider in their appraisals of the contexts in which they practice. In the next section, we draw from this literature to develop a more complete view of the environment that also takes into account the analytical frameworks and organizing perspectives of empowerment practice.

Rethinking the Environment for Empowerment Practice

In social work practice, as in life itself, there is a tendency to think of environments primarily in terms of their most obvious, surface, and external characteristics. Assessment questions tend (not surprisingly) to reflect this view of the world: What is the physical condition of a particular home or neighborhood? What amenities are available? What kinds of connections do people who live here seem to have with one another? To answer these questions, social workers are encouraged to use their observational skills, as well as a range of methods that capture and organize information about clients in relation to their larger social and environmental contexts (see, for example, the assessment tools in Mattaini, 1993).

Although valuable, such assessments tend to place social workers in the role of supposedly neutral observers of client environments, which in turn are assumed to be open to external evaluation through their "objective" features and attributes. These dual assumptions—that environments are knowable by external observers and that this knowledge can be ascertained validly by way of their external characteristics—shape a preponderance of the environmental assessment tools and frameworks available to social work practitioners and researchers.

There are several difficulties with this reliance on environmental information that is derived largely from observers' perceptions of an environment's external features. First, even brief reflection on our own experiences in everyday environments tells us that there is more to these environments than appears on the surface. Second, what the observer sees may be very different than the participant's lived experience. Third, the tendency to catalog environments in terms of their external features tends to obscure not only the highly diverse ways in which different people experience the same environment, but also the extent to which environments express social power relationships.

In the framework presented here (see Figure 2.1), we conceptualize environments as having both multiple dimensions and many layers within these dimensions. In addition to those dimensions typically included in environmental typologies (such as the physical environment and the social/interactional environment), we emphasize: (1) the ideological and cultural messages and assumptions embedded and encoded in environmental experience, including the ways in which spatial arrangements reflect and reinforce relations of social power; (2) the meaning, or symbolic significance, of the environment to individuals and groups; and (3) the dialectical relationship between social space and physical space, including the ways in which the environment shapes and is shaped by human experience.

This typology is informed by an ecological systems perspective, which draws attention to the multiple contexts and levels of human development and activity. Bronfenbrenner (1979), a primary architect of contemporary ecological systems thinking, conceptualized the contexts of human life as a series of environments nested, like a set of Russian dolls, one within the other, from the intimate environments of home, family, and friends, to more distal environments, such as social welfare institutions and po-

---

FIGURE 2.1   *Dimensions of Environment*

- Physical environment, both natural and built
- Social/interactional environment
  - Personal social networks
  - Family
  - Group
  - Neighborhood and community
- Institutional/organizational environment
- Sociopolitical and cultural environment
- Environment as constructed in individual and collective systems of meaning and belief

---

Source: From *Person-Environment Practice*, by Susan P. Kemp, James K. Wittaker, and Elizabeth M. Tracy, 1997, (p. 86) New York: Aldine de Gruyter. Copyright 1997 by Aldine de Gruyter. Reprinted with permission.

litical structures. Translated into social work practice, the ecological perspective brings into sharper focus the dynamic interactions between person and environment over time and across settings, and it makes clear that these interactions are reciprocal, that people both shape and are shaped by their environmental contexts (Germain & Gitterman, 1995; Meyer, 1983). Also reflected in our expanded conceptualization of the environment are critical, feminist, and postmodern theories and perspectives, which variously and in combination draw attention to the contextual nature of relations of power, diversity, and difference (for a full discussion of these theoretical influences, see Kemp, Whittaker, & Tracy, 1997).

The Physical Environment, Natural and Built

The physical environment includes the natural world and the human-made, or built, environment (for classic discussions of the salience of the physical environment to social work practice, see Germain, 1978, 1981). Large bodies of research indicate that aspects of the physical world, such as noise, crowding, privacy, or aesthetics, profoundly affect people's experiences of the world and their well-being within it. In a series of recent studies in a troubled public housing project in Chicago, for example, researchers found relationships between the presence of green and habitable outdoor spaces, neighborhood social ties, and residents' senses of safety and adjustment (Kuo, Sullivan, Coley, & Brunson, 1998).

Careful evaluations of the physical environment are an important element of comprehensive environmental assessments (Gutheil, 1992). The physical world is particularly relevant to the many social work clients who face considerable impediments within it, such as persons with mental and physical disabilities, the elderly, children, or clients whose marked identities (as racial minorities, gays, or even women, for example) constrain their free use of both natural and built environments.

The Social/Interactional Environment

In the social/interactional environment we include the range of people's human associations, from the intimate interpersonal environment of the family or personal social networks of extended family and friends, to more distant connections, such as the weak but significant connections (Granovetter, 1973) that come through schooling, employment, or membership in various communities of interest. As with the physical environment, large bodies of empirical and anecdotal evidence underscore the central importance of the social environment, particularly social networks and supports, in the human life course. The social dimensions of the environment, furthermore, interact with physical realities to influence personal and social outcomes. A physically deteriorated neighborhood that nonetheless is rich in social supports, for example, will likely result in different outcomes for residents than one in which physical disorganization combines with social alienation (Moos, 1996). In our own work (Kemp, Whittaker & Tracy, 1997; Tracy & Whittaker, 1990), we have emphasized the importance of social networks as potent sources of support and demand and as a central focus of social work practice.

The Institutional/Organizational Environment

In this domain we include the many institutional and organizational contexts that intersect and interact with people's lives, not always to their benefit. Encompassed here are those organizations with which clients have direct contact (one's own social work agency, for example, or the public welfare office or the local school) and those at a distance from people that nonetheless have important impacts on life opportunities and outcomes. This latter group is encompassed in what Bronfenbrenner (1979) termed the *exosystem:* those settings that from a distance shape and structure the nature and capacities of primary environments. Too often, the impact and involvement of external systems, both proximal and distal, are overlooked in social work assessments and related intervention planning. As Imber-Black (1988) has so usefully argued, however, helping professionals neglect this dimension at our peril, given the number and complexity of institutions involved in the lives of our clients and constituencies.

The Cultural and Sociopolitical Environment

In contextual social work practice, we are particularly interested in the ways in which everyday environments support or constrain access and opportunity, a focus that brings us to questions of power. Everyday places and spaces both produce and reinforce wider social patterns of privilege and oppression. As "landscapes of power," environments are deeply implicated in patterns of exclusion and inclusion, of denial and privilege (Sutton, 1996). Environments can be understood, in other words, as cultural artifacts, shaped, as Weisman (2000) has pointed out, "by human intention and intervention, a living archeology through which we can extract the priorities and beliefs of the decision-makers in our society" (p. 1).

Examples of the potent relationships between daily environments and larger social arrangements can readily be found. Consider, for example, formal and informal mechanisms of residential segregation—from legalized racial segregation to the more subtle processes by which residents, banks, realtors, and city governments interact to restrict residency on race and class grounds—or the many ways in which built environments tend to express male preferences and to reinforce male power and privilege. From the design of office buildings to the layout and facilities in public spaces such as airports and parks, feminist critics have documented the extent to which the built environment has long reflected the primacy of men's views and needs over those of women (Darke, 1996; Ruddick, 1996; Spain, 1992; Weisman, 1992). Patterns of social inclusion and exclusion can similarly be seen in the management and use of public spaces and amenities, particularly in relation to restrictions on the use of such environments by populations who for various reasons are considered to be difficult or deviant (e.g. the mentally ill [Parr, 1997]).

In considering the spatial dimensions of social power, we must bear in mind that everyday environments are implicated in the construction and maintenance of patterns of privilege, as well as of oppression. To understand this, it is helpful to think in dynamic terms of environmental or spatial relationships, in contrast with the static environmental entities (buildings, parks, litter, greenery) that more commonly are the building blocks of contextual analyses. One community's ability to resist the siting of a waste transfer station or to effectively protest the routing of air traffic over its residential neighborhoods, for example, is directly and reciprocally related to the likelihood that some other, typically less powerful, community will have to accommodate these environmental threats.

Everyday environments also express and reinforce cultural norms and expectations. In American society, many environments are constructed in White cultural terms. Peters (1998) explores, for example, the marginality of indigenous First Nations people in urban environments, a process of exclusion that can be related to social beliefs that locate First Nations people as belonging in rural (and segregated) environments. Kay Anderson's (1987) compelling historical study of "Chinatown" in Vancouver, Canada, similarly illuminates the complex links between spatiality and the construction of social and racial categories. Anderson argues that the spatial separation of Chinatown, its historical association with vice, danger, dirt, and immorality, and its implied cultural inferiority, has enabled dominant White groups to intensify their sense of self (to define "us" in contrast with "them") and to justify particular social and political practices toward Chinese people and property. From this perspective, Chinatown is understood as being as much a construction of White European thought as it is an ethnic enclave shaped by Chinese cultural norms and aspirations: "The significance of 'Chinatown' is . . . that it has been, like race, an idea with remarkable cultural force and material effect—one that for more than a century has shaped and justified the practices of powerful institutions toward it and toward people of Chinese origin" (Anderson, 1987). Closer to home, Western aesthetics and cultural norms frequently dominate the structure and furnishings of social service agencies, creating environments that many clients perceive as unwelcoming at best, and oppressive at worst.

The Experienced Environment

"The environment," which so often we treat as though it is a unitary and universally experienced reality, in fact is perceived and experienced in many different ways, depending on a person or group's view of the world, position within it, and current circumstances. At the same time, there are aspects of environments—physical conditions, for example, or danger, or beauty—that people largely agree on. Social scientists have long struggled to understand this relationship between the environment in an objective sense—the world "out there" that we can evaluate, measure, and describe with some degree of consensus—and the world as we experience it subjectively, mediated and thus individualized by our perceptions, history, beliefs, expectations, developmental stage, and even mood. Kurt Lewin (1935) used the concept of "life space" to capture the particular, individualized ways in which each person understands and constructs his or her physical and social world. Phenomenologist Husserl (1970) similarly wrote about the "lifeworld" and the ways in which people make meaning within the experienced world. More recently, cognitive and constructivist theorists and researchers have contributed greatly to our understandings of the ways in which people make sense within their larger environmental and social milieus (Berlin, 1996).

In assessing and intervening in client's environments, therefore, it is important that we pay careful attention to the *experienced environment*—the environment as it is perceived and constructed in individual and collective systems of meaning and belief. Personal, collective, and cultural meanings give shape to people's experiences in their everyday environments. People are active interpreters of the world they live in, and the lenses they bring to these interpretations are shaped by factors such as life history, culture, social beliefs and values, and age—all of which contribute to the "meaning, intention, felt value, and significance that individuals and groups give to places" (Gesler, 1992, p. 738).

The environment can be thought of as a symbol (Sutton, 1996), as well as an externally experienced reality. Take our earlier example of children's environmental experiences. Recent scholarship suggests that children understand their key everyday environments in particular and specific ways that may be quite different from adult perspectives on the same contexts (Burton & Price-Spratlen, 1999). Efforts to understand and "read" children's environments should, therefore, incorporate children's own views of their most important life settings, their sense of what their everyday worlds mean and symbolize. For both children and adults, this view from the inside out is essential, not only to efforts to fully understand clients' environmental experiences, but also to the construction of social work practices that connect with and support the foundations of people's efficacy and agency in everyday life contexts.

Environmental Strengths and Resources

A holistic understanding of the environment requires us to focus on environmental strengths and resources, as well as on barriers and challenges, and to integrate what we know about environmental assets with our related, but differently oriented, concern with relations of power and equity. An asset-based approach is consistent with prevailing emphases in social work practice on client strengths and capacities. It also reflects a respect for diversity, because very often a lack of attention to resources and strengths involves a dominant cultural misreading of what is available in particular contexts (Delgado, 1999).

A focus on environmental strengths, resources, and capacities is identified as an essential component of strengths-based practice (Saleebey, 1997; Sullivan, 1992; Weick & Saleebey, 1995). This focus represents a deliberate attempt to balance, if not overcome, the more common tendency in social work to focus primarily on environmental threats and deficits. The framing assumption here is that all persons and environments contain resources and strengths, actual and potential, that can be harnessed to improve quality of life and that can be used as foundations for change.

> A strengths perspective of social work practice offers an alternative conception of the environment. This perspective promotes matching the inherent strengths of individuals with naturally occurring resources in the social environment. . . . Recognizing, recruiting, and using these strengths can help maximize the potential of our clients and our community. In addition, when the environment is viewed as a source of opportunities, rather than an ecology of obstacles, the sheer number of helping resources we perceive expands dramatically. (Sullivan, 1992, 148–149)

In conceptualizing environmental strengths and resources, we include people's individual and collective agency and resilience within their everyday environments. In even the most difficult and challenging of contexts, many examples can be found of the varied and creative ways that people resist and transcend their environmental circumstances. Parr (1997), for example, has documented the ways in which people with mental health problems claim and inhabit public spaces at the same time as they are subject to scrutiny, surveillance, and often, outright harassment. Despite their parents' best efforts, most children similarly find many ways to find and use the physical environment for their own purposes, as all of us who have created private childhood places well know. To keep in mind that people are active shapers of and participants in their environments, and are not simply acted upon, is an essential element of empowering practice.

To focus on environmental strengths does not, however, mean that we intend to deny the real challenges that everyday environments present to many of social work's clients. Our goal is to encourage a more complex view, which incorporates both increased awareness of the negative impacts of environmental structures and conditions and increased efforts to acknowledge, replenish, and enhance environmental strengths and resources.

Implications for Empowering Practice

In empowering practice, this expanded understanding of the environment translates into conscious efforts to bring critical appraisal of everyday environments more fully into the work that social workers do, including analysis of the power relations embedded in clients' everyday environments and careful attention to environmental resources and strengths, as well as to environmental barriers and constraints. Although we emphasize the social and structural aspects of environmental contexts, our framework is sensitive also to the meanings that environments have for the people who live in them, to the many and detailed ways that people make places for themselves in the world, and to human agency, ingenuity, and persistence in even the most devastating and toxic of environments. Our focus, in other words, is on person–environment transactions and negotiations in all their richness and variability. How, then, do these expanded understandings translate into the practicalities of assessment and intervention in social work practice?

Contextual Assessment

A contextual approach to assessment draws on our expanded environmental typology to develop more complex understandings of the relationships between client issues and social and environmental contexts. These expanded understandings are particularly important, given that assessment establishes the framework for intervention. Assessments that incorporate textured and multidimensional readings of clients' social and physical environments make interventions at multiple systems levels more likely (Meyer, 1993). Assessments that attend adequately to the multiple layers in environmental contexts, including issues of power, are also essential to the development of intervention strategies directed to empowerment and social justice.

Consistent with the focus in empowerment practice on client participation, our approach emphasizes assessment methods that actively allow for this in the process of generating information. The goal is an engaged process, in which clients, key members of their social networks and communities, and professionals develop shared understandings of salient environmental experiences and realities as a foundation for collaborative decision-making. Supporting such participation in practice requires enriched understandings of people's "personal geographies"—who and what is meaningful to them in their everyday environmental contexts (Kemp, 2001). It also assumes that social workers will consistently and actively involve clients and communities in the process of gathering environmental information (through, for example, participatory research methods or collaborative assessment strategies).

In constructing contextual assessments, workers should

- focus on both personal and environmental issues
- gain a better understanding of issues of concern and available resources
- include personal social networks, which open up important opportunities for active consultation, collective exchanges, and empowerment
- consider both workers and clients as partners in the process of knowledge development

Not surprisingly, we consider personal and collective narratives of environmental experiences as important components of an accurate and comprehensive environmental analysis. Narratives of everyday life are invariably rich in environmental content. In particular, such stories contain vital information on the ways in which personal and cultural beliefs and values interact with the external world to produce the experienced environment—an environment that has particular meaning to a client and her reference group. Systematic efforts to listen for, draw out, and explore such stories are essential to knowing the environmental context as it is understood and explained by the client.

Accessing such information requires the use of narrative methods that are deliberately attentive to the contexts in which personal experience is embedded. Leigh's (1998) work on ethnographic interviewing, for example, uses open-ended questions ("Would you tell me about the living conditions of people in your neighborhood?" "I'm interested in how people in your neighborhood help each other.") to explore key life domains, including environmental and spatial experiences. Such questions broaden the focus of assessment and affirm clients as cultural guides who are both knowledgeable about their social and environmental experiences and able to teach others about them.

Narrative information, which pivots around meaning and experience, can and should be supplemented by information that builds a picture of the environment from the outside. There are many types and sources of environmental information, from data collected by government and social agencies, to local-level efforts to survey environmental resources and constraints. Tools for environmental assessment that incorporate expressive and/or graphic modalities, such as writing or drawing, also add dimensionality and specificity to the verbal methods at the core of most social work assessments. Leigh (1998) asks clients to draw pictures of their neighborhood or of a room in a typical house in their community. Useful assessment models also can be found in other disciplines. Geographer Melissa Gilbert (1998), for example, used a simple map to contrast the lived geographies of two low-income women, one White and one African American. This straightforward but powerful graphic vividly conveyed information about the nature of the women's social and environmental resources, the location and spatial range of their daily activities and social network members, and the patterns the women made as they went about their lives in particular geographical and community settings.

Ecomapping (Hartman, 1978) and social network mapping (Tracy & Whittaker, 1990) are likewise of considerable value as sources of contextual information. Used in combination, these assessment tools help workers and clients better understand who is in a client's personal social network and the distribution of resources and challenges in the network and the surrounding environment. This dual focus is important, given that the strengths and limitations of personal networks are inextricably shaped by larger social and environmental patterns of resources and constraints. When networks and the environmental contexts in which they are located are depleted by the demands of chronic poverty, for example, it is unrealistic and ultimately destructive to look only to local resources as a source of change (Halpern, 1995b).

Social workers can reach beyond descriptive data and narrative accounts to critical analysis by consistently providing clients with opportunities to make connections between their environmental experiences and larger social conditions. Strategies for the development of critical perspectives build on the work of Paulo Freire (1973), who emphasized the use of "problem posing" and reflective dialogue as a basis for exploring the relationships between everyday lived experience and social and political arrangements. Central to this process is deliberate attention to questions of power and agency, including both the constraints that clients experience in their everyday environments and the multiple and creative ways that they resist or negotiate these challenges (Korin, 1994).

At the core of empowerment practice, as we have stressed already, is an understanding of environments from the perspective of power and social justice. Hagan and Smail (1997) have described a process that they term *power-mapping*, which involves three key steps. First, it is necessary to map the distribution of power and resources in a particular environmental context, across key domains. Second, it is important to analyze how conditions of power or powerlessness affect those within this setting. Third, it is essential to identify sources of actual or potential power. Such an analysis enhances critical consciousness of the social and environmental distribution of power and its consequences, provides important information on resources and strengths available to support interventions, and opens up perspectives on what needs to be done in order for people to obtain power in key life domains.

Contextual Intervention

As with assessment, the process of intervention should be consistent with a larger philosophy of practice. In contextual social work practice, activities that enhance awareness of, connectedness to, and efficacy within the environment (broadly defined) are central to improved outcomes for vulnerable individuals, groups, and communities. Emphasis is also placed on the fit between potential interventions and the commitment in this approach to issues of client system inclusion, empowerment, and equity.

In general interventions should

- make sense to the client
- be feasible with available resources
- include clients as active participants
- encourage the development of competence
- be positive rather than punitive
- strengthen personal and collective expectations and sources of efficacy
- build on client, network, and community strengths
- be empowerment oriented
- utilize personal social networks as sources of social support, as tangible resources, and for their potential power as collectivities
- be supported by evidence of their effectiveness (derived from research *and* practice)

Of central importance, we suggest, is a view of environmental intervention that extends beyond social work's conventional focus on modifying environments (to improve environmental conditions, for example, or to remove clients from difficult or dangerous environmental circumstances). Both recent scholarship in other disciplines and emerging perspectives within social work indicate that environmental intervention should be reconstructed to include both action in the environment and the related process of transforming individual and collective perspectives through critical analysis of the impact of environmental conditions. Of particular importance is critical awareness of and action in relation to the ways in which power relationships, including those pertaining to race, gender, and class, are articulated in spatial arrangements and experience. Also central are interventions that enhance the development of ecological competence (Maluccio, 1981) in clients and communities and that provide a platform for effective action in relation to oppressive social and environmental conditions. Many robust and well-tested interventions, ranging from empowerment practice (Breton, 1984) to cognitive-behavioral strategies (Berlin, 1996), focus on strengthening client system skills and competencies in navigating the external world.

In intervention as well as in assessment, contextual practice must be thoroughly grounded in the ways in which individuals, groups, and communities interpret and define their everyday experiences and environments. Here, as in much of social work practice, the line between assessment and intervention blurs: Many of the strategies we propose are tools for change as well as for gathering data. We stress, however, the value and importance in working with clients and communities to envision the possible as well as the actual. Sutton (1996) emphasized, for example, the practical and democratic value in working with children to envision and rewrite their environmental texts, whether these are texts of privilege or texts of marginality. In recent work in urban elementary schools undergoing reconstruction, we collaborated with children to imagine, design, and lobby local officials for the funding of child-centered playground environments (Sutton & Kemp, in press). In the process, children not only imagined their worlds differently, but they developed tangible skills and competencies in domains ranging from design skills to the practice of citizenship.

A central challenge in contextual practice is to ensure that connections are made between individual experiences and perspectives and collective issues. At one level, this has to do with diligent attention to the development of critical consciousness (Freire, 1973). It includes, however, the need to forge links across systems levels and among different communities of interest. Without conscious efforts by practitioners, environmental issues can all too easily be identified and managed only at the individual or family level. Though valuable on their own terms, interventions at only these levels delimit opportunities for clients, communities, and agencies to partner around changing underlying environmental conditions. This link from private to public is particularly important, as Fisher and Karger (1997, p. 4) point out, in a world dominated by "private individuals, private spaces, and private institutions."

We envision, therefore, practice that actively attends to the environmental dimensions of client issues, that carefully explores both the tangible *and* the subjective contours of these contextual factors, that provides opportunities for clients to imagine and be involved in producing more equitable and empowering environments, and that routinely connects local and personal experiences in everyday environments to larger coalitions and efforts. Such practice is possible, we believe, from within the mandates and structures of direct practice, as well as from within those positions more typically defined in community or macrolevel terms (for a more expansive discussion of this position, see Kemp, Whittaker, & Tracy, 1997).

Continuing the Conversation

For social workers, a renewed focus on contextuality is illuminating but also challenging. It is relatively easy to grasp the importance in social work practice of a complex and critical understanding of the relationships between people and their everyday environments. Apparent also is the need for a greater appreciation of the contradictory, multidimensional, and inherently power-laden nature of environmental experience. Less clear, however, is the position of the social worker in the dialectics of space and place. How, for example, can social workers, who so often represent institutional authority, fully participate in the creation and maintenance of emancipatory spaces? Is it possible to build bridges between transformative experiences in local, everyday environments and larger social structures? What will it take to move social service systems driven by risk assessment and person-centered diagnostic imperatives to a more complex view of the characteristics of everyday environments? These and related questions require careful attention as social workers struggle to articulate the rhetoric of strengths, empowerment, and social justice in their daily practice.

References

Anderson, K. J. (1987). The idea of Chinatown: The power of place and institutional practice in the making of a racial category. *Annals of the Association of American Geographers, 77*(4), 580–598.

Antonovsky, A. (1979). *Health, stress, and coping.* San Francisco: Jossey-Bass.

Berger, P. L., & Neuhaus, R. J. (1977). *To empower people: The role of mediating structures in public policy.* Washington, DC: American Enterprise Institute for Public Policy Research.

Berlin, S. B. (1996). Constructivism and environment: A cognitive–integrative perspective for social work practice. *Families in Society, 77*(6), 326–335.

Boyer, P. (1978). *Urban masses and moral order in America, 1820–1920.* Cambridge, MA: Harvard University Press.

Breton, M. (1984). A drop-in program for transient women: Promoting competence through the environment. *Social Work, 29*, 542–546.

Briar, S., & Miller, H. (1971). *Problems and issues in social casework.* New York: Columbia University Press.

Brodsky, A. E. (1996). Resilient single mothers in risky neighborhoods: Negative psychological sense of community. *American Journal of Community Psychology, 24*(4), 347–363.

Bronfenbrenner, U. (1979). *The ecology of human development: Experiments by nature and design.* Cambridge, MA: Harvard University Press.

Burton, L. M., & Price-Spratlen, T. (1999). *Through the eyes of children: An ethnographic perspective on neighborhoods and child development.* In A. Hasten (Ed.). Cultural processes in child development (pp. 77–96). Mahwah, NJ: Lawrence Erlbaum & Associates.

Coulton, C. J., Korbin, J. E., & Su, M. (1996). Measuring neighborhood context for young children in an urban area. *American Journal of Community Psychology, 24*(1), 5–32.

Coulton, C. J., & Pandey, S. (1992). Geographic concentration of poverty and risk to children in urban neighborhoods. *American Behavioral Scientist, 35*(3), 283–257.

Darke, J. (1996). The man-shaped city. In C. Booth, J. Darke, & S. Yeandle (Eds.), *Changing places: Women's lives in the city.* London: Paul Chapman.

Delgado, M. (1999). *Social work practice in nontraditional urban settings.* New York: Oxford University Press.

Fisher, R., & Karger, H. J. (1997). *Social work and community in a private world.* White Plains, NY: Longman.

Freire, P. (1973). *Education for critical consciousness.* New York: Seabury Press.

Garbarino, J., Kostelny, K., & Dubrow, N. (1991). *No place to be a child: Growing up in a war zone.* Lexington, MA: Lexington Books.

Germain, C. B. (1978). Space: An ecological variable in social work practice. *Social Casework, 59*, 515–522.

Germain, C. B. (1981). The physical environment in social work practice. In A. N. Maluccio (Ed.), *Promoting competence in clients: A new/old approach to social work practice* (pp. 113–124). New York: Free Press.

Germain, C. B., & Gitterman, A. (1995). Ecological perspective. In R. L. Edwards & J. G. Hopps (Eds.), *The encyclopedia of social work: Vol. 1* (18th ed., pp. 816–824). Silver Spring, MD: National Association of Social Workers.

Gesler, W. M. (1992). Therapeutic landscapes: Medical issues in light of the new cultural geography. *Social Science in Medicine, 34*, 735–746.

Gilbert, M. (1998). "Race," space, and power: The survival strategies of working poor women. *Annals of the Association of American Geographers, 88*, 595–621.

Gitterman, A., & Germain, C. B. (1976). Social work practice: A life model. *Social Service Review, 50*(4), 601–610.

Gould, K. H. (1987). Life model vs. conflict model: A feminist perspective. *Social Work, 32*, 346–351.

Granovetter, M. (1973). The strength of weak ties. *American Journal of Sociology, 78*(6), 1360–1380.

Gutheil, I. A. (1992). Considering the physical environment: An essential component of good practice. *Social Work, 37*(5), 391–396.

Gutiérrez, L. M. (1990). Working with women of color: An empowerment perspective. *Social Work, 37*(5), 149–153.

Gutiérrez, L., & Lewis, E. (1999). *Empowering women of color.* New York: Columbia University Press.

Hagan, T., & Smail, D. (1997). Power-mapping I: Background and basic methodology. *Journal of Applied and Community Psychology, 7*(4), 257–267.

Halpern, R. (1995a). *Rebuilding the inner city: A history of neighborhood initiatives to address poverty in the United States.* New York: Columbia University Press.

Halpern, R. (1995b). Children on the edge: An essay review. *Social Service Review, 69*(1), 131–151.

Hamilton, G. (1958). A theory of personality: Freud's contribution to social work. In H. Parad (Ed.), *Ego psychology and dynamic casework* (pp. 11–37). New York: Family Service Association of America.

Hartman, A. (1978). Diagrammatic assessment of family relationships. *Social Casework, 8,* 467–474.

Husserl, E. (1970). *The crisis of European sciences and transcendental phenomenology.* Evanston, IL: Northwestern University Press.

Imber-Black, E. (1988). *Families and larger systems: A family therapist's guide through the labyrinth.* New York: Guilford Press.

Kemp, S. P. (1994). *Social work and systems of knowledge: The concept of environment in social casework theory, 1900–1983.* Unpublished doctoral dissertation, Columbia University School of Social Work, New York.

Kemp, S. P. (2001). Environment through a gendered lens: From person-in-environment to woman-in-environment. *Affilia, 16*(1), 7–30.

Kemp, S. P., Whittaker, J. K., & Tracy, E. M. (1997). *Person–environment practice: The social ecology of interpersonal helping.* New York: Aldine de Gruyter.

Korin, E. C. (1994). Social inequalities and feminist relationships: Applying Freire's ideas to clinical practice. *Journal of Feminist Family Therapy, 5*(3/4), 75–98.

Kuo, F. E., Sullivan, W. C., Coley, R. L., & Brunson, L. (1998). Fertile ground for community: Inner-city neighborhood common spaces. *American Journal of Community Psychology, 26*(6), 823–849.

Leigh, J. W. (1998). *Communicating for cultural competence.* Boston: Allyn & Bacon.

Lewin, K. (1935). *A dynamic theory of personality.* New York: McGraw-Hill.

Lynch, K. (1979). The spatial world of the child. In L. Michelson & I. Michelson (Eds.), *The child in the city, today and tomorrow* (pp. 102–127). Toronto, Canada: University of Toronto Press.

Maluccio, A. (1981). *Promoting competence in clients: A new/old approach to social work practice.* New York: Free Press.

Mattaini, M. A. (1993). *More than a thousand words: Graphics for clinical practice.* Washington, DC: NASW Press.

Matthews, M. H. (1992). *Making sense of place.* Hemel Hempstead, UK: Harvester Wheatsheaf.

McDowell, L. (1999). *Gender, identity, and space: Understanding feminist geographies.* Minneapolis: University of Minnesota Press.

Meyer, C. H. (1983). *Clinical social work in the ecosystems perspective.* New York: Columbia University Press.

Meyer, C. H. (1993). *Assessment in social work practice.* New York: Columbia University Press.

Moos, R. H. (1996). Understanding environments: The key to improving social processes and program outcomes. *American Journal of Community Psychology, 24*(1), 193–201.

Nurius, P. S., & Markus, H. (1991). Situational variability in the self-concept: Appraisals, expectancies, and asymmetries. *Journal of Consulting and Clinical Psychology, 9,* 316–333.

Parr, H. (1997). Mental health, public space, and the city: Questions of individual and collective access. *Environment and Planning D: Society and Space, 15,* 435–454.

Parsons, R. (1991). Empowerment: Purpose and practice principle in social work. *Social Work with Groups, 14*(2), 7–21.

Peters. E. J. (1998). Subversive spaces: First Nations women and the city. *Environment and Planning D: Society and Space, 16*(6), 665–685.

Proshansky, H., Fabian, A. K., & Kaminoff, R. (1983). Place-identity: Physical world socialization of the self. *Journal of Environmental Psychology, 3,* 57–83.

Pulido, L., Sidawi, S., & Vos, R. O. (1996). An archeology of environmental racism in Los Angeles. *Urban Geography, 17*(5), 419–439.

Rappaport, J. (1987). Terms of empowerment/exemplars of prevention: Towards a theory for community psychology. *American Journal of Community Psychology, 15*(2), 121–148.

Riger, S. (1993). What's wrong with empowerment? *American Journal of Community Psychology, 21,* 279–292.

Ruddick, S. (1996). Constructing difference in public spaces: Race, class, and gender as interlocking systems. *Urban Geography, 17,* 132–151.

Saegert, S., & Hart, R. (1978). The development of environmental competence in boys and girls. In M. Salter (Ed.), *Play: Anthropological perspectives.* Cornwall, NY: Leisure Press.

Saleebey, D. (Ed.). (1997). *The strengths perspective in social work practice* (2nd ed.). New York: Longman.

Soja, E. W. (1989). *Postmodern geographies: The reassertion of space in critical social theory.* New York: Verso.

Spain, D. (1992). *Gendered spaces.* Chapel Hill: University of North Carolina Press.

Specht, H., & Courtney, M. E. (1994). *Unfaithful angels: How social work has abandoned its mission.* New York: Free Press.

Stanton-Salazar, R. D. (1997). A social capital framework for understanding the socialization of racial minority children and youths. *Harvard Educational Review, 67*(1), 1–40.

Sullivan, W. P. (1992). Reconsidering the environment as a helping resource. In D. Saleebey (Ed.), *The strengths perspective in social work practice* (pp. 148–157). New York: Longman.

Sutton, S. E. (1996). *Weaving a tapestry of resistance: The places, power, and poetry of a sustainable society.* Westport, CT: Bergin & Garvey.

Sutton, S. E., & Kemp, S. P. (in press). Youth as responsible, culturally responsive citizens: A social justice perspective on children and the environment. *Journal of Environmental Psychology.*

Tracy, E. M., & Whittaker, J. K. (1990). The social network map: Assessing social support in clinical practice. *Families in Society, 71,* 461–470.

University of Washington School of Public Health. (2000). *The state of Washington's children.* Seattle, WA: Author.

Valentine, G., & McKendrick, J. (1997). Children's outdoor play: Exploring parental concerns about children's safety and the changing nature of childhood. *Geoforum, 28*(2), 219–235.

Wakefield, J. (1996). Does social work need the ecosystems perspective? Part 1: Is the perspective clinically useful? *Social Service Review, 70*(1), 1–32.

Weick, A., & Saleebey, D. (1995). *A postmodern approach to social work practice.* The 1995 Richard Lodge Memorial Lecture, (unpublished paper), Adelphi University, New York.

Weinstein, C., & David, T. (Eds.). (1987). *Spaces for children: The built environment and child development.* New York: Plenum Press.

Weisman, L. K. (1992). *Discrimination by design: A feminist critique of the man-made environment.* Urbana: University of Illinois Press.

Weisman, L. K. (2000). Women's environmental rights: A manifesto. In J. Rendell, B. Pennell, & I. Borden (Eds.), *Gender space architecture: An interdisciplinary introduction* (pp. 1–5). New York: Routledge.

Zimmerman, M. A., & Rappaport, J. (1988). Citizen participation, perceived control, and psychological empowerment. *American Journal of Community Psychology, 16,* 725–750.

3

Challenging Injustice and Oppression

David G. Gil

The emotional and intellectual roots of this essay reach back to my own experiences of injustice and oppression after the German occupation of Austria in 1938. At that time, our family's business was coercively "aryanized," our livelihood was destroyed, my father was imprisoned in a concentration camp, and I was expelled from my school and placed in a segregated school for Jewish children. Eventually, my mother sent me abroad with a "Kinder-transport" of refugee children. Our family was never reunited.

These experiences and the trauma of separation from my family at age fourteen led me to raise a difficult question that has become a major focus of my work: "How can we overcome and prevent injustice and oppression, regardless of who the victims are?" My quest has led me gradually to a philosophy of social equality, liberty, real democracy, individuality through community, cooperation, and active nonviolence (Buber, 1958; Freire, 1970; Gil, 1998; King, 1992; Kropotkin, 1902/1956; Tawney, 1931/1964).

This essay is based on my quest for answers to this question. It clarifies the meanings of injustice and oppression, sketches their sources and history, and examines their consequences for key institutions of social life. It then discusses strategies to overcome these dehumanizing social conditions.

Meanings of Injustice and Oppression and Their Opposites

Oppression refers to social structures and relations involving domination and exploitation of individuals, classes, and communities within a society and of peoples

This essay is based on the author's book, *Confronting Injustice and Oppression*. New York: Columbia University Press, 1998.

beyond a society's territory. Domination serves to institute economic, social, psychological, and cultural exploitation and to establish privileged conditions of living for certain social classes and peoples. The goals of domination and exploitation are implemented by expropriating resources and products of dominated classes and peoples and by controlling their work and productivity.

Domination and exploitation usually have been initiated by force, followed by socialization and ideological indoctrination. Over time, these processes, backed by systems of social control, resulted in the internalization of the perspectives and culture of dominant classes and peoples into the consciousness of their victims and in willing submission of the latter to the expectations of the former.

Injustice refers to the consequences of domination and exploitation: multidimensional inequalities and development-inhibiting, discriminatory, and dehumanizing conditions of living. These coercively established and maintained conditions include, but are not limited to: slavery, serfdom, and wage labor; unemployment, poverty, hunger, and homelessness; discrimination by race, ethnicity, age, gender, sexual orientation, disabilities, and so forth; and inadequate health care and inferior education.

Justice means the absence of domination and exploitation. It implies equal liberty and equal rights, responsibilities, and constraints for all. Domination, exploitation, and injustice, on the other hand, involve unequal liberties, rights, responsibilities, and constraints of oppressed individuals, groups, classes, communities, and peoples.

Oppression within and beyond societies and conditions of injustice have always been results of human choices and actions, rather than inevitable expressions of human nature. Evidence in support of this proposition is provided by the existence throughout history of human groups whose ways of life and social relations were shaped by values of equality, liberty, solidarity, and cooperation, rather than by dynamics of domination, exploitation, and competition (Kropotkin, 1902/1956).

Being results of human choices and actions, domination, exploitation, and injustice, therefore, were never, nor are they now, inevitable. People could always have made different choices, and they can now and in the future chose to transcend oppression and injustice. Indeed, people have often challenged such dehumanizing conditions and relations, and they are likely to do so again by spreading critical consciousness and organizing liberation movements (Freire, 1970).

Societies that evolved internal relations of domination and exploitation tended to extend these relations beyond their populations and territories. Colonialism, genocide of native peoples, and slavery, as well as contemporary economic and cultural imperialism, illustrate this tendency. Such oppressive practices intensified over time as a result of resistance by victims and reactive repression by perpetrators, as well as competition for dominance among different colonial and imperialistic powers. By now, relations of domination and exploitation and conditions of injustice have penetrated most branches of humankind in the name of neoliberal, globalized, "free" market capitalism.

Relations of domination and exploitation from local to global levels have come gradually to be reflected not only in social, economic, political, legal, and cultural institutions, but also in the consciousness, values, attitudes, and actions of most people, including victims of oppression. Overcoming oppression and injustice, therefore, would require not only transformations of the institutions that maintain them (liberation of institutions), but also transformations of people's consciousness, values, attitudes, and actions (liberation of consciousness and practice).

Societies whose human relations are shaped by oppressive tendencies usually are not divided simply into oppressors and oppressed people and classes. Rather, people in such societies, regardless of their class position, tend to be oppressed in some contexts and oppressors in others.

Key Institutions of Social Life in Both Free and Oppressive Societies

To discern characteristics of just and free, and of unjust and oppressive, societies, one needs to examine how individuals and social classes participate in and are affected by key institutions of social life, including the following:

- Stewardship, ownership, and control of life-sustaining natural and human-created resources
- Organization of work and production
- Exchange and distribution of concrete and symbolic goods and services and of civil and political rights and responsibilities
- Governance and legitimation
- Reproduction, socialization, and social control (Gil, 1992)

The way these interrelated, key institutions function shapes the circumstances of living and relative power of individuals and social classes, the quality of human relations among individuals and classes, and the overall quality of life in society. Characteristics of just and free, and of unjust and oppressive, societies are sketched next, with reference to these key institutions.

Just and Free Societies

In just and free societies, all people are considered to be of equal intrinsic worth, in spite of individual uniqueness and differences, and are, therefore, entitled to equal rights, liberties, and responsibilities concerning participation in the key institutions of social life.

In such societies, exchanges of work and of products do not involve exploitation, everyone's individual needs and potential are considered equally important, and all are treated as equals in the distribution of concrete and symbolic goods and services and of civil and political rights and responsibilities. Marx's pithy phrase, "to each according to needs, from each according to capacities," seems an apt characterization of just and free societies (Tawney, 1931/1964; Tucker, 1978).

Unjust and Oppressive Societies

In unjust and oppressive societies, on the other hand, people are not considered to be of equal, intrinsic worth, and, therefore, are not entitled to equal rights, liberties, and responsibilities concerning participation in the key institutions of social life.

In such societies, people belonging to different classes are entitled to different rights and are subject to different expectations and conditions of work. Also, exchanges of work and of products involve economic and social exploitation. Furthermore, the needs and potential of members of dominant classes are deemed more important than the needs and potential of members of dominated classes. Hence, the former receives routinely preferential treatment in the organization of work and in the distribution of concrete and symbolic goods and services and of civil and political rights, liberties, and responsibilities. Establishing and maintaining such inequalities concerning the key institutions of social life are usually not possible without coercion, that is, social-structural violence (Gil, 1999).

Variability of Oppression and Injustice

Oppression and injustice tend to vary among societies and over time in the same society. These variations reflect differences in social values and in degrees of inequality concerning the key institutions of social life in particular societies at particular times. The higher the degrees of inequality, the higher are the levels of coercion necessary to enforce them, as well as the levels of resistance from dominated classes and the levels of reactive repression by dominant classes.

Although variations are possible in degrees of oppression and injustice, variations logically are not possible concerning justice and nonoppressive relations, which are predicated on equality of rights, liberties, responsibilities, and constraints. Equality, however, is not a continuum, but the zero point on the continuum of inequality, therefore, it cannot vary by degrees.

It follows that whenever inequalities are present in a society, its ways of life involve oppression and injustice, its people are not free in a meaningful sense, and its political institutions are essentially undemocratic and coercive, in spite of elections and claims, such as "being part of the free world."

Historical Notes

The story of social evolution reveals that oppression and injustice did not become institutionalized until the spread of agriculture and crafts, about 10,000 years ago. These major changes in ways of life resulted gradually in a stable economic surplus, which was conducive to the emergence of occupational and social classes, differentiations into rural and urban settlements, and centralized forms of governance over defined territories (Eisler, 1987).

Preagricultural, Egalitarian Communities

For several hundred thousand years before the development of agriculture and crafts, people lived in isolated communities that subsisted by hunting, gathering, and fishing. Internal relations in these communities were usually based on egalitarian, cooperative, and communal principles, and they did not involve institutionalized domination, exploitation, and injustice.

Stewardship over resources was exercised collectively to meet people's basic needs. Organization of work was based mainly on age, gender, physical conditions, and individual capacities, but not on criteria such as caste and class. Everyone had roughly equal rights and responsibilities to work in order to secure the survival of the community. The exchange and distribution of goods and services did not involve exploitation. Civil and political rights, liberties, and responsibilities tended to be shared equally, and people were subject to equal constraints. Everyone's needs were deemed equally important and were met, subject to limits set by natural resources and collective productivity.

The ways of life of early communities were not conducive to economic exploitation such as slavery, because their simple technologies did not enable people to produce more than they consumed. They, therefore, were not able to generate a reliable surplus for appropriation and exploitation by others—the material base and precondition for oppressive systems.

I do not mean to idealize preagricultural ways of life, nor to advocate a return to that stage of social evolution in order to overcome contemporary oppression and injustice. I am aware that human relations then were not free from oppressive tendencies, especially in relations between men and women, older and younger persons, and community members and strangers. Also, relations between different societies were not always peaceful.

However, from what is known from archeology and anthropology about the preagricultural period of human evolution, domination and exploitation were not institutionalized policies and practices then. We could, therefore, derive important insights from the values and ways of life of early human communities.

Postagricultural Societies

Gradual increases in population, which upset the balance between people and life-sustaining resources, led to the development of agriculture and animal husbandry. This had revolutionary consequences for the ways of life of nomadic communities and for their internal and external relations.

Gradually, people settled into permanent communities that generated food supplies beyond their consumption needs. It was, therefore, no longer necessary for everyone to engage in food production, and many people were able to pursue alternative occupations. This led to the emergence of occupational and social classes, including peasants, artisans, and traders; priests, scholars, professionals, and artists; and civilian administrators, soldiers, and ruling elites.

Occupational differentiations led also to spatial differentiations—the emergence of cities and neighborhoods—and to social, economic, political, and cultural differentiations, all of which resulted in differences in ways of life, consciousness, interests, values, and ideologies among subgroups of societies.

The new ways of life evolved tendencies toward expropriation of resources and complex divisions of labor that yielded an economic surplus—the base for the emergence of domination, exploitation, and injustice. These changes led to changes in modes of exchange and distribution and in overall social organization, values, and ideologies. Illustrations of these developments are the ancient civilizations of Mesopotamia and Egypt (Durant, 1935).

To be sure, these developments took centuries and millennia and involved at any stage many choices, none of which was ever inevitable. Indeed, other societies that developed agriculture and animal husbandry made different choices and developed different patterns of key institutions, values, and ideologies. Rather than developing patterns of oppression and injustice, they used the economic surplus from their increased productivity toward enhancing the quality of life for all their members. They also continued to organize work and production, as well as exchange and distribution in accordance with egalitarian, cooperative, and communal values. Illustrations of this tendency have been identified among native peoples in the Americas, Africa, and elsewhere. Many of these native societies preserved just and nonoppressive ways of life until, and often beyond, the violent conquest of their lands by colonizing European empires (Farb, 1968; Zinn, 1980).

Types of Societal Oppression and Injustice

The ways by which oppression and injustice were established varied among societies. Two related and interacting types may be distinguished: (1) dominating and exploiting strangers—that is, other societies and their people—and (2) dominating and exploiting fellow citizens. Societies that have practiced domination and exploitation have usually done so at home and abroad, as both types involve similar assumptions, value premises, and ideologies, and as internal and external human relations interact with and influence one another. It is, nevertheless, useful to differentiate conceptually between internal and external oppression and to analyze their emergence separately.

Dominating and Exploiting Strangers
Crops ripening in the fields of people who had preceded others in developing agriculture attracted nomadic tribes to invade peasant villages to appropriate their products. These invasions were the beginnings of warfare motivated by efforts to achieve control over economic resources. Invasions of ancient European villages by Asian nomadic tribes, the Kurgans, illustrate this process (Eisler, 1987).

These violent encounters were not inevitable. The discoverers of agriculture might have been ready to share their knowledge and skills peacefully (as native peoples actually did in the Americas) when European explorers and conquerors first arrived.

The invasions of peasant communities around harvest time resulted gradually in their enslavement by nomadic tribes, who became accustomed to securing their food supplies by appropriating the fruits of other people's work. With time, the invaders realized the advantage of keeping the peasants alive, rather than killing them, and of coercing them to continue raising crops and to turn over much of the product to the invaders. Eventually, nomadic societies not only coerced conquered communities into giving up their surplus products, but they captured men and women from conquered villages, enslaved them, and exploited them sexually.

One can identify the typical elements of oppression and injustice in these early relationships between nomadic peoples and the peasant communities they dominated and enslaved. The motivating factor is exploitation of the victims. This is accomplished by controlling their resources—their territories and their knowledge and skills—and forcing them to work.

With time, social, psychological, and ideological dimensions evolved around the economic roots of oppressive relationships. The prestige of work performed by enslaved people declined relative to the activities engaged in by the dominant people, regardless of the objective importance of the work and activities, and the status and prestige of dominated, enslaved workers declined relative to that of members of dominant societies. These perceptions of the relative status and prestige of work and workers were internalized into the consciousness of everyone involved in exploitative relations. They became the core of discriminatory ideologies and practices concerning different social groups, classes, and peoples. Phenomena such as racism, sexism, and classism are contemporary manifestations and expressions of this ancient tendency.

Imposing oppressive relations and unjust conditions on other societies in order to exploit their resources, their work potential, and their human-created goods and services has gradually become the model for building colonial empires during antiquity, the Middle Ages, and modern times. Historical details have varied from case to case, but institutional practices concerning resources, work and production, and exchange and distribution, have remained essentially the same throughout history, and so have the social, psychological, and ideological dimensions, as well as the secular and religious rationalizations for domination, exploitation, injustice, and discrimination (Frank, 1977; Magdoff, 1977).

Dominating and Exploiting Fellow Citizens

Oppression and injustice emerged within many but not all societies as a consequence of occupational, social, and spatial differentiations. Whether these differentiations resulted in oppressive relations and unjust conditions seems to have depended largely on the terms of exchange between peasants and people pursuing newly emerging crafts and other occupations.

If exchanges were balanced in terms of work and material resources invested in products, then relations between peasants and groups pursuing other occupations (and living mainly in cities) could evolve along nonoppressive, synergetic patterns, with everyone benefiting equally (Maslow & Honigman, 1970).

If, on the other hand, exchanges were imbalanced, establishment and maintenance of such conditions required physical and ideological coercion. In these situations, urban dwellers were bent upon exploiting the peasantry and gradually also each other, as occupational specializations and social differentiations multiplied and as each occupational group aspired to appropriate as much as possible of the economic surplus by claiming privileged shares of available goods and services.

Unjust and oppressive societies that were based on coercively maintained exploitative exchanges among social classes engaging in different occupations and performing different roles (and enjoying different levels of rights, responsibilities, and liberty) were not as stable as preagricultural, egalitarian, cooperative communities. They were changing continuously, due to gradually intensifying competition and conflicts among individuals and social and occupational groups. These groups gained control over different shares of resources and different roles in the work system and were able to command different shares in the distribution of goods and services, civil and political rights, and power.

During the early stages of the emergence of unjust and oppressive relations, the egalitarian, cooperative, and communal values, ideology, and consciousness of preagricultural societies were gradually transformed into their opposites. These value changes toward inequality, competition, and selfishness were conducive to the ongoing development and reproduction of occupationally, spatially, and socially fragmented and stratified societies.

Perpetuation of Inequality

Once inequalities concerning the key institutions of social life were established in a society, they tended to be perpetuated, because individuals and groups who controlled disproportionally larger shares of resources and access to preferred work were in advantageous positions to assure continuation of their privileges and even to increase them. Also, emerging legal and political institutions tended to reflect established inequalities and power relations among competing interest groups and classes, and they were, therefore, unlikely to upset temporary equilibria among them.

The processes and logic of conflict and competition within societies originated in minor, initial inequalities in exchanges among individuals and occupational and social groups, which barely required coercion. However, the emerging tendency to legitimate, institutionalize, and increase minimal inequalities did require coercion. This resulted usually in resistance from victimized groups, to which privileged groups reacted with intensified coercion. The vicious circle of oppression, resistance, and reactive repression intensified with time. People tended to react to the latest violent stages in the circle, but they did not trace the sources of these destructive interactions, and they usually lacked insights and motivation for reversing their course and moving in alternative, constructive, nonexploitative directions.

The tendency for inequalities to intensify once they are initiated on a small scale has important implications for people who advocate reduction, rather than elimination of inequalities: As long as inequalities, at any level, are considered legitimate and are being enforced by governments, competitive interactions focused on restructuring inequalities tend to continue among individuals, social groups, and classes, and a sense of community and solidarity is unlikely to evolve.

One reason for the constant intensification of coercion in unjust and oppressive societies has been that people's motivation to work declined in proportion to the increase in exploitation. Work discipline, therefore, had to be assured by ever more overt and covert coercion. Expectations concerning a "work ethic" became typical elements of socialization and of religions and ideologies that interpreted and justified established, inegalitarian conditions of life and work. Socialization and indoctrination were routinely backed up by elaborate systems of submission-inducing rewards and sanctions and by open and secret police and military forces (the instruments of "legitimate violence" within inegalitarian societies and among societies of unjust and exploitative world systems).

The history of oppression and injustice within and among societies over the past 10,000 years is essentially a series of variations on the theme of coercively initiated and maintained exploitative modes of resource stewardship, both in work and production, and in exchange and distribution. This history is a tragic one indeed. The mere mention of coercive work systems, such as ancient and recent slavery, feudal serfdom, and early and contemporary industrial and agricultural wage labor, brings to mind images of toiling people transformed, not by their own choice, into dehumanized "factors of production," dominated and exploited by tyrants and slave masters, absolute rulers and aristocracies, and individual and corporate, capitalist employers. Such work systems could never have been established and perpetuated without massive coercion and violence in the form of civil and foreign wars, genocide, murder, torture, imprisonment, starvation, destitution, unemployment, and ever-present threats of these and other oppressive measures (Gil, 2000; John Paul II, 1982; Tucker, 1978).

Social-Change Strategies to Overcome Injustice and Oppression

An important insight gained from the history of social change is that activists need to differentiate short-range from long-range goals. Short-range reforms, such as transition policies based on U.S. President Franklin Roosevelt's proposals for a Bill of Economic Rights and on the United Nations' Universal Declaration of Human Rights, will not be discussed here, as our focus is on eliminating the roots of oppression and injustice (Gil, 1998).

It is important to emphasize, however, that pursuing short-range goals is not only necessary but is also ethically valid, in order to reduce the intensity of injustice and oppression as far and as soon as possible, even before eliminating their institutional sources. Pursuing short-range goals need not be an obstacle to the pursuit of long-range goals and can be connected strategically with the pursuit of fundamental social transformations, as long as activists do not confuse these different goals.

Long-Range Visions

Fundamental social transformations toward just and free societies are unlikely to come about through spontaneous, brief, revolutionary events. Rather, they require lengthy processes involving countercultural education toward critical consciousness, initiated and sustained by social movements seeking to transform development-inhibiting institutions into development-conducive alternatives. Such transformation processes and movements require long-range visions to guide them.

Transformation visions need to identify essential attributes of just and free societies and of strategies toward their realization. The visions should reflect the common interest of all peoples to meet their human needs. Accordingly, the visions must include the following institutional attributes (Gil, 1992; Maslow, 1970; Tawney, 1931/1964).

Establishing a Public Trust of Productive Resources.   Natural and human-created, concrete and nonconcrete, productive resources would be considered and administered as "public trust," or "commons," available to everyone on equal terms for use in productive, life-sustaining, and life-enhancing pursuits. Stewardship of the public trust would be carried out through decentralized, horizontally coordinated, democratic processes, from local to global levels. Although the public trust would replace private and corporate ownership and control of productive resources, consumption goods could be owned by individuals, households, and groups of people.

Redefining Work and Production.   Work and production would be reorganized, redefined, and redesigned to meet the actual needs for goods and services of all people, anywhere on earth (Gil, 2000). Education for, and participation in, work and production, in accordance with individual capacities, would be assured to all throughout life. All people would have the rights, responsibilities, and opportunities to become self-directing "masters of production," using their faculties in an integrated manner, rather than being forced to labor as hired hands, or "factors of production," under alienating conditions in the perceived interest and at the discretion of individual or corporate employers.

Furthermore, all people would have equal rights, responsibilities, and constraints, to choose and change their occupations, to design, direct, and carry out their work, and to share by rotation in socially necessary work, not chosen voluntarily by enough people. Work would be redefined to include all activities conducive to the maintenance and enrichment of life and would exclude life-impeding activities. Thus, caring for one's children and dependent relatives would be considered and rewarded as socially necessary work, while weapons manufacture—to use an extreme example—might be considered as "counter-work" and phased out. All socially necessary work would be deemed to be of equal worth and rewarded accordingly.

Finally, work would be in harmony with nature, with requirements of conservation, and with global demographic developments. It would, therefore, have to produce high-quality, long-lasting goods, use renewable resources when possible, and avoid waste.

Exchanging Goods and Services Nonexploitatively.　Goods and services would be exchanged and distributed on fair, nonexploitative terms. All people engaging in socially necessary work would have equal rights to have their needs acknowledged and met by obtaining goods and services in adequate quantity and quality. Social, civil, cultural, and political rights, responsibilities, and constraints would be assured to all on equal terms.

Developing Democratic Structures and Processes of Governance.　Structures and processes of governance, on local and translocal levels, would be truly democratic, nonhierarchical, decentralized, horizontally coordinated, and geared to assuring equal rights, responsibilities, and constraints, and to serving the real needs and interests of everyone living now and in the future. Government service would not entitle elected and appointed officials to privileged living conditions relative to the conditions of the people they represent and serve.

Applying Egalitarian Socialization Processes.　Socialization practices during all stages of life would be shaped by egalitarian and democratic values, so all children and adults would have equal rights, responsibilities, and opportunities to develop in accordance with their innate potential, with due regard for individual differences in needs, capacities, and limitations.

Feasibility of Realization of Long-Range Visions.　When people encounter long-range visions like the one sketched here, they tend to doubt that such visions actually can be realized. Such skepticism is understandable, given people's lifelong experiences with prevailing social, economic, political, and cultural realities, and their adaptation to and identification with these realities.

　　People living long ago would have been similarly skeptical concerning the possibility of ever realizing long-range visions involving comprehensive transformations toward contemporary ways of life. Yet such transformations did come about, not quickly and spontaneously, but through lengthy processes involving efforts and struggles by critical thinkers, social activists, and popular movements. By analogy, one may hypothesize that visions of just and free societies, which seem to most people unrealistic and utopian, could eventually be realized through persistent efforts and struggles over lengthy periods of time by contemporary and future thinkers, activists, and social movements.

Theoretical Perspectives on Transformation Strategies

Social transformation toward long-range visions of just and free societies involves discerning and eventually overcoming forces and processes that maintain and reproduce existing unjust and oppressive societies and cultures. Human societies and their particular institutional systems have always been shaped by the actions and social relations, and by the consciousness of their members. Hence, the forces and processes that liberation movements must target for transformation include

- patterns of action, interactions, and social relations of the members of societies
- processes of consciousness that underlie, motivate, and facilitate the existing patterns of actions, interactions, and social relations

Transformation of unjust and oppressive societies into just and free ones would require major changes in patterns of people's actions, interactions, and social relations. In turn, such changes seem to depend on prior changes of people's consciousness that would be conducive to alternative patterns of actions and relations. Activists pursuing long-range visions of social justice and freedom ought to devise and implement strategies aimed at facilitating the emergence of "critical consciousness," in order to induce and sustain appropriate changes in people's actions, interactions, and social relations (Freire, 1970).

Critical Consciousness: Key to Fundamental Social Change

To advance visions of just and free societies by noncoercive, voluntary, truly democratic means (the only strategic mode likely to be effective), rather than by coercive, authoritarian, nondemocratic ones, seems to require transformation of the status quo–reproducing consciousness of most people into alternative, status quo–challenging critical consciousness. Social movements pursuing the elimination of injustice and oppression would have to make intense efforts to facilitate the spreading of such critical consciousness. These efforts would involve dialogical, educational processes to promote changes concerning

- images of social reality that most people now hold
- ideas, beliefs, and assumptions people tend to take for granted without critical examination
- perceptions of individual and collective needs and interests that underlie and motivate the actions, thoughts, and social relations of most people
- values and ideologies that derive from the perceptions of needs and interests and affect the choices, actions, thoughts, and social relations of individuals, groups, and classes

Images of Social Reality
As for changes in the images of reality, people have to be helped to discover that social realities are results of human actions and thoughts, that people have changed realities in the past and will change them in the future, and that by acting together, people have power to influence the directions of future changes, even though as individuals they feel and are powerless to do so.

People also have to be helped to realize that prevailing social inequalities were established, and are being reproduced, by coercion and socialization, rather than by democratic choices. "Law and order" in the context of "legitimate" social inequalities does not imply justice and freedom because the existing legal system tends to uphold injustice and oppression.

Unexamined Assumptions and Beliefs

Ideas, beliefs, and assumptions that people have to be helped to examine include the views that humans are compelled by nature, rather than merely enabled, to be selfish, greedy, competitive, and violent, and that just, nonoppressive, egalitarian, cooperative, and nonviolent societies, therefore, have never existed, nor is it possible to establish such societies in the future.

People also would have to examine the social and individual dimensions of human nature. Once they come to understand these intrinsic aspects of the human condition, they are likely to realize that individuality can develop optimally only in the context of communities. It fails to develop adequately in the context of individualistic pursuits unrelated to or damaging to a community (Fromm, 1955; National Conference of Catholic Bishops, 1986).

Other widely held beliefs to be challenged are that everyone who tries can secure adequate living conditions by working within the established social order, that, therefore, no major structural changes, only marginal adjustments, may be necessary, and that people who fail to secure adequate conditions may be inherently deficient and should blame themselves (Ryan, 1971).

Furthermore, people ought to examine Adam Smith's controversial, yet influential, assumptions (which have not been supported by history) that the public good tends to appear spontaneously, as if created by an "invisible hand," when individuals act selfishly and competitively in pursuit of material gain, and that governments should not interfere with supposedly "free markets," nor should they plan for and attempt to promote the public good (Smith, 1961).

Underlying Perceptions of Individual and Collective Needs

As for perceptions of individual and collective interests, people have to be helped to realize that institutionalized inequalities are incompatible with their true interest to satisfy their real human needs. Given the dynamics of contemporary capitalist societies and cultures, many people may be able to satisfy their needs for biological-material necessities, though often under alienating and stigmatizing conditions and at substandard levels. However, given these dynamics, people are usually unable to meet their social-psychological, productive-creative, security, self-actualization, and spiritual needs at adequate levels (Gil, 1992; Maslow, 1970). The consistent frustration of human needs due to the dynamics of injustice and oppression in contemporary societies is a constant source of social, emotional, and physical pathology and violence and of individual and community underdevelopment.

It is important to note that being successful in economic terms, under prevailing social and cultural conditions, does not imply that one's nonmaterial needs are being realized adequately and that one's development is not inhibited. Affluent people are now as unlikely as poor people to fulfill their nonmaterial needs adequately. They, too, would have to reexamine the current perceptions of their needs and interests, and they, too, might discover that they would be more likely to meet their real needs in a just and free society shaped by different perceptions of individual and collective needs and interests.

Values and Ideologies

Finally, people would have to be helped to reexamine the dominant values and ideologies of their cultures, which they internalized into their consciousness while growing up and interacting with others in everyday life. Once people internalize these values and ideologies, they come to perceive their interests in adapting to the practices and expectations of their society, and they are motivated to think and act in ways that continuously reproduce the institutional status quo.

When people are helped to discover that their real needs are being frustrated consistently in the context of established unjust and oppressive institutions, they are also likely to realize that transforming these institutions into just and nonoppressive ones would serve their interest, as it would be conducive to their personal development by enabling them to meet their real needs. These insights would enable them also to recognize the necessity of shifting currently dominant values and ideologies, which sustain unjust and oppressive ways of life, toward alternative values and ideologies that affirm equality, liberty, individuality, community, cooperation, and harmony with nature.

Strategies to Expand Critical Consciousness

Expanding critical consciousness through everyday social and professional encounters involves initiating political discourse in social gatherings and in places of work. When people interact socially or professionally in everyday life, their actions and communications can either conform to or challenge the social status quo and prevailing patterns of human relations. When people speak and act within the range of "normal" expected behavior, they reinforce the existing social order and its "commonsense" consciousness. On the other hand, when people's words and acts transcend "normal" behavioral ranges by questioning and challenging the status quo, they create opportunities for the emergence of reflection and critical consciousness on the part of others with whom they interact.

Based on these considerations, the strategy suggested here involves efforts by activists to "deviate" in everyday social and professional encounters from system-reinforcing behaviors, to pose challenging questions and to engage people in reflection and dialogue concerning consequences of prevailing social, economic, political, and cultural realities for the quality of their lives.

As dialogues evolve, activists could identify themselves as advocates of social and economic justice and real democracy—feasible alternatives to capitalism and plutocracy. They must not practice self-censorship concerning their political views, as people tend to do in unjust and oppressive realities. One cannot help others to extricate themselves from the dominant ideology and culture unless one is comfortable with acknowledging one's alternative perspective.

In pursuing this strategy, activists need to be sensitive to the thoughts, feelings, and circumstances of people with whom they engage in dialogue. As the goal of these encounters is to stimulate reflection, one needs to be sure that people are ready to communicate. Also, activists have to be tolerant of positions they reject. Whatever positions people hold do make sense to them in terms of their life experiences and frames of reference. People have to be respected in these encounters, even when their positions and values conflict with those of the activists.

There are many opportunities to act in accordance with this strategy. Were many activists to use these opportunities routinely, many people might become involved in political discussions, and the taboo against discourse that challenges capitalism might be overcome. Gradually, growing numbers of people might undergo transformations of consciousness, join transformation movements, and carry on this strategy.

It is important that people pursuing this strategy do not try to do too much too soon, but develop their skills and sensitivity gradually, in order to avoid burnout. People using this strategy are likely to benefit from joining support groups whose members can help one another to examine and improve their political practice. Applying this strategy to "radical" practice of social work and other professions requires a separate essay (Gil, 1998).

From Conventional Politics to Politics of Common Human Needs

Conventional politics concerning workplace and community issues, the rights of groups subjected to discrimination, protection of the environment, electoral politics, and so forth tend to pursue short-term goals rather than long-range visions of fundamental social change. However, radical activists can use participation in conventional politics to help people trace connections between apparently separate issues and discern their common roots in the prevailing social order. When exposed to such insights, people may realize that they would have to confront root causes in order to deal effectively with the separate issues they intend to solve.

Expanding people's consciousness concerning the connections and the common roots of discrete problems (around which interest groups tend to form) could enable them to overcome fragmentation and competition for limited resources. Such fragmentation and competition are politically dysfunctional because they reinforce the status quo of power by reducing the potential collective strength of separate interest groups. The goal of radical activists in these situations, therefore, is to transform conventional interest-group politics into politics of common human needs.

Beyond Critical Consciousness: Changing Behavior and Institutions

Unless shifts in consciousness cause individuals and groups to evolve new patterns of actions and social relations, the process of social change could stall on the level of ideas. New patterns of action and social relations depend on self-transformation by individuals, as well as on institutional transformations carried out collectively by individuals and groups and the networks among them.

Individual Changes

Changes in the consciousness of individuals could gradually lead to changes in attitudes and relations toward people with whom they live and work and toward the natural environment on which all life depends. People could try to avoid dominating, exploiting, and competing with others and to reduce socially structured inequalities and benefits derived from racism, sexism, and other types of discrimination. In their everyday social relations, people could foster cooperation, solidarity, and community as far as possible, in spite of prevailing social structures and dynamics.

People could modify their actions and social relations in accordance with their transformed consciousness by testing and expanding accepted limits in settings and situations over which they exercise some influence. They could create "liberated spaces," prefiguring possible futures. People could also reduce their personal involvement in wasteful and destructive consumption of the earth's limited resources, and they could aim to adjust personal lifestyles to principles of global distributive justice and environmental sustainability. Through such socially less unjust and ecologically less damaging practices, people could reduce somewhat the contradictions between their newly evolving values and everyday realities (Simple Living Collective, 1977).

Collective Changes

The transformation of the oppressive institutions and culture of globalized capitalism could be furthered by gradual emergence of alternative economic practices that transcend the principles of capitalism and by simultaneous spread of emancipatory philosophical and ideological systems, such as democratic socialism.

A renaissance of cooperative economic enterprises began in the eighteenth and nineteenth centuries and became a worldwide phenomenon during the twentieth century (Buber, 1958; Thompson, 1994). Modern cooperative institutions include consumer cooperatives; cooperative financial services such as credit unions, cooperative banks, and rotating community loan funds; producer cooperatives and networks of producer cooperatives for bartering and marketing; and "total" cooperatives, which combine cooperative production and consumption with living cooperatively (Blum, 1968; Buber, 1958; Gil, 1979; Lindenfeld & Rothschild-Whitt, 1982; Morrison, 1991).

Consumer cooperatives are not as significant a challenge to capitalism as producer cooperatives and total cooperatives. However, consumer cooperatives demonstrate the value and ideology of cooperation, and in this way they challenge the dominant, competitive ideology of capitalism.

Producer cooperatives and their marketing associations challenge a basic capitalist principle: the separation of ownership and control of enterprises from workers employed by them. In producer cooperatives, workers own the means, skills, and knowledge of production, and they control and design the processes of production and marketing. While capitalism exists, producer cooperatives are forced to function as capitalist units, responsive to dynamics of capitalist markets. However, internally, they are a cooperative alternative to the dominant competitive economic model. Their spread in many parts of the world could, in theory, replace capitalism gradually from within, and they are, therefore, a significant action strategy toward a just and non-oppressive economy, society, and culture.

Total collectives, like the kibbutz and kibbutz networks in Palestine and Israel and other religious and secular communes in the United States and elsewhere, transcend and challenge capitalism not only as an economic system, but also in social, political, cultural, and philosophical-ideological terms. They are models that prefigure just and nonoppressive societies, and they demonstrate the feasibility of creating such comprehensive alternatives within prevailing realities. They also reveal the difficulties involved in creating such alternatives. Yet, like producer cooperatives, they are important elements of a comprehensive strategy for social transformation because they combine into a living reality the transformation of consciousness, actions, and social relations (Buber, 1958; Gil, 1979; Fellowship for Intentional Community, 1990; Kanter, 1972, 1973; Spiro, 1970).

Violence and Social Change

It is widely assumed that violence and armed struggle are necessary to overcome injustice and oppression. It is, therefore, important to examine this assumption when developing strategies for human liberation.

When analyzing the origins and dynamics of injustice and oppression, we concluded that societal violence was used in establishing unjust and oppressive social orders and that maintaining and reproducing these orders depends on subtly coercive processes of socialization, as well as on overt and covert, coercive social control. Coercion and societal violence are constant features of life in unjust and oppressive societies. Poverty, homelessness, exploitative work, unemployment, inadequate health care, poor education, and individual and social underdevelopment are but some of the symptoms of persistent societal violence of established ways of life in unjust and oppressive societies.

Societal violence is also used by dominant social classes to defend the established way of life against challenges from dominated and exploited classes. Social movements struggling against injustice and oppression are likely to encounter coercive and violent measures used against them by the legal system and the armed forces of the established order. It follows that when liberation movements engage in armed struggle, in self-defense against an unjust and oppressive state or in order to gain control over centers of state power, they are not initiating violence, but are reacting with counter-violence to the initiating societal violence used against them by agents of the state (Gil, 1999).

Whether coercion and violence are present in liberation struggles is, therefore, a moot question. They are inevitably present as constant societal violence used by dominant social classes to maintain unjust social orders. The proper questions liberation movements ought to consider when planning their strategies are whether, when, under what conditions, and toward what targets and ends they should use counterviolence and whether counterviolence can actually achieve just and nonoppressive social orders.

There are no universally valid answers to some of these questions because the conditions of injustice and oppression vary greatly in different situations, places, and times, and because strategies of liberation movements need always to be designed in relation to specific societal realities and opportunities. Moreover, only people involved in and affected by particular unjust and oppressive realities, rather than distant supporters and observers, have a moral right to determine what means to use in their struggle. They alone must live (or die) with the consequences of their strategic choices. To illustrate this point, outsiders could not have determined the mode of struggle of American colonists against the British, revolutionaries against the French monarchy, the African National Congress against the apartheid system, the Bolsheviks in Russia, the Maoists in China, and Castro's movement in Cuba.

Students of social change can, and should, however, examine the consequences of the use of counterviolence in armed struggles in various historic situations. They should also compare the consequences of armed struggles with those of active, nonviolent struggles, and they should study theoretical and philosophical positions concerning armed and nonviolent struggles.

Such studies suggest that although armed struggle can be effective in dealing with intense injustice and oppression in the short term, it is unlikely to eliminate domination and exploitation, the root causes of injustice and oppression. It has, at times, overpowered dominant classes who oppress people and benefit from coercively maintained injustice, but, so far, it has not eliminated the practice of domination and exploitation, and it is unlikely to do so in the future. It has merely changed the agents and victims of oppression.

The implication of such studies is that armed liberation struggles, whatever their apparent achievements, may have to be followed by long-term, unarmed, active, nonviolent liberation struggles aimed at overcoming the root causes of injustice and oppression, rather than merely their most severe manifestations (Bruyn & Rayman, 1979; King, 1992; Lakey, 1987; Sharp, 1973, 1979).

Continuing the Conversation

In this essay, I have presented my tentative insights into the nature, dynamics, and perpetuation of injustice and oppression and into strategies to struggle against these destructive social practices. It is important that readers examine these issues critically for themselves in order to develop their own perspectives. The following questions, along with others that may occur to readers, should be useful in such an examination:

• Do the concepts and definitions of oppression and injustice in this essay make sense? Would you suggest others?

- Is the concept of key institutions of social life useful in understanding oppression and injustice and in developing strategies to overcome them?

- Is the sketch of the history of oppression and injustice useful in reflecting about strategies to overcome them?

- Do the strategies suggested in this essay make sense? Would you suggest others?

- Does armed struggle fit into a comprehensive strategy against injustice and oppression, and if so, when and how?

I have referred to my insights as tentative because the search for understanding injustice and oppression and modes of overcoming them is a lifelong process. Certainty will be reached only when social movements succeed, sometime in the future, to create and maintain just societies. Only then will people know what has worked and what insights and strategies were valid. Until then, our views on these matters will be, at best, informed hypotheses.

References

Blum, F. H. (1968). *Work and community.* London: Routledge & Kegan Paul.

Bruyn, S. T., & Rayman, P. (1979). *Nonviolent action and social change.* New York: Irvington Publishers.

Buber, M. (1958). *Paths in utopia.* Boston: Beacon Press.

Durant, W. (1935). *The story of civilization I: Our oriental heritage.* New York: Simon and Schuster.

Eisler, R. (1987). *The chalice and the blade.* New York: Harper and Row.

Farb, P. (1968). *Man's rise to civilization.* New York: Avon.

Fellowship for Intentional Community and Communities Publication Cooperative. (1990). *Intentional communities—1990/1991 directory.* Evansville, IN: Fellowship for Intentional Community, and Stelle, IL: Communities Publication Cooperative.

Frank, A. G. (1977). *World accumulation, 1492–1789.* New York: Monthly Review Press.

Freire, P. (1970). *Pedagogy of the oppressed.* New York: Herder and Herder.

Fromm, E. (1955). *The sane society.* Greenwich, CT: Fawcett.

Gil, D. G. (1979). *Beyond the jungle.* Cambridge, MA: Schenkman, and Boston: G. K. Hall.

Gil, D. G. (1992). *Unravelling social policy.* Rochester, VT: Schenkman Books.

Gil, D. G. (1998). *Confronting injustice and oppression.* New York: Columbia University Press.

Gil, D. G. (1999). Understanding and overcoming social structural violence. *Contemporary Justice Review, 2*(1), 23–35.

Gil, D. G. (2000). Rethinking the goals, organization, designs and quality of work in relation to individual and social development. *Contemporary Justice Review, 3*(1), 73–88.

John Paul, II. (1982). *Encyclical on human work.* Boston: Daughters of St. Paul.

Kanter, R. M. (1972). *Commitment and community.* Cambridge, MA: Harvard University Press.

Kanter, R. M. (1973). *Communes: Creating and managing the collective life.* New York: Harper and Row.

King, M. L., Jr. (1992). *I have a dream: Writings and speeches that changed the world.* San Francisco: Harper.

Kropotkin, P. (1956). *Mutual aid.* Boston: Porter Sargent. (Original work published 1902).

Lakey, G. (1987). *Powerful peacemaking: A strategy for a living revolution.* Philadelphia: New Society Publishers.

Lindenfeld, F., & Rothschild-Whitt, J. (Eds.). (1982). *Workplace democracy and social change.* Boston: Porter Sargent.

Magdoff, H. (1977). *Imperialism: From the colonial age to the present.* New York: Monthly Review Press.

Maslow, A. (1970). *Motivation and personality.* New York: Harper and Row.

Maslow, A. H., & Honigman, J. J. (1970). Synergy: Some notes of Ruth Benedict. *American Anthropologist, 72,* 320–333.

Morrison, R. (1991). *We build the road as we travel: Mondragon, a cooperative social system.* Philadelphia: New Society Publishers.

National Conference of Catholic Bishops. (1986). *Economic justice for all*. Washington, DC: Author.

Ryan, W. (1971). *Blaming the victim*. New York: Pantheon.

Sharp, G. (1973). *The politics of nonviolent action*. Boston: Porter Sargent.

Sharp, G. (1979). *Gandhi as a political strategist*. Boston: Porter Sargent.

Simple Living Collective, American Friends Service Committee, San Francisco. (1977). *Taking charge*. New York: Bantam Books.

Smith, A. (1961). *The wealth of nations*. Indianapolis, IN: Bobbs-Merrill.

Spiro, M. E. (1970). *Kibbutz—Venture in utopia*. New York: Schocken Books.

Tawney, R. H. (1964). *Equality*. London: Allen and Unwin. (Original work published 1931).

Thompson, D. J. (1994). Co-operation in America. *Co-operative Housing Journal*.

Tucker, R. C. (Ed.). (1978). *The Marx-Engels reader* (2nd ed.). New York: Norton.

Zinn, H. (1980). *A people's history of the United States*. New York: Harper and Row.

Ethical and Inescapable: Politicized Social Work

Pamela Long

So I wonder who you are, reading this chapter. Are you like I was as a social work student in the early 1970s and again in the early 1980s? Did you enter the field to enhance the well-being of individuals and families? As you register for the requisite policy courses, are you endeavoring to "get through them" so you can then take "more relevant" courses you believe will benefit your interpersonal practice with individuals and families more than social welfare policy? Or do you think that although it may be helpful for you to know what policies exist to meet human needs, you will not seek changes in policies because you are interested primarily in direct practice?

These were my thoughts as an undergraduate student in the early 1970s. Although I found social welfare policy mildly interesting, I did not understand the relevance of policy to social work practice—especially direct practice. Intervention methods at the time included casework, group work, and community organization. My undergraduate practicum placement in a public child welfare agency was, to me, about helping people—most of them poor—with their individual problems using the casework methods I had learned from a text by Florence Hollis (1972). After I graduated, I continued to seek individual solutions to what impressed me as personal problems in public child protective services. Far from seeing myself as a policy advocate, I acted apolitically. Like most of my colleagues, I saw my role as a social worker to be one of evaluating needs and providing and coordinating services to families. To become entangled in policy or political issues, I believed, would serve to undermine attention to my primary working relationship with families. Yet I recall that I lived with a nagging feeling (for which I had no cognitive life raft) that what I treated were symptoms of larger problems and that social workers maintained social order by managing certain disregarded groups.

Later, as a graduate student in the early 1980s, I plowed through two required policy courses and completed research exploring critical gaps in services to families, demonstrating the need for policy change. After graduation, however, I planned to seek employment in community mental health and to focus on the development of direct practice skills. In my advanced policy course, I recall one of my policy professors asking those of us intending to work with individuals and families what kind of questions we might ask a stay-at-home mother considering divorce after nine years of marriage. Our class responded with questions designed to explore the marital history, stresses in the marriage, and concerns about the coparenting relationship. The professor took issue with our responses and introduced a policy issue, pointing out that this woman's future economic security was at stake. Should this hypothetical client divorce before ten full years of marriage, she would be ineligible to receive social security benefits on her former husband's work record. This was something I needed to know. I began to realize how what Jansson (1999) refers to as policy sensitive practice was important to "good client service."

After graduation, I practiced as a clinical social worker within a mental health center. I continued to try to be policy sensitive, but I did not see social work as political. Neither did my colleagues. Indeed, Alexander (1982) found that most social workers at that time favored the separation of professional activities and political activities. Given the conservative nature of the times and my "quest for professionalism," it would be some time before I began to understand Abramovitz's (1993) assertion that all of social work is "political because it deals either with consciousness or the allocation of resources" (p. 6). In contrast, apolitical social work "typically blame[s] the victim and deflects attention from the more systemic causes of many personal and social problems" (p. 6).

Integrating policy with practice is necessary to work with client systems in carrying out the mission of social work as articulated in the preamble of the National Association of Social Workers (NASW) *Code of Ethics* (2000):

> The mission of the social work profession is to enhance human well being and help meet the basic human needs of all people, with the particular attention to the needs and empowerment of people who are vulnerable, oppressed, and living in poverty. . . . Social workers promote social justice and social change with and on behalf of clients. . . . Social workers also seek to promote the responsiveness of organizations, communities, and other social institutions to individuals' needs and social problems. (p. 1)

The history of the profession provides a rich tradition of confronting oppression and promoting a just society. The current political and postindustrial economic climates call for political sensitivity at all levels of practice and a commitment to social action and change.

My hope in writing this chapter is to deepen your appreciation and understanding of the political nature of social work practice. It is essential for us as social workers to develop our own consciousness about the connections between personal issues and sociopolitical and economic realities. I hope to inspire you to intentionally practice with a "politicized consciousness." Additionally, this chapter provides guidelines for examining your own work and the practice within your agency setting from a political perspective and suggests strategies for you to successfully intervene for social justice.

The Political Nature of Social Work Practice

Social workers are sensitive to social welfare policy because it affects clients' lives and provides the context for practice. Social welfare policy determines who receives services, for how long, and where. However, when we speak of "promoting social justice and social change with and on behalf of clients," as the NASW (2000) Code charges, we refer to issues of power and policy and enter a political arena. Cowger (1994) writes, "clinical practice that considers social and economic justice suggests a type of practice that explicitly deals with power and power relationships" (p. 263). Fisher (1995) asserts that social work "is fundamentally about power, ideology and social justice" (p. 195). Whether you agree with these assertions depends on your underlying political ideology. From a progressive view, social work is about social change and social justice, whereas a conservative stance holds that politicizing social work is unprofessional (Fisher, 1995).

Some practicing social workers take a position that political involvement is hurtful or at best irrelevant to clients. Referring to the 1980s, Fisher (1995) observed, "much of social work practice was depoliticized, personalized, and decontextualized" (p. 194). These were conservative times, when many social workers conveyed a dislike of public agency social work practice and were attracted to individual counseling and private practice. Alexander (1982) found that most social workers in the early 1980s favored the separation of professional activities from political activities. When social workers were politically active, they tended to promote their own welfare, addressing guild issues—those focused on improving professional status—instead of a social justice agenda. A later study by Salcido and Seck (1992) found that the NASW chapters' political activities "act on behalf of goals related to promoting the profession and to a lesser extent on those promoting social services legislation . . . [suggesting] advocacy for disenfranchised groups is not a high priority" (p. 564).

Having the understanding that all social work practice is political—that is, having to do with power—and recognizing the interdependence of practice and policy is a less-accepted position. Despite "increased literature, political social work or politicized social work practice is still viewed as atypical, aberrant, temporary and/or unprofessional at the turn of the millennium" (Haynes & Mickelson, 2000, p. 4).

The perspective expressed in this chapter stands in stark contrast to this conservative view of an apolitical social work, asserting that every intervention is a political action. A decision to *act* apolitically is a decision to support the status quo, impede opportunities for change, and further participate in the oppression of vulnerable client systems. Practicing ethical social work means attending to power and political issues at every system level and intervening in ways to promote social justice and to ensure full client self-determination.

The Political Nature of Direct Practice

The "personal is political" in the person of the social worker. The beliefs, values, and practices of the social worker have political implications. Social workers who focus only on individual behaviors and who believe clients are best served by working with them only to *adapt* to their environment impede their clients' abilities to fully exercise self-determination. Cowger (1994) asserts

> client power is achieved when clients make choices that give them more control over their presenting problem situations and their own lives . . . Social work practice based on the notion of choice requires attention directed to the dynamics of personal power, the social power endemic to the client's environment, and the relationships between the two. (pp. 263–264)

Consider the social worker in an inner city hospital emergency room where a high incidence of young children are seen for various injuries related to poor public housing conditions. An individual focus may include attention to "parental deficits" in parental care and supervision of children, with a consequent referral to a parenting group or child welfare services. Within this framework, clients may exercise limited self-determination by either electing to accept or reject the referral. A more complete opportunity for client self-determination evolves when the social worker collaborates with parents to advise them of the high incidence of injuries among children who reside in public housing. The social worker may then involve parents to consider an array of available options to parents of children who are injured, including social advocacy. In this case, parents may choose to advocate for necessary repairs to their homes and thereby exercise self-determination in affecting institutional change. Through their collaborative work with parents, social workers also realize social and economic justice goals.

The Power of Defining the Problem
A practitioner's theoretical formulation and practice approach are political choices. When a practitioner comes from an "expert" role, oppression and injustices clients experience in the world are reinforced in the power differential established within "therapeutic" relationships. The medical model, around which much of our current system of reimbursement is based, pathologizes adaptive behavior, decontextualizes persons from their environment, and points up individual failures and inadequacies. Despite a growing body of empowerment literature and a strengths focus, conventional social work practice continues to focus on deficits, disorder, and dysfunction, often cloaked within a presumption of neutrality and objectivity.

Decades ago, in *Politics of Therapy*, Halleck (1971) concluded that any professional practicing psychotherapy is neither objective nor neutral and has taken "positions on issues that have political implications . . . issues that involve the distribution of power within social systems" (p. 34). Helping professionals enforce social control by treating persons stressed by environmental conditions, by turning their attention from those environmental stresses to internal processes, by labeling as mentally ill those who do not "fit," therefore depriving them of power, and by patholgizing certain oppressed groups.

How much has changed since the time of Halleck's critique? Not much! Kutchins and Kirk (1997) examine the politics of certain diagnostic categories from the American Psychiatric Association's *Diagnostic and Statistical Manual of Mental Disorders (DSM-IV)* (1994) and find that the "definitions of mental illness often mask gender and racial bias . . . [and that the] interpretation of scientific data is often distorted to serve the purposes of powerful professional groups" (p. 17). They identify three key themes in *Making Us Crazy: DSM: The Psychiatric Bible and the Creation of Mental Disorders:*

- Everyday behavior is pathologized. More and more human problems are being defined as mental disorders under "medical jurisdiction." (p. 16)
- "Political negotiation and advocacy—as well as personal interests—are just as, and often more, important in determining whether a mental disorder is created."
- *DMS-IV* is "an instrument that pathologizes those in our society who are undesirable and powerless." (p. 16)

The authors conclude that "the development of diagnostic categories has been similar to other types of professional decision making, where status, reputation, and turf are dominant considerations" (p. 18).

In the context of managed mental health care, the *DSM-IV* (1994), and the subsequent revised edition, the *DSM-IV-TR* (2000), are increasingly used by social workers, many of whom do not critically consider their origins and context or the political ramifications of diagnosis. Based on this matrix, McQuaide (1999) advises us to remember

> that the *DSM* syndromes are actually social constructions, not scientific facts free from a political agenda; remaining always cognizant of the individual's uniqueness; recognizing that the *DSM*, while privileging certain knowledge, subjugates other knowledge; and remembering that the person is not the problem, the problem is the problem. (p. 410)

The problems that people face are frequently oppression, discrimination, and social injustice.

Contrasting Paradigms

The practitioner's consciousness shapes the interaction with the client system. In interpersonal practice, social workers can choose to operate within models of deficits, disorders, and dysfunction, or they can focus on the strengths and capabilities of client systems. Focusing on the strengths and resilience of clients promotes an ability to place in perspective the sociopolitical realities in which our clients live. "Clinical social work, including private practice, can promote compliance and adjustment to the status quo or liberate individuals from internalized oppression using consciousness-raising and self-empowerment processes that link personal problems to social conditions" (Abramovitz, 1993, p. 9).

Multicultural practice models and feminist social work approaches insert power dynamics into work at the personal level. Land (1995) discusses feminist practice as a method that acknowledges the political nature of personal issues and how personal issues reflect power inequalities. "Many times, the components of the political context are multifaceted, covert in nature, and defined by those in power as problems residing within the individual rather than in the system" (p. 9).

Place yourself in the following scenario, which characterizes the manner in which workers are invited to pathologize clients, even though opportunities exist to support them and collaborate with them in an empowering process.

You work in an agency in which nonvoluntary clients referred to the clinic, usually by the judicial system, have "not been engaging very well" with their assigned therapists. This "problem," coupled with long clinic waiting lists, leads to an administrative plan for "pre-client group services" with the goal of "socializing these court-ordered persons to clienthood." Of your last twenty initial client appointments, nine have been women—poor, single parents, who have said they were depressed. Your clinic protocol is to provide individual services in which you teach clients how to "manage their depression" and to consider a referral for medication. You have read of an innovative group model in which clients find support in discussing common issues, begin to make connections between personal problems and social policy issues, and advocate change. However, no such service is available within the clinic.

In this example, the "expert role" of the social work practitioner and the power of the agency are evident. Clients are forced to adapt to coercive, deficit-based assessment and treatment services. This furthers the power differential between clinicians and clients, utilizing authority as a social control. The medical model used to assess depression fails to acknowledge the political and economic sources of depression. Consequently, there is no imagination for "treatment" at an environmental level. The implementation of group services would serve to promote the participants' understanding that their "life chances and choices are significantly curtailed by inequalities in the distribution of social, economic, and political power and resources" (Breton, 1994, p. 24).

Apolitical social work practice, with its incomplete understanding of client self-determination, results in reinforcing the status quo. Conventional social work continues to support the existing social, economic, and political systems (Carniol, 1992). In contrast, the empowerment-based, constructionist, and feminist models promote the understanding of a politicized practice. The social work values of self-determination and the promotion of social justice are more effectively met when practicing within these models.

Acknowledging Power and Privilege

In considering the political nature of social work practice, we have discussed theory, practice models, and ethical issues, but we also need to consider who we are as social work professionals. Good social work practice calls on us to critically reflect on our cultural history, social location, and degree of privilege. To persons and groups holding it, privilege is invisible (Swigonski, 1993). Consider, for example, whether your background provided you with more privilege than many of the clients you see in your practice. Frequently, our middle-class values and professional training distance us from the everyday lives and realities of many of our clients. Without a politicized consciousness and critical reflection, our values are likely to lead us to work with clients in ways that further oppress and pathologize them. Day (2000) writes:

> We become society's way of enforcing conformity to norms that may not be relevant to the problem at hand. Norman Goroff has called social workers 'soft cops' because our work often hides values that society, the agency or we ourselves want to impose on our clients. (p. 26)

As we deal, then, with the "personal issues" of clients, we are either agents of social control or social change. There is no middle ground. The vulnerabilities of clients in direct practice settings are frequently exploited, both in the relationship established by the practitioner and by the beliefs, practices, and privilege that have become the culture of institutions vested with the authority to "help."

Power in Organizational Structures

Some years ago, family members of young adults with severe and persistent mental illness who were served by a rural mental health agency wanted to form a group and to ultimately associate with the National Alliance for the Mentally Ill (NAMI). They asked the agency to provide space for their meetings. The agency agreed, but it also provided two clinical facilitators for these meetings. The facilitators practiced what they knew best: attention to thoughts and feelings and "faulty family relationships." As a result, the family members persisted in dealing with crises and guilt around their young adult children. There was no opportunity to make claims to further needed services. The group did not move to join with the state and national advocacy organization and never advocated improvements in locally based services for their adult children, who needed and deserved so much. The group's original purpose was thwarted. These family members could have been supported in sharing their strengths to mobilize advocacy efforts for the community resources desperately needed by their family members who have mental illnesses.

Consider another example. As a school social worker in a bilingual community, you want to introduce a district, monthly parent newsletter. You are surprised to find some school administrators disapprove your plan to disseminate a Spanish version of the newsletter to non-English-speaking Hispanic families. Your supervisor suggests you drop your plans for the Spanish version. The supervisor feels the elementary students can translate this for their parents, as they do all other school material.

These examples illustrate issues of power and politics at the agency level. In both examples, agencies reinforce the one-down position of client groups who are oppressed and preserve the privilege of "helping professionals." In neither instance is client self-determination promoted, and in the latter example, the administrative directive clearly denies opportunities for full participation as required by the NASW code.

The regulations and policies of an employing agency direct social workers in that agency. Ethical social workers must assess the appropriateness of agency practices as they relate to politicized client service. When practitioners believe agency procedures are not helpful to clients, they can discuss this with colleagues and their supervisors and seek change. Agency-based social workers at any level can find a voice to discuss concerns with agency supervisors and administration. A social worker's status as an agency employee does not diminish a sense of professional practice. "A profession of 'agency employees' is not a profession at all. . . . That a professional . . . is employed by an institution need not diminish the freedom to think straight and practice with craftsmanship" (Meyer, as cited in Schorr, 1985, p. 191).

Power in Social and Political Institutions

Social welfare in the United States serves to both assist persons in need and to maintain social, political, and economic institutions. According to Day (2000), if social welfare programs were "assessed only on client benefit, most would be considered failures, for the lives of clients are not changed much by most social welfare programs" (p. 36). On the other hand, with respect to control, they may be judged as a success. For example, public assistance programs "relieve society of the burden of adequate support and provide employers with sufficient workers at low wages and minimum benefits" (p. 36).

Social welfare and tax policies do little to redistribute income and redress inequality in social structures. Gilbert and Terrell (1998) discuss how, in the past forty years, the welfare state has benefited the middle class. Although most citizens consider "welfare" as Temporary Assistance for Needy Families (TANF) and food stamps, these programs are modest in comparison with Social Security benefits that create "a network of medical and income entitlements aimed at providing economic security over the life cycle of ordinary families" (p. 43). The tax system also tends to benefit taxpayers who are more well off, providing the greatest dollar value to those in the highest tax brackets. A 1996 study by the Citizens for Tax Justice (Ettlinger et al., 1996) found that nationally, low- and middle-income families pay a disproportionately higher percentage of their income on state and local taxes than families who are very well off.

The conservative movement in social welfare policy has had and will continue to have negative consequences for groups that are structurally oppressed. With challenges to affirmative action and the restrictive and time-limited benefits of welfare reform, vulnerable populations are further marginalized and often targeted as "the problem." Consider the following case example.

The agency employing you has just received a contract to provide group parenting education to all welfare mothers who are near the end of their benefit time limits. You realize this process, in itself, sends a message to these potential participants that they are not "good mothers," and further, that they are "personally responsible" for their lack of economic resources. You are told you may adapt the curriculum to fit the needs of this group. You have a political choice. The last worker lectured on children's developmental needs and methods of child discipline. However, you have just completed a social welfare policy course and believe this mandatory training will further victimize these mothers.

What a wonderful opportunity to design an empowerment-oriented approach that fits the reality of your clients. Essentially, the group can become a vehicle in which individual and family stories can be told, strengths acknowledged, and political realities discussed. Keeping in mind that political awareness, social action, recognition of competence, and the use of power are components of empowerment, you, as a social worker, can seek to become a partner to the change process initiated by the group (Breton, 1994).

"Social change efforts," "participation in decision making," and "equality of opportunity" are key responsibilities charged to social work professionals by the NASW (2000) code. Ethical social work practice is informed by an understanding of power at all system levels.

Political Pathways for Policy Change

Reisch (1997) calls for social work to recognize the inextricable connection between politics and social work practice: "The linkage of politics and social work requires social workers to reconceptualize the nature of our practice roles" (p. 89). A politicized practice is an integrated practice in which social workers assess and intervene at all system levels, client situations are contexualized, personal issues are linked with policy and social issues, and client empowerment is an outcome (Fisher, 1995).

Although becoming aware of the politics of direct practice is a first step, we also need to incorporate political skills into our practice. The current political environment calls for social work practice roles to include political behavior. Reisch (1997) offers the following general recommendations for political practice:

- Identify and publicize impediments to the delivery of quality social services and those working conditions that interfere with service delivery or create hardships for clients and workers at all levels of practice.

- Use both intra- and interorganizational groups to strengthen the political efforts of our agencies and schools.

- Link efforts to improve our agencies' services to larger underlying issues in our advocacy, political, and public education work—for example, by engaging in research on the impact of public policies on poverty and inequality.

- Work for increased political action within established professional organizations such as NASW and CSWE [Council on Social Work Education], while creating activist social work organizations to complement the efforts of mainstream professional associations.

- Form internal support groups in agencies and schools to discuss the political aspects of practice and education.

- Enter power entities, especially those that establish social policy priorities such as political parties, while building stronger relationships with low-power clients around issues that they define as important and helpful.

- Reemphasize the role of the political environment in the conceptual frameworks and modes of intervention that underlie our practice, scholarship, and teaching. (p. 89)

Within a politicized consciousness, agency-based social workers are able to encourage and work with colleagues and client systems for social change. Starting from a position of policy sensitivity, social workers become further aware of pathways for political social work practice.

Applying Practice Skills at the Policy Level

Social workers are trained in assessment and planning, working with groups, collaboration, and using research to inform practice. These generalist skills can all be exercised to advance a policy agenda within agency practice. Expertise in policy analysis is not a requirement. Politicizing social work practice can be a collaborative effort with agency colleagues and, in some instances, with client systems.

To politicize your direct practice, watch for linkages between the "personal and political" and discuss these issues with colleagues and clients. Orient case reviews to consider the common needs and issues for clients that may identify the need for policy change at some level. It is also important to examine theories by which we practice, as well as our policies and organizational procedures. As we have already discussed, theories and practice models may function to maintain privilege and social injustice in both interpersonal practice and practice with larger systems. Critically evaluating our theories, policies, and procedures in terms of empowerment practice promotes more-ethical responses to the clients with whom we work.

Although you may choose to politicize your practice on your own, Reisch (1997) emphasizes collaboration at a number of levels. For example, he recommends working within the professional organization while also creating an activist organization. He also advocates joining an established political party while working with "low-power client groups" around their identified common issues. Associating with established power entities is beneficial while creating opportunities for alternative voices to be heard.

Documentation as a Political Tool

Case documentation is an arena in which direct service workers and supervisors are invaluable because they are in a position to examine needs, issues, and trends. Haynes and Mickelson (2000) encourage agencies to construct documentation systems to include political activities, to supplement management information and clinical data. In most cases, agencies utilize information systems to characterize staff activity, in addition to client characteristics, problems, and case plans. Perhaps a group of social workers in your agency would be interested in meeting to discuss critical issues in service delivery or hardships for clients and to determine how current information systems could be used to collect data to identify service gaps and unmet needs. Either individually or in groups, practitioners can develop case profiles and other information to depict an area of concern.

I attended the 1997 NASW national convention in Baltimore, Maryland, where Mary Bricker-Jenkins gathered a group of social workers from across the country and asked what changes they had observed in their practices as a result of welfare reform legislation. Several social workers discussed increased absences of elementary children from school. In these cases, because their mothers could not miss work, children from second through fifth grades stayed home to watch a younger brother or sister in the absence of available day care. Documenting these types of outcomes and needs is an important observation most visible to the practitioner.

Participatory Action Research
Social work research guides theory development, informs practice, substantiates claims for needed services, and provides evidence of fiscal and program accountability. As an agency-based social work practitioner, you will undoubtedly participate in developing research questions and in designing programs, services, and outcome studies. Promoting an opportunity for client involvement in agency research is a way to link personal with policy issues. Clients' participation in research issues promotes "unity among research, practice and policy as one collaborative process" (Sohng, 1996, p. 82). Clients, whose lives are affected by research findings and outcomes, ethically should have a say in identifying the research question and process. "Guided by the spirit of the settlement movement" (Malekoff, 1994, p. 47), participatory action research is "founded on the principle that those who experience a phenomenon are the most qualified to investigate it" (DePoy, Hartman, & Haslett, 1999, p. 561).

A participatory action research project might evolve from providing clinical group services to a disenfranchised population. For example, the group services previously discussed to "depressed," low-income mothers or to parents nearing the end of welfare benefit time limits might find therapeutic benefit in participating in an exploratory action research study. Common features between participatory research and practice approaches are evident in Sohng's (1996) discussion of participatory action research, including its politicized perspective and social justice value base:

> Both researcher and participant are actors in the investigative process, influencing the flow, interpreting the content, and sharing options for action. Ideally, this collaborative process is empowering because it (1) brings isolated people together around common problems and needs; (2) validates their experiences as the foundation for understanding and critical reflection; (3) presents the knowledge and experiences of the researcher as additional information upon which to critically reflect; (4) conceptualizes what have previously felt like "personal," individual problems or weakness; and (5) links such personal experiences to political realities. The result of this kind of activity is living knowledge that may get translated into action. Participatory research reflects goal oriented, experiential learning, and transformative pedagogy. (p. 83)

Marlow (2001) suggests that the elements of the empowerment-based approach to social work practice developed by Miley, O'Melia, & DuBois (2001) are closely associated with the steps related to research. For example, participatory methods parallel the initial step, forming partnerships in empowerment-based social work practice. Marlow contends that participatory action research provides one way of achieving this purpose and "is rapidly becoming the preferred approach to social work research" (p. 21).

Becoming More Knowledgeable about Policy

Many authors provide comprehensive information and guides for gathering information and resources for learning about social welfare policies (Gilbert & Terrell, 1998; Karger & Stoesz, 1998; Segal & Brzuzy, 1998). To incorporate knowledge of social welfare policies that drive your practice and the political context in which these policies take shape, there is no one right place to begin. However, consider beginning by talking with your agency supervisor or director. Your local or school librarian can assist you in locating reference information about public policies and show you where to retrieve government documents at the local, state, and federal levels. Elected officials, their aides, and advocacy organizations are also willing to provide policy information, opinion, and analysis. The Internet is an invaluable resource to learn more about policy. Advocacy organizations, think tanks, and professional associations provide detailed policy information on the World Wide Web (WWW). Also on the WWW, national newspapers, such as the *Christian Science Monitor*, the *New York Times*, the *Washington Post*, and the *Wall Street Journal* provide excellent sources for background information. Finally, federal and state governments post extensive web pages, and many policies may be downloaded directly.

Policy Analysis for the Social Work Practitioner

Social welfare policy texts (Gilbert & Terrell, 1998; Karger & Stoesz, 1998; Segal & Brzuzy, 1998) offer frameworks for policy analysis. Two primary considerations in analyzing social welfare policy are important to consider in a politicized practice. The first is to analyze the "political process and likely outcomes of those processes" (Haynes & Mickelson, 2000, p. 67). This includes assessing legislation, both the intended benefits and effects and the potential, unintended consequences. Second, from a social justice perspective, you will want to examine "issues of equity in eligibility and adequacy in provision [as these are] . . . directly related to the criteria of social justice" (Figueira-McDonough, 1993, p. 185). "Furthermore, underlying and subtle influences of institutional racism, sexism, homophobia, and ageism, as well as destructive elements of social control, punitive measures, or regressive redistribution of resources should be examined" (Haynes & Mickelson, 2000, p. 67).

An example chronicled by Gladwell (2000) in the *New Yorker* reveals the political process in the allocation of public health funds and the negative influences of racism. In both of the previous years, the U.S. Centers for Disease Control requested from Congress an extra $15 million to eradicate syphilis. The incidence of the disease had been at an all-time low, having last peaked in 1990. The window of opportunity to easily eliminate syphilis might be passed in a short time. So why, in a time of "fiscal plenty," would Congress not approve funds to eliminate a disease that increases the transmission of HIV disease, harms infants of infected mothers, and "costs the country two hundred and fourteen million dollars a year" (p. 21)? Two answers became evident when examining the political process and considering social-justice issues. First, resources available for medical research had increased since groups concerned with certain diseases had lobbied directly on Capitol Hill. For example, actor Michael J. Fox had spearheaded the campaign for funding and research for Parkinson's disease, and actor Christopher Reeves had brought a good deal of attention to the needs of persons with spinal cord injuries. Constituencies without voice or power, whose needs were perhaps greater, were more likely to be slighted. "That syphilis is a sexually transmitted disease primarily affecting very poor African Americans only makes things worse—sex, race and poverty being words that the present Congress has difficulty pronouncing individually, let alone in combination" (pp. 21–22).

Testimony at Public Hearings

Public hearings are an excellent way for clients and social workers to express opinions and perspectives to legislators and other elected officials about particular topics. The purpose of testimony before a legislative committee or in a public hearing is not simply to inform, but to persuade. Effective testimony is well prepared and clearly articulates the proposal you are advancing. It combines personal experience with more-objective information documenting the impact of the issue. If you have an opportunity to testify at a public hearing or before a legislative committee about proposed policies, consider encouraging the voices of client groups who are affected by proposed policy change.

If you are asked to testify, it is important to prepare well. The National Committee for the Prevention of Elder Abuse (2000) offers the following suggestions:

- Describe personal situations with generalizations and statistics about the population and connect them with the proposal you are advancing.
- If you are testifying about proposed legislation, ask for the committee's analysis and address questions committee members have previously raised.
- Prepare your remarks in advance and be brief and specific unless asked to elaborate.
- Be polite, but be sure to clarify your point and distinguish irrelevant examples.

Written statements, sometimes required several days prior to the testimony, should be carefully completed so the information is objective, easy to understand, and supports the testimony (Jansson, 1999).

Lobbying

Lobbying is a generic term referring to activities used to persuade legislators and officials in the executive branches of government. Professional lobbyists and lobby teams "are hired by corporations, trade associations, professional organizations or groups representing specific populations and issues" (Jansson, 1999, p. 99). For example, the NASW lobbies in Washington, D.C., and in the state capitols to advance the association's advocacy agenda. Figueira-McDonough (1993) identifies two potential shortcomings in institutional lobbying. "First, it might confine legislative advocacy to a limited number of officials, and second, given the nature of the organizations, the interests represented may more likely be those of the profession than the clients" (p. 82). The NASW has indeed been criticized for advancing the cause of professional social work licensure and other guild issues while neglecting disenfranchised groups (Specht & Courtney, 1994).

In addition to supporting institutional lobbying, social workers and client groups can participate directly in lobbying activities. Haynes and Mickelson (2000) contend "that lobbying is a legitimate, fundamental and powerful practice in a pluralistic society and that social workers and their clients will continue to lose politically if they do not enter this arena" (p. 89). Mary Andrus, MSW, legislative director for Congressman James Leach of Iowa, encourages social work students and social workers to participate in legislative arenas because they bring an active perspective from the field:

> They have much to share with legislators about the needs of individuals and organizations in their communities. They are often the ones who see where programs are not meeting the needs of individuals or where policy decisions are not bringing about the desired outcomes. They can shed light on how programs work or not as the case may be. This information is invaluable to legislators who debate programs and their funding. . . . This is a perspective that legislators should never overlook nor underestimate. (Special Interview, 1999, p. 13)

A great deal of information exists to guide social workers' lobbying efforts (Dear & Patti, 1981; Haynes & Mickelson, 2000; Jansson, 1999; McInnis-Dittrich, 1994; Richan, 1996). It is important to remember, though, that social workers do not require any special training to begin to practice in this arena. Your assessment and communication skills, along with your professional experience, provide you with a strong beginning point for advocacy.

Personal Meetings

Personal meetings with legislators or their staff members can be scheduled at any district office. Although you could meet with an official individually, small groups work well. Segal and Brzuzy (1998) recommend including media coverage. "This can be as simple as informing the staff member making the arrangements that you will have a photographer with you to take pictures for a newsletter" (p. 251). Consider the following suggestions:

- Determine your agenda and objectives. Be clear on what topics you are going to address and what you would like the outcome of the visit to be.
- Be prepared, identify yourself as a constituent, and articulate your knowledge and experience about your issue. Link the concerns of your clients, colleagues,

and members of the community to your issue. If you have prepared a fact sheet, be prepared to leave this, along with a business card.

- Be brief, concise, and polite. If the official cannot meet with you, meet with the staff person to articulate your position. If the official's position is different from yours, do not argue, but restate your position. Seek closure on your issue and follow your visit with a thank you note, briefly outlining again your issues. (NASW, New York Chapter, 2000; Segal & Brzuzy, 1998).

Letters and E-Mails

Letter writing is a powerful and effective tool in advocacy work. Your individual letter to a legislator or your generation of a letter-writing campaign can make a significant difference in influencing an elected official's vote. If you belong to an advocacy group, you may receive Action Alerts from that group with sample letters, asking you to contact your legislator. In these cases, it is good practice to write your own letter so you can add your individual perspective and experience.

Although legislative advocates generally agree that legibly handwritten or typed letters are the most effective, the use of electronic mail is increasing and provides an effective avenue for communicating important areas of concern. Whether you write and post a letter, fax correspondence, or mail electronically, your message should focus on one bill or issue and be brief. Use recommended forms of salutation. Begin the letter by identifying yourself and articulating your relationship to the subject or issue. If there is a bill number, reference this early in your communication. State your position on the bill and support your position with reasons and examples. Close your correspondence by requesting specifically what action you want from the elected official (Mickelson, 1995). Be sure to include your name, address, and phone number, and keep a copy of the correspondence for your own advocacy records.

Citizenship and Activism

Organizational restraints may require you to work outside of your agency in some cases. For example, if you are employed by a nonprofit organization recognized by the U.S. Internal Revenue Service under tax-code section 501(c)(3), your advocacy as an identified agency employee may be limited to educating elected officials about social conditions or program needs. Influencing the vote of an elected official, or endorsement of any kind to a political candidate or political party as an agency employee, may jeopardize your agency status with the Internal Revenue Service. It is best to review the law to clearly understand the regulations and how they may affect political activities as an agency employee.

However, social workers are also citizens and have rights and responsibilities to participate as informed and empowered citizens. The political process is open to all citizens, and social workers with a politicized consciousness may exercise partisan politics individually as citizens or as members of a professional or advocacy organization.

Electronic Advocacy

Social workers and clients with access to the Internet can gain access to pending legislation, voting records, committee activities, and links to the home pages of elected officials. For example, using THOMAS (http://thomas.loc.gov), the Library of Congress search engine for legislative information on the Internet, one can access public laws by number, bill summaries and status, congressional records, committee information, House and Senate directories, and links to state and local governments. Project VoteSmart (http://www.vote-smart.org), a nonpartisan, voter information organization, provides factual information about candidates and elected officials at all levels of government. From these web pages, one can easily identify public officials, access their voting records, and either send e-mails to elected officials or procure the street addresses for conventional letters.

Even though electronic advocacy is in the early stages of development, "electronic techniques, particularly those that utilize Internet-based technologies, are changing the way that advocacy is practiced" (McNutt, 2000, p. 1). Changes in technology or the political system "push the envelope of political participation into cyberspace," (p. 1) therefore enhancing the electronic-advocacy environment. McNutt notes that changes in technology and the political system call for social workers to learn about electronic-advocacy techniques because they provide an opportunity to become more effective in changing social systems and in joining with clients to advocate for social justice.

Professional and Political Alliances

Although the voice of one constituent makes a difference to an elected official, the power of a professional organization or an interorganizational alliance wields greater political power. Allying with organizations provides you with information on current policy issues and the opportunity to support policy with other persons who are interested in advocating for the same cause. The NASW is the largest professional organization for social work. Join your local district and state chapter. Become active in the Legislative Electoral Advocacy Network (LEAN), Political Action for Candidate Endorsement (PACE), or the Advocacy Listserv. Identify advocacy organizations within your field of social work practice and participate in defining a policy agenda. For example, a school social worker may want to explore such organizations as the Council for Exceptional Children or the School Social Work Association of America.

Voting and Voter Registration

Most U.S. citizens eighteen years and older have the right to vote. Yet, many do not register, and not all registered voters participate in elections. The percentage of registered voters participating in elections in the United States was 53 percent in the 1980s. When compared with other democracies during the same decade —67 percent in Canada and 94 percent in Italy—we can see the rate of voter participation in the United States is very low (U.S. General Accounting Office, 1990, as cited in Segal & Brzuzy, 1998). Census data reveal that younger adults are much less likely to vote than older adults. African Americans and Hispanics are less likely to vote than Whites. In the 1994 election, 47 percent of Whites voted, but only 37 percent of African Americans and just 19 percent of Hispanics voted. Finally, people earning higher annual incomes are significantly more likely to vote than persons making lower incomes. Politicians, of course, are aware of these patterns "and are more likely to tailor their positions to the preferences of those most apt to vote" (Segal & Brzuzy, 1998, p. 247).

The implication of these voting patterns is clear. Persons of privilege maintain their privilege through voting. The outcome of elections could be different if more people who are registered to vote did so. Perhaps even more important, the results of elections could be very different, not only if a higher percentage of people voted, but also if persons voting were truly representative of the population in the country. The National Voter Registration Act (NVRA) of 1993, a federal mandate requiring all states to offer voter-registration opportunities at driver's license and motor vehicle bureaus, welfare offices, and military recruiting stations, was enacted to compel states to adopt more-accessible voter registration procedures. The intent of the legislation was to target young people, new residents, and persons in poverty when they were applying for a driver's license or for public assistance so "the disenfranchisement of those populations might be partially overcome" (Martinez & Hill, 1999, p. 297).

Registration alone does not address the issue of nonvoting behavior. Martinez and Hill (1999) assessed the short-range impact of the NVRA in the 1996 election results and found almost no effect on voter turnout and equality in participation. One explanation for this low impact is the notion of voting as a two-step process. Persons who were not previously registered to vote were disinclined to participate. People participate in electoral politics because they are inspired to do so. Political parties and candidates, who provide this inspiration, tend to target voters who are easier to reach by conventional means—in factories, offices, and interest groups and in the mass media (Rosenstone & Hansen, 1993). As a result, persons who have been disenfranchised are less likely to be mobilized by political parties and candidates.

Client empowerment means supporting clients to act on their own behalf and to assert their rights. Encouraging voting is a way to increase a client's right to self-determination. An example of voter registration and support comes from the National Mental Health Association, which has recently accepted sponsorship of the Mental Health Voter Empowerment Project. The Project was begun in 1994 in an "effort to create a nationwide constituency of people with mental illness by locating potential voters, registering them, educating them about mental health issues, and making sure they get to the polls on Election Day" (Goode, 1999, A-1). In addition to registration, this project addresses potential barriers to voting—transportation, education, and fear.

Voter registration as a nonpartisan activity is an advocacy activity in which all social workers can participate. Social workers employed by the federal government or in state and local executive agencies are subject to the Hatch Act, which prohibits employees from influencing the votes of others, but does not preclude assisting in voter registration. Likewise, "social workers and human service agencies that have a tax-exempt 501(c)(3) status can participate in voter registration as long as the drive remains nonpartisan" (Haynes & Mickelson, 2000, p. 80).

Continuing the Conversation

My intention in this paper has been twofold: (1) to inspire you to practice with a politicized consciousness, and (2) to provide guidelines for you to organize your own practice from a political perspective. "Social workers need to understand and become involved in the political process in order to enhance our effectiveness and expand clients' capacity for self-determination" (Reisch, 1997, p. 90). The cherished social work value of promoting client self-determination is only actualized in a context in which alternatives exist.

Think about your own life to understand the need for political practice. As you make choices among options to reach your goals and aspirations, what opportunities are available to you? How do you account for the options you have? Can you trace your own privileges—your opportunities for education, for career advancement, and for professional status—to the political efforts of others? If you look closely enough, you will likely discover that your own reach is higher because you stand on the shoulders of those who came before you. Now look around at those less advantaged with whom you are likely to work as a social work professional. What will you do to extend their reach?

Perhaps in reading these pages you have determined to develop further policy sensitivity or to lobby in association with an advocacy organization. To paraphrase how we begin to work with clients, we "start where the social worker is." We also recall that we consciously politicize our practice because it is ethical and because, in doing so, we intervene for social justice and promote client self-determination.

References

Abramovitz, M. (1993). Should all social workers be educated for social change? Pro. *Journal of Social Work Education, 29,* 6–11.

Alexander, C. (1982). Professional social workers and political responsibility. In M. Mahaffey & J. W. Hanks (Eds.), *Practical politics: Social work and political responsibility* (pp. 15–31). Washington, DC: National Association of Social Workers.

American Psychiatric Association. (1994). *Diagnostic and statistical manual of mental disorders* (4th ed.). Washington, DC: Author.

American Psychiatric Association. (2000). *Diagnostic and statistical manual of mental disorders* (4th ed., revised). Washington, DC: Author.

Breton, M. (1994). On the meaning of empowerment and empowerment-oriented social work practice. *Social Work with Groups, 17*(3), 23–37.

Carniol, B. (1992). Structural social work: Maurice Moreau's challenge to social work. *Journal of Progressive Human Services, 3*(1), 1–20.

Cowger, C. D. (1994). Assessing client strengths: Clinical assessment for client empowerment. *Social Work, 39,* 262–269.

Day, P. J. (2000). *A new history of social welfare* (3rd ed.). Boston: Allyn & Bacon.

Dear, R. B., & Patti, R. J.(1981). Legislative advocacy: Seven effective tactics. *Social Work, 26,* 289–296.

DePoy, E., Hartman, A., & Haslett, D. (1999). Critical action research: A model for social work knowing. *Social Work, 44,* 560–569.

Ettlinger, M. P., McIntyre, R. S., Fray, E. A., O'Hare, J. F., King, J., & Miransky, N. (1996). *Who pays: A distributional analysis of the tax systems in all fifty states.* Washington, DC: Citizens for Tax Justice; Institute for Taxation and Economic Policy. Retrieved January 14, 2001, from the World Wide Web: http://www.ctj/whop/whop_txt.pdf

Figueira-McDonough, J. (1993). Policy practice: The neglected side of social work intervention. *Social Work, 38,* 179–188.

Fisher, R. (1995). Political social work. *Journal of Social Work Education, 31*(2), 194–203.

Gilbert, N., & Terrell, P. (1998). *Dimensions of social welfare policy* (4th ed.). Boston: Allyn & Bacon.

Gladwell, M. (2000, July 10). Comment: Cheap and easy. *New Yorker,* pp. 21–22.

Goode, E. (1999, October 13). Gentle drive to make voters of those with mental illness. *New York Times*, pp. A-1, A-18. Retrieved on July 8, 2000, from the Wide World Web: http://nytimes.com

Halleck, S. L. (1971). *Politics of therapy*. New York: Science House.

Haynes, K. S., & Mickelson, J. S. (2000). *Affecting change: Social workers in the political arena* (4th ed.). Boston: Allyn & Bacon.

Hollis, F. (1972). *Casework: A psychosocial therapy* (2nd ed.). New York: Random House.

Jansson, B. S. (1999). *Becoming an effective policy advocate: From policy practice to social justice* (3rd ed.). Pacific Grove, CA: Brooks/Cole.

Karger, H. J., & Stoesz, D. (1998). *American social welfare policy: A pluralist approach* (3rd ed.). New York: Longman.

Kutchins, H., & Kirk S. A. (1997). *Making us crazy: DSM: The psychiatric bible and the creation of mental disorders*. New York: Free Press.

Land, H. (1995). Feminist clinical social work in the 21st century. In N. Van Den Bergh, (Ed.). *Feminist practice in the 21st century* (pp. 3–19). Washington, DC: NASW Press.

Malekoff, A. (1994). Action research: An approach to preventing substance abuse and promoting social competency. *Health and Social Work, 36*, 46–53.

Marlow, C. R. (2001). *Research methods for generalist social work* (3rd ed.). Belmont, CA: Brooks/Cole.

Martinez, M. D., & Hill, D. (1999). Did motor voter work? *American Politics Quarterly, 27*(3), 296–315.

McInnis-Dittrich, K. (1994). *Integrating social welfare policy and social work practice*. Pacific Grove, CA: Brooks/Cole.

McNutt, J. G. (2000). Coming perspectives in the development of electronic advocacy for social policy practice. *Critical Social Work, 1* (1). Retrieved November 29, 2000, from the World Wide Web: http://www.criticalsocialwork.com/00coming_mcn.html

McQuaide, S. (1999). A social worker's use of the "Diagnostic and Statistical Manual." *Families in Society, 80*(4), 410–418.

Mickelson, J. S. (1995). *Speaking out for Houston's children*. Houston: Children at Risk.

Miley, K. K., O'Melia, M., & DuBois, B. (2001). *Generalist social work practice: An empowering approach* (3rd ed.). Boston: Allyn & Bacon.

National Association of Social Workers (2000). *Code of ethics*. Washington, DC: Author.

National Association of Social Workers, New York Chapter (2000). *How to lobby: Developing an advocacy agenda*. Retrieved July 3, 2000, from the World Wide Web: http://www.naswnys.org/legislative/howtolobby.html

National Committee for the Prevention of Elder Abuse. (2000). *Techniques for legislative advocacy*. Retrieved July 9, 2000, from the World Wide Web: http://www.presentelderabuse.org/frame/online/techniquesleg.htm

Reisch, M. (1997). The political context of social work. In M. Reisch & E. Gambrill (Eds.), *Social work in the 21st century* (pp. 80–92). Thousand Oaks, CA: Pine Forge Press.

Richan, W. C. (1996). *Lobbying for social change* (2nd ed.). New York: Haworth Press.

Rosenstone, S., & Hansen, J. M. (1993). *Mobilization, participation, and democracy in America*. New York: Macmillan.

Salcido, R. M., & Seck, E. T. (1992). Comments on currents: Political participation among social work chapters. *Social Work, 37*(6), 563–564.

Schorr, A. L. (1985). Professional practice as policy. *Social Service Review, 59*, 178–196.

Segal, E. A., & Brzuzy, S. (1998). *Social welfare: Policy, programs and practice*. Itasca, IL: F. E. Peacock.

Sohng, S. S. L. (1996). Participatory research and community organizing. *Journal of Sociology and Social Welfare, 23* (4), 77–97.

Specht, H., & Courtney, M. E. (1994). *Unfaithful angels: How social work has abandoned its mission*. New York: Free Press.

Special Interview with Ms. Mary Andrus, MSW. (2000). *Influence, 1*(4), p. 13.

Swigonski, M. E. (1993). Feminist standpoint theory and the question of social work research. *Affilia, 8*(2), 171–183.

Community Action Research

Marge Reitsma-Street and Leslie Brown

This chapter examines Community Action Research (CAR), an approach we have developed as social workers, as researchers, and as social work educators over the past two decades. Both originally trained in positivistic quantitative methods, we each took our own paths of discovering the limitations and even dangers of such a research approach. In this chapter we first present our journey to CAR, drawing upon conversations we had with each other in June 2000 and using short illustrations of the approach as used by Marge Reitsma-Street in urban settings in northern Ontario. Next is a description of CAR, its characteristics, values, and processes, followed by a detailed example of Leslie Brown's work in a British Columbia Aboriginal reserve community. The chapter ends with several questions we are pondering while continuing our journey and conversations.

Our Journey to Community Action Research

Understanding how and why we engage in research is an important place to start the story of our journey. Early on in our respective journeys we realized that our enjoyment in thinking about ideas and solving puzzles increased if they were useful to people. People have to be in the "absolute centre of the useful action," we said in our June conversations. The context for our research was people in relationships with one another who wanted to think creatively about concerns and do things that were useful for themselves and their communities. Doing good science and good community

The authors wish to acknowledge with deep appreciation the teachings, patience, and encouragement of our many teachers, in particular Pat Rogerson, Harry Street, Mabel Jean Rawlins-Brannan, Bobby Joseph, and Bruce Parisian.

works, therefore, are connected to one another, both situated within relationships and reflective practice. Leslie summed up this part of the journey:

> If you don't know how you have come to be, if you are not reflective about how you got here, and if you enter a research relationship only as an expert with the power to name, you haven't got it. We are just on a journey, personally and professionally, and how you enter a relationship is part of that journey. There has to be respect for the expertise of the whole persons that we engage with and the gifts they bring as a mother, a researcher, or a fifteen-year-old girl to the research relationships. Research may be the reason to begin the relationships, but it goes beyond that. Building relationships with participants is not just a research technique. That approach contaminates relationships. You have to be well-known in the community, be part of it before engaging in research.

An Example of Useful Research

Our commitment to useful research and social change prompted us to experiment with research activities that are helpful to people as they make pressing decisions on behalf of a community. Here is one example that shows how low-cost research activities were designed to help a group of people representing diverse constituents in two, poor, multicultural northern Ontario neighbourhoods decide about program directions for a proposed community resource centre (Reitsma-Street & Arnold, 1994).

> The planning group had many ideas, but there was neither coherence to the ideas nor agreement within the group about which program ideas made the most sense to the community. Twenty members of the planning group volunteered to interview people who lived or worked in the area to find out what program directions would make sense. Simple, fun questions suggested by parents who lived in the neighbourhood were used in short interviews, including, for example, "What would you do with a million dollars for the children in your neighbourhood?"
>
> The group began interviewing local people they knew, who recommended others to talk to. Everyone was asked the same questions, and answers were written down in a manner appropriate to each interviewer. In three weeks, 302 children and parents were interviewed, including every tenth household in the 600 public housing units in the neighborhoods, and sixty-two of the social-service professionals working in the area.
>
> After a long, informal afternoon of sharing data and suggesting interpretations, three people analyzed the recorded data more systematically and reported back to the group in a subsequent meeting. These research activities helped to clarify the specific concerns in the community and to build a consensus about program directions. All members of the neighbourhoods wanted children to play in safe places. All wanted good schools and help for children to complete their schooling. Furthermore, there was agreement that not just one, but several small neighbourhood centres were needed for adults and children to meet, play, and work. Lastly, culturally appropriate activities and services were necessary for the Aboriginal and Francophone families living in the community. Three members of the planning group volunteered to write up these findings to direct the creation of a funding proposal. The proposal was funded for five years. The program directions generated through the community action research initiative guided the centre's development during its initial years.

The Political Nature of Research

As we each traveled through different experiences with people-centred, useful research for communities, we learned to leave the certainty of traditional methodologies behind. Each of us in our own way had to challenge the authority of who knows best (Becker, 1970). By displacing authoritative accounts (Lather, 1991) and the centrality of scientific expertise, there emerged space for the experiences, knowledges, concerns, and expertise of many people, especially those most vulnerable to exclusion and oppression. We both gravitated to doing research with peoples pushed to the margins of our society—Leslie with Aboriginal communities and Marge with people living on low incomes or in marginalized communities. The political nature of our social work research began to emerge.

Fundamental to the politics of research is the careful and continuous negotiation about whose voice one emphasizes, what research strategies are selected, and on whose behalf one engages in research. It also is a political act to examine who benefits from particular information and how. In the example presented later in this chapter, Leslie clearly chose, and contracted, not to work for the federal Department of Indian Affairs, which funded the project, but reported to and was held accountable by the Aboriginal community.

In an initiative to shut down a welfare snitch line in an Ontario city, Marge and others used action-oriented research processes to mobilize energies among those who opposed the snitch line and to provoke uncertainty among decision-makers as they faced an anniversary review of the line's installation (Reitsma-Street, 1996). For instance, financial data were collected that failed to demonstrate any financial savings since installation of the snitch line. Also collected were qualitative examples of implications of the snitch line to community pride, to neighbourliness, and to people falsely accused of welfare fraud. Information on who actually benefited and who paid for the snitch line was released in story form to the press, in report form to bureaucrats, and in letters to politicians.

Our journey is not over. Feminist scholarship and current work in multicultural and Aboriginal communities continue to challenge us to explore what is good, useful research for a community. Leslie speaks of how a Kwakwaka'wakw elder helped her development as a researcher.

> He told me that research is a way for non-Aboriginal people to understand what Aboriginal people already know. I came to reframe research as a means of communication and understanding. It is a political tool that can be used to oppress or to liberate. This view was compatible with my feminist approach to research. I also wanted to make the links with social work practice and realized that I found the activism I desired in community development approaches to social work practice.

After many years of very different experiences, we practice and teach research in ways that reflect both our unique journeys and our common understanding of research. Marge teaches a graduate course titled "The Practice of Action-Oriented Human Service Research," and Leslie teaches a graduate course titled "Decolonizing Methodologies." The next part of this chapter explains the common research approach that underpins our individual work. We have chosen to name it Community Action Research. It is not a new name, as others speak of community-based action research (Stringer, 1999) and community action-research (Banks & Mangan, 1999). What is unique is our naming the following characteristics, values, and processes of CAR.

What Is Community Action Research?

The interest in naming and debating this approach to research draws from an appreciation of the congruence between social work values and the values of participation, reflectivity, empowerment, relationships, and change espoused in action-oriented, community-based research traditions. The interest also stems from a need to sharpen the possibilities of CAR, to share specific strategies, and to examine the difficulties. CAR is a useful, action-oriented, community-based approach for change. It is a value-based approach inspired by the emancipatory work of education activists like Paulo Freire (1993) and bell hooks (1994); the feminist social work scholarship of Patti Lather (1991) and Janice Ristock and Joan Pennell (1996); the critical analysis of everyday living in a globally restructured world by writers like Linda Tuhwai Smith (1999) and Sheila Neysmith (2000); and the practical social action work of community organizers conceptualized by Marie Mies and Vandana Shiva (1993), Joan Kuyek (1990) , and Nancy Naples (1998). CAR is an approach to research that can promote the self-discovery of individuals, build communities, and serve as a catalyst for social change. We have come to use the term CAR as a way to reflect the importance of the community building and the political activism in our research. As critical curiosity and self-discovery are promoted for all those engaged in CAR, we, too, continue to reflect on the meaning and limits of CAR and are critical of the naming of it.

The "Community" in Community Action Research

Community is the context for the work of CAR. Community well-being is its purpose. The *lifeworlds* of a community are its focus (Banks & Mangan, 1999). Lifeworlds are the collection of traditions, networks, and material realities created in part by interrelated individuals, but existing apart and beyond them. Community is often, but not necessarily, situated in a geographical local space. We do not assume community is made up of permanent members. Transient membership, lukewarm allegiance, and volatile living situations are common patterns in poor communities, in the virtual-cyberspace communities of youth, and in the marginalized communities of workers disconnected from regular jobs or isolated in their work spaces. Also, there are not one, but several lifeworlds in any community. We assume that in most communities there are sharp differences in the lifeworlds and futures of its members, shaped by gender, race, class, and ability. CAR, along with community organizing and other social justice initiatives, aims to make visible the inequities in these differences and to work toward a more just distribution of the resources needed for adequate lifeworlds for all citizens in a community.

Within the complex and diverse lifeworlds of a community, the contribution of CAR is to focus on understanding and changing that that enhances and that that destroys the *common grounds*. The common grounds is a metaphor for the necessities of life that all people need in order to survive and to make humane choices. The grounds must be protected and cared for in common through collective means, whether laws, customs, or relationships. The common grounds could be the land, air, and water that have become the foci of the work of public health activists and the Aboriginal land rights and environmental movements (e.g., Barndt, 1999; Krauss, 1998). The common grounds could be the legal and political freedoms sought by the slavery abolitionists of the nineteenth century and the economic rights sought by the unionists and unemployed workers of the twentieth century. Those participating in a CAR initiative choose to work with, for, and on behalf of not only themselves and their families, but also those outside their homes and places of work. It is this other-regarding character toward people (Milroy & Wismer, 1994) and toward the common grounds that is crucial to shaping the strategies of CAR and to evaluating their impact.

The "Action" in Community Action Research

The focus on action is inherent in any action research. This action could be nurturing growth in people and community relationships, abolishing unjust policies, or constructing new ideas and structures. What may be unique to CAR is its intentional, strategic actions that aim to include the active contributions of many participants and the reactions of multiple audiences. The action in CAR is geared to the present and to the future. Each step of the research project encourages participation of those interested in or affected by the project's focus. Opportunities for active engagement are a key part of the work in designing CAR activities. The researchers do not reserve for themselves the funds or the tasks of thinking about ideas, gathering and interpreting data, or strategizing dissemination. Thus, the immediate foci for action are the research processes themselves. Other related but longer-term foci for action include changes in relationships, ideas, and structures.

As in other empowering types of action-oriented research approaches (e.g., Reason, 1988; Park, Brydon-Miller, Hall, & Jackson, 1993), a central site for action is the self of those who participate most directly in a CAR project. Changes in the confidence and skills of individuals occur in part because members of the CAR initiative nurture a broader web of respectful relationships. The nurturing of relationships builds on specific, immediate research and change tasks, as well as the ongoing, daily, informal work of centre people and activist mothers in a community. The work of building research and other relationships spirals out to include family members, neighbours, and selected allies in positions of power (Naples, 1998).

Changing ideas is another site of intentional action in CAR. In each step of CAR, rather than only at the end of a project, conversations and tasks help to break the frames of accepted, unitary ideas of why people are poor, for example, or the unquestioned beliefs about the responsibilities of parents. Broadcasting results does not just happen at the end of a CAR venture. Our assumption is that the new ideas spawned by CAR activities are needed to solve practical problems. New ideas are also needed to challenge the distortions and *veils* that enslave imagination and ensnare people into thinking crazy, unhealthy ideas (Comstock & Fox, 1993). Furthermore, we search in CAR for what Mathiesen (1974) calls unfinished, competing, and contradictory ideas. The contradictory ideas help to abolish the certainty of current practices and open up spaces for community members to imagine other possibilities. Thinking about competing, but not finished, alternatives supports the opportunities for people to go beyond reaction and into creation, to take control of their own destiny.

Changes in people and ideas may be short-lived unless action is taken to embody the changes in practice, policies, laws, and institutions (Banks & Mangan, 1999; Chambers, 1997; Reinharz, 1992). This is the strongest reason for doing CAR. It is also very difficult to achieve. LeCompte (1993) argues that successfully embedding change in institutions can be obscured by our own rhetoric and thwarted by the real difficulty in moving beyond awareness to activism. She warns that "bringing about change is not a quiet academic pursuit; to empower is to get into trouble" (1993, p. 15). Nonetheless, we also argue that knowledge about an institution, an unjust law, and the nature of power may only come through the struggles to change them. As Mies states, one "comes to know the naked face of aggression through struggles versus it" (1993, p. 40). Thus, there are risks in CAR and in other forms of empowering action research. CAR practitioners learn to be strategic. They engage in realistic, and often modest, change activities that build momentum and feed the commitment to action. At the same time, they select tasks to serve as steps toward more fundamental change.

The "Research" in Community Action Research

A hallmark of CAR is its use of a variety of methods for a variety of audiences. Using several methods and sources of information increases the possibility of understanding complex phenomenon. Multiple methods and triangulation also help to uncover evidence that may convince different audiences (Moss, 1995).

Three sets of multiple methods are used in CAR. The first set is the now-common set of qualitative and quantitative methods, each with their own disciplines and standards of rigour. Examples include life-history narratives of people living in poverty (e.g., Banks & Bangan, 1999) and statistical analysis of the numbers of people in a community living below national poverty lines (Reitsma-Street, Hopper, & Seright, 2000). The second set of research methods is sustained, democratic dialogue on one hand and on the other, shorter research activities, such as community mapping, that fit with procedures people are comfortable with. The democratic dialogue is geared to small but changing groups of people, including the researchers, who help to facilitate CAR and take responsibility for ensuring momentum and productivity (Maguire, 1987; Reason, 1988). By way of contrast, informal, speedy methods are introduced into CAR in order to invite more people to participate in a project, to contribute their unique pieces of local knowledge to the larger puzzle, and to gather evidence useful to different audiences (Chambers, 1997; Mavalankar et al., 1996; Riley, 1997).

The third set of methods deals with the theorizing work in research. There is the local, public process of interpretation and making sense of the data through democratic dialogue, with provisional hypotheses and multiple explanations relevant to different audiences. Hours of private thinking and writing by the researchers and others are needed to interpret, for example, the statistical analysis of the specific impact of toxic materials on people's health (Merrifield, 1993) or the deconstructive analysis used by Ristock and Pennell (1996) in their empowerment, community-based research project on unionization drives among workers in shelters for battered women.

As in all research, CAR uses methods that can account for how conclusions are reached. This account needs to be accessible to public scrutiny. Good research also includes standards against which information can be compared and evaluated. Standards used in CAR include subjective interpretations of relevance and authenticity; evaluations comparing results to community principles or to international covenants of rights; qualitative research standards of trustworthiness and congruence; and quantitative statistical standards of reliability, validity, and generalizability. What is more unique to CAR is the strategic attention to broadcasting and dissemination of what is happening, what has been learned, and what the implications are. As developed in the next section on values and processes of CAR, results are presented in various styles and forums, carefully selected to reach specific audiences who can make decisions or apply pressure for change.

The Values and Processes of Community Action Research

This section presents the values of CAR and a brief summary of key processes common to CAR initiatives. We have selected a wheel as a symbol, with the centre hub of values, the ten spokes of processes, and the rim of relationships that connects the activities together and to the hub. A wheel also captures the dynamic and nonlinear nature of CAR. The hub, spokes, and rim are all necessary for the wheel to turn and for the project to move forward. The hub of values is the center circle to which the CAR processes are attached. All the processes are necessary for the wheel to turn, but they are not initiated in any fixed order and can be conducted simultaneously. The rim of relationships among people connects the processes together and makes CAR possible.

The Centre: Values of Community Action Research

CAR is a value-driven activity. The values that underlie it are not a discrete list of attributes, but rather they are an integrated set of concepts that, taken together, provide direction for the planning, implementation, and utilization of CAR (Figure 5.1). A circle, with four directions to it, is illustrative of how each value of social justice, agency, community connectedness, and critical curiosity come together to inform the work of CAR.

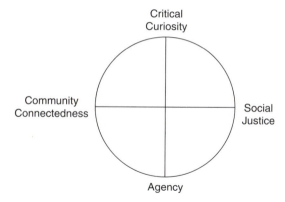

FIGURE 5.1 *The Values of Community Action Research*

Social Justice

To begin understanding the values, start with the concept of social justice. CAR is undertaken in the pursuit of social justice. It is not a neutral activity. Rather it is research that has a very overt political intention. This means that those involved in a CAR project are deliberately taking a particular stand on the topic of interest. Whether it is poverty research that aims to reduce poverty in a community or health research that intends to improve the lives of persons with HIV, there is a clear agenda that is understood by those participating. Some people may consciously choose to be neutral in their research work, but when people are working on a CAR project, it is conscious that even the choosing of neutrality is a political choice that is aimed at furthering the social justice goals of the project. CAR is research for social change. It is not about simply any kind of change, however; it is change that seeks to work for the elimination of injustice and oppression. This distinguishes CAR from other types of action research that desire to change organizational behaviour or to have participants involved in the exploration of a topic of academic interest. CAR is a visibly political act.

Agency

CAR is about the doing; it is not only about reflecting or theorizing. In order for social justice to be pursued, there needs to be an action component to any CAR project. Agency refers to the ability to act. Again, the action that takes place in a CAR project is informed by the values of social justice and therefore manifests itself as activism. CAR is politically active, and many CAR practitioners consider themselves activists as much as they consider themselves researchers. We differ from Stringer's (1999) view that the researcher should not be an activist, but rather a facilitator. Facilitation is a key role for a Community Action Researcher. Yet activism to us means supporting the philosophical and political beliefs of those one works for and with while engaging in such facilitation roles. It is action with a social justice agenda.

There is a fundamental belief in the agency of the community. Researchers respect the abilities of communities to define and answer questions of importance. There is individual expertise within communities of all kinds, and CAR attempts to utilize the strengths within communities. The value of agency goes beyond simple participation. It is the recognition of the agency and the power of the participants to act. As argued earlier in this paper, having a commitment to action means more than simply making recommendations for change. It means engaging in action at all stages of the research process. As such, agency is a value that motivates one to look continually for opportunities to act, to engage others, and to advocate for justice.

Community Connectedness

A primary strategy to maximize a community's capacity to act on its own behalf is to develop collective expertise and connections. The power of coalitions in community collectivity is respected. CAR values relationships and the connections that are built and maintained within a community as part of a CAR project. This value necessitates participation by a community in the action research. Participation is not sought only for the provision of data. Rather, the social justice value that interacts with community connectedness and participation means there is a team approach to the research that respects the contributions of all participants and pays attention to the power relationships between participants, which includes the researchers. A feature of CAR is the democratic dialogue based on participation and relationships.

Valuing community connectedness does not imply that more participation is always better. As feminists learned when we first began working together with ideals of inclusion and consensus, progress can be very conservative if everyone has to be consulted. The values of social justice and agency need to inform the value of connectedness. There is often an inherent tension in a CAR project between the involvement of people and the need to progress toward the goals of social justice. Sometimes, the involving of more people is not prudent, but who gets to decide if and when this is so? Maintaining the dialogue among participants that attempts to hold the values of CAR in an integrative and purposeful manner can inform such decisions.

Critical Curiosity

Finally, there is the value of critical curiosity. CAR is about research, and research aims to discover, explore, and explain. Research is often undertaken in response to a curiosity or puzzlement. Curiosity also motivates CAR. In addition to being a political tool, it is an academic pursuit in that it seeks to respond to a curiosity. The interaction of the other values makes this curiosity a critical curiosity. Understanding power and injustice is part of the academic and personal reflections that accompany CAR. CAR, while aiming to contribute to social science knowledge, is firmly grounded in the daily experiences of people and communities. As such, it is a reflexive practice.

The Spokes: Processes of Community Action Research

At first glance, the work processes of CAR are similar to those in other research approaches presented as stages or components of a project, including clarification of a research question and review of the literature, establishment of the method, collection and interpretation of data, and writing and sharing results. However, the work of CAR makes visible other processes, such as the decision to join together to address a community concern and the work of broadcasting results to engage people in change actions. CAR also features visiting research principles and developing relationships among people who participate in the action research processes. Throughout each of the CAR processes, attention is paid to designing opportunities so that those committed to the community concern are invited and helped to participate when they wish to in the research activities and decisions. We have found that the CAR processes are not necessarily efficient research procedures, although they can be inexpensive and speedy, as was the three-week needs assessment presented in the example opening this chapter. The processes are, however, intended to sponsor action while implementing the values of social justice, agency, community connectedness, and critical curiosity. How the processes of CAR are conducted, we argue, is an essential part of building momentum to create new ideas, new relationships, and new institutional changes. We have identified ten processes. They are not numbered, as that would give the illusion of linearity. Rather, they are processes that participants in a CAR project move back and forth through. The processes are

- decide to join together to address a community concern
- enter the experiences and expertise of those concerned
- devise, revisit, and reinvent principles
- develop decision-making procedures
- negotiate resources, access, and allies
- design research procedures
- gather and inspect data
- analyze data and debate interpretations
- broadcast results to engage multiple audiences
- experiment with actions

Decide to Join Others to Address a Community Concern

This process is almost invisible, yet fundamental to CAR. Without at least two or three people deciding to spend time thinking about a concern and addressing it, there would be no CAR. The concern that prompts the decision to begin may be an unjust practice, such as a welfare snitch line, or a pressing decision, such as the site for a new community. The concern may also be vague, huge, and complex, such as poverty or racism in a neighbourhood. It may take a few weeks, months, or even years to gain sufficient momentum for a few people to decide to engage in CAR processes around a community concern. Deciding to begin is a process that continues throughout the life of a CAR project, as new people decide to join and others need to leave. Usually, the original few people decide also to form an organizing or steering group made up of interested people who vary in skills but have a common commitment and willingness to work together on the community concern. The organizing group makes initial decisions to facilitate several of the CAR processes; it can expand, shrink, evolve, divide, or disband as the needs of the CAR change. One of the many tasks that are embedded in this decision to address a community concern is negotiations around the specific research foci, purpose, and questions.

Enter the Experiences and Expertise of Those Concerned

Before the research questions and action tasks can be clarified, we argue it is important to enter the experiences and appreciate the expertise of the original few and the organizing group who decide to make a concern something they want to address. Why are people concerned? What do they know? What motivates people to learn more and to take action? People need to take time to discuss and explore their experiences and expertise and to invite interested others to join in this exploration. Particular attention is paid in this process to the knowledge and reality of those most affected by a concern. The academic and popular literature on ways of understanding the concern and responses to it are also reviewed. Entering the experiences and knowledge needs to be revisited several times throughout the course of a CAR, especially as new people join or another round of data gathering or sharing results is launched.

Devise, Revisit, and Reinvent Principles

People decide to work on a community concern for different reasons and with varying energy, skills, and time. It is essential that common principles are negotiated early on in a CAR venture and as new people join, whether as community citizens, agency representatives, or researchers in a university position, as was Marge for the CAR project in northern Ontario, or on a funded contract, as Leslie was in the Aboriginal community example. These principles will guide the activities of those engaged in this value-based approach to doing action research in a community. The values of CAR regarding social justice, agency, community connectedness, and critical curiosity are the centre from which specific principles are debated, negotiated, and agreed to. Perhaps only a few principles can be agreed to early on, such as "care for members of the project by providing mutual support, learning, and personal development opportunities" and "do research in a way to help build skills that we can carry with us." These are examples of principles that were agreed to by the organizing group in the first example presented in this chapter (Reitsma-Street & Arnold, 1994, p. 234). Other principles emerge or old ones are reinterpreted when specific work is needed, as relationships develop, or after unanticipated situations necessitate a change in direction. So, for example, in a poverty project, the principle of "accurate, comprehensive data will be made available and accessible at minimal cost" was agreed to early on. Two years later, however, this principle was revisited and interpreted to mean that the final report had to be made free, and fund-raising efforts had to be launched to raise money for the report (Reitsma-Street, Hopper, & Seright, 2000).

Develop Decision-Making Procedures

Although decision-making is a part of each of the processes of CAR, one of the readers of the first draft of this chapter, a community development social worker, brought to our attention that it deserves to be articulated as a process in and of itself. Initially, decisions are needed about who joins the project and what are the project purposes and principles. These types of decisions are revisited as the project moves through time and encounters new or unexpected situations. Also, other decisions must be made: about research design, interpretation and ownership of data, and use of the research results for specific actions. If there are funds and people to hire, personnel and accounting decisions are needed.

There is no preferred mode of decision-making. We have participated in designing procedures that make decisions by consensus, by majority votes, and by executive fiat. What is necessary for CAR, however, is developing and revisiting decision-making procedures that are congruent with the values of social justice, agency, connectedness, and critical curiosity. Decision-making also needs to respect the cultural norms of the community, as well as be congruent with the specific principles that the community devises for a particular research project. That is, because connections within the community is one of the core values in CAR, then decision-making procedures must include ways and time for people to sort out how best to develop relationships with their chosen community and to determine how to maintain authentic representation and accountability. Or, if participation is a key principle of a project, then procedures about determining the research direction, personnel hiring or firing, and the release of results must promote opportunities for people to participate in those decisions. Furthermore, as the unexpected is expected, and as serious differences of opinion are inevitable when researching complex topics that evoke strong feelings, it is also necessary to design procedures for conflict resolution, healing of tensions, and revisiting key decisions. For instance, if the participants have chosen to make decisions by consensus, then a procedure is needed for when consensus breaks down. If voting is used to make decisions, there need to be procedures to revisit decisions in the event of a vote that alienates a large minority of participants or threatens the credibility of the project. If only a few people are mandated to make particular decisions, such as members of a technical committee responsible for statistical procedures or a media committee in charge of a press conference, there need to be processes whereby the scope of decisions is reviewed, supported, or revised.

Negotiate Allies, Resources, and Access

CAR ventures may be funded in part or for a time period. Much of CAR, however, is unfunded. The preparatory work leading to the decision of people to join together to address a concern, the work of building relationships and gaining access to information, and the work of communicating results and initiating actions depend heavily on existing resources, the time of people with paid jobs, and the volunteer energies of many people. These negotiations cannot be rushed. Principles emerge from these negotiations; these principles in turn become a guide to further the CAR work. In addition, each negotiation over resources and access with an individual, with an Aboriginal government, or with an agency's board of directors becomes an opportunity for developing allies. Allies are key players who may play small roles in a CAR venture and larger roles when research results are communicated and actions are debated.

Design Research Procedures

In this process we find the familiar research steps of sample selection, design of instruments, development of responses to ethical and organizational requirements, and pilot work to test feasibility of procedures. In CAR, however, there is awareness that the strategic selection of methods can enhance the possibility of people listening to the findings and taking subsequent action. As multiple methods are a hallmark of CAR projects, it is not uncommon to invite those with expertise in qualitative and quantitative procedures to join or teach members of the organizing group. Using multiple methods means that nearly everyone will learn something new. An atmosphere of sharing and learning new procedures enhances critical curiosity. Various procedures are needed to answer complex questions and convince different audiences.

Gather and Inspect Information

This process is also familiar. As in other community-based or action-oriented research projects, so, too, in CAR ventures particular attention is paid to creating opportunities for people to participate in gathering data and inspecting it. The opportunities can include activities as varied as collecting water samples, conducting interviews, distributing questionnaires, participating in focus groups, and debating the collected numbers, words, and ideas spread over the ground or on the walls. We have found that the more people who have the "data inside them," the stronger their interest in owning the results. As different individuals or groups figure out a piece of the results for themselves, they are more likely to translate data into action. For theoretical purposes, it is important at this stage to develop procedures so that the provisional hypotheses, hunches, and early analytical insights of those engaged in gathering and inspecting data are recorded and made available for additional analysis.

Analyze Data and Debate the Interpretations

This process begins early on and is visited several times as people join the CAR venture and try to make sense of the information—how much to believe, what is missing, and what is biased or incomplete. We have learned to seek out the most sophisticated technical assistance necessary to help analyze certain data at the same time as we develop opportunities for simple ways of analyzing information. Part of the analytical process is to place the information continuously in context of the experiences of the people most affected by a community concern and in the context of what openings there are for change. More problematic to this process are figuring out what the information means to individuals personally or as a group and what responsibility flows from what people have learned.

Broadcast Results to Engage Multiple Audiences

As mentioned previously, unique to CAR is the strategic attention to broadcasting and dissemination of results. Nearly from the beginning of a project and parallel to the process of gathering and inspecting information, a strategic plan is developed and revisited on how to present results and how to encourage debates on implications. The intent is to think about specific audiences who can make decisions or apply pressure for change. Printed or electronic fact sheets and community forums are strategically designed, as are reports, speeches, workshops, press releases, curriculum readers, popular plays, and academic articles.

The audiences for the results are often multiple, as a community concern is usually complex and many actions are needed to respond. Thus careful time is spent understanding how politicians, the public, grassroots advocacy groups, and business organizations hear information and respond to it. Up to one-third, and sometimes more, of funds and energy in the CAR projects we have completed were dedicated to publicizing results, including, for example: discussions in kitchens, presentations in agency board rooms, long conversations with allies, press conferences, and academic speeches. Broadcasting results does not just happen at the end of a CAR venture. This process can begin early on in a CAR, when a few simple preliminary results are shared to help the original organizing group reach out to expand their core group and to develop connections to potential allies and sympathetic decision-makers. Broadcasting results to indifferent or unsympathetic decision-makers takes place, but later in a CAR venture, once solid relationships have been built and strong data analyzed. The first audience that needs to hear and debate results, however, includes people closest to the information and to the processes of gathering and analyzing it. Although we have sensed the impatience of academics and bureaucrats needing the finished products for their use, we argue that the values of CAR, especially those of community connectedness, imply that a community needs to digest the results first, to figure out responses and possible action. In the example in the next section, Leslie found that, in order to show respect for those who had given information and to facilitate the community-building process, she had to discuss the survey results over time with members of the Aboriginal community individually and in small groups, and then wait for a time before releasing the formal, complete report to the band council and community as a whole.

Experiment with Actions

This process is not the last one in a CAR initiative. As with the other CAR processes, work begins early on thinking about actions: what changes in research procedures, relationships, ideas, and institutions would be helpful to address the community concern. If, for example, the presence and magnitude of poverty is denied among some leaders in a community or is invisible to its policy-makers, one action could be the construction of a strong coalition of influential groups, including popular media, who could give legitimacy to a solid statistical analysis of the extent of poverty in the community. To address the causes of poverty will need many more actions, such as abolition of punitive government regulations that limit combining welfare and job payments or revisions to municipal zoning that restricts renovating homes to include affordable suites. The following example illustrates the values and processes of CAR, including the successful completion of an action.

CAR in an Aboriginal Community: Where to Move the Community?

An Aboriginal community requested Leslie's assistance in conducting a survey of their membership to determine the location of a new village site. The existing village site had been forced on them by the Canadian federal government about forty years prior and had not proven to be a healthy place. Many people had moved away due to the lack of space, the poor environment (due to a location next to a pulp mill that polluted their air and water), and other social and political reasons. They had talked on and off for years about moving the village site, but the current administrative and political leadership of the community was ready to push once again for such an initiative. They saw the move as not only a way to get away from an environmentally unsafe location, but as an opportunity to rebuild a community. They wanted a survey of the community members to determine where the new village should be located. The research team, consisting of Leslie, a non-Aboriginal woman, and an Aboriginal man from another Nation, responded to the request of the Band Chief and Council with a CAR approach to the proposed survey. The researchers had previous relationships with people in this community and knew from many discussions with people there that moving the village was only one of many interrelated problems that faced this community. Administrators were frustrated with the apathy, infighting, and general negative attitudes that permeated the community. They thought that moving the village would be a catalyst to improving the overall well-being of the community. They were hopeful that the proposed research approach would motivate the community to work together to make the move possible.

This CAR project was owned and operated by the people in the community. As such, there is a tension for the researcher in writing or talking about it for purposes outside the community, such as this chapter. The data belong to them, not to the researchers. Knowing that Leslie is an academic, they had given permission for her to talk about the process for educational purposes, but they expect that the relationship established between them and the researcher will be honoured in choosing how to do this. With respect, this illustration is offered in order to demonstrate the potential of CAR to facilitate social change and justice. After commenting on the use of CAR values in this venture, the major activities engaged in are listed. These activities illustrate the CAR processes, although not all ten are specifically addressed.

The Values

This project was framed by the values of CAR. Social justice was an ongoing motivator of the project. This community had been forced to live in an environmentally unhealthy place. They had subsequently become unhealthy socially and culturally as well. The intent of the project was to facilitate empowerment through consciousness raising about health status and the possibilities for the future. The collection of data from individuals was also an opportunity to engage in dialogue with people about their lives, their hopes, and their fears. As Freire (1993) characterizes such work, the researchers are educators who come to know with the participants about the reality of their lives.

The value of agency was a conscious one that had to be constantly rekindled. From the initiation of the project, the community was pushed to be involved and to take real ownership of the process and outcome. After years of dependency, community members often just wanted the researchers to do the work and to simply make a recommendation on their behalf to the federal government. The researchers had to work hard to resist this and work actively at every step to keep the ownership of the project in the community. Consciousness raising occurred at the individual, family, and community levels through personal discussions, regular meetings with administrators and politicians, community meetings, and so on. As the project progressed, the responsibility for maintaining the action shifted from the researchers to others in the community.

The belief in the capacity of the community to act and determine its future was a fundamental belief. Outsiders could not fix the problems for the community. The community members had to take hold of the issues and solutions, and then they were able to negotiate with outsiders such as the federal government for what they had decided was needed. The potential power of the community was a fundamental value that was often challenged by apathy and internalized oppression and dominance among the community members. Maintaining this value of agency was strengthened by the other values of social justice and connectedness. The role of the researcher really was one of activist.

Rebuilding this community necessitated a commitment to connecting community members with each other in the visioning of a new community. Valuing the connections despite family feuds and long geographic or time distances did not make it easy. However, through using processes that encouraged interactions between people, the community members developed a collective understanding of their health and social issues. Community members were also made aware of the resources within their community that could be utilized as they rebuilt their cultural, social, and economic society.

Finally, the value of critical curiosity was ever present. There had been rumors about the poor health and living conditions, but no studies had been done to substantiate them. The community had complained for years to the government, which had minimized the affects on the entire community. Once the health status for all was compiled, the community was amazed at the results. They were outraged, but now they had the data upon which to act. They also now knew the people's beliefs about moving were not as divisive and controversial as people had feared. They saw in the data the potential to come together as a community and act.

The Processes

The community members owned the research. This meant that the researchers had to do a lot of talking and listening in the community about the proposed research so that people committed themselves to participating as owners of the research and not as passive subjects. Whenever the research was referred to, it was as community research—the researchers' names were not attached. The Band Council and others were consulted at every step, from designing the questions to planning how to conduct interviews. The process was transparent, including being referred to continually at band meetings, in newsletters, and on the local community television station.

The commitment of the researchers went beyond a contractual commitment to conduct a survey. The community made it clear that the researchers had a relationship with them and that conducting research this way meant that the researchers, too, were a part of their future. Developing new personal associations with people is often a part of doing research. A social relationship among researchers and participants was a particular feature of this CAR project. The researchers have a connection with those people forever.

Every band member, on and off reserve, was involved. Because building community connectedness was important, the researchers had to track down people who had left the local area and invite them to participate. Individual interviews of about three hours each were conducted with more than 300 adults. Forums for youth and children were also held several times. Involving band members from all over the region was important to the rebuilding enterprise. As one person said, "It's hard to be scattered and a family."

The survey instrument was designed to elicit information on community health and social issues, as well as to get indicators of what would be important to people in choosing a new site for the village. The instrument aimed to set the tone of community building, not only the selection of a physical site. People interviewed offered three levels of information to the researchers. The survey questions were discussed and, together with a researcher, the respondents would decide what would be written down as their responses to the formal questions (i.e., the official responses that would appear in a report that could be submitted to outside agencies such as the Department of Indian Affairs). Also written down were other points that the respondent wanted the community to know but that should not go outside the community. Respondents had control over what was written. Some chose to do the writing themselves; others reviewed what the researcher had written. In many cases it was a cooperative task. Finally, there were comments that the respondents wanted the researchers to keep confidential. All interviews were tape recorded, with the control of the on/off button in the hands of the respondent. Tapes were the property of the respondent, not of the community or the researcher.

As data were collected, workshops and meetings were held to present the data and engage the community in analysis. This not only enabled the construction of the analysis and recommendations in the research, but it also galvanized the community members to take ownership and action. They were angered by what they had discovered—that their people were unhealthy and that they had to do something about it.

As community ownership of the project increased, the role of the researchers diminished. Eventually, the researchers were not needed as researchers. The data had been collected and presented in various forms and forums. Subsequent meetings, reports, and strategy papers were conducted and written without the researchers having to initiate them or even be present.

The Aboriginal reserve community in this project agreed on the need to move to a new village site and took the necessary steps for this to be realized a few years later. Four years after the relocation was realized, at the time of writing this chapter, the commitment to building a healthy community that was sparked in part by the values and processes of the CAR venture remains. The relationships that rimmed the project continue to be the glue that holds this ongoing community work together.

Continuing the Conversation

Community Action Research is the name we have given to a value-based approach to politicized research processes that address community concerns. Based on experiences and the literature, we have conceptualized values and processes of this dynamic approach that are responsive to the need for useful community-based research. We continue to debate the limits of CAR and to experiment with its promise in order to understand how research can on one hand build and empower communities, and on the other, examine the hidden, messy, fundamental forces that destroy the common grounds and lifeworlds required by diverse people to live in community with each other.

From our experience and reflections, we suggest there is a need to understand and debate the implications of dualities and contradictions in the core values and specific work processes within empowerment types of research, such as CAR. We are debating what these dualities are, what tensions they provoke, and how much they are inevitable, necessary, or problematic. Is it possible that the obvious tension between action and research, for example, or between too much information and not enough, or between making opportunities for individuals to participate within a CAR project and the needs of research to be rigorous and legitimate can help to clarify what tasks are most important, when, and for whom? We contend that attention needs to be given to these types of debates and consideration given to both poles of a duality in them. Peter Reason (1994) speaks, for example, of the need to articulate the opposing poles of a concern for the participants' need for identity and participation and the need for research perspective.

> Too much concern for participative identity among co-researchers will lead to loss of perspective; too much concern for perspective will leave co-researchers alienated from each other and from their experience. The dialectic involves both a movement between the two poles and a simultaneous articulation of the two poles. (p. 91)

The contradictions and the dualities, however, add a complexity to what may already be a difficult, unwieldy endeavour. We have engaged in short, efficient CAR ventures, and we know that solid research and relevant action on a community concern can begin and end in a few months—if, and it is a big if, the relationships, context, and energy are available (Reitsma-Street, 1996). Others, such as Chambers (1997) and Riley (1997), have developed efficient, rigorous research instruments that have been used effectively to make decisions within an authentic participatory framework. However, the processes of developing relationships, broadcasting results, and debating action strategies in CAR ventures can take a long time and encounter paralyzing difficulties. We need to debate when a CAR project would make sense and for whom. When, for example, is a community development initiative, not a CAR project, needed? Or when would a top-down, science-driven research approach be appropriate, without the additional CAR processes that pay attention to relationships, principles, opportunities for participation, broadcasting results, and strategizing change? Are the critical curiosity value of CAR and the rigorous research activities added primarily to legitimate an initiative for the sake of academics? Budd Hall (1993) argues that university researchers, and probably social workers, are not necessary to participatory research.

> Countless groups make use of processes which resemble participatory research every day without naming it or certainly without asking for outside validation of the knowledge which is produced. (p. xx)

Another debate we have is about resources. To conduct CAR in a substantial and not token manner takes time, skill, and funds. Too often it depends on professionals adding something to their already full days or community members giving volunteer time. Our experience is that people, even those with limited incomes and minimal energies, will give a great deal and far more than expected when they feel they can negotiate freely what to give and when, and if they feel they can withdraw their contributions without shame or retribution (Reitsma-Street & Neysmith, 2000). Nonetheless, CAR is not possible without material resources, especially time. There also is an injustice or imbalance in paying funds and honouring the expertise of academic, technical skills while expecting those with other expertise, in the experience of poverty or Aboriginal traditions, for instance, to give it freely.

Further debate and clarity on such issues are needed as the popularity of action-research and community-based research traditions grows (Brown, 1994; Fetterman, Kaftarian, & Wandersmand, 1996; Fleming & Ward, 1999; King, 1995; Levin, 1999). With the legitimization of such research approaches, there is an accompanying worry that CAR will be coopted for the benefit of those already holding privilege and power. Accompanying popularity are attempts to transform community research for change into an unrealistic, depoliticized service. There is also the pressure to simplify the processes, making them into technical prescriptions focusing, for instance, on people as clients and beneficiaries, not as citizens. More insidious are claims of authentic collaboration when only token or restricted participation of the community in action research is possible or desired (Smith, 1999; VanderPlaat, 1997). Just as there is the strong possibility for CAR to be a strategy for liberation, it also has the potential to be used to further oppress. Research is a political tool.

References

Banks, C. K., & Mangan J. M. (1999). *The Company of Neighbours: Revitalizing community through action-research*. Toronto, Canada: University of Toronto Press.

Barndt, D. (Ed.). (1999). *Women working the NAFTA food chain: Women, food & globalization*. Toronto, Canada: Second Story Press.

Becker, H. S. (1970). Whose side are we on? In J. D. Douglas (Ed.), *The relevance of sociology* (pp. 99–111). New York: Appleton-Century Crofts.

Brown, P. A. (1994). Participatory research: A new paradigm for social work. In L. Gutiérrez & P. Nurius (Eds.), *Education and research for empow-*

erment practice (pp. 293–303). Seattle, WA: University of Washington, Center for Policy and Practice Research, School of Social Work.

Chambers, R. (1997). *Whose reality counts? Putting the last first.* London: Intermediate Technology Publications.

Comstock, D. E., & Fox, R. (1993). Participatory research as critical theory: The North Bonneville, USA, experience. In P. Park, M. Brydon-Miller, B. Hall, & T. Jackson (Eds.), *Voices of change* (pp. 103–124). Toronto, Canada: Ontario Institute for Studies in Education Press.

Fetterman, D. M., Kaftarian, S. J., & Wandersmand, A. (Eds.). (1996). *Empowerment evaluation: Knowledge and tools for self-assessment and accountability.* Thousand Oaks, CA: Sage.

Fleming, J., & Ward, D. (1999). Research as empowerment: The social action approach. In W. Shera & L. M. Wells (Eds.), *Empowerment practice in social work: Developing richer conceptual foundations* (pp. 370–389). Toronto, Canada: Canadian Scholars Press.

Friere, P. (1993). *Pedagogy of the oppressed* (Rev. ed., M. B. Ramos, Trans.). New York: Continuum.

Hall, B. (1993). Introduction. In P. Park, M. Brydon-Miller, B. Hall, & T. Jackson (Eds.), *Voices of change* (pp. xii–xxii). Toronto, Canada: Ontario Institute for Studies in Education Press.

hooks, b. (1994). *Teaching to transgress: Education as the practice of freedom.* New York: Routledge.

King, J. A. (1995). Bringing research to life through action research methods. *Canadian Journal on Aging, 14*(Suppl. 1), 165–176.

Kuyek, J. (1990). *Fight for hope: Organizing to realize our dreams.* Montreal, Canada: Black Rose Books.

Krauss, C. (1998). Challenging power: Toxic waste protests and the politicization of white, working-class women. In N. A. Naples (Ed.), *Community activism and feminist politics.* (pp. 129–150). London: Routledge.

Lather, P. (1991). *Getting smart: Feminist research and pedagogy within the postmodern.* New York: Routledge.

LeCompte, M. D. (1993). A framework for hearing silence: What does telling stories mean when we are supposed to be doing science? In D. McLaughlin & W. G. Tierney (Eds.), *Naming silences lives: Personal narratives and processes of educational change.* (pp. 9–27). New York: Routledge.

Levin, M. (1999). Action research paradigms. In D. J. Greenwood (Ed.), *Action research* (pp. 25–38). Amsterdam: John Benjamins.

Maguire, P. (1987). *Doing participatory research: A feminist approach.* Amherst, MA: University of Mass-achusetts, Center for International Education, School of Education.

Mathiesen, T. (1974). *The politics of abolition.* Oslo, Norway: Universitagaet.

Mavalankar, D. V., Satia, J. K., & Sharma, B. (1996). Experiences and issues in institutionalizing qualitative and participatory research approaches in a government health programme. In K. de Koning & M. Marton (Eds.), *Participatory research in health* (pp. 216–228). London: Zed Books.

Merrifield, J. (1993). Putting scientists in their place: Participatory research in environmental and occupational health. In P. Park, M. Brydon-Miller, B. Hall, & T. Jackson (Eds.), *Voices of change* (pp. 65–84). Toronto, Canada: Ontario Institute for Studies in Education Press.

Mies, M. (1993). Feminist research: Science, violence and responsibility. In M. Mies & V. Shiva (Eds.), *Ecofeminism* (pp. 36–54). Halifax, Canada: Fernwood.

Mies, M., & Shiva, V. (1993). *Ecofeminism.* Halifax, Canada: Fernwood.

Milroy, B. M., & Wismer, S. (1994). Communities, work and public/private sphere models. *Gender, Place and Culture, 1*(1), 71–90.

Moss, P. (1995) Embeddedness in practice, numbers in context: The politics of knowing and doing. *The Professional Geographer, 47*(4), 442–449.

Naples, N. A. (1998). *Community activism and feminist politics: Organizing across race, class and gender.* New York: Routledge.

Neysmith, S. (Ed.). (2000). *Restructuring caring work: Power, discourse and everyday life.* Toronto, Canada: Oxford University Press.

Park, P., Brydon-Miller, M., Hall, B., & Jackson, T. (Eds.). (1993). *Voices of change: Participatory research in the United States and Canada.* Toronto, Canada: Ontario Institute for Studies in Education Press.

Reason, P. (Ed.). (1988). *Human inquiry in action: Developments in new paradigm research.* London: Sage.

Reason, P. (1994). Participation in the evolution of consciousness. In P. Reason (Ed.), *Participation in human inquiry* (pp. 16–29). London: Sage.

Reinharz, S. (1992). *Feminist methods in social research.* Toronto, Canada: Oxford University Press.

Reitsma-Street, M. (1996). Activist research contributions to shutting down a welfare snitch line. *Atlantis, 21*(1), 123–132.

Reitsma-Street, M., & Arnold R. (1994). Community-based action research in a multi-site prevention project: Challenges and resolutions. *Canadian*

Journal of Community Mental Health, 13(2), 229–240.

Reitsma-Street, M., Hopper, A., & Seright, J. (Eds.). (2000). *Poverty and inequality in the Captial region of British Columbia*. Victoria, Canada: University of Victoria.

Reitsma-Street, M., & Neysmith, S. (2000). Restructuring and community work: The case of community resource centres for families in poor urban neighbourhoods. In S. Neysmith (Ed.), *Restructuring caring labour: Power, discourse and everyday life* (pp. 142–163). Toronto, Canada: Oxford University Press.

Riley, D. A. (1997). Using local research to change 100 communities for children and families. *American Psychologist, 52*(4), 424–433.

Ristock, J. L., & Pennell, R. (1996). *Community research as empowerment: Feminist links, postmodern interruptions.* Toronto, Canada: Oxford University Press.

Smith, L. T. (1999). *Decolonizing methodologies: Research and indigenous peoples.* London: Zed Books.

Stringer, E. T. (1999). *Action research* (2nd ed.). Thousand Oaks, CA: Sage.

VanderPlaat, M. (1997). Emancipatory politics, critical evaluation and government policy. *Canadian Journal of Program Evaluation, 12*(2), 143–162.

6

Cultural Competence: A Requirement for Empowerment Practice

Salome Raheim

Why? Why were so many people of African descent around the world poor and not in control of their countries, their communities, or their lives? From enslavement in the United States to colonization in the Congo, how was it possible for one group of people to have such a history? Was it because of an internal defect? Were the stereotypes true that we were less intelligent, less ambitious, and less capable? Was the myth true that we were cursed by God because of some sin committed in ancient times? How could we regain control of our lives? How could we improve them? These were the questions that haunted me growing up in inner-city Baltimore in the 1960s. My search for answers marked the beginning of my interest in empowerment.

Barbara Solomon's (1976) *Black Empowerment* provides the conceptual framework for understanding the persistent and widespread poverty and powerlessness of African Americans and other oppressed groups. Solomon and others (Gutiérrez, 1990; Gutiérrez & Lewis, 1999; Pinderhughes, 1989) explicate the mechanisms of social control—direct and indirect power blocks—that minimize, marginalize, and prohibit group members from accessing resources, services, and opportunities to improve and control their lives. These mechanisms of oppression may result in internalized oppression, whereby target-group members come to believe the prevailing stereotypes and negative valuations of themselves (Frye, 2001). This internalized oppression may lead to hopelessness and further disempowerment, disconnecting them from the knowledge of their strengths, capacities, and internal resources.

Achieving the aims of empowerment practice with vulnerable, stigmatized, and marginalized populations requires cultural competence. Without specific cultural knowledge, skills, and attitudes, empowerment practice in cross-cultural situations may be ineffective at best, and harmful at worst. This chapter examines the application of principles of cultural competence to empowerment practice, which is called here *culturally competent empowerment practice.*

Empowerment and Cultural Competence

Empowerment has become widely accepted in social work and other helping professions as a preferred process and outcome (Gutiérrez, 1990; Rappaport, 1984; Simon, 1994; Zimmerman, 1995). Drawing on the work of Staub-Bernasconi (1991), Lee (1996) explains that empowerment practice with vulnerable, stigmatized, oppressed, and marginalized populations addresses problems of direct and indirect power blocks, poverty, asymmetrical exchange relationships, powerlessness, and contrary social criteria or values. After twenty years of explicating empowerment in the practice literature, practitioners may fail to recognize the multiple meanings of empowerment among client groups from diverse cultural backgrounds and social identities.

Empowerment: Variations in Meaning

Culture, racial-ethnic group membership, gender, sexual orientation, and socioeconomic status are key factors that influence clients' definitions of, desires for, and preferred pathways to empowerment (Foster-Fishman, Salem, Chibnall, Legler, & Yapchai, 1998; Hill Collins, 1986; Rappaport, 1984; Zimmerman, 1995). Foster-Fishman and colleagues remind us that empowerment has multiple forms for different racial, gender, and other social groups. "Because personal history emerges from the intersection of demographic characteristics and social opportunities, we should expect individuals with different racial, gender, ethnic, class, and social backgrounds to desire different forms of empowerment" (p. 509).

The metaphor of culture as an iceberg illustrates the relevance of culture in empowerment practice (Fowler & Mumford, 1995). The tip of the iceberg, the part of culture that can be seen, includes all of the material aspects of culture, such as music, dance, clothing, food, and artifacts. Misunderstanding these differences is not the most frequent and significant source of cultural missteps in practice. Rather, it is below the tip of the iceberg, hidden from direct observation, where the more significant "deep culture" lies, shaping attitudes, behavior, and interpretations of the world. When practitioners are unaware that culture is operating to guide their own and others' attitudes, preferences, and behavior, practice will be ineffective.

The meanings of the concepts of power and empowerment within varying cultures lie below the tip of the iceberg, beyond our view. When this is recognized, we are reminded that we must not assume that the meanings of these concepts are the same for our clients as they are for practitioners, personally or professionally. Because of empowerment's broad acceptance as a preferred process and outcome and the many efforts to define it in the practice literature, practitioners may forget that clients' meanings, preferences, and goals related to empowerment may differ dramatically from our own. Practitioners can engage in culturally competent empowerment practice only if we seek to understand and honor clients' notions of power and empowerment. Otherwise, we may impose our own definitions, working against the self-determination we are seeking to support.

Empowerment in Cultural Context

Time and contextual factors also influence desires for empowerment and how empowerment is manifested. Drawing from findings of several studies (Bartunek, Foster-Fishman, & Keys, 1996; Bartunek, Lacey, & Wood, 1992), Foster-Fishman and colleagues report that amount of experience within a specific context affected individuals' definitions of empowerment. Citing a participatory decision-making process as an example, those new to the process found a directive leader empowering, whereas those with more experience defined empowerment as real influence over decisions (Foster-Fishman et al., 1998).

A study of employees in a human service organization found that multiple forms of empowerment exist across people and contexts, and it identified six distinct pathways to employee empowerment (Foster-Fishman et al., 1998). These pathways were: (1) a degree of job autonomy, (2) freedom to be creative, (3) acquisition of job-relevant knowledge, (4) feeling trusted and respected, (5) a sense of job fulfillment, and (6) opportunities to participate in decision-making. Although employees' empowerment experiences were categorized into these six pathways, the nature of the experiences within each category was diverse. For example, some employees experienced job autonomy as working at their own pace, whereas others felt autonomous when they were allowed to make independent decisions about their cases. Additionally, the combinations of these pathways were unique to each individual. For one employee, job autonomy alone was sufficient for his empowerment. For others, autonomy along with trust, respect, opportunities for creativity, and other pathways were required elements for their empowerment.

Empowerment practice requires an understanding of how culture and context affect the definition of empowerment (Rappaport, 1987; Trickett, 1994; Trickett, Watts, & Birnam, 1994). Trickett suggests that this understanding impacts our implementation of empowerment practice principles:

> If, however, empowerment is conceptually bound to local context, it is not possible to pre-ordain what kind of helping relationship, set of activities, or criteria of success, can be used to define either empowering process or outcomes. . . . Further, it suggests that the same activities, may, in different communities and with different groups, either serve or inhibit empowerment goals. (p. 588)

Advancing the value of a constructivist approach to understanding empowerment, Zimmerman (1995) asserts that empowerment must be connected to people's experience as they state it and contextually grounded in their life experiences. Therefore, effective practice challenges us to go beyond our ideological commitment to empowerment principles to understand "the sociocultural terrain" (Trickett, 1994, p. 591). Clearly, empowerment practice requires an ecological perspective.

Empowerment practice is likely to occur in the context of significant difference between client and worker. The vulnerable, stigmatized, and oppressed populations that we serve may be of different cultural, racial-ethnic, and socioeconomic backgrounds than our own. It has been well documented that practitioners are often uncomfortable in the face of such differences (Atkinson, Morten, & Sue, 1998; Lum, 2000; Pinderhughes, 1989). Worker discomfort can be an impediment to exploring the critical issues of racial-ethnic identity, racism, sexism, heterosexism, and other oppressions that empowerment practice demands. In cultural competence workshops I have conducted with human service professionals, White workers frequently express discomfort with discussing these issues. Many have shared that they do not feel equipped to discuss issues of race, ethnicity, and other differences and that they do not discuss these issues unless a client "brings it up." One worker shared that she had never discussed racial-ethnic identity with an African American adolescent girl in a long-term residential facility where there were no other African American clients. Another shared that she had never explored issues of culture and ethnicity with a family that included a White father, a Puerto Rican mother, an adolescent son (identified client) from the mother's previous marriage to a Puerto Rican man, and a younger son from the current marriage. The family lived in a predominantly White county with few Latinos and no other Puerto Ricans. In both cases, the practitioners' lack of knowledge, skill, and comfort in the context of cultural difference prevented them from exploring critical issues required for empowerment practice.

Requirements for Culturally Competent Empowerment Practice

According to Lum (2000), cultural competency is the fifth and latest step in the development of "culturally diverse social work practice" theory (p. 21). Lum marks the beginning of this development with Solomon's (1976) *Black Empowerment* and charts its course through the contributions of Devore and Schlesinger's (1981) *Ethnic-Sensitive Social Work Practice* and Green's (1982) *Cultural Awareness in the Human Services* to his own *Culturally Competent Practice* (1999). Lum (2000) states, "To be culturally competent, one must understand the historical oppression of ethnic minorities, the similarities and differences among people of color, the practice principles of ethnic sensitivity and cultural awareness, and the practice emphasis on cultural diversity" (p. 22).

Simply stated, cultural competence at the individual practitioner level is "the state of being capable of functioning effectively in the context of cultural differences" (Cross, 1995/1996, p. 4). It is a developmental process that may be conceptualized as a six-point continuum (Cross, Bazron, Dennis, & Isaacs, 1989; Mason, Benjamin, & Lewis, 1996). At the least desirable end of the continuum is cultural destructiveness, in which difference is stigmatized and efforts are made to eliminate cultural difference through assimilation or genocide. Cultural incapacity and cultural blindness, the next two points on the continuum, reflect worker ineffectiveness due to ethnocentrism, prejudice, and discrimination. Next, pre-cultural competence involves recognition of worker deficits in cross-cultural practice and beginning efforts to improve. At the most desirable end of the continuum is basic and advanced cultural competence, in which practitioners accept and respect difference and are skilled in cross-cultural practice. Those at the advanced level are engaged in relevant knowledge building and dissemination and program development. A practitioner may be located at different points on the continuum with different populations. For example, an African American practitioner who grew up in a multiethnic neighborhood composed of African Americans, Latinos, and Whites may be at an advanced level of competence with Latinos and Whites but at a pre-cultural competence level with a new group of immigrants, such as Sudanese refugees.

Cross, Bazron, Dennis, and Isaacs (1989) have identified several principles for culturally competent practice. These include

- View clients and their experiences in the context of their cultural group.
- Determine clients' involvement and connection to their culture, including levels of acculturation/assimilation. This is a requirement for "starting where the client is."
- Recognize that minority populations must be at least bicultural for effective social functioning and that this status creates a unique set of mental health issues.
- Consider that individuals and families make different choices based on cultural forces.
- Acknowledge, accept, and adjust to dynamics that are inherent in cross-cultural interactions.
- Understand that few interventions are culturally blind or culturally free.

Cross and colleagues (1989) outline five elements required for an individual practitioner to be culturally competent: (1) awareness and acceptance of difference, (2) awareness of own cultural values, (3) understanding the dynamics of difference, (4) cultural knowledge, and (5) adaptation of practice to the client's cultural context. A description of these elements and their relevance to empowerment practice follows.

Awareness and Acceptance of Difference

A fundamental requirement for culturally competent practice is "to acknowledge cultural differences and to become aware of how they affect the helping process" (Cross, et al., 1989, p. 32). Although similarities exist, the differences are likely to become the cause of cultural missteps in the helping process if ignored. Cultural blindness will hinder practitioners from exploring "below the tip of the iceberg," to understand clients' values, perceptions, and worldviews. Lee (1996) asserts that blindness to differences and attempts to treat all clients the same inhibit practitioners' abilities to see client strengths and are not useful. Instead, "empowerment means that both workers and clients draw strength from working through the meaning of [their] different statuses, enabling them to be who they are: persons with a rich heritage" (p. 230).

Included in this awareness and acceptance is acknowledgement that the clients' desires for empowerment and preferred pathways to empowerment may be significantly different than those of the practitioner. For example, self reliance and independence may be central to the practitioner's view of empowerment. These concepts may conflict with the client's cultural values of commitment to family and community. Accordingly, the goals of the practitioner may be incongruent with the goals of the client. Similar misjudgments can be made in program development. Strawn (1994) studied a program intended to facilitate the empowerment of low-income women that unintentionally undermined their natural sources of support and strength. The program provided individual case management services based on the program developer's values of American individualism. The program design ignored the importance of community and social interaction in some of the targeted communities. By inaccurately defining what empowerment meant to these women and which processes would facilitate their empowerment experience, the program unintentionally increased their alienation. Becoming aware of and accepting difference in our clients' views of empowerment may be more challenging than we anticipate.

Awareness of Own Cultural Values

Closely related to awareness and acceptance of difference is practitioners' awareness of their culture and its influence on their attitudes and behavior. Understanding the influence of culture on our own thoughts, perceptions, interpretations, and actions is a prerequisite for understanding the complexities of cross-cultural interactions (Cross et al., 1989; Lecca, Quervalú, Nunes, & Gonzales, 1998; Lum, 2000; Lynch & Hanson, 1992). Cross and colleagues explain:

> Many people have never acknowledged how their day-to-day behaviors have been shaped by cultural norms and values and been reinforced by families, peers, and social institutions. How one defines family, determines desirable life goals, views problems, and even says hello is influenced by the culture in which one functions. (p. 33)

Without cultural self-awareness, ethnocentrism leads practitioners to view their values and resulting behaviors as normal and others' as deviant. Such a view encourages practitioners to fix, reform, or eliminate clients from their caseloads, rather than develop empowering partnerships with them. Ethnocentrism has motivated segregated human services (Stehno, 1982) and the inappropriate removal of children of color from their families (Pinderhughes, 1991), and it has forced assimilation (U.S. Civil Rights Commission, 2001) and removal of people of color from their property (Joe & Malach, 1992). Gutiérrez and Lewis (1999) note that such ethnocentrism has persisted throughout the development of social work practice. Ethnocentrism, prejudice, and other biased attitudes are a major barrier to worker engagement in empowerment practice (Gutiérrez & Lewis, 1999; Shera & Page, 1995). Developing cultural self-awareness is a critical step in eliminating ethnocentrism and prejudice against clients.

Understanding the Dynamics of Difference

There are two levels at which the concept of "dynamics of difference" is relevant to culturally competent empowerment practice. The first level involves client–worker interactions in which cultural differences may lead to misinterpretations of behaviors and intentions. The prior contact each has had with the other's cultural group, the stereotypes each holds about that group, and each person's culturally prescribed rules of social interaction may lead to misjudgements of the other (Cross et al., 1989; Lecca et al., 1998; Leigh, 1998). Cross et al. illustrate this point:

> One clear example of the dynamics of difference is when two persons meet and shake hands. If someone from a culture in which a limp hand is offered as a symbol of humility and respect (as in some Native American groups) shakes hands with a mainstream American male (who judges a person's character by the firmness of their grip), each will walk away with an invalid impression of the other. (p. 33)

Although both may misinterpret the meaning of the other's behavior, it will be the client, not the worker, who is disadvantaged by the misinterpretation.

The second level of dynamics of difference involves how clients are targets of oppression due to their cultural, racial-ethnic, or other group status and the corresponding power and privilege that are afforded to dominant group members (McIntosh, 2001; Swigonski, 1996). "Empowerment [practice] challenges the status quo and attempts to change existing power relationships. . . . It requires of the worker the ability to analyze social processes and interpersonal behavior in terms of power and powerlessness" (Pernell, 1986, p. 111). Lee (1996) explains:

> Two conditions are needed for empowerment: a worker with a raised consciousness and a client who seeks to be empowered. . . . To help empower, we must first learn to speak openly about power with clients and then engage in examination of power bases stemming from personal resources and articulation power, symbolic power, value power, positional power, or authority and organizational power. (p. 225)

An understanding of this oppression–power–privilege dynamic is essential for practitioners to engage in the power analysis that empowerment practice demands (Gutiérrez, 1990). Practitioners can develop a "raised consciousness" only through engaging in analysis of ways we are privileged and ways we lack privilege, based on racial-ethnic group membership, gender, sexual orientation, socioeconomic status, education, professional position, and other social identities. Practitioners must also examine how cultural differences influence power dynamics and the power differential in relationships with clients. Practitioners without this self-knowledge are ill-prepared to undertake a power analysis with clients and will be ill at ease with issues of racism, sexism, classism, and other forms of oppression.

The second level of the dynamics of difference involves clients' responses to oppression, what Cross and Bazron (1996) call "responses to a hostile world." These responses range from self-hatred, an extreme form of internalized oppression, to hatred of and violence toward the oppressor. Central to both cultural competence and empowerment practice is understanding these dynamics of difference and their potential effects on clients and our relationships with them.

The Development of Cultural Knowledge

Understanding the dynamics of difference requires acquiring specific knowledge of the client's cultural group, including the historical and contemporary patterns of oppression experienced by group members and their responses (Cross et al., 1989; East, 2000; Gutiérrez, 1991). This history, along with other cultural information, provides the context for understanding the client's values and behavior, including views of empowerment. What does power mean in the client's culture? According to cultural beliefs, is the locus of power internal? External? Both? How much control should one strive to have over one's life? The development of cultural knowledge guides the practitioner in understanding how empowerment principles might be applied with a specific client group, what approaches are consistent with the cultural beliefs of the group, and what might undermine members' empowerment. Although clients may not hold all the beliefs of their cultural group, knowledge of the cultural group can guide the practitioner in the exploration of relevant cultural issues with individual clients. Until this exploration is done, the relevance of cultural patterns to a specific client is unknown. Cultural knowledge is a useful starting point in understanding clients' desires for and preferred pathways to empowerment, but practitioners must avoid making assumptions about clients based on knowledge of the client group.

Adapting Practice to the Cultural Context of the Client

Finally, practitioners must use their knowledge of self, of the dynamics of difference, and of the client's culture to engage in culturally competent interactions and interventions that promote client empowerment. Ethnographic and constructivist approaches are especially consistent with this aim. Leigh (1998) notes:

> Ethnographic interviewing holds much promise for social workers who wish to attain cultural competence. [It] can be very helpful when working with ethnic minority persons of color. . . . By ethnographic methods of inquiry, the social worker elicits the story. The story of a person can be seen as narrative through which the storyteller's perspective is revealed. (pp. 12–13)

Using this approach, practitioners are positioned to learn clients' strengths, challenges, and desired outcomes. As clients tell their stories, they become what Freire (1973) describes as subjects, active participants in the world versus powerless objects of social processes. This may empower them to participate in the change process. As the experts on construction of meanings of their own culture and lives, clients' views of empowerment can be elicited through their narrative. Through seeking to understand the clients' world from the clients' perspective, the practitioner is entering the clients' world, understanding it from their perspective instead of imposing the practitioner's values and worldview (Leigh, 1998).

An ethnographic approach can help practitioners begin the conversation about the significance of race, ethnicity, cultural identity, and other client characteristics that may make them targets of discrimination and oppression. Initiating the exploration of such topics can communicate that the practitioner has the capacity and the willingness to understand the client's experience from the client's perspective. In the case noted earlier of the worker with an African American teenage girl in residential treatment, a simple statement like "I wonder what it is like for you to be the only African American who lives here?" is sufficient to introduce the topic. Practitioners who fail to explore these topics communicate that they lack understanding of their significance or are uncomfortable or unwilling to address them. Additionally, such omissions may signal clients that such topics are not appropriate for discussion with the practitioner and may discourage them from raising these issues.

Similarly, the constructivist approach is well suited for exploring sensitive issues of difference and disempowerment. This approach may facilitate empowerment through de-emphasizing therapeutic-hierarchical power and control and emphasizing collaboration (Greene, Jensen, & Jones, 1996). The collaborative interaction between practitioner and client becomes the vehicle for understanding, constructing, and reconstructing knowledge, and clients are positioned as the experts in their own lives (Foster-Fishman et al., 1998; Guba & Lincoln, 1989; Swigonski, 1994). From this potentially empowering relationship, practitioner and client can explore critical issues needed for facilitating client empowerment: ethnic and cultural identity, bicultural awareness, and power and privilege. With the new awareness gained through this therapeutic process, clients can successfully restory their lives to include the unique elements needed for their empowerment.

Beyond specific practice approaches, practitioners must actively seek opportunities to adapt practice to the cultural context of the client. These adaptations may be as simple as removing one's shoes when entering a client's home where everyone's shoes are lined up at the entrance. More-complex adaptations may involve culturally specific interventions, such as Native American talking stick circles or rites of passage programs for African American youth (Monges, 1999). In any case, practitioners' cultural knowledge will guide such adaptations.

The diversity of U.S. cultural groups, as well as within-group diversity, make it impossible for practitioners to have comprehensive knowledge of all client groups we may encounter. In addition to collaborating with clients as cultural guides, it is useful to enlist the assistance of cultural consultants who can assist in gaining and interpreting cultural knowledge. These individuals may be community leaders, elders, clergy, or healers (Cross, 1995/1996).

Organizational Support for Culturally Competent Empowerment Practice

Practitioner efforts to engage in culturally competent empowerment practice are most effective when supported by a parallel process at the organizational level. Organizations must also become culturally competent (Cross et al., 1989; Mason, 1994; Mason et al., 1996) and empowering (Gutiérrez, GlenMaye, & DeLois, 1995; Gutiérrez & Lewis, 1999; Shera & Page, 1995). A culturally competent organization is one that has "a set of congruent practice skills, attitudes, policies and structures . . . that enable that system, that agency, or [its] professionals to work effectively in the context of cultural difference" (Cross, 1995/1996, p. 4). An empowering organization is one that has "a process of enhancing self-efficacy among organizational members through the identification of conditions that foster powerlessness and through their removal by both formal organizational practices and informal techniques which provide efficacy" (Shera & Page, 1995, pp. 2–3). These organizational characteristics of cultural competence and empowerment are mutually supportive, but not always co-occurring.

Similar to individual practitioners, organizational cultural competence can be assessed along the same six-point continuum, ranging from cultural destructiveness to advanced cultural competence (Cross et al., 1989; Mason et al., 1996). Corresponding to the elements needed for individual cultural competence, Mason and colleagues (1996) identify five elements for organizational cultural competence:

1. *Valuing diversity.* Diversity must be understood as a strength at the client level, as well as at all levels of the organization, including staff, administrators, board members, and volunteers.

2. *Organizational self-assessment.* Measures should be used to assess the agency's effectiveness in serving diverse populations and dealing with diversity issues.

3. *Managing the dynamics of difference.* The organization must understand the challenges involved when people of diverse backgrounds interact and must modify its core culture to develop an environment of acceptance and inclusion.

4. *Institutionalizing cultural knowledge.* Agencies must provide a mechanism for continued access to cultural information.

5. *Adapting to diversity.* Organizational structures, policies, services, and attitudes must be modified to reflect a commitment to culturally competent empowerment practice and to match the cultural context of the populations served.

When organizations use empowering process to systematically address these elements, practitioner-level efforts are simultaneously encouraged and supported.

Organizations that attempt to increase their cultural competence without attending to empowerment principles may minimize worker effectiveness. Top-down, bureaucratic approaches are likely to increase practitioners' sense of loss of control, helplessness, and vulnerability (Shera & Page, 1995). Disempowered practitioners are less able to engage in culturally competent empowerment practice (Gutiérrez & Lewis, 1999; Pinderhughes, 1983; Shera & Page, 1995).

Empowering processes, such as promoting shared leadership, trust and respect, participatory decision-making, creativity, autonomy, training, and horizontal and vertical communication and interactions (Foster-Fishman et al., 1998; Gutiérrez & Lewis, 1999; Shera & Page, 1995) can support organizational cultural competence efforts. These processes increase workers' knowledge, as well as encourage them to share their knowledge of the organization's needs to improve practice with diverse populations. Their participation parallels the empowerment process of clients, fostering their empowerment through involvement in the change process. Employing these processes in the context of value and respect for difference decreases the potential for marginalization of staff who are members of underrepresented groups, encouraging them to share their perspectives. Using empowering processes to design cultural-competence initiatives is an organizational cultural-competence empowerment intervention.

Continuing the Conversation

During social work's twenty-five years of exploring empowerment with diverse populations, our profession, along with other helping professions, has developed a useful knowledge base. Yet, we are seeking to understand and intervene in dynamic social phenomena that are changing with new political, economic, and social conditions. The landscape continues to shift, and each shift demands that practitioners acquire new knowledge and adapt their skills. A constructivist approach encourages us to continually revisit our previously constructed meanings and reshape our understandings.

The profession of social work has made important advances in developing the requisite practice knowledge, skills, and attitudes to engage in culturally competent empowerment practice. Our challenge is to further develop this knowledge, disseminate it, and inspire the commitment to operationalize it. Practitioners can play a vital role in shaping human service organizations that have the will and the means to advance empowerment practice with diverse populations. In partnership with individuals, families, communities, other practitioners, administrators, and policy makers, our commitment and efforts will continue the empowerment tradition of social work practice.

During my forty years of seeking answers to my childhood questions, I have found some answers and raised new questions. I now know that the oppressive forces of racism, sexism, and classism conspired to accomplish the slavery of Africans in the Americas and the colonization of Africans on our own continent, not an internal defect, sin, or inadequacy. I know our history is longer and larger than our contact with Europeans and its consequences. I know our strengths, our contributions to the world, and our resiliency, despite centuries of oppression. I know the parallels and intersections of African American oppression with the oppression of other peoples of color, of women, of gay men and lesbian women, of poor people of all colors and ethnicities, and of people with disabilities. I know this knowledge is a source of power.

There are several questions before us in the twenty-first century: How do we eliminate the conditions that cause today's children to ask my childhood questions? How can we proactively facilitate the empowerment of members of stigmatized and oppressed groups, before power blocks create debilitating effects in their lives? How do we inspire and maintain the personal and professional commitment to meet this challenge? I believe that there are answers to these questions. I believe practitioners can find these answers through collaborative work with each other and with those whom it is our mission to serve.

References

Atkinson, D. R., Morten, G., & Sue, D. W. (1998). *Counseling American minorities.* Boston: McGraw Hill.

Bartunek, J. M., Foster-Fishman, P., & Keys, C. B. (1996). Using collaborative advocacy to foster intergroup cooperation. *Human Relations, 49,* 701–733.

Bartunek, J. M., Lacey, C. A., & Wood, D. R. (1992). Social cognition in organizational change: An insider-outsider approach. *Journal of Applied Behavioral Science, 28,* 204–223.

Cross, T. (1995/1996). Developing a knowledge base to support cultural competence. *Family Resource Coalition Report,* 14(¾), 2–7.

Cross, T., & Bazron, B. J. (1996). *Developing cultural competence: Training of trainers workshop curriculum.* Washington, DC: Georgetown University Child Development Center, National Technical Assistance Center for Child Health and Mental Health Policy.

Cross, T. L., Bazron, B., Dennis, K., & Isaacs, M. (1989). *Towards a culturally competent system of care. A monograph on effective services for minority children who are severely emotionally disturbed: Vol. 1.* Washington, DC: Georgetown University Child Development Center, CASSP Technical Assistance Center.

Devore, W., & Schlesinger, E. (1981). *Ethnic sensitive social work practice.* Columbus, OH: Merrill.

East, J. F. (2000). Empowerment through welfare rights organizing: A feminist perspective. *Affilia, 15*(2), 311–328.

Foster-Fishman, P. G., Salem, D. A., Chibnall, S., Legler, R., & Yapchai, C. (1998). Empirical support for the critical assumptions of empowerment theory. *American Journal of Community Psychology, 26*(4), 507–536.

Fowler, S. M., & Mumford, M. G. (Eds.). (1995). *Intercultural sourcebook: Cross-cultural training methods: Vol. 1.* Yarmouth, ME: Intercultural Press.

Freire, P. (1973). *Pedagogy of the oppressed.* New York: Seabury.

Frye, M. (2001). Oppression. In P. S. Rothenberg (Ed.), *Race, class, and gender in the United States: An integrated study* (5th ed., pp. 139–143). New York: Worth Publishers.

Green, J. W. (1982). *Cultural awareness in the human services.* Upper Saddle River, NJ: Prentice-Hall.

Greene, G. J., Jensen, C., & Jones, D. H. (1996). A constructivist perspective on clinical social work practice with ethnically diverse clients. *Social Work, 41*(2), 172–180.

Guba, E. G., & Lincoln, Y. S. (1989). *Fourth generation evaluation.* Newbury Park, CA: Sage.

Gutiérrez, L. M. (1990). Working with women of color: An empowerment perspective. *Social Work, 35,* 149–155.

Gutiérrez, L. M. (1991). Empowering women of color. In M. Bricker-Jenkins, N. Hooyman, & N. Gottlieb (Eds.), *Feminist social work practice in clinical settings* (pp. 199–214). Newbury Park, CA: Sage.

Gutiérrez, L. M., GlenMaye, L., & DeLois, K. (1995). The organizational context of empowerment practice: Implications for social work administration. *Social Work, 40,* 249–258.

Gutiérrez, L. M., & Lewis, E. A. (1999). *Empowering women of color.* New York: Columbia University Press.

Hill Collins, P. (1986). Learning from the outsider within: The sociological significance of Black feminist thought. *Social Problems, 33,* 514–532.

Joe, J., & Malach, R. S. (1992). In E. W. Lynch & M. J. Hanson (Eds.), *Developing cross-cultural competence: A guide for working with young children and their families* (pp. 89–119). Baltimore: Paul H. Brookes Publishing.

Lecca, P. J., Quervalú, I., Nunes, J. V., & Gonzales, H. F. (1998). *Cultural competency in health, social, and human services.* New York: Garland Publishing.

Lee, J. A. B. (1996). The empowerment approach to social work practice. In F. J. Turner (Ed.), *Social treatment: Interlocking theoretical approaches* (4th ed., pp. 218–249). New York: Free Press.

Leigh, J. W. (1998). *Communicating for cultural competence.* Boston: Allyn & Bacon.

Lum, D. (1999). *Culturally competent practice: A framework for growth and action.* Pacific Grove, CA: Brooks/Cole.

Lum, D. (2000). *Social work practice and people of color: A process stage approach* (4th ed.). Belmont, CA: Wadsworth.

Lynch, E. W., & Hanson, M. J. (Eds.). (1992). *Developing cross-cultural competence: A guide for working with young children and their families.* Baltimore: Paul H. Brookes Publishing.

Mason, J. L. (1994). Developing culturally competent organizations. *Focal Point, 8*(2), 1–7.

Mason, J. L., Benjamin, M. P., & Lewis, S. A. (1996). The cultural competence model: Implications for child and family mental health services. In

C. A. Heflinger & C. T. Nixon (Eds.), *Families and the mental health system for children and adolescents: Policy, services, and research* (pp. 165–190). Thousand Oaks, CA: Sage Publications.

McIntosh, P. (2001). White privilege: Unpacking the invisible knapsack. In P. S. Rothenberg (Ed.), *Race, class, and gender in the United States: An integrated study* (5th ed., pp. 163–168). New York: Worth Publishers.

Monges, M. (1999). Candace rites of passage program: The cultural context as an empowerment tool. *Journal of Black Studies, 29*(6), 827–840.

Pernell, R. B. (1986). Empowerment and social group work. In M. Parnes (Ed.), *Innovations in social group work* (pp. 107–118). New York: Haworth Press.

Pinderhughes, E. E. (1983). Empowerment for our clients and for ourselves. *Social Casework, 64*(6), 331–338.

Pinderhughes, E. E. (1989). *Understanding race, ethnicity, and power: The key to efficacy in clinical practice.* New York: Free Press.

Pinderhughes, E. E. (1991). The delivery of child welfare services to African American clients. *American Journal of Orthopsychiatry, 61*(4), 599–605.

Rappaport, J. (1984). Studies in empowerment: Introduction to the issue. *Prevention in Human Services, 5,* 1–7.

Rappaport, J. (1987). Terms of empowerment/ Exemplars of prevention: Toward a theory for community psychology. *American Journal of Community Psychology, 15*(2), 121–148.

Shera, W., & Page, J. (1995). Creating more effective human service organizations. *Administration in Social Work, 19*(4), 1–13.

Simon, B. L. (1994). *The empowerment tradition in American social work history.* New York: Columbia University Press.

Solomon, B. B. (1976). *Black empowerment.* New York: Columbia University Press.

Staub-Bernasconi, S. (1991). Social action, empowerment, and social work: An integrating theoretical framework. *Social Work with Groups, 14*(3/4), 35–52.

Stehno, S. M. (1982). Differential treatment of minority children in service systems. *Social Work, 27*(1), 39–46.

Strawn, C. (1994). Beyond the buzz work: Empowerment in community outreach and education. *Journal of Applied Behavioral Science, 30,* 159–175.

Swigonski, M. E. (1994). The logic of feminist standpoint theory for social work research. *Social Work, 39,* 387–393.

Swigonski, M. E. (1996). Challenging privilege through Africentric social work practice. *Social Work, 41*(2), 153–161.

Trickett, E. J. (1994). Human diversity and community psychology: Where ecology and empowerment meet. *American Journal of Community Psychology, 22*(4), 583–592.

Trickett, E. J., Watts, R., & Birman, D. (Eds.). (1994). *Human diversity: Perspectives on people in context.* San Francisco: Jossey-Bass.

U.S. Civil Rights Commission. (2001). Indian tribes: A continuing quest for survival. In P. S. Rothenberg (Ed.), *Race, class, and gender in the United States: An integrated study* (5th ed., pp. 436–440). New York: Worth Publishers.

Zimmerman, M. A. (1995). Psychological empowerment: Issues and illustrations. *American Journal of Community Psychology, 23*(5), 581–599.

7

Building Community Collaboratives

Tania Alameda-Lawson and Michael A. Lawson

As an experienced social worker, what makes you to want to become a part of something new and innovative? What makes you want to stay a part of something new and innovative over time? These simple questions frame the complex process of building community collaboratives, in vulnerable, low-income communities. They are the questions that we have learned to systematically ask ourselves and those we work with every day.

As you may have experienced, finding ways for people from diverse backgrounds, with diverse perspectives and interests, to come together for the purpose of achieving *any* group task can be an extremely tall order. After all, have you ever had a difficult time figuring out with your friends or family what to have, or where to go, for dinner on a Friday night? Have you ever struggled to find a convenient time for people to get together for a meeting or study group? Have you ever found yourself having to work with someone that you disagreed with or disliked so strongly that you literally wanted to strangle them? If you have experienced any or all of these, then you are familiar with some of the basic challenges confronting many collaboratives and collaborations serving low-income communities.

A Perspective on Collaboration

Now consider this scenario. You walk into a community-planning seminar and the facilitator, after assigning each of you a unique professional role (such as counselor, law enforcement officer, probation officer, city planner, educator, psychologist, and so forth), issues this challenge: You and your colleagues are collectively charged with developing a systematic action strategy for ameliorating poverty in a gated, low-income housing community of 5,000 residents.

On one hand, this may seem like an overly idealistic task for a group your size. On the other hand, it is the very task that similar numbers of frontline workers and middle-management helping professionals are asked, or mandated, to do collaboratively every day.

So, where will you and your colleagues start? If you are like many collaboratives, you may start by trying to identify or operationalize the defining features or manifestations of poverty. Depending on your worldview, professional background, and training, some of you may talk about the challenges related to school failure and substance abuse. Others may want to talk about substandard housing, unemployment, and lack of meaningful job opportunities available to vulnerable residents. Still others may talk about parental neglect and child abuse, teenage pregnancy, gangs, and a lack of role models in low-income communities. Others may talk about delinquency, crime, lack of businesses in communities, or institutional racism, classism, sexism, and oppression.

You ask the facilitator about the defining features of the community. "Depending on your worldview," the facilitator replies, "all of them are present."

Your entire group wonders in silence. How will you accommodate and integrate these diverse views of what constitutes or contributes to poverty? How will you translate them into practice strategies that will make things better for our most vulnerable?

You decide to break the silence and suggest to the group that all of the above manifestations of poverty are salient barriers to making things better for vulnerable people. In so doing, you suggest breaking down the challenges related to poverty into subgroups, committees, or action teams. Thankfully, everyone agrees on this approach. You collectively decide to divide into four action teams to accommodate all of the areas. Together, you organize your efforts under the following titles: housing and community development, social services, education, and probation. You all agree to reconvene in four weeks to individually present, then collectively integrate or incorporate, your plans.

Four weeks later, you report back. The housing and community development team has generated an exciting strategy of linking community development corporations with the Department of Housing and Urban Development and the local housing authority to provide home-ownership opportunities so that vulnerable residents can feel a sense of ownership in the communities in which they live. They suggest that true empowerment starts with giving people real ownership over their lives.

The social services team doesn't look as excited. One member of the social services team suggests that economic empowerment is great. But, she continues, economic empowerment is impossible unless people are able to function sufficiently in order to keep their jobs and manage their finances responsibly. Another member of the team suggests that the members of this community probably lack the psychosocial well-being to make such an economic-empowerment agenda work.

When asked from the housing and community development team what their solution is, the social services team says they have had a hard time trying to find where to start. Do they focus on providing interventions aimed at erasing specific problems or disorders? Or do they promote prevention and early intervention strategies as a means of helping the innocent children who are victimized by the environments in which they live?

One member of the team talks about the obvious needs for counseling and mental health services, citing the pathologies inherent in the ways that many poor families function. Another talks about rampant substance abuse. Together, they suggest that treating habitual users is not only difficult, but most of the female abusers are also using when they are pregnant with their babies, which has dire effects on the healthy development of the community's children. Another member of the social services team mentions that child abuse and neglect are frequent offshoots of so much drug use.

At that point, a member of the education team chimes in, saying that drug use is prevalent at the schools. She says that the team talked not only about kids using drugs (and not succeeding in school), but they think that many kids are showing up at school with empty stomachs and dirty clothes—all because their parents either don't care about their welfare or because they are too strung out on drugs.

A member of the probation team then enters the discussion, saying that the primary problem is that most kids in the community simply do not have anywhere to go where they can undertake positive activities. As a combined result of sheer boredom and not wanting to go home to households that are either abusive or dysfunctional, kids are taking to the streets, where they become involved in gangs, loot and steal from small, local businesses and shops, use drugs and alcohol, have premarital sex, and participate in other delinquent behaviors. These behaviors not only result in kids entering the system at early ages, but unwanted babies are being conceived as a consequence.

Another member of the probation team concludes that the team feels that if a community center were placed somewhere central in the community, combined with a wealth of activities and flexible hours, then youth delinquency and substance abuse could be curtailed and community safety could be improved.

Excitedly, a member of the social service team suggests that perhaps some of the intervention, early intervention, or prevention services that they have talked about could be placed at the community center. A member of the education team then wonders aloud, would it be possible for a Boys and Girls Club or a like organization to provide role models, as well as tutoring and mentoring for kids at that center? A member from the housing and community development team suggests that maybe the housing authority could help fund a community center.

The group exhales. You all did it! You broke out into action teams, dissected complex problems, found commonalities, and integrated your programs all into one space that met everyone's objectives. You collaborated! Congratulations!

Now, consider a quote from a parent we have worked with as she reacted to a similar process undertaken in her community.

> You know, it's nice to see all of these resources and supports poured into our community. And I mean our (the resident's) community. But what makes me really mad is that no one is asking us what we think about all of this. And once again they (professionals) are going to do what they think that we need and nothing is going to change. The only thing that changes here is them (professionals). More agencies just comin' and going. And you know what, we need those drug and alcohol services. But people won't use what they have, because nobody is going to go to some central location so that every-

one can see what they're doing and what their business is. And nobody is going to go and get services at 2:00 in the afternoon. People are going to want services when they are about to do drugs. In this community, people are jonesin' (wanting to use) about 2:00 in the morning or so. So, who's gonna be there then? Only us community members, that's who. But where are we in all of this? Nowhere. And soon they'll be gone, and we'll all still be here. *(parentheses added)*

This parent's voice captures the need for the model of community collaboration advanced in this chapter. Although derived from the important points of knowing evident in the literature, much of our discussion flows from our practice experience over the past decade or so. Readers should be mindful that, as practitioners, we have both been centrally involved in collaborative processes that have failed to capture the imagination, attention, and aspirations of professionals, residents, and clients alike. On the other hand, we have also been a part of collaboratives that have helped transform the way that professionals, residents, and clients view themselves, each other, and their communities.

The difference between our successful and unsuccessful collaborative experiences has largely been determined by the nature and scope of client and resident participation. In our early work, professionals were the central participants. The collaboratives spent much time trying to integrate services that, in spite of seemingly innovative collaborative practices, clients and residents still seldom accessed. However, when we developed means that enabled residents and clients to become centrally involved, each collaborative largely flourished.

In order to highlight the strengths and action strategies included in community collaboratives, a common frame of reference about what community collaboration is—and specifically, what community collaboration is not—is needed. To address this challenge, we begin our discussion by introducing the dominant conception and model of professionally driven collaboration. Once advanced, the framework and problems identified through professionally driven collaboratives provide a mechanism of comparison to the unique client and resident-driven features and power-sharing activities found in community collaboratives. We conclude by offering a continuing conversation from our learnings and worldviews.

Professionally Driven, Service-Centered Collaboratives

Many collaborative processes like the preceding scenario originate with a group of helping professionals charged with solving monumental social, sociopolitical, sociocultural, and socioeconomic problems. When helping professionals convene for the purpose of collectively finding ways to solve challenges in low-income communities, their efforts are referred to in some circles as *professionally driven, service-centered collaborations* (Aspen Institute, 1997). They are called professionally driven because the collective conceptions generated about the challenges, problems, and needs of vulnerable children, youth, and families are largely determined by professionals. In addition, they are also often called service-centered because the action strategies employed by members of the collaborative can largely be defined and measured as services that are rendered to vulnerable communities from paid and highly trained professionals.

Organizing a Professional Collaborative

When helping professionals serving low-income communities gather to collaborate, some standard products are often developed. For starters, collaboratives usually begin by formulating some sort of vision statement. This visioning process often provides collaborative members with the opportunity to collectively develop an image for how the community will be improved as a result of their collective effort. An example of a vision statement for a community-based, safety- and law enforcement-focused collaborative could be:

> For our community to be crime- and drug-free within the next five years.

The next process is often the drafting of a mission statement. When completed, this 25 to 35 word (or less) statement guides the group on its general direction and purpose. An example of a mission statement for a school-linked services collaborative could be:

> To provide our community with case-management services and responsive community supports so that children can do better in school, stay in school, and become productive citizens of tomorrow.

Thirdly, collaboratives also often draft Memorandums of Understanding (MOUs, sometimes also called Letters of Agreement, LOAs), which are crafted to explicitly state the formal contribution that each agency, institution, or stakeholder will make to the larger whole. Sometimes, these MOUs are developed to state formal agency arrangements for the sake of legal and liability purposes. In other instances, MOUs are drafted to develop *norms of reciprocity*, whereby agency professionals develop explicit means for how they will treat and interact with one another.

The development of explicit norms of reciprocity is particularly evident and useful in communities where there are long histories of interagency conflict and skepticism (Hooper-Briar & Lawson, 1994). They are also frequently developed in collaboratives that bring together professionals representing several different disciplines or service sectors—especially when they have never before worked together. Oftentimes, larger-scale collaboratives—ones that include twenty or more agencies—hire consultants to help them draft vision and mission statements and MOUs, as well as to provide team-building exercises to help ready the group for developing and drafting formal norms of reciprocity. However, although these benchmarks, and the ways in which they are achieved, are important to the ongoing success of collaboratives, the "real work" of collaboration begins when participants or members from each agency leave each collaborative meeting or session and return to their "real jobs."

Professional Collaboration—Real Change?

Tyack and Cuban (1995) explain the systematic failure of school reform in the United States. In their book, *Tinkering Toward Utopia: A Century of Public School Reform*, they coined a phrase, *real school*, to refer to the daily roles, rituals, responsibilities, and happenings that occur in schools each day. Tyack and Cuban argued that, in spite of significant developments in knowledge and practice related to school reform, reform efforts in this country systematically fail because they rarely meaningfully impact what really happens in and around schools and schooling every day.

Similar to school reform efforts, collaborations between and among a community's professionals are largely convened to positively impact what are perceived to be structurally ineffective practices of helping professionals and helping systems (Wood & Gray, 1991). The majority of professionally driven, service-centered collaboratives and collaborations are convened to address the following structurally related problems to the delivery of services:

• Services are often difficult for community residents, who often lack transportation and child care, to access.

• Services are often delivered in a competing and categorical manner, leaving families with as many as fifteen agencies that they need to visit or attend simultaneously—many of them court mandated—without coordination between and among the different agencies or services.

• Agencies often compete for clients and fiscal resources—resulting in some clients being "overserviced," others left without receiving supports, and unstable grant-funded agencies and community-based organizations that are opening up and shutting down monthly in many communities.

Consequently, the dialogues and processes found in many professionally driven, service-centered collaboratives are largely focused on addressing these three interdependent problems and challenges.

When the collaborative centers on improving service access and coordination, these efforts are often referred to as *service integration* initiatives (Hasset & Austin, 1997). They focus on improving the ways in which professionally driven services can be more consumer or customer friendly to low-income and vulnerable populations. Questions and comments asked and directed at many of these collaboratives include

"How can we get community residents to access our services?"

"The problems and challenges our clients are confronting are due to the fact that services in this community are fragmented."

"If we are going to continue to offer these services to this community, we need to have more referrals. Otherwise, we are going to have to shut down."

The outward focus of the dialogues inherent to many professionally driven collaboratives and collaborations makes sense. After all, if counseling services are located ten miles away, the weather is atrocious, and a family of four needs to take a bus to those services while lacking bus money, with three different route transfers added to the fold, then the chances that clients will access that service are slim. Likewise, clients who are mandated to attend multiple agencies and service providers who are not aware of each other often have their well-being compromised by the different and often-competing interests, directives, and diagnoses provided by the agencies or professionals.

We have found that one of the primary and critical challenges endemic to professionally driven, service-centered, and service-integration-focused dialogues stems not from the apparent validity of the problems they address, but from a systematic failure to impact what we refer to as changes in *real-service delivery*. Their practices often tend to neglect a meaningful examination of the assumptions (and limitations therein) that define and underscore the day-to-day work practices of their participants (Alameda-Lawson & Lawson, 2000).

Single Problems and Single Solutions

Many service-centered collaboration models are staffed and convened by professionals trained to develop single-problem, single-solution or categorical programs (Gardner, 1992). They are professionalized experts in developing projects, programs, and initiatives to improve the lives of targeted individuals who demonstrate, through some form of assessment, a need for professionally driven services. Although this expertise is vitally important in many ways, it also poses limitations to collaboration.

Because of the nature of this conventional program development, professionals with backgrounds in categorical programming often view the outcomes of their services in terms of changes in the specific behavior of individuals (Schön, 1983). As a consequence, outcome data and "success stories" generated through categorical programming measure how specific interventions result in specific psychosocial improvements (Lodge, 1998).

For example, a social worker employed by a county drug and alcohol bureau is charged with addressing community challenges related to substance abuse. The primary mandate is to develop programs that provide specific interventions to targeted substance abusers that alleviate individual wants or needs to use a controlled substance, usually through drug and alcohol counseling and self-help. Over time, and through years of training and work-related experience, professionals become socialized into the overall problem domain of their work. In this instance, the problem domain of this social worker's practice becomes substance abuse. The solution to improving abusive behaviors becomes substance abuse counseling and treatment. This is a single-problem, single-solution mindset.

Single-problem, single-solution mindsets are generated from professionalized worldviews. These worldviews are created, shaped, and shaded by particular conceptions of the problems facing our society. They are maintained by market-driven forces that demand expertise over specific, and often singular, conceptions of what ails us, what we need, and what is good for us (Brint, 1994). These professionalized worldviews start in schools that educate helping professionals and are, in turn, reenforced by agencies and institutions charged with solving single-sector-related problems and issues (Lawson, 1997).

This is not to suggest that expertise and expert knowledge is not an important part of helping people. It is. However, such mindsets or professionalized worldviews are often problematic to collaboration because the very nature of bringing diverse professional groups together from different service sectors stems from the notion that the challenges in many low-income communities are not separate. They are interrelated!

As a consequence, many service integration-focused efforts wrestle constantly with the implicit mandate of collaboration (namely, the need to view problems and interventions as interrelated and interdependent) against what their professional experience and professional training has taught them: specific problems need to be targeted with specific and separate interventions.

This dissonance manifests itself in many collaboratives through the coordination of existing services without sacrificing the ways in which professionals conduct much of their day-to-day business (Adelman & Taylor, 1997). At the end of the day, real-service delivery does not change much, if at all, through professionally driven collaboratives. Also, because the ways in which professionals conduct much of their business do not change, community conditions tend not to be impacted much either (McKnight, 1995).

Professional Collaboration—The Benefits

What does change, however, in the short term through these collaboratives is that professionals from different specializations, professions, disciplines, and service sectors often do engage in dialogues about the problems and challenges facing individuals and families on their case loads. *Multidisciplinary, service-integration,* or *resource-coordination* teams are close companions and common offshoots of broader, professionally driven collaboratives. These teams focus on coordinating services and programs to better the lives of those they share as clients (Gardner, 1992). In other instances, these teams act as their own collaboratives. We have seen as many as five of these separate collaboratives exist in the same community.

The extent to which professionally driven collaboratives are able to meaningfully change the lives of individuals and families often depends on whether their helping professionals can agree on shared conceptions of the problems facing their client populations (Himmelman, 1996). Because of the different professional socialization and professionalization practices outlined earlier, collaboratives sometimes remain stuck in the problem-setting stage, when they try to collectively agree on a point of departure for collaboration, for quite some time.

Nevertheless, when helping professionals can agree on a shared description of problems, the following events are believed to eventuate as a result of collaborating:

• If (policy and practice) infrastructures are created to ensure that services can be and are integrated and coordinated properly, then service-related access, assessment, treatment, follow-up, and follow-through will improve.

- When (service) access, assessment, treatment, follow-up, and follow-through improve, individual behaviors and outcomes will improve and problematic behaviors will decrease.

- When problematic behaviors decrease in individuals, community conditions will improve as a consequence.

This chain of events defines the foundation of a *theory of helping* for professionally driven, service-centered, and service-integration-focused collaboration. This theory rests on the notion that community revitalization can be achieved by helping one person at a time through a project-by-project development strategy bolstered by the strategic linking or integration of services for families that have multiple needs (Shiffman & Motley, 1989). Its approaches are also based on the notion that communities can be more readily improved through an outside-in change and development strategy: Professionals working from the "outside" can systematically affect individuals on the "inside" so that, ultimately, communities can be improved to the core.

Community Collaboratives: An Alternative

> Here they go talking about all the things they (service providers) are providing. But what are they really providing? More jobs for them and theirs, that's what. And that's why no one will ever really use what they're providing, 'cause it's not for us, it's for them. Just a bunch of things they think we need, not what we think we need to better us, you know what I'm saying?
>
> —Low-income Community Parent, Sacramento, CA

Thirty-five years ago, new approaches to community development emerged and began to change the ways in which problems facing low-income communities were framed. Instead of looking at being poor as an affliction on families and their individual members, the broader notion of poverty was advanced as a systematic phenomenon that affects and afflicts whole communities. Problematic manifestations of poverty—such as deteriorated housing, impaired health, poor health-care access, nonexistent or low wages, the welfare assault on self-respect, high crime rates, low tax base, reduced police and school services, child neglect, family abuse, and the continued divestment of financial capital—all feed off of each other to create communities with multiple and multilevel challenges that span across several sectors and systems (Shiffman & Motley, 1989).

From this perspective, critical masses of scholars, practitioners, and policy makers developed community-based and comprehensive approaches to improving the social, physical, economic, and environmental conditions of vulnerable communities simultaneously. These approaches continue to be based today on the notion that the lives of vulnerable populations can only get better when communities are built from the inside out, rather than trying to fix each individual so they can escape, or persevere in spite of, difficult environments (McKnight, 1995).

Distinctive Qualities of Community Collaboratives

Nondominant approaches to collaboration—called *community collaboration*—differ from the dominant, professionally driven, service-centered, and service-integration-focused models in several ways. They differ in orientation because the focus of professionally driven efforts are narrowed to improving the lives of individuals and targeted families. On the other hand, community collaboratives focus on promoting and facilitating the collective well-being of all members of a community (Aspen Institute, 1997).

They also differ in stakeholder participation. Professionally driven collaboratives tend to be staffed largely by helping professionals from specific service sectors (although cross-sector, or multisector collaborations do exist), some business leaders and policy makers, and occasionally, residents. Community collaboratives begin with the explicit inclusion of community residents, in addition to helping professionals, policy makers, and business leaders (Armstrong, 1997).

Although professionally driven collaboratives will likely address community challenges through categorically and/or programmatically driven action teams, community collaboratives address broad conceptions of community challenges in joint settings. Whereas mental health and policing would often be delegated to separate committees, action teams, or even distinct collaboratives in professionally driven collaboratives, in community collaboratives, the mental health of a community would be viewed as inseparable from the police protection afforded (or not afforded) to a community's residents (Alameda-Lawson & Lawson, 2000). Professionally driven collaboratives focus on ways that professionals can help individuals through their services, but community collaboratives focus on developing strategies to create opportunities for residents to play central roles in community development and revitalization.

These differences in orientation and practice frame the foundation of a theory of helping that underscores many community collaboratives

• If practice and policy infrastructures are created to ensure that community supports and resources are brokered and provided by community professionals in response to needs directly voiced by clients and community residents, community challenges can be addressed in a truly comprehensive and integrated manner.

• When collaboration occurs between members of different service systems and sectors with clients, residents, and families as central participant–guides, then formal and informal support networks will develop that enable *communities of systems* to develop, overlap, and complement one another.

• When families, agencies, institutions, and systems are mutually supported and supportive, then community conditions improve, and strong and healthy communities are developed.

A particularly salient strength of the theory of helping of community collaboratives is the central inclusion of resident community members as equal partners and participant–guides. When clients are central participants, they guide community collaboratives in determining *what* services are provided to a community, *where* they are provided, *how* they are provided, and in some instances, *if* they are provided at all. Indeed, community collaboratives support a framework in which the lived experiences of clients and community residents provide the blueprint from which community resources and supports can be developed, redeveloped, and implemented in a comprehensive and integrated way (Alameda-Lawson & Lawson, 2000). How is this possible?

When collaboratives elicit the voices and experiences of clients, collaborative members quickly realize that the nature of client struggles exceeds the scope of individual, categorical programs. Because clients rarely compartmentalize their lives according to a particular service sector or professional interests, the ways that they frame problems demand integrated solutions or solution sets (Smale, 1995). For countless residents of low-income communities, their children's psychosocial well-being is as central to them as their children's health, success in school, or their ability or inability to be or feel safe while playing outside. One cannot be addressed without the others.

These simple and intuitive, albeit holistic, perspectives, coupled with the cumulative impact of community challenges being addressed separately for decades, afford clients and residents the ability to often readily envision how things can and should be done differently. Community collaboratives recognize these lived experiences of clients as invaluable strengths. This is why some community collaboratives refer to client or resident participants as *client* or *family experts.*

Professional Stances in Community Collaboratives

Although there are far too many professionals who still believe that clients have no business determining the ways in which professional services are delivered or rendered, many professionals do increasingly value the contributions of their clients. The problem that professionals frequently encounter in promoting the ongoing participation of clients often can be traced to the reasons why they want client participation in the first place. In many professionally driven collaboratives, the rationale for client or resident participation, in effect, is to find *client ambassadors* to sell the innovative work undertaken by professionals collaborating for the first time. Under this top-down model, clients and residents are brought into the collaborative fold before the implementation of new services, but after collaborative assessment and planning has occurred (Mondros & Wilson, 1994).

For example, in a western state, a group of professional service providers underwent a nine-month planning process in an effort to revitalize a particularly challenged low-income community. Although they were mindful that resident "buy in" was a requisite resource for the success of their project, they waited to include (low-income) residents until their action plan was completed. Once they had mobilized all of the community's service providers, formalized MOUs, and secured facilities and space in the local community, they invited residents to a presentation with the hope that they would "spread the good news" of their drug and alcohol counseling services throughout the community. The result: only three families attended the planning team's meeting. Eight months later, only two families had accessed the planning team's substance abuse counseling program.

Conversely, community collaboratives are built on the notion that clients need to be central in collaborative, programmatic planning and development, implementation, operation, and evaluation (Halpern, 1997). This focus differs qualitatively from wanting client or resident input to rubber stamp professional notions or conceptions of what is needed in a community. Instead, proponents of community collaboration believe that collaboration cannot begin until families are explicit guides in the redevelopment of their communities.

Consider this example: In one southern state, a group of professionals convened to develop a service collaborative based out of an elementary school. Their goal was to promote and improve resident access to formal services. After professional workers were repositioned to work at the school, the community's families still did not access the resource center that the service collaborative created. However, months later when community residents were recruited to help run and redefine the resource center's services, service access to the resource center tripled. Why? Under the new community collaborative design, residents identified legal services as a chief community need. When the collaborative helped implement legal services at the resource center, residents not only accessed legal services in large numbers, but they also became more aware of other services available to them. Service access in all areas increased as a result. Moreover, community access to legal services helped to change housing statutes in the community, which, in turn, helped reduce community transience!

Unfortunately, it is commonplace to find clients and/or community residents disengaged from formal institutional processes. Indeed, many clients have had considerable difficulty and hardship in their previous interactions with professionals. For community collaboration to occur, then, professionals need to reverse this trend by restructuring some, if not many, of their conventional practices.

Professionals as Resource Brokers and Providers
The extent to which a community collaborative functions (or is responsive to the voices and needs of its clients or residents) is dependent on whether professional collaborative members can recast their conventional roles as service providers to *resource brokers* and *providers*. Resource brokers and providers differ from service providers in both ideology and function. For example, service providers' practices tend to operate from a deficit model that suggests that vulnerable populations have problems that can best be addressed through professionally run services. In other words, the way in which professionals view or value clients is through a lens of dependency; clients are dependent on professionals' abilities to help them lead productive lives (Brint, 1994; McKnight, 1995).

Resource brokers and providers have a different value set that underscores their practices. Instead of viewing clients as dependency-laden individuals burdened by (intergenerational) pathology, clients are considered by resource brokers and providers as a part of a community of systems in need of support. These systems—including families, faith-based organizations, schools, social service agencies and institutions, community-based nonprofit groups, businesses, professionals, clients, and community residents—are viewed as integral parts of a comprehensive whole. Without the development of an infrastructure that supports and links these systems, they break down (Gardner, 1994). Vulnerable children, youth, families, and the professionals who serve them are victims of systematic and cyclical hardship and failure (Lawson, Briar-Lawson, & Lawson, 1997). However, when supported and integrated in a meaningful and responsive way, a community of systems possesses the capacity to transform and revitalize communities. This value orientation and epistemology of practice guide resource brokers and providers to target, implement, and render their services as one component needed to support the well-being of families and communities. Over time, this practice of brokering and providing community resources—as identified from the lived experiences and direct voices of clients—becomes the central thrust of helping professionals conduct their day-to-day business. Real-service delivery changes.

Engaging Clients through Outreach

For community collaboration to be successful, clients are not only brought into the fold, but they are explicitly placed at the center of collaboration. For agency professionals working in community collaboratives, restructuring their work practices begins by leaving the confines of their offices, going out into the community, and conducting door-to-door outreach (Alameda-Lawson & Lawson, 2000).

The process of going door-to-door and walking the streets is not only time consuming, but for many, it represents the type of work that is not suitable for professionals with a terminal degree. For others, outreach simply represents an intimidating and outright scary prospect. In addition, the horror stories that frequent professional agencies serving vulnerable communities about community shootings, violence, gangs, substance abuse practices, and so forth never help. Although mindful of these important warnings, we have found that over time, the process of reaching out into a community to talk with unfamiliar people in unfamiliar scenarios becomes easier and less threatening.

It is important to keep in mind that the people with whom practitioners conduct outreach are often as frightened, if not more frightened, than the professionals. As a result, the extent to which professionals can find a way to implicitly recognize their vulnerability determines the degree of engagement generated through door-to-door outreach (Hooper-Briar, Lawson, & Alameda, 1996). The theory of engagement here is intuitive: If one person is scared of another, and the other person is scared (of the other) as well, then if both parties learn of each other's fears, they will be less fearful of one another and will interact with more facility as a consequence.

One way to begin to convey this metamessage of vulnerability to clients is to explicitly tell them that our ability to do our jobs effectively depends on their active input and participation. The subtext of this message, if delivered in a sincere fashion, is easily decoded by clients. *I need you in order to do my job. Without you, I can't do my job well.*

Without you, I have no job. This subtext tends to reveal a vulnerability to the client that is engaging, or at the very least, less threatening.

Nevertheless, if clients are to truly buy into this message that we need them, there needs to be some formal mechanism by which we can convey to them that our efforts represent a different approach from what they may have previously experienced. This different approach needs to be couched in a way that is engaging to, and not exploitative of, the clients, their needs, and their aspirations.

Opportunity-Focused Engagement Strategies

We have found that when clients feel they are afforded an opportunity to utilize their expertise and knowledge to impact positive change in their community, their ongoing engagement can be facilitated and generated over time. However, if clients feel pressured to fulfill an obligation that they are alleged to have (e.g., parenting, civic engagement/concerned citizen, and so forth), then disengagement and lack of client turnout or follow-through can be expected.

Perhaps the best method for beginning an engagement strategy that is opportunity-focused is to put our (professional) money where our mouths are: Pay clients to attend special planning meetings. Although this practice is sometimes viewed by professionals as providing an incentive for what clients or residents should be doing in the first place, we think that providing a little something in agency budgets to monetarily recognize client contributions is a way to build a community culture supporting collaboration. By providing stipends, organizations at least implicitly recognize the value of clients and residents by making room in what are always tight budgets. Over time, clients feel more valued by and less skeptical about professionals when their input and participation is explicitly honored in a way that benefits them (Alameda-Lawson & Lawson, 1999).

Whatever means are used to create an opportunity-focused—in lieu of an obligation-focused—outreach strategy, we have found that community collaboratives that are successful in keeping clients involved over time often manifest three salient practices and values in regard to outreach

• Outreach is a systematic, central, and continuous part of programmatic or agency operation.

• Outreach is something undertaken by multiple agencies and is considered separate from service-centered home visits designed to inform clients of compliance mandates or to perform therapy or assessment.

• Monetary compensation provided to residents recognizes their expert contributions and the sacrifices they make by participating on their own time.

Sustaining Community Engagement

Once client interest is peaked through opportunity-focused outreach, three additional critical components are needed to sustain community engagement in collaboratives.

The first of these components provides a mechanism by which clients create the agenda to guide the ways a collaborative solves problems and conducts its primary operations. This process is facilitated through *nominal group techniques* or *nominal needs assessments*. The second component involves facilitated *role playing* so that clients, lacking experience as participants in professional settings, can learn to decode the often convoluted, hidden rules and metamessaging process that can confuse all of us. Finally, the third sustaining element casts social workers in the roles of *community advocates* or *professional change agents*, who build mechanisms to facilitate collaborative problem-solving and retain the active participation of all members.

Nominal Group Techniques

Perhaps more than any other process, nominal group techniques allow for the initial agendas of community collaborative meetings to be grounded in the needs of communities (Alameda-Lawson & Lawson, 2000). Following outreach, nominal group techniques entail mobilizing clients to collectively identify the challenges or problems impeding the wellness of themselves, their children, and their community. It is a process that has three distinct and interdependent foci:

- to provide clients with an explicit opportunity to talk about their lives in a way that values and validates their experiences

- to provide clients with an opportunity to talk about their conceptions and perceptions of community challenges in a group context so that clients can recognize each others' (similar) worldviews and experiences

- to provide a foundation for developing a client or resident group that can support—both formally and informally—its client members, as well as the collaborative as a whole

In professionally driven collaboratives, similar meetings of community residents are often called focus groups. From our experience, focus groups are employed by collaboratives annually or biannually to generate information about what services community residents need so professionals can levy them on behalf of families (Aspen Institute, 1997).

In community collaboratives, focus groups and other forms of community assessment also are conducted annually in an effort to reach as many people as possible. However, nominal needs assessments are conducted on a monthly basis so clients and residents are prepared to address their own tangible challenges directly to the collaborative as participants. This process whereby clients consistently define and present their own needs in community collaboratives results in several buzzwords in practice. Among these labels are client-driven, consumer-driven, resident-driven, consumer-guided, customer-guided, family-centered, and family-focused. Whatever label is used, this distinct feature of community collaboratives rests in the lived experiences of clients, their families, and community as accessed through collaborative group processes.

Nominal group techniques provide professionals with the opportunity to hear tangible client and resident needs so that they transition from service providers to resource brokers or providers (Bruner & Chavez, 1998). In so doing, community collaboratives are always bottom-up. Client and resident aspirations become the central, guiding, and unifying component of integrating community resources. This distinct difference in process enables community collaboratives to deviate from the complex, albeit oftentimes linear, focus of integrating services to integrating support systems or integrating community systems.

Role Playing

In many ways, community collaboratives represent a framework within which clients and residents are able to negotiate, alter, or transform the way that systems work. Role playing is a vital step in preparing clients and community residents to learn how to advocate for themselves and their community in situations and contexts often resistant to their views, values, and expertise. Role-playing exercises should focus on helping clients and residents learn basic tasks related to professional meetings and contacts, including

- how to ask for clarification when an issue or stream of words seems confusing
- how to decode acronyms that they do not understand
- how to engage elusive professionals and collaborative members

Attempts at community collaboration and community engagement that are unsuccessful often spend a great deal of time focusing on what clients do not know instead of focusing on how to enable others to hear what they do know. By using client and community-resident expertise as the unit of analysis in role playing, the process of teaching meeting-related or etiquette-related skills can be couched within an overall framework that is strength-based. As a result, clients and community residents can enter meetings with confidence and competent skills, a critical step to their long-term engagement in the collaborative.

When community collaboratives are formed (and clients and residents first present needs and action strategies to professionals) professional members tend to delegate many responsibilities and tasks to clients. Clients are asked to make telephone calls to key agency contacts, to write letters to agency officials—even to write grant proposals and planning documents. These delegation processes, if gone unchecked, create power differentials in community collaboratives that are both problematic and harmful in two ways. First, when professionals delegate tasks to clients, they implicitly define client and resident participation as carrying out the directives of agendas of professionals (Briar-Lawson, 1998). In turn, clients and residents are removed from the center of collaboration and placed on the fringe (Alameda-Lawson & Lawson, 1999). Second, when professionals simply delegate tasks to clients, those tasks may exceed the scope of clients' current capacities or levels of empowerment, thus creating a framework for clients, and as a consequence the collaborative, to fail. Moreover, when delegation processes define the primary outputs of professional participation, their day-to-day work practices stay the same. Real-service delivery does not change.

Over time, if these top-down practices continue, client and resident participation often wanes, and community collaboratives become either professionally driven, service-centered collaboratives, or they dissolve altogether (Himmelman, 1996).

Role-playing exercises can help clients develop the confidence and methods to politely ask professionals to assume responsibility for the tasks they delegate to others. In so doing, clients help professionals make the normative leap from resource brokers—when professionals identify contacts or resources that can help communities address their challenges—to resource brokers and providers—when professionals not only identify contacts and resources that can help clients and communities but also make the collaborative provision of those resources a central part of their work. Role playing, then, is a central mechanism to recast professional work routines in ways that respond to the needs and voices of consumers. It should be considered a critical component and facilitator of community collaboration.

Social Workers As Community Advocates

Community advocates are professionals charged with developing the capacities of families and existing service systems. Community advocates model a new type of collaborative professionalism that supports the development of client and resident groups and casts a new framework for collaborative practice. This reprofessionalization of sorts requires both complex thinking and simple intuition. In more esoteric terms, it necessitates multimodal thinking and multilevel practice (Lawson & Alameda-Lawson, in press).

Framing a Collaborative Environment

A key role of the community advocate is to provide professionals with a new framework for collaborative practice. Because many helping professionals have spent a lot of time working in isolation, trying to "save the world" by themselves, many professional communities in low-income contexts have an implicit sense of learned helplessness or hopelessness that sometimes pervades their work routines (Gardner, 1992). As a consequence, some helping professionals—particularly those who have worked in the system for several years—have a difficult time moving beyond what appears to them as seemingly insurmountable community problems to developing collaborative solutions to the challenges identified by their clients (Himmelman, 1996).

> One way that community advocates help move skeptical professionals away from these paralyzing mind-sets is to provide a process from which "success stories" can be generated today from the daunting problems of yesterday.

Successful community collaboratives are able to create positive collaborative environments filled with purpose and agency when they replace victim blaming with paradoxical thinking (Lawson & Alameda-Lawson, in press). Deficit-oriented views toward clients blame the victim and often result in clients resisting and disengaging from institutions and helping systems. Likewise, indictments toward professional practices, whether implicit or explicit, can also spawn worker disengagement from community collaboratives. Community advocates need to focus dialogue toward ways that *existing* professional and client expertise can be used to help the challenges and action strategies of both clients and professionals.

To avoid deficit views, think paradoxically. Einstein said that for every action there is an equal and opposite reaction. In community collaboratives, for every negative experience incurred by a member, there is an equal and opposite expertise or strength that has developed as a consequence. Thus, a homeless client who might be blamed for irresponsibility, poor resource management, not taking care of her children, and drug use could instead be viewed as an expert on surviving the perils of homelessness, on identifying the barriers faced by homeless populations, and on knowing the struggles and suffering of homeless parents and children. Similarly, a helping professional viewed as difficult, disengaged, uncaring, or noncollaborative may alternatively be recognized as an expert on what is needed to better support professionals.

Constructing a Collaborative Process

Another important function of a community advocate is seemingly linear: to develop mechanisms in a collaborative to ensure that the voices and visions of community residents are central to the collaborative and its practices. However, finding ways and means to develop these mechanisms and infrastructures can be difficult and complex.

Community advocates need to help provide measures to ensure that clients are constantly understanding and decoding the interactions and subtexts of each meeting. This includes eliciting the cues and action strategies identified by clients during nominal group techniques and role playing. Sometimes, making sure that clients and residents are "up to speed" appears to slow down the collaborative. Over time and upon reflection, community advocates tend to realize that professionals are also often confused by the buzzwords and esoteric dialogues present at collaborative meetings. Community advocates help members identify how to address questions and concerns without being or feeling silly, stupid, or condemned. This is an important first step in building a group culture that supports collaboration. Formally developing functional and meaningful norms of reciprocity—through MOUs or LOAs—that are responsive to this need can also be a vital component to sustaining initial client and professional engagement in communities fraught with histories of conflict and poor relations (Hooper-Briar & Lawson, 1994).

Helping collaboratives develop accountability for problem solving is another task of the community advocate. Community collaboratives that are able to consistently problem-solve keep the interest, attention, and attendance of their members over time (Aspen Institute, 1997). One way to provide such an accountability structure is through the strategic use of minute-taking and agenda-setting activities (Alameda-Lawson & Lawson, 2000). Highly detailed and accurate minutes taken in collaborative meetings emphasize to members who said what, when, and why, and how each member committed to address each action strategy. Community advocates can meet with clients after each meeting to debrief them on the events and implications associated with the meeting. These debriefing sessions provide a means of revisiting the happenings of the meeting so that clients can generate an agenda for the next meeting. At the next meeting, problem-solving activities can be systematically addressed.

Continuing the Conversation

As you can see, the processes involved in building a community collaborative are challenging, daunting, and at times defeating for its members. Yet, community collaboration also involves successes that define and typify why many helping professionals choose to enter their professions. Although this chapter offers a few methods for making this process easier or more manageable, we believe that it is important to keep at the forefront of your mind and your practice when undertaking such complex endeavors the values and worldviews that you bring to them. Critical questions such as, What am I ultimately trying to accomplish? and Why is that important? need to be asked throughout collaborative practice and development. Such questioning demands critical attention and reflection, not only to what you think, but to what you see, feel, and hear as trite or mundane every day. Constantly challenge the assumptions you take for granted as valid.

However, if your worldview dictates to you that the primary challenges confronting vulnerable populations stem from poor service access, coordination, or fragmentation, then you will probably gravitate toward the conventional, professionally driven, service-centered, and service-integration-focused collaborative model. You will also probably gravitate to this conventional model if you believe that parents are a primary detriment or limiting factor to their children, or if you believe that broad changes can only occur in a community by helping one person at a time.

If your worldview dictates to you that the vulnerability of low-income communities stems from a community of systems that have broken down, AND if you believe that facilitating the development of strong families is the best way to help all children, AND if you believe that strong communities are the requisite resource for strong families, AND if you believe that the best way to build healthy communities is to develop an infrastructure that represents and recognizes the diverse facets, assets, and limitations of each community and its members as strengths, THEN you will probably find yourself on the path toward building community collaboratives. In so doing, you will undertake and embark on the complex journey of trying to build a mutually supporting and supportive community of systems. Although immensely challenging, we believe it is the way of the future. We believe it is the way to a brighter tomorrow and a better world. What do you believe?

References

Adelman, H., & Taylor, L. (1997). Toward a scale-up model for replicating new approaches to schooling. *Journal of Educational and Psychological Consultation, 5,* 197–230.

Alameda-Lawson, T., & Lawson, M. (1999, March). *Parents as the guiding and unifying component for restructuring educational support services.* Paper presented at the Council on Social Work Education Annual Program Meeting, San Francisco.

Alameda-Lawson, T., & Lawson, M. (2000, February). *Consumer-led community collaboratives: Building social cultural capital and promoting cultural democracy.* Paper presented at the Council on Social Work Education Annual Program Meeting, New York.

Armstrong, K. (1997). Launching a family-centered, neighborhood-based human services system: Lessons from working the hallways and street corners. *Administration in Social Work, 21*(3/4), 109–126.

Aspen Institute Roundtable on Comprehensive Community Initiatives for Children and Families. (1997). *Voices from the field: Learning from the early work of comprehensive community initiatives.* Washington, DC: Aspen Institute.

Briar-Lawson, K. (1998). Capacity-building for family-centered services and supports. *Social Work, 43,* 539–550.

Brint, S. (1994). *In an age of experts: The changing roles of professionals in politics and public life.* Princeton, NJ: Princeton University Press.

Bruner, C., & Chavez, M. (1998). *Getting to the grassroots: Neighborhood organizing and mobilization.* Des Moines, IA: NCSI Clearinghouse.

Gardner, S. (1992). Key issues in developing school-linked, integrated services. *The Future of Children, 2,* 85–94.

Gardner, S. (1994). Conclusion. In L. Adler & S. Gardner (Eds.), *The politics of linking schools and social services* (pp. 189–200). Washington, DC, & London: Falmer Press.

Halpern, R. (1997). Good practice with multiply vulnerable young families: Challenges and principles. *Children and Youth Services Review, 19,* 253–273.

Hassett, S., & Austin, M. (1997). Service integration: Something old and something new. *Administration in Social Work, 21* (3/4), 9–29.

Himmelman, A. (1996). *Communities working collaboratively for a change.* Minneapolis, MN: Himmelman Consulting.

Hooper-Briar, K., & Lawson, H. (1994). *Serving children, youth and families through interprofessional collaboration and service integration: A framework for action.* Oxford, OH: Institute for Educational Renewal at Miami University and the Danforth Foundation.

Hooper-Briar, K., Lawson, M., & Alameda, T. (1996). *Partnerships for vulnerable children and families: Empowering families and communities to develop educational and life success for poor children* (Institute on Race & Ethnicity Report). College Station, TX: Texas A&M University Press.

Lawson, H. (1997). Children in crisis, the helping professions and the social responsibilities of universities. *Quest, 49*(1), 8–32.

Lawson, H., Briar-Lawson, K., & Lawson, M. (1997). Mapping challenges for vulnerable children, youth, and families: Implications for university-assisted community schools. *Universities and Community Schools, 5*(1–2), 80–94.

Lawson, M. & Alameda-Lawson, T. (in press). What's wrong with them is what's wrong with us. *Journal of Community Practice.*

Lodge, R. (1998). *California's healthy start: Strong families, strong communities for student success.* Davis, CA: University of California, Davis, Healthy Start Field Office.

McKnight, J. (1995). *The careless society: Community and its counterfeits.* New York: Basic Books.

Mondros, J. B., & Wilson, S. M. (1994). *Organizing for power and empowerment.* New York: Columbia University Press.

Schön, D. (1983). *The reflective practitioner: How professionals think in action.* New York: Basic Books.

Shiffman, R., & Motley, S. (1989). *Comprehensive and integrative planning for community development.* Pratt Institute Center for Community and Environmental Development. Retrieved September 15, 1999, from the World Wide Web: http://www.picced.org/advocacy/compplan.htm

Smale, G. (1995). Integrating community and individual practice: A new paradigm for practice. In P. Adams & K. Nelson (Eds), *Reinventing human services: Community and family-centered practice* (pp. 59–80). New York: Aldine De Gruyter.

Tyack, D., & Cuban, L. (1995). *Tinkering toward utopia: A century of public school reform.* Cambridge, MA: Harvard University Press.

Wood, D., & Gray, B. (1991). Toward a comprehensive theory of collaboration. *Journal of Applied Behavioral Science, 27,* 139–162.

Creating an Affirming Community

Steve Stickle and Kim Gibson

Looking back through her diaries, Joyce Wiley recalls how her son Jason told her while he was in middle school that he was struggling with his sexual orientation. Like many parents, Joyce thought that given enough time, Jason's same-sex attractions would pass. When he was 16, Jason told Joyce and her husband, Jack, that he was definitely gay. Joyce and Jack recall their response to Jason as something like, "That's fine," and then swiftly moved on to the next topic of conversation. Though they believed Jason's declarations, neither Jack nor Joyce fully realized how much help their son needed. On Valentine's Day of his senior year of high school, Jason's struggle came to a head. On that cold winter's afternoon, Jack and Joyce Wiley were rushing their son Jason to the hospital as he was on the verge of putting a very final end to his suffering. As Joyce explains it, "We really began to listen then. We heard Jason saying that he thought being gay was somehow a nearly unbearable way to be." From that moment on, the lives of the Wileys would never be the same; neither would the Quad Cities.

Situated on the Mississippi River, the Quad Cities is a community that for many years was the farm-implement capital of the world, producing more farm machinery in local factories than anywhere else. Even today, it continues to be the world headquarters for John Deere and Company. The Quad Cities is probably not the place where you would expect to find cutting-edge work in the area of gay and lesbian community services.

Twenty-one years after the Stonewall Rebellion changed the face of the gay community in New York City and other major metropolitan areas, Jack and Joyce Wiley would use their personal experience as the parents of a gay son as a galvanizing force to create change in the Quad Cities. Recognizing that many other parents must be going through a similar situation, the Wileys organized fellow members of the local

Unitarian Church's Social Action Committee to respond. They called the initial meeting of what would first be called the Coalition Concerned for Gay and Lesbian Youth (and later Quad Citians Affirming Diversity).

Within this first meeting are the roots of the success of Quad Citians Affirming Diversity (QCAD). The story of QCAD is one of continuing success. We share our story as an example and, hopefully, as an inspiration. Within this chapter we trace the origins of QCAD and, in doing so, vividly illustrate the power that a motivated individual can assert. We also demonstrate the geometric expansion of power developed in collaborative alliances with others. In this chapter we reveal our vision of an affirming community—a community that celebrates all citizens regardless of sexual orientation and that provides equal and safe access to community resources and support. We describe the evolution of an opportunity structure and its integration into an existing community framework of citizen support. From its inception, QCAD's members envisioned that the organization would not be exclusively gay; rather, it would include both gay and straight members. This integration of gay and straight within the organization provides the model for the community we are working to create.

The QCAD Model for GLBT Advocacy

Any effective model for GLBT (gay, lesbian, bisexual, and transgender) advocacy has to begin with an understanding of why GLBT individuals and families need advocacy—namely, the impact of homophobia. Homophobia is defined as the "irrational fear, hatred, prejudice or negative attitudes towards homosexuals or homosexuality, felt or expressed by a person or group" (Ryan & Futterman, 1998, p. 12). This definition also includes institutional forms of homophobia "that result in invisibility, discrimination, neglect and mistreatment" (Ryan & Futterman, 1998, p. 12). The consequences of homophobia for GLBT people are considerable. For example, research indicates GLBT youths encounter difficulties in schools leading to higher dropout rates, are at greater risk for substance abuse and addictions, and are more likely to attempt and to complete suicide (DeLois, 1998; Garofalo, Wolf, Kessel, Palfrey, & DuRant, 1998; Hunter & Schaecher, 1995; Proctor & Groze, 1994; Ryan & Futterman, 1998). Homophobia affects adults, too. The lack of social sanction undermines the durability of their relationships, and legalized discrimination in employment, housing, and credit directly affects their abilities to maintain their livelihoods (Berger & Kelly, 1995; Poverny, 2000; Tully, 2000). In essence, the communitywide problem of homophobia calls for advocacy. To respond, we at QCAD set out to provide the needed advocacy and to alter the entire community climate by undermining the impact of homophobia whenever possible.

Vision

Unlike most organizations that focus on the needs of a minority, QCAD, from its beginning, drew members both from the minority group whose rights it advocates and from the majority, involving both gay and straight community members on its board and working committees. Recognizing that significant community change must tap into traditional sources of power, we brought into our movement a number of powerful people in the community. In drawing influential members to the organization, QCAD was able to legitimize itself quickly as a community institution.

The institutionalization of QCAD as a community force and resource coincided with actions to create change within the larger community. As our guiding mission, we at QCAD focused on creating broad-based change in existing community organizations. By accomplishing this, it would not matter what organization a GLBT person might contact, because that entity would be able to interact supportively and provide diversity-sensitive services. In other words, we focused on changing institutional capacity across the entire community to facilitate existing organizations in constructing a GLBT-affirming climate.

Original Structure

QCAD began as and continues to be an organization of contributing members who pay yearly dues. Early members of our organization were typically straight, gay, clergy, service providers, and anyone else who agreed with the mission. Members convened at First Thursday meetings at the Unitarian church. These monthly general membership meetings provided an orientation to the issues and purposes of our group. The First Thursday meetings were the primary vehicle for education, support, and membership building during those early years. Out of this membership, we formed a board of directors. Initially the board of directors consisted of several members of the Unitarian church, a Lutheran minister, the director of the local YWCA, social workers, homemakers, a small-business owner, and a former Metropolitan Community Church minister. We were a band of merry dedicated souls committed to the cause, meeting in the Wiley dining room at 7:00 on Saturday mornings!

In these meetings, we shared ideas about what we hoped to accomplish. We recognized that the process of systemic change requires an organization that adapts to the facets of the community that it seeks to enhance. With the concept of institutional change in mind, we established several working committees: the Religious Concerns, School Relations, Public Policy, and Library Committees.

Religious Concerns Committee.   The Religious Concerns Committee brought together clergy committed to GLBT affirmation. These committee members were already involved in Progressive Clergy, a group concerned about social justice issues. Involved clergy members included Unitarians, Presbyterians, Lutherans (ELCA), American Baptists, Reformed Jews, and those from the United Church of Christ. Banding together to address the effects of homophobia in religious institutions, the committee focused on educating both their peers and the general public about more affirming religious views of GLBT persons. To address the need for more community education on the diversity of viewpoints regarding homosexuality (and simply to point out the often-overlooked fact that not all religions stigmatize homosexuality), the committee created public forums and programs featuring nationally known authorities in the field.

School Relations Committee. The School Relations Committee sought to create changes in area schools, a task they soon discovered was formidable. As recently as the mid-1990s, the counseling staff at one area high school insisted that there could be no gay or lesbian youth among its student body of more than 1,000 students. However, by cultivating individual contacts with sympathetic community members, this committee made incremental progress in area schools. Among its early accomplishments was gaining permission to present a biannual program on GLBT issues to a high school class on gender studies. Another early effort placed representatives from QCAD as presenters at the annual area Youth Conference, where nearly one hundred junior high and high school students participated in a program on anti-GLBT harassment. Youth Conference planners continued to request this same program each subsequent year.

Public Policy Committee. The Public Policy Committee focused its energy on public education as a "two-way street." On one hand, the committee spent substantial time talking to legislators, city council members, and other elected officials to educate them about the needs of GLBT constituents. On the other hand, they also worked to educate the GLBT and allied community members about the positions of public office candidates on GLBT issues. In doing so, the committee sought to increase the dialogue between GLBT constituents and their elected officials (and candidates for such offices) in the larger arena of public debate.

Library Committee. The work of the Library Committee acknowledged that much oppression and stigmatization of GLBT people and families is grounded in ignorance. To begin to address that ignorance, the Library Committee sought to raise public awareness of GLBT topics in public libraries. The committee created displays about selected topics. One such topic, "Gay Men and Women Who Enrich the World," featured biographies of famous GLBT people supplemented by a selection of relevant books available in the library's collection. In subsequent years, this outreach expanded to include displays for Gay Pride Month (June) in all Quad City libraries.

The Library Committee also compiled, cataloged, and maintained QCAD's own library, now housed in the organization's community drop-in center. Over the years, the library has grown to more than 1,000 volumes, including materials for general circulation as well as journals and other references for consultation by staff members and area professionals.

Evolution and Development

QCAD was well served by this early board and committee structure to carry out its mission for many years. Over time, we began to look at how we might increase the intensity of our work and restructure to facilitate this transformation. Until the fall of 1997, we had administered the organization entirely with volunteers and had operated with a very limited budget. At that time, we hired a development consultant to guide the organization on a path toward a more sustainable and intensive community action.

The consultant helped the board of directors identify the organization's priorities and create a strategic plan. With a clear vision for the future, the board then set about finding the resources to carry out that mission. In the spring of 1998, we hired a part-time (10 hours per week) employee to reestablish the youth program and to develop resources to support the organization as a whole. By late summer 2000, we expanded our operations to include four full-time employees and approximately 50 volunteers.

The dramatic growth of QCAD as an organization in less than three years began with a coordinated plan for sustainable change. As a step toward implementing this plan, we risked moving from our meeting place in the basement of the Unitarian church to space rented for a community center. The location was very carefully considered. In contrast with the usual move by other community centers, we purposely looked for space that was not a storefront because we knew that a storefront location would likely make entrants feel identified as gay, and thus scare off the very people who might need our services most—those still closeted. Instead, we chose a space on the third floor of a downtown office building. Consistent with the inclusive vision of QCAD, this accessible and safe space allowed us to further integrate into the community.

The first source of funds for our community space came from the local county health department, which was seeking to target HIV-prevention services for gay youths. The QCAD organization was in a unique position to provide service to such a hard-to-identify population. The theme of prevention also fit nicely with QCAD's vision of creating a community of safety for GLBT citizens. With that initial funding, we were able to hire a part-time staff member to develop the youth program and lay the foundation for organizational expansion.

A Strategy of Institutional Change

QCAD's organizing strategy begins with a startlingly simple concept: The community, not the GLBT individual, has a problem that needs to be addressed. Though this assumption seems so simple on its face, the implications of this strategy are still being fleshed out. To understand our progress requires understanding how we have operationalized this nonpathological assumption about our constituents into a working strategy for creating community change. Because homophobia permeates every community institution in various ways, we at QCAD believe that every community institution must be assisted to correct the way in which homophobia has impaired its ability to serve GLBT persons equitably. Specifically, we have developed a strategy that addresses schools, families, religious congregations, governments, and social service agencies.

Working with Schools

In keeping with our goals to support GLBT youths, QCAD's school intervention efforts have increased dramatically. In the 1999–2000 school year, we trained all 200 staff members at two area high schools, including the largest high school in the state of Iowa (Quad Citians Affirming Diversity, 2000). As a result, teachers and other school personnel now recognize their responsibilities to meet the needs of GLBT students in their classes and hallways. In the process, we have continued to strengthen our referral networks with area teachers. Thus, when teachers, counselors, and administrators find themselves working with GLBT youth, they now call on QCAD for technical assistance.

In a climate in which an assumption of "recruitment" into homosexuality continues to hold for some people, creating change in schools takes on additional challenges when the topic is the safety and affirmation of GLBT students. In order to address the ways in which schools have failed to equitably treat their GLBT students, we have developed formal and informal strategies.

Policy Development and Implementation

One element of the formal strategy has focused on the dual nature of policy change: that work must focus on both policy development and policy enforcement. Obviously, some uncertainty exists about whether the unmitigated harassment that GLBT students experience is the consequence of inadequate policy or inadequate enforcement. It is equally unclear whether the root cause of such harassment is even uniform across school buildings and districts.

Although school administrators and board members often will defend their current antiharassment policies as sufficient to protect all students regardless of sexual orientation, GLBT students in local schools report otherwise. In the area of policy development, we have lobbied school administrators and board members to change antiharassment policies to specifically include sexual orientation. In the area of policy implementation, we have advocated more stringent enforcement of existing policies. For example, we asked school officials to include specific examples of derogatory names for GLBT students (such as *dyke, fag,* or *queer*) in handbooks and to require enforcement of zero-harassment policies when GLBT students are called such pejorative names in hallways and classrooms. This advocacy has also included sensitivity education to the plight of GLBT students, as well as information about the legal consequences of ignoring harassment of GLBT students. Targets of this advocacy have included all the superintendents in three Iowa counties as part of their regularly scheduled in-service meetings, an open forum for teachers and administrators that featured a representative of Lambda Legal Defense and Education Fund, and all the Iowa area school social workers and counselors.

Educating Key Personnel

Another element of our formal strategy includes the provision of faculty in-services to area schools. These 90- to 120-minute training sessions begin in territory familiar to educators, focusing on adolescent development. However, as the discussion unfolds and faculty begin to understand how GLBT students are blocked in traditional school settings from completing their developmental tasks, the proverbial "light bulbs" begin to go on. As the discussion continues, the connection between the obstruction of normal development and the increased risk factors among GLBT youth becomes transparent. These training sessions then turn consultative, encouraging faculty members to connect how their responses to GLBT students and to anti-GLBT harassment have real consequences for the lives and well-being of their students.

One of the keys to QCAD's expansion into more school districts has been the success of these in-services. Demonstrating that we can address the topic of the needs of GLBT students in a meaningful and nonconfrontational manner has prompted school administrators to feel safe in their decision to allow such training. The other key to the success of these presentations has been a consistent focus on teachers' responsibilities to all students. Recognizing that faculty members come from diverse backgrounds and hold varying perspectives on GLBT issues, we construct a common ground that allows for all to meaningfully participate. We focus on the issue of safety for all students. Although some faculty may personally withhold affirmation of GLBT students, professional obligations require that these teachers must ensure the safety of all students. From that starting point, we can examine how the safety of GLBT students can include both physical and emotional dimensions. The feedback has been consistently positive—"better than at least 90% of the presentations seen on any topic," according to one teacher. We have learned that the topic of GLBT students, even though one might think of it as one of those to-be-avoided, hot button issues, can be discussed even in conservative schools in small midwestern cities.

QCAD's work within schools also extends to informal strategies, such as networking information and resources to teachers who wish to become stronger allies for GLBT students. In practice, our collaboration with many area teachers and counselors has mutual benefits. QCAD benefits because we are able to reach more GLBT youths through referrals from these faculty members. For teachers and counselors, QCAD's technical assistance and resources enable school personnel to more effectively serve their GLBT students. Using these informal networks, we continue to work within the existing structures without being confrontational. Before these informal collaborations were established, we needed to take the initiative to market our presentations. Now, most schools seek us out as a resource for staff development in their efforts to create a safe and nurturing school environment.

Religious Institutions

Although we must certainly acknowledge the reality that some of the most virulent rhetoric opposing the equality and affirmation of GLBT people has come from religious institutions, participation in faith-based communities can also offer some of the most significant support for GLBT people. In that spirit, we at QCAD have incorporated outreach into communities of faith to build support for the full inclusion of

GLBT congregants into the lives of area churches and synagogues. Outreach components include identifying supportive clergy and initiating a program, the Affirmation Project. To identify our base of clergy support, we compiled and published a list of affirming clergy in the QCAD newsletter and incorporated this list into posters distributed to area congregations. These clergy have publicly acknowledged their belief that GLBT persons should be welcomed and affirmed within communities of faith. Clergy on these lists are categorized by their institutional affiliation and denomination of ordination/training so that GLBT people may identify supporters from a particular tradition.

The Affirmation Project

In keeping with our philosophy of systems change at multiple levels, we work with lay people in area congregations as well as clergy. Recognizing that sometimes members of congregations are able to take controversial stands without risking the potential repercussions that clergy might face, we have established the Affirmation Project as a second strategy within the faith-based community. Because clergy may feel bound to uphold doctrinal stances (even if they don't personally agree with them), the Affirmation Project trains two lay members in as many area congregations as possible to be "Affirmation Allies." These members welcome GLBT people into their congregations. They also advocate a GLBT-friendly climate through their activism on church committees and task groups. Affirmation Allies act as catalysts for creating an affirming and more inclusive environment for GLBT persons in their respective congregations.

The Affirmation Allies training program includes components dealing with religious traditions regarding homosexuality, offers information about sexual orientation, and includes experiential exercises. In developing this training, the Religious Concerns Committee was especially concerned that we deal both with "the heart and the head." Because homophobia is so woven into the fabric of our culture, intellectual acceptance of GLBT people often occurs before emotional acceptance. Thus, committee members recognized that although it might be easy for well-intentioned people to intellectually believe that GLBT persons were worthy of inclusion and affirmation, the same might not be said about their emotional acceptance. With that concern in mind, the training for Affirmation Allies prepares participants for the rigors and potential hazards of acting as change agents on behalf of GLBT inclusivity. In addition, for ongoing support as they express views that may not be particularly popular within their respective congregations, allies meet monthly to exchange ideas and experiences.

Political Institutions

QCAD also works to change how governmental entities treat GLBT people. Because of the restraints that IRS regulations place on not-for-profit organizations incorporated under article 501(c)(3) of the U.S. tax code, we have historically limited our political activities in order not to jeopardize our legal status. More recently, to ensure compliance and to give greater clarity to the scope of our political strategies, the

QCAD board: (1) registered QCAD as a 501(h) organization with the IRS, and (2) set policy that the organization would not be formally or legally involved in various political groups targeting statutory changes at the local and state level.

Electing to file for the 501(h) status gives an organization greater flexibility and predictability about legal boundaries regarding lobbying. By filing for such status, QCAD takes advantage of congressional action in 1976 that "influencing legislation is an appropriate and legitimate activity for charitable organizations" (Alliance for Justice, 2000, p. 2). The 501(h) status legitimizes lobbying activities subject to certain limits—in QCAD's case, 20 percent of the agency's budget. This figure excludes expenditures of funds received from governmental bodies, no part of which may be used for political purposes. We have made cautious use of the freedoms offered by our 501(h) status to facilitate political change, most recently in our alliance with the efforts of the Equity Project.

Equity Project

An example of how QCAD protects its nonprofit status yet still supports political efforts is its relationship with the Equity Project. The Equity Project is a group of community activists focused on effecting statutory changes in local communities to protect the rights of GLBT citizens. One notable achievement of the Equity Project is its successful effort in adding sexual orientation to the civil rights ordinance in Davenport, Iowa. Members of the Equity Project attended city council meetings, testified at hearings regarding changes in the local civil rights ordinance, directly lobbied city council members, and successfully worked to elect political candidates supporting the ordinance change.

QCAD supported the work of the Equity Project in limited, but significant, ways. In keeping with our empowerment philosophy, we at QCAD always encourage members to be active citizens at all governmental levels, to vote and exercise their rights in influencing governmental actions. Specifically in regard to the Equity Project, we provided emotional support and guidance for members, particularly youth members, who wished to testify at public hearings about the proposed ordinance change. As we do with all information relevant to the GLBT community, we also kept our membership informed about the work of the Equity Project through our newsletter and support service network.

Social Service Delivery Systems

Area social service agencies represent yet another challenge for QCAD's work in transforming community institutions. As area social service providers themselves have conceded, agencies are very often ill-equipped to deal with GLBT clients. The challenge, although by no means unique to social service agencies, begins with the "identification problem." Given the hostility that all levels of community institutions have exhibited historically toward GLBT people, one should not be surprised to learn that many GLBT people may not readily identify their orientation to service providers, even when such information is relevant to appropriate service provision. That reluctance to self-disclose is intensified still further when service providers ask, for example, gender-specific questions about personal relationships.

GLBT Sensitive Services Committee

As with many of our initiatives, the impetus to intervene in local social service delivery came from members within the QCAD organization. In February 1999, one youth program participant came to us with a serious crisis: he was about to be kicked out of his home by his mother who disapproved of his sexual orientation. As QCAD staff struggled to find housing for this youth, we quickly realized that there was a larger need to be addressed: residential services for any homeless youth who was not formally involved in the state child protective system. Seeing the opportunity to link the needs of GLBT youth with other youths in the community, we brought together the executive directors of many of the most powerful area social service agencies to address this communitywide concern. The resulting discussion and others that followed became part of successful efforts in both the Iowa and Illinois Quad Cities to increase residential options for all homeless youths in the area, with special assistance targeted for those youth dealing with issues involving sexual orientation. This community activism also defined QCAD as part of the human service network.

From this series of meetings, QCAD launched a new committee, the GLBT Sensitive Services Committee, to continue to address the needs of GLBT clients throughout the social service delivery system. This committee, comprised of directors and senior staff members of many area social service providers, is perhaps the most innovative of QCAD's committees. We have created a supportive atmosphere in which service providers feel comfortable discussing their own agency's deficiencies in services to GLBT persons without fearing that the acknowledgement will have negative repercussions. Instead, through a series of focus groups and discussions, we have parlayed their input and influence to construct a model of technical assistance for improving social service delivery in the community. The most substantial achievement of this committee has been the development and successful funding of the Rainbow Referral Network.

Rainbow Referral Network

The Rainbow Referral Network is a collaboration among QCAD and member agencies joined in the purpose of sensitizing social service delivery to the needs and aspirations of GLBT clients. Within this collaboration, QCAD provides training, a monthly news and information letter, and technical assistance to member agencies. Training services include both an orientation for new agency employees in demonstrating acceptance and providing support for GLBT clients and more-advanced training for experienced employees in working with the emotional, social, and legal issues unique to GLBT clients. The newsletter offers general information about GLBT issues and specific announcements of programs and activities implemented by QCAD. Technical assistance focuses on creating organizational contexts that are GLBT-friendly in the areas of organizational policy, nonheterosexist language in paperwork and publications, and office environments that communicate acceptance of diverse lifestyles and family structures. Our goal is to formalize membership in the Rainbow Referral Network through a certification process in which a member's certificate can be displayed prominently in waiting rooms and on agency brochures and publications. This certification will announce a safe and supportive environment in which GLBT clients can identify themselves without risk of bias, rejection, or retaliation and in which they can receive informed and affirming services.

Direct Support for Individuals and Families

The original intent of QCAD to focus on broad-based institutional change has evolved into a dual focus on creating institutional change while providing direct support to persons in the GLBT community. Over time, we have witnessed that other community institutions are not yet at the point at which they can provide sensitive services. With that recognition, QCAD has expanded its scope of direct service provision without sacrificing its efforts to create the systemic change necessary to lessen the need for those direct services in the future. In fact, these strategies complement each other because direct support services to GLBT clients activate widespread participation in QCAD and inform the organization's efforts in working toward community change.

Revisiting again the idea that the community has the problem because of its homophobia, QCAD's direct services have not set therapeutic goals per se but instead focus on empowering GLBT people to thrive in spite of the prejudice that confronts them. This paradigm allows for validation of a GLBT sexual orientation as a normal and natural identity and provides a framework for supporting GLBT individuals and their families in successfully navigating environments that are not consistently affirming. Current support activities for GLBT persons and their families include programs for youths, activities for adults, and services for parents and family members.

Youth Support Services

A local health department grant for youth programming led to hiring the organization's first full-time employee, a director whose background included GLBT activism, academic training in both sociology and philosophy, and extraordinary skills in grant writing. Taking a multidisciplinary approach to the development of the youth program, initial steps were geared toward educating the public and creating marketing materials to bring youths into the community center. One step in the process was meeting with the counseling staffs at each of the nine area high schools to educate them about the needs of gay youths, to provide them with educational materials and posters advertising a Sunday "drop-in," and to put a face to the program, reassuring them that any referrals that they made to QCAD would not be ill-advised.

The Youth Program initially included two offerings: a Saturday afternoon support group and a Sunday evening drop-in. The format for a support group drew heavily from what has traditionally been offered for gay youth: a facilitated group with its accompanying levels of professionalism and quasi-clinical style. The drop-in, on the other hand, was designed to be a very informal setting in which youth participants would experience support and assistance in a less clinical atmosphere. Interacting with adult staff, volunteers, and other youths, participants would receive support, affirmation, and information through a more organic process. The drop-in gave the youths the power to make decisions for themselves about what they might choose to do for the evening—perhaps learning more about their identity, perhaps approaching an adult volunteer for discussion about a problem, or perhaps simply choosing to "be" in a space in which their sexual orientation did not alienate them from their peers. With this freedom, these youth have been able to develop age-appropriate relationships and to engage in the same rites of passage as their peers. We provided them the opportunity to complete their adolescent developmental tasks—the same developmental tasks that all teens must complete to successfully and healthily pass into young adulthood.

Listening to Youth

In practice, we found that youth participants were not interested in the support group concept because they believed that support groups were for people with problems (such as alcoholics). Because they did not have a problem, they did not feel the need to attend a group for people with problems. Though it was clear from their interactions during the drop-in that they were receiving the benefits that support groups offer, they were free to take that support as they chose. In effect, we were offering the same service in two contrasting forms. However, one packaging (the support group) was unappealing because of its forced nature and pathological focus, whereas the other package (the drop-in), with its potential for choosing how to receive that support, was very appealing. From a Sunday in late May 1998 when two youths participated, the drop-in group grew very steadily each week to 40 or more youths per night by the end of the summer. At the same time, no one participated in the support group, and it was eventually dropped from the programming lineup.

The original idea for a drop-in actually came from tuning into the needs of gay youth. Before developing the youth group, we had observed that gay kids in the community were finding each other and hanging out at coffee shops. Because we were not in a position to offer drop-in services at area coffeehouses, we used additional funds from the local health department to create a modified coffeehouse in the community center. The "coffeehouse" was comprised of a few tables (with unlit candles), two cappuccino machines, and supplies to make various coffees. Drop-in participants took turns making the drinks, learning how from one youth who worked at a coffeehouse.

Currently, the Youth Program is thriving. Participants show a great deal of ownership of the program's development and agenda. They have organized a youth advisory council to coordinate activities within the drop-in center, as well as to develop activities in the wider community. Their idea for an Alternative Prom is a noteworthy example of their innovation. Annually in the spring, QCAD's Youth Program hosts a dance open to gay and straight couples from any of the area high schools, offering a "traditional" social opportunity to GLBT youth not openly available in the local school systems. Local news coverage of this event has been extensive. Youth Program participants also elect two members to represent the views of youth constituents on QCAD's board of directors.

Adult Support Services

Although youth services have become a very significant portion of QCAD's program services (and a magnet for program funding), QCAD has not abandoned the importance of providing support services to adults. In that first year of operation in the community center space, we authorized a group of four men to establish a "Coming Out/Being Out" group for gay and bisexual men. The meetings focused on preselected topics related to the particular concerns facing group members. This group provided opportunities for sharing personal experience among a cross-section of men who were at different stages in the coming out process.

Similarly, we empowered a local couple interested in starting a transgender support group with the space and resources to do so. Even within the GLBT community, transgender individuals and their families tend to be marginalized. With that recognition and consistent with our philosophy of inclusion, we offered support to transgender individuals and their families and also set out to further educate our own membership. Using our existing program of monthly general meetings, we held a series of presentations on transgender issues to educate QCAD's membership and other interested community members.

With a subcontract from the local AIDS service organization, we also established a stronger program of HIV-prevention activities and services for adult men. This program enhanced the existing men's group and transgender support group and initiated new services as well. Borrowing from the successful model we used with youth, we developed a drop-in program for adults. Although the drop-in was open to adults of both genders, the drop-in quickly became predominantly male. The adult drop-in eventually developed into "theme night," with some evenings featuring a communal dinner at which participants would gather together to prepare and eat a meal. In creating such a program, we provided an opportunity for socializing and community building without alcohol, an environment that is somewhat rare given the historical presence of bars as de facto community centers for the adult GLBT community.

QCAD's HIV-prevention services also include outreach to area gay bars and bookstores by developing a series of posters promoting safe sex. What has made these posters especially powerful is the fact that local community members created them. Rather than relying on outside assistance to develop messages that might not fit the community, QCAD utilized its executive director (a gay man) and a youth drop-in participant (a young gay man) to develop posters that resonated with their sensibilities as gay men in our particular community. Thus, the messages contained in the posters recognized the importance of validating and affirming sex between men while still stressing the importance of practicing safe sex.

One of QCAD's most significant challenges in addressing the needs of GLBT adults has been finding ways to effectively serve lesbians. Over the years, several volunteers have made attempts to establish women's groups to serve the needs of lesbian and bisexual women. Although some groups have met with initial success, they have often faltered after a brief period. QCAD continues to explore new avenues for meeting the needs of lesbian and bisexual women.

Family Support Services

The needs of the families of GLBT persons also have been another important programmatic focus for QCAD. Here the primary emphasis is on the families of GLBT youth. Although the teen years often represent a time of decreased dependence on parents, basic support and affirmation from parents nevertheless remain a constant and enduring need for all youths. In working with parents, QCAD seeks to provide them with a number of services. At the most basic level, parents need information about sexual orientation and its meaning for their GLBT children. As we often point out in community presentations, neither high school parenting classes nor most parenting books mention the possibility that one's child might be GLBT. In spite of the fact that many parents report they suspect that their child might be gay or transgender before their children come out to them, many are still unprepared to cope with the reality of the news.

Working with parents as they learn to affirm their children who are GLBT produces tangible benefits for the community. Our experience has documented a number of GLBT youths who are homeless either as a result of being directly thrown out or indirectly driven out by hostile living conditions at home. Working within their families prevents such crises and reduces the demand for social services. This work also gives us access to yet another core institution within the community—the family—a key element of creating a more affirming and inclusive environment for GLBT youths and adults. However, actual delivery of this important service is an ongoing challenge. From its inception, QCAD has provided a parents' support and discussion group, but in reality the vast majority of the parents who seek assistance choose to meet individually with either our professional staff or with another parent of a GLBT youth.

Continuing the Conversation

We at QCAD take pride in our accomplishments and see the need for continuing development to expand and solidify our efforts. Our organizational structure, program, and self-governance embody core concepts of empowerment. Our strategy reflects an affirmation focus and demonstrates an ecosystemic approach to social change. We identify four key components that we believe contribute to our current success: a focus on institutional change rather than individual adaptation, a consistent philosophy of inclusion, cooperation with existing community resources and institutions, and self-governance of the organization by its members.

As the QCAD organization continues to grow, our membership faces the new challenge of being true to our "grassroots" while meeting the increasingly bureaucratic demands required by national, state, and local funding bodies. In recent planning retreats, the board of directors has struggled with questions related to this balance. How do we maintain a posture of social activism that targets community institutions for change when at the same time we depend on these same institutions for support in our funding efforts and in providing services to our constituents? How do we continue to provide direct services to members of the GLBT community to mitigate the impact of oppression while maintaining the philosophy that the problem is rooted outside of the person in need? How do we meet the demand for increasing professionalization within our organization without silencing those members who are only now beginning to find their voices?

These are not questions with easy answers. However, perhaps it is not the answers themselves that are so significant but the processes with which we work to answer them. True to our mission, we at QCAD approach these questions in a way consistent with our core philosophy of inclusion, involving our members and the community at large in a dialogue that acknowledges that we are all in this together. The advantages for a community that affirms GLBT individuals are not contained solely within a minority population but instead contribute to a socially just context that benefits us all.

References

Alliance for Justice. (2000). *Worry-free lobbying for non-profits: How to use the 501(h) election to maximize effectiveness.* Washington, DC: Author.

Berger, R. M., & Kelly, J. J. (1995). Gay men overview. In R. L. Edwards (Ed.), *Encyclopedia of social work: Vol. 2* (19th ed., pp. 1064–1075). Washington, DC: NASW Press.

DeLois, K. A. (1998). Empowerment practice with lesbians and gays. In L. M. Gutiérrez, R. J. Parsons, & E. O. Cox (Eds.), *Empowerment in social work practice: A sourcebook* (pp. 65–71). Pacific Grove, CA: Brooks/Cole Publishing.

Garofalo, R., Wolf, R. C., Kessel, S., Palfrey, J., & DuRant, R. H. (1998). The association between health risk behaviors and sexual orientation among a school-based sample of adolescents. *Pediatrics, 101*(5), 895–902.

Hunter, J., & Schaecher, R. (1995). Gay and lesbian adolescents. In R. L. Edwards (Ed.), *Encyclopedia of social work: Vol. 2* (19th ed., pp. 1055–1063). Washington, DC: NASW Press.

Poverny, L. M. (2000). Employee assistance practice with sexual minorities. *Administration in Social Work, 23*(3/4), 69–91.

Proctor, C. D., & Groze, V. K. (1994). Risk factors for suicide among gay, lesbian, and bisexual youth. *Social Work, 39,* 504–512.

Quad Citians Affirming Diversity. (2000). *QCAD progress report to the Gill foundation.* Rock Island, IL: Author.

Ryan, C., & Futterman, D. (1998). *Lesbian and gay youth: Care and counseling.* New York: Columbia University Press.

Tully, C. T. (2000). *Lesbians, gays, and the empowerment perspective.* New York: Columbia University Press.

Pushing the Boundaries in Empowerment-Oriented Social Work Practice

Marcia B. Cohen

I have been a teacher and practitioner of empowerment-oriented social work for many years. I am deeply committed to the values of empowerment but often find myself struggling with contradictions, quandaries, and questions, such as: What if the client is making a really dangerous choice? What if my agency claims to be client centered but imposes enormous obstacles to client autonomy? What if being true to my empowerment principles will get me fired? As my students struggle to integrate empowerment theory with their practice in the field, they are plagued with similar questions. They express concerns that the empowering practice principles they are learning in school may not be valued or even relevant in "the real world." This chapter will explore some of these issues and probe the structural limitations faced by the empowerment-oriented worker in an environment characterized by inequality.

What I Learned from Josie

I have always been acutely aware of the power inherent in the social work role. I have found it awe inspiring when used to help unleash clients' potency, dangerous when used against clients' interests, and often quite limited when used in any way that might threaten the status quo of existing organizational structures. As an empowering social worker, I have always seen my primary role as helping clients increase their control over their environment (Breton, 1994a; Rose & Black, 1985). The practice of empowerment seemed deceptively simple, at least conceptually. After all, I possessed a strengths orientation, knowledge of community resources, and some basic skills that I could use to help clients become more powerful in their lives.

As the director of a mental health program in a residence for homeless women, I trained staff and students to work from an empowerment perspective. We developed our program in collaboration with our clients and took pride in our partnership approach to service delivery (Cohen, 1989). It was easy to be proud of our work helping clients become actors in their own lives, make individual choices, and set their own directions (Miley, O'Melia, & DuBois, 2001). It was easy, that is, until the night that Josie threatened to jump off the roof.

Involuntary commitment and empowerment practice don't mix very well, but what is an empowering practitioner to do when a client stands on the roof of a six-story building, shouting that the voices are telling her to jump?

I knew Josie well. She was a middle-aged Latina who had been labeled schizophrenic and mentally retarded. She was, in my experience, an insightful and clever woman, a survivor of many years of sexual abuse, homelessness, and other untold horrors. Josie cared deeply about the other women in the residence and about the staff and would do anything to help and protect us. I knew that Josie had made a number of serious suicide attempts in the past, including a jump from a fire escape that almost succeeded in killing her. I was also aware of her extensive history of psychiatric hospitalizations.

It was a Saturday evening and I was not even supposed to be at the residence. But, I knew Josie was having a rough time, so I decided to stop by and see her. That was when I discovered her on the roof. She told me to go away, to leave her alone, that she was going to jump. When I tried to persuade her to come inside where we could talk, she became agitated and responded, "I can't come inside; I have to listen to what the voices tell me." All my collaborative, partnership, client-centered skills could not get Josie off that roof. In contrast, my call to 911 resulted in a rapid response: five police cars and twice that many large, armed police officers who physically forced Josie from the roof and put her in handcuffs. They transported her to the emergency room at Bellevue Psychiatric Hospital. The night ended with Josie hospitalized against her will, a direct result of my using my power as a social worker to generate the even greater police power that ensued. The process was further facilitated by the power of the young psychiatric resident who committed her.

I can argue that I used my power over Josie's voices and not over Josie. I can claim absolution because, as Josie told me later, I had "saved her life." I don't really need absolution and I am glad Josie survived that night. I will never forget this experience or feel comfortable about my role in it, but I would certainly do much the same thing over again.

It seems important for me to take responsibility for the vast power imbalance in this situation. I had the power to call for police. I had the power to have someone locked up against her will. I had an incredible amount of power, in part, because Josie was Latina and I was White, because Josie was poor and I was middle class, and because Josie had a history of psychiatric hospitalizations and I did not. Mostly, however, I had the power to curtail Josie's freedom because I was the worker and Josie was the client. As social workers, we have to acknowledge this power imbalance. As empowering social workers, we have to own it and seek to minimize it, while knowing that some inequality will always be present. Finally, we need to accept the responsibility to use our power wisely, in client-centered ways.

In situations like the one involving Josie and me, there is often an opportunity, after the crisis is over, for dialogue. Josie and I were eventually able to talk together about how and why I had used my power, why I had this power, what she would have wanted me to have done differently, and how terrifying the experience had been for both of us. Nevertheless, my experience on that rooftop begins to suggest some of the dilemmas of the worker's role in empowerment-oriented practice.

Organizational Barriers to Empowerment Practice

Although Josie's story is a dramatic one, it does not fully convey the more structural obstacles to empowering social work practice. My students frequently remind me of the institutional barriers they face in the field. One student, whose internship was in a recovery program for women with addictions, experienced strong disapproval from her supervisor when she employed client-centered interventions. She was told that her strengths-oriented approach in helping clients identify their problem-solving and coping skills was serving to enable their manipulative behavior. Another student was discouraged from offering a voluntary support group in a residence for adolescent males where the norm was for groups to be mandatory. A third student, who was in a criminal justice setting, was appalled to discover that her role was more one of social control agent than of helper.

Some social work students and practitioners conclude that the problem is in the setting itself, and they seek greener pastures where empowerment work is valued. However, as many come to discover, there are inherent contradictions and organizational barriers to empowerment, even in agencies that pride themselves on their empowering approach to service delivery.

Research on Client/Worker Relationships

Several years ago, I studied the perceptions of client/worker relationships from the standpoint of residents and staff members in five programs for homeless, mentally ill people (Cohen, 1998). I was particularly interested in how power differentials were viewed and how the agency's stated commitment to empowerment was put into practice within its larger organizational environment. My interviews with residents and staff members directly explored issues related to client and worker perspectives on power dynamics, particularly experiences with goal setting and treatment planning.[1]

---

[1]Details on the study's methodology and findings can be found in Cohen, 1998.

Treatment Planning and Goal Setting: Whose Goals Are They Anyway?

As a means of exploring perceptions of power in client/worker relationships, residents and staff members were asked about their experiences with the treatment planning process. State Medicaid funding required treatment plans for all of the residents. These plans included a template of required categories into which the residents' goals had to fit. In addition to discussing the process of goal setting and the experience of negotiating different points of view, respondents were asked whose goals they felt were reflected in the plans: clients, worker, and/or agency.

Very few residents or staff members experienced treatment plans as predominately client-goal driven. Most described the treatment plans as reflecting a combination of client and worker goals. These participants described treatment planning as a collaborative process. Donna, a female resident in her thirties, described it this way:

> With the worker I have now, I have a say in what happens to me. We set the goals together. The goals reflect my ideas about what I want for myself and also her ideas. It's a combination, we do it together. This is much better than what I had in the past. It's easier now because I have some say in what the goals are.

Some residents voiced a preference for relying on their workers' expertise:

> We do the plans together, but my worker comes up with most of the goals. I trust her judgment, so I don't mind her coming up with goals for me. (Craig, a male resident in his forties)
>
> I would say that for the most part, the treatment plans are based on the residents' goals, but the workers have a lot of influence on them. I think that is a good thing because the workers usually know what's best for us. (Serena, a female resident in her forties)

A small number of residents described their plans as strongly worker-driven:

> My worker came up with all the goals. They were written for me before I ever saw them. I was asked for input before I signed them, and I think my input was taken seriously. Still, it wasn't me coming up with the goals. It wasn't me writing them down. (Geoff, a male client in his thirties)
>
> With my most recent worker, the goals on my plan were mostly her goals. She had an idea of what my goals should be because she knew me pretty well, but it would have been much better if she could have listened to me. (Loretta, a female client in her thirties)

Only a small number of residents and staff described the plans as reflecting a combination of client, worker, and agency goals. Theresa, a female client in her twenties, saw all three as playing a role but identified stronger, external forces influencing the goal-setting process:

I guess the goals are ultimately mine, but my worker writes them up and doesn't always give me much input. So, I guess it depends on who the agency assigns to be your worker. But the whole treatment plan format comes from the state and Medicaid, not from the agency. . . . These plans aren't really for our benefit. They are for the state, for Medicaid reimbursement. The workers have to make up a plan that looks good on paper, that looks good to Medicaid.

Several staff members articulated a similar viewpoint. These workers tended to describe their role as mediating between client interests, agency protocol, and Medicaid demands. Jill, one of the program directors, put it in these words:

The residents here are intimidated by treatment plans. It's a real struggle to meet Medicaid requirements and also make the plan a user-friendly tool. The trick is to talk to the residents, find out what they want to be doing, and turn that into Medicaid goals, get them on paper, and then show it to the client.

Joe, a house manager in one of the residences, described treatment planning as wholly imposed on clients and workers by the agency and the state. He described a greatly diminished role for workers and clients in the goal-setting process:

I have a hard time with treatment planning. I spend a lot of time doing the plan and wording it in a certain way to satisfy the agency, the Department of Mental Health, Medicaid. . . . My role in writing the plan is really a technical one. And, nine times out of ten, the client reads it and doesn't understand what it says because I have written it to satisfy the agency or the government. It's not for the client.

Although residents and staff members varied in their perspectives, it seemed that all had thought about who controlled the goals and who had power. One staff person and one resident were particularly emphatic in articulating their struggles with the power imbalances and imposed authority they saw as inherent in the residential context:

I think every day of my role and my power. Staff has a lot of power. Residents often have nowhere else to go; we are their last chance. They know if they don't follow the rules, they won't be able to stay. So, we have a great deal of power over them. It is important to acknowledge that we have power, even if it makes us uncomfortable. We need to be very fair in how we use our power. Sometimes you need to step back and take a deep breath and make sure you are using that power in a good direction, in terms of the program and the people in it, and not use it to intimidate people. (Marie, a program director)
   The staff certainly has more power than you when you are under their roof. You have to try and go along with what they think is best, otherwise you might be asked to leave. . . . So, all of these house rules are being imposed on me, which I don't like. I'm not that happy about my discharge plan either, but, I am cooperating. It's not what I really want, but I am trying to believe that they know what is best. (Kellie, a female resident in her forties)

As Kellie and Marie's comments imply, power differentials emanating from unequal control over crucial resources such as housing have the potential to bring elements of authoritarian control into relationships, even when participants prefer collaboration and mutuality. The magnitude of the power to withhold housing resources from people who have been homeless cannot be overstated. Neither can the power to bestow such resources. This may, in part, explain the willingness of many of these clients to give up some of their power in exchange for residential services.

One of the conclusions I drew from this research is that even agencies that take pride in being client-centered are not immune from elements of coercion in relationships with clients. There were distinct power imbalances identified by many of the workers and clients who I interviewed. The clients I talked to cared about their relationships with their workers and had strong opinions about the extent to which power was shared. They were clear about their preference for having input into decisions that impacted their lives. Many of the staff members felt painfully torn between their commitment to empowerment practice and the constraining demands of the agency and the statewide mental health system. As Hasenfeld (1987) points out, agencies exert considerable power over their workers, controlling their decision-making, constraining the type of information they process, limiting the range of alternatives available, and dictating the rules by which they will choose among alternatives.

This brings us to a question my students have raised, namely whether empowerment-oriented social work can fully realize the goals of shared power, mutuality, and collaboration as long as client/worker relationships are embedded in a hierarchical power structure? Organizational change practice may hold some of the answers to this thorny question.

Changing Organizations from Within

The literature on organizational change practice (Brager & Holloway, 1978; Netting, Kettner, & McMurphy, 1997, Patti & Resnick, 1972) provides analytic tools and strategizing techniques for the "low power actor" wishing to affect agency change in order to better meet clients' needs. Students in my practice courses have employed organizational change methodology to make their field placement agencies more receptive to empowerment-based practice. This work has included: gathering information on formal and informal organizational structure, culture, and ideology, teasing out the forces that can facilitate change goals and the forces that can inhibit them; identifying actors within the agency system with the potential to influence the success of the change goal; and determining appropriate change strategies and tactics (Brager & Holloway, 1978). Examples from two students' organizational change papers will illustrate some ways in which we can foster more-empowering agency environments.

Brendan's field placement was in a residential care facility providing assisted living to elderly people. Brendan observed that although the facility had a residents' council that provided a forum for client input into organizational decisions, the "second-floor residents," all diagnosed with Alzheimer's disease, were systematically excluded from participation in most of the facility's activities, including the residents' council. Brendan's organizational change project began with collecting relevant data on the preferences of second-floor residents, which he did through focus-group interviews with those residents. Based on what he learned from the interviews, Brendan established the goal of integrating second-floor residents into the activities of the larger organizational environment, including the residents' council. Brendan wrote in his organizational change paper

> For the purposes of assessing the organizational environment and the viability of my change goal, I did a force field analysis, as described by Brager and Holloway (1978). I saw the CEO of the facility and the Director of Health Services as being the two Critical Actors, they had the final say on what the second floor residents could participate in and their support was essential for the change goal to come to fruition. The Facilitating Actors, who were in a position to influence the critical actors, were identified as being the Director of Social Services and the Care Manager for the second floor unit. These individuals are potential allies who have much informal power within the facility, above and beyond their formal positions as management team members. . . . My next step was to tease out the balance sheet of forces for and against the change goal. It seemed that agency ideology, as reflected in the emphasis on client autonomy in the mission statement, was a potentially positive force. Other positive forces were the interest of second floor residents in fuller participation, the minimal resources needed to implement this change, and the management team's expressed desire to enhance quality of life for all residents. . . . In terms of the forces potentially restraining the desired change, I identified the organization's natural resistance to change, resistance that has been voiced on the part of second floor staff who indicate that their residents do not have the capacity for an increased role and also some fear on the part of some second floor residents that they will not be accepted by the other residents. I believe that I can bring enough influence to bear in order to reduce both of these restraining forces. The second floor Care Manager can work with her staff, since she supports the change goal, and the director of Social Work and I can work with the second floor residents.

After a thorough force field analysis, ascertaining whether each force was potent, predictable, and amenable to change, Brendan determined a course of action, relying heavily on the support of the director of social work and his other allies in the facility. He maintained the involvement and commitment of the second-floor residents, who became more confident in their ability to participate in community life and advocate for themselves within the organization. At the time of writing his paper for school, Brendan was confident that the desired agency change was under way.

Marna's internship was in an agency associated with the criminal justice system. It was a court diversion project in which individuals who had not yet been adjudicated could receive social services and monitoring by case managers as an alternative to remaining in jail while awaiting a court date. Marna's organizational change project focused on training staff in the principles and skills of empowerment-oriented practice. She defined the problem for change as follows:

> The glaring organizational problem that I am painfully aware of is the lack of client-centered, strength focused services for individuals who come to the agency for help. . . . The agency is doing a disservice to its clients by not helping them be more empowered

in making decisions and choices about their lives. . . . The agency's services are technically voluntary but the clients are referred by the court; it's either come to us or stay in jail. So, on top of that, when the case managers go ahead and develop contracts for clients without the clients' involvement, clients lose any sense of autonomy they might have had. The case managers at the agency end up perpetuating the cycle of powerlessness and worthlessness that caused these individuals to be incarcerated in the first place. . . . I got the idea for this change project after struggling to write my papers for practice class last semester. I was having a hard time making a connection between writing a strengths oriented assessment and doing empowerment-based practice, as I was being taught to do in school, and the work I was actually doing in my internship which felt more like checking up on people and being a social control agent. It was pretty hard to reconcile the two approaches. For a while I thought about leaving, switching to a more client-centered agency, but then I decided to stay and see if I could make a difference. . . .

Marna's change project involved developing training materials and organizing an all-day workshop on empowerment practice for the agency staff. She went through the same process as Brendan: collecting data, analyzing the driving and restraining organizational forces, identifying critical and facilitating actors, cultivating allies, and developing an overall change strategy. She was successful in her immediate goal. The executive director and the board approved the expenditure of funds for a one-day staff training that was favorably received by the majority of staff. Whether case management practice at this agency will become more empowering, as a result, remains to be seen. The framing force (highly consistent and not very amenable to change) of the agency's culture, emanating from its ties to the criminal justice system, will not be overcome by training alone. The agency's clients were, in the eyes of the court and the jail, "perps" to be monitored and controlled. The case managers in Marna's agency are caught in much the same bind as the staff in the mental health agency I researched: They are held hostage to the demands of a larger system, which, far from embracing the values of empowerment, is strongly committed to social control.

Students and practitioners need to appreciate the power of organizational change practice as well as its limitations. Organizational change is usually incremental in nature. Brendan is hopeful that next year's intern will pick up where he left off in his work with the second-floor residents. The executive director at Marna's agency has made a commitment to future staff training on client empowerment. These kinds of environmental changes, although certainly meaningful, are relatively small scale. They do not threaten the larger power structures that these settings are a part of, such as the health care and criminal justice systems. Larger system change requires going beyond the boundaries of an individual agency. It requires concerted social action and work with large and small groups.

Social Action Group Work

Just as the skills of organizational and community work can be used to extend the boundaries of empowerment practice, so can social action group work. The central goals of social action group work are systemic change and the empowerment of oppressed populations. This practice approach is quite comprehensive, encompassing individual, interpersonal, and social change (Breton, 1995; Cohen & Mullender, 1999; Mullender & Ward, 1989). Although social change goals predominate, participants in social action groups also achieve significant personal and interpersonal benefits. As Canadian group work author Margot Breton (1994a) has observed, "Good empowerment work . . . requires that all levels of work, the personal, interpersonal, and structural/political, be addressed" (p. 31).

A community action group in a homeless day shelter program provides an illustration of this kind of multilevel group work (Cohen & Johnson, 1997). This group used the medium of poetry to educate the public about homelessness, writing poetry together weekly and holding periodic poetry readings that were open to the community at large. The poetry group members experienced considerable personal growth and interpersonal support while raising public awareness about poverty and oppression. The creative energy, engagement with feelings, and development of mutual support through writing about painful experiences served to revitalize rather than distract from the group's social change goals (Cohen & Mullender, 1999).

The role of the social action group worker is an active but nondirective one. It includes facilitating opportunities for the empowerment of group members, assisting group members in the process of determining social action goals and strategies, and challenging internal and external forms of oppression. This is consistent with social action's empowerment orientation, which has been defined as "having the choice to participate in the decisions that affect one's life, and the life of one's society and community" (Breton, 1994b, p. 27).

The Self-Directed Group Work Model

Self-directed group work is one of the most fully developed of the empowerment-oriented social action approaches being used today. This model, developed in Britain by Audrey Mullender and David Ward (1985, 1991), targets external goals identified by group members through a process that involves them in focusing, in turn, on what the major problems in their lives are, why these exist, and how to tackle them. A notable feature of the approach is a clear value base that is outlined in the form of six practice principles emphasizing: the avoidance of labels, the rights of group members, basing intervention on a power analysis, assisting people to attain collective power through coming together in groups, opposing oppression through practice, and workers facilitating rather than leading groups.

Inherent in these values is a social structural analysis of the issues facing oppressed and marginalized groups. Self-directed groups do not have therapeutic purpose, per se. Indeed, these groups seek to challenge the fact that group members can become negatively labeled as a result of interventions that inappropriately seek change at the individual or family level, rather than working to empower a group to tackle wider injustices. Intrapersonal and interpersonal change do come about, however, as a consequence of participation in self-directed groups. The poetry group, for example, consciously utilized the six practice principles of self-directed group work.

Though anger and despair were writ large in the poetry and were evident in the group's internal discussions and public presentations, the members did more than get in touch with and support each other through these emotions. The group moved into an enthusiasm for struggle and pursuit of social change, taking control of their own group goals and taking action toward meeting those goals. Although this did not result in major structural change, it did have an impact on the larger community and its attitudes and actions toward poor and homeless people.

The role of the worker in this model is that of active but non-directive facilitator. The worker uses her or his skills to help the group discover the means to achieve their own ends. Mullender and Ward (1991) describe this delicate balance as one in which "the worker must be directive about being non-directive," while avoiding the trap "of going too far and becoming totally non-interventive" (p. 129). The degree of worker involvement will vary with the needs of the group, but the non-directive focus must be consistent if the group is to be truly self-directed. This requires that the worker be actively observing the group at all times in order to tune into and monitor its changing needs for intervention. This kind of group facilitation requires an array of tuning in, assessment, and interventive skills. The self-directed group worker's role has the fluidity of a dance, in which the worker's movements are supple and flexible, moving forward and stepping back with the rhythm of group needs (Cohen & Johnson, 1997).

Pushing the Boundaries

As with organizational change practice, social action group work can push the traditional limits of our practice by bringing about empowering changes in people, their environments, and the larger social structure. There remain finite limits to empowerment practice, however, and the most we can do is actively struggle to push them wider. This is no small undertaking. It requires confronting and acknowledging our own roles as agents of social control and of social change.

Social workers are frequently expected to exert power over clients—to control their behavior, their compliance with agency regulations, their violations of the law and the terms of parole, their use of substances, their adherence to medication regimens—in short, to control their conformance with the dominant society's norms and mores. The social work profession has tended to embrace many of these societal norms. Social workers themselves are frequently subjects of social control in their workplaces, where their behavior and compliance with organizational regulations are often closely monitored. In my study of client/worker relationships, the workers felt intense pressure to comply with state Medicaid regulations. They experienced a strong conflict between their commitment to the values of client self-determination and the agency's demand that they impose these regulations on clients.

Workers in many settings are also subject to organizational control over their attire, their use of substances (in some cases off the job as well as on), their expressed loyalty to their institutions, and their ability to maintain professional distance from clients. In my experience, social workers are not infrequently chastised for overidentifying with their clients but never for overidentifying with their agencies.

Empowerment practice cannot fully realize its goals of shared power, mutuality, and collaboration when client/worker relationships are embedded in a hierarchical power structure that simultaneously transcends and impacts on power relationships within the dyad. Practitioners seeking to practice from an empowerment base would be well advised to examine and confront the sometimes-subtle sources of power within their agency contexts and within their relationships with clients. Acknowledging this power can help us to more fully realize our historical role as agents of social change, in collaboration with our colleagues and in alliance with our clients.

It is critical that empowerment-oriented social work practice clearly identify and acknowledge *all* sources of power over clients in a collective effort to struggle against them. We must also examine and resist the sources of power that are imposed over us, particularly organizational constraints that limit client empowerment. Acting as an agent of social change may require combating the power of agency hierarchies, funding sources, accrediting bodies, and even our own power as professionals. As suggested previously, organizational change practice and social action group work represent two models for resisting structural power on behalf of our clients and ourselves. Other collective approaches, such as joining with our clients in social protest activities or asserting our rights as workers through union organizing, represent similar avenues for client and worker empowerment.

Confronting power imbalances in client/worker relationships and increasing client power include helping clients to assert their legitimate claims to entitlement and rights within our agencies, increasing their expertise in manipulating the environment in order to achieve desired outcomes, and linking them to supportive social networks outside agency structures. Empowerment-oriented social work practice also includes organizing client resistance and protest in situations in which disruptive tactics are effective in obtaining needed resources (Hasenfeld, 1987). In order to reduce the power disparities between clients, social workers, and larger organizational structures, we will have to confront, and be prepared to renounce, some of our power in relationship to our clients while simultaneously seeking to increase our power in relationship to our agency bureaucracies.

Continuing the Conversation

This chapter has raised a series of tough questions: How can empowering social workers recognize, address, and reduce the power imbalances that exist between social workers and clients? How can we use our professional power in concert with clients to help them achieve their goals? How can we help change organizational environments to increase their responsiveness to client needs? How can workers recognize their own disempowerment within organizational hierarchies and collectively struggle against it? Although some beginning answers have been suggested through such practice approaches as organizational change and social action group work, none of these questions has been fully answered. We are left with the contradictions of empowerment-oriented social work practice in a fundamentally unjust society. We remain a profession characterized by the opposing forces of social control and social change.

The challenges to the empowering social worker are many. They include navigating the powerful undercurrents of worker and agency control over clients while seeking out opportunities for action for social change. No one of us can meet these challenges alone. They require group efforts and the power of numbers. They require workers and clients acting together for collective empowerment and structural change.

Such action is not simply a vision that sounds good in a social work textbook. It is being realized, at least to some extent, in what my students refer to as "the real world." The current welfare-rights movement is a good example of a fledgling social movement in which workers and clients have come together as allies in order to fight welfare cuts and bring about political change. As Baptist, Bricker-Jenkins, and Dillon state in their article about the 1998 "Freedom Bus," which took the struggle on the road, transporting poor adults, families on welfare, and social workers all over the country to participate in a series of social protest efforts

> Social workers have a material and moral stake in the struggle to end poverty—not as 'supporters,' but as 'partners in crime'. . . . Increasingly social workers are asked not only to implement programs that criminalize poverty, but are themselves victimized by layoffs, downsizing, and privatization. (1999, p. 25)

Empowerment-based social work takes us to rooftops, to people's homes, to the highways, and to the streets. As we work within an often-oppressive system to promote client empowerment, we will find ourselves continually challenged by unequal distribution of power and resources. Although many of the questions posed in this chapter cannot be fully answered, it is important that they be raised, engaged, and struggled with.

References

Baptist, W., Bricker-Jenkins, M., & Dillon, M. (1999). Taking the struggle on the road: The New Freedom Bus—Freedom from unemployment, hunger, and homelessness. *Journal of Progressive Human Services, 10*(2), 7–29.

Brager, G., & Holloway, S. (1978). *Changing human service organizations.* New York: Free Press.

Breton, M. (1994a). On the meaning of empowerment and empowerment-oriented social work practice, *Social Work with Groups, 17*(3), 23–35.

Breton, M. (1994b). Relating competence-promotion and empowerment. *Journal of Progressive Human Services, 5*(1), 27–44.

Breton, M. (1995). The potential for social action in groups. *Social Work with Groups, 18*(2/3), 5–13.

Cohen, M. B. (1989). Social work practice with homeless mentally ill people: Engaging the client. *Social Work, 34*(6), 505–509.

Cohen, M. B. (1998). Perceptions of power in client/worker relationships. *Families in Society, 79*(4), 433–442.

Cohen, M. B., & Johnson, J. (1997). Poetry in motion: A self-directed community group for homeless people. In J. Gill & J. Parry (Eds.), *From prevention to wellness through group work* (pp. 131–142). New York: Haworth Press.

Cohen, M. B., & Mullender, A. (1999). The personal in the political: Exploring the group work continuum from individual to social change goals. *Social Work with Groups, 22*(12), 13–31.

Hasenfeld, Y. (1987). Power in social work practice. *Social Service Review, 61,* 470–483.

Miley, K., O'Melia, M., & DuBois, B. (2001). *Generalist social work practice: An empowering approach* (3rd ed.). Boston: Allyn & Bacon.

Mullender, A., & Ward, D. (1985). Towards an alternative model of social groupwork. *British Journal of Social Work, 15,* 155–172.

Mullender, A., & Ward, D. (1989). Gaining strength together. *Social Work Today, 20*(50), 14–15.

Mullender, A., & Ward, D. (1991). *Self-directed groupwork: Users take action for empowerment.* London: Whiting & Birch.

Netting, F. E., Kettner, P. M., & McMurphy, S. L. (1997). *Social work macro practice.* New York: Longman.

Patti, R., & Resnick, H. (1972). Changing the agency from within. *Social Work, 17*(7), 48–57.

Rose, S., & Black, B. (1985). *Advocacy and empowerment.* Boston: Routledge and Kegan Paul.

10

Shutting Off That Damn Bell: Raising the Voices Within

Kathy Weiman, Carolyn Dosland-Hasenmiller, and Jane O'Melia

Susan, age twenty one, had just joined our agency for services. When we met Sue, it was clear that she lived in a world separated from others, even from her family. The list of Sue's diagnoses and disabilities seemed endless: profound mental retardation, cerebral palsy, vitamin D–resistant rickets, seizure disorder, scoliosis, cortical blindness. She was seated in a wheelchair, wearing straps to help her sit up. She could see no more than shadows, and she was unable to speak. In other words, Sue was totally dependent on others for every aspect of her life.

In a book about empowerment, there are many examples of people speaking up for themselves and initiating positive change. Speaking up for oneself is a substantial challenge for many people. Yet, what if you were Sue? Even if you could find the courage to tell your caregivers that you did or did not like something, how could you get your message across? How can someone like Sue ever connect with the world when she cannot talk or use sign language? Sue is doubly challenged, first by her total dependence on others and second by her physical inability to talk.

These are obstacles familiar to many of the clients supported by the staff at the Association for Retarded Citizens (ARC) of Rock Island County.[1] In fact, more than two-thirds of the clients we serve have few if any expressive language skills. We will share with you how someone like Sue came to speak with us and how she and others actually transformed our agency. Although we at ARC were proud of the effectiveness

---

[1]ARC of Rock Island County, located in Rock Island, Illinois, is a not-for-profit community-based agency with a mission to serve individuals who have a primary diagnosis of mental retardation. Services first offered in the mid-1950s have evolved since that time into a broad base of supports, including day services, community employment, residential support, and auxiliary services.

of our interventions and training, we have recently learned that we are really only as effective as our ability to listen. Susan has taught us how to listen. It sounds so simple, doesn't it? "Shhh . . . just listen! "

Yet simple it is not. Learning to listen was only the beginning of an exciting journey to open communication pathways throughout our agency. We can now look back and see that our agency was transformed through this journey. Beginning with a philosophy of fixing others, we adopted a model of listening and translating, and finally we evolved to our current approach of *connecting* on multiple levels. This transformation is one aspect of a cultural shift in the organization that culminated in a new empowerment initiative called Skill Blocks.

Fixing

Those familiar with the history of services for persons with developmental disabilities can trace the evolution of services from state institutional care into a more-palatable model of community services. The intent of this movement is to support clients in environments in which they can connect with other people and enjoy a web of personal relationships. Unfortunately, even in the community, we find ourselves with remnants of the very clinical, impersonal style of institutional service provision. This institutional style is sustained by a myriad of regulations governing what services are delivered and how.

The Expert Model

Many of these regulations required licensed experts to design specific interventions for staff to provide to clients. In other words, we would take a client with an identified problem to an expert in that area who would advise us on how to fix the problem. For example, regulations mandated that clients with identified deficits in communication receive professional assessment from licensed speech pathologists. In some instances, our speech consultants drew from their experience with young children with speech problems, applying a developmental model to prescribe speech training. In other instances, some speech clinicians recommended no training whatsoever, believing that the client would gain no benefit.

Here is a typical scenario from the Fixing phase:

- An agency staff person escorted a client to an appointment with a speech pathologist.
- The pathologist conducted a standardized speech assessment, a process requiring approximately fifteen minutes.
- The pathologist completed a report. The report would include a notation that the person could not speak and a recommendation that the staff should work to teach the person to say "ba" to get a ball.
- The recommendations were incorporated into a formal program for the staff to teach the client.

- Once each day, agency staff would conduct this program with the client according to the written instructions.
- One year later, the client might say "ba" and might not.

How frustrating for all of us. We knew that our clients could communicate in "non-speaking" ways. We had seen that spending day after day teaching a fifty-year-old gentleman to repeat vowel sounds was futile. If he had not learned to speak in fifty years, would he ever? Even if he did learn to say "ball," would that change the quality of his life? Would he then be able to tell us how he feels? To be frank, applying a developmental model of speech training aimed at fixing deficits was a waste of time.

Distributing Expertise

There are so many things wrong with the Fixing approach. First of all, notice how far removed the client is from the expert making recommendations. Those recommendations are crafted from a clinician's knowledge of the field, not knowledge of the client. The persons closest to the client (family members, friends, caregivers) had no input into the goals or approaches. Staff members were required to follow the program, rather than contribute their own thoughts and observations.

> "Learners" in this model are generally assumed to be ignorant, passive, empty vessels who can be effectively filled up by the expert expounding knowledge. . . . It also implies a one way flow of information which precludes an opportunity for the "expert" to learn from the "learner" or, more importantly, for the "learner" to learn from their own inner-knowing. (Ryan, 1995, p. 279)

And that was that. Clients received training that failed to improve their communication skills but met all the regulatory standards. Staff members conducted training sessions by rote and provided no input. Information flowed one way.

In the Fixing phase, we focused on the problems of clients and asked the clinical experts to recommend ways to solve those problems. The model assumes there is something wrong with clients that should be fixed. Clients disagree. "Self-acceptance is a challenge to those of us who believe that the individual with a disability is something like a lump of clay that can be programmed into an individual. They [clients] stated they are OK at the start of the process" (Hingsburger, 1990, pp. 7–8). These deficit-focused approaches solved nothing for us. Rather, they worked to maintain the status quo of clients dependent on our staff and staff dependent on knowledge outside of themselves in the form of an expert.

Jim Gets a Break

The contrast between a Fixing approach and one that listens to the people involved is stark. Consider the example of Jim. Jim had a communication board consisting of black-and-white line drawings on a board about one foot high by two feet wide. The pictures on the board were eat, drink, toilet, yes, no, happy, exercise, work, good, and bad. These were the items selected by a speech clinician at the school Jim attended before coming to us. Jim would point to the pictures during training, but he rarely used them for actual communication. Jim also exhibited some fairly dangerous outbursts when he was angry, including throwing objects, screaming at others, pushing others, and running away from his work area. Observing him for a while, we saw that he was able to work for approximately half an hour. When staff would give him more work and prompt him to continue, he would show signs of agitation. It seemed to us that he needed a break, yet he had no way to tell us. Finally, the team gave him a bright red stop sign. Each time he would hand a staff member the sign, he could take a break. Within a month, Jim was using the stop sign to take a break. Interestingly, over time he requested fewer and fewer breaks; in addition, we began to see a dramatic reduction in his outbursts. Most importantly, Jim gained comfort from knowing he could communicate his need for a break and get one.

It is embarrassingly simple. No one had ever asked Jim what he wanted on his communication board or observed him long enough to determine what might be important to him. The expert designers simply picked out the things they thought would be most important to communicate, and we accepted that. It appears that when you are stuck in a Fixing mode, as we were, few people question what might work better. Like the clients we serve, we were stuck in a dependency rut, a dependency on the experts above us who determined what we would do each day.

Translating

We sought to teach communication in different, more useful ways. Our new approach was simple. Find a way, any way to help clients communicate. Don't waste their time trying to teach them to speak when they are not physically capable.

> If environmental accommodations and support can be used to enhance self-determination, even for those with severe disabilities . . . a myriad of intervention possibilities open up that have yet to be considered. No longer will interventions need to solely be conceptualized as efforts to change the person. Rather, they can focus on providing clients with the environmental accommodations they need to take greater control over their lives. (Sands & Wehmeyer, 1996, p. 137)

We began to turn our system upside down by starting from the client's point of view. We also began to use experts in different ways than we had in the past. First, we observed and interacted with each client for quite some time. Second, we talked with the staff members who worked most closely with the client and wrote down all they said. Third, we developed a communication training system that integrated what we interpreted from the client with approaches that staff believed would work. In other words, we started from the client's point of view, incorporated the staff's input, and then consulted with experts as necessary to create effective means of communication. This was when we began to move from fixing to translating.

Implementing the New Perspective

A change in perspective requires new tools for implementation. In collaboration with the University of Illinois at Chicago's Assistive Technology Unit, we developed an assessment tool that we could use to gather information on each person's communication skills. After we answered several very simple, functional, and easily interpreted questions, the tool itself acted as a guide toward best-practice interventions. In other words, we incorporated our consultant's expertise into a tool that "nonexperts" could use. What we saw after adopting this tool was phenomenal. By answering the assessment questions, staff members gained an understanding of the underlying concepts of functional communication. For example, one section on the inventory asks whether the person can make choices with objects, with photos, with black-and-white drawings, and so forth. By answering these questions, the staff members began to think of ways to incorporate objects, photos, or drawings into the client's life. All of a sudden, there were homemade picture boards, object schedules, switches, stop signs, and texture cards showing up everywhere in our programs. And, almost as quickly, maladaptive behaviors such as aggression or screaming began to diminish.

Our direct service staff are not licensed or degreed experts. Yet they were making communication happen for the clients they supported. What was going on? Very rapidly, we had moved from the Fixing phase to one in which useful information flowed from and to the right places. The experts provided information to the staff, who integrated it with their unique knowledge of the client. Staff members were listening to their assigned clients and developing augmentative communication systems to understand them better.

Phillip's Point of View

After completing an assessment for Phillip, Phillip's team determined he would benefit from an object box to communicate his preferences. His box would have three compartments holding objects that represent activities. Staff member Louisa would encourage Phillip to choose what he wanted to do next by taking an object out of the compartment. Initially, Phillip just sat there. He would look up and down and over to the staff member, but he would not point to, touch, or pick up any object. After repeated attempts, Louisa noticed that Phillip scanned up and down when presented with the box. She turned the box on its side so the three compartments ran up and down in front of him instead of side to side. Phillip immediately grabbed a switch, which was used to turn on some music.

It's simple isn't it? Louisa heard Phillip. It was just a matter of "listening" to Phillip by observing him. Phillip helped the staff create communicative opportunities for him. No expert consultant could pick up such subtle nuances about Phillip through a brief assessment meeting. Although we still collaborate with clinical experts to provide guidance on technical challenges, we have found that direct input from clients and the people closest to them is our most important resource.

Susan's Voice

Let's go back to Susan at her preadmission staffing. Observe the shift in perspective as Director of Team Services Kathy talks with Susan's mother.

Kathy: What can you tell us about Sue?

Mom: Well, Sue is very easygoing, very easy to take care of, and will be happy wherever you take her. She's very healthy.

Kathy: How does she communicate with you?

Mom: Communicate? Oh, Sue doesn't communicate at all. Like I said, we do everything for her.

Kathy: Are there things you know she likes or dislikes?

Mom: Oh sure. She loves mashed potatoes and gravy. She really doesn't like people who feed her too fast, and she doesn't like loud music.

Kathy: How do you know what she likes or dislikes, you know, if she doesn't communicate?

Mom: Oh, I don't know, I just *know* I guess.

Kathy: What does she do when she's eating mashed potatoes and gravy that tells you she likes it?

Mom: Well, she moves her head toward the food as if wanting more, and she smiles and makes a humming sound.

Kathy: And what does she do when there is loud music that is annoying to her?

Mom: Oh that's easy, she rubs her head and moans.

Without a doubt, Susan is communicating effectively with her mother. Mom just didn't call it "communication." After spending quite a bit of time talking with her mom, we determined that Sue had several gestures and sounds she used to communicate various emotions. As soon as Mom understood that this type of information was helpful, she began watching more carefully for other ways she could interpret Sue's messages. We compiled this information into a "Gesture Dictionary." This dictionary is basically an outline of specific cues that Susan employs and what each one means. Knowing Sue's basic gestures and different sounds opened everyone's eyes and ears to even more subtle cues. Sue's family and her support staff know how to respond when they see or hear Sue using any of these cues. When you enter the area where Susan works, you can see the staff members successfully modify their interactions with her in response to her language.

So, here's the big question: Did we teach Sue how to communicate? Did we teach Phillip how to make choices with objects? No, we did neither. Nor did we teach Jim how to ask for a break. Each of these folks taught us how to listen to them. Listening does not only mean hearing words. Listening does not mean deciding what is best for someone. Rather, listening entails watching, guessing, trying, modifying, and supporting. Our focus changed. Instead of working to teach others to talk, we were working to hear what they were already saying. We had successfully arrived at the Translating stage. Clients were being heard by their support staff, and the support staff were adapting information from the clinicians.

It may seem a small thing for people to have the ability to communicate that they want the music turned down or that they want to take a break. However, this is just the starting point for clients who have had no voice before. They were moving from no voice to some voice, and that was beginning to change the quality of their lives.

Connecting

> *"umuntu ngumuntu nagabantu" (a person is a person because of other people)*
> —a Zulu folk saying

We had arrived at communication utopia in our agency, right? We had certainly improved from the Fixing model, but there was still something missing. We were doing a good job of maximizing communication for many of the clients we served, yet we were still "talking" to them. While they were pointing to pictures with us, we were yakking away at them. We were not joining them in their world to have a two-way conversation.

Consider the situation of Tashia. Tashia helped design her own communication book. The format was simple. The book contained approximately seven or eight pages of pictures, words, and drawings. She was adept at pointing to these items to communicate what she wanted, and she used it quite successfully for a couple of months. Then it seemed that almost out of the blue, Tashia stopped using her book altogether. When we sat down with her to try to figure out what was wrong with her book, we noticed that she frequently looked over at Bob, who had a voice-output communication device. We hypothesized that Tashia wanted to "talk" like everyone else. Her book had no voice, yet the only way people interacted with her was by talking. So, she stopped using her book and lost her voice. Tashia and her team decided to get her a small voice-output device that she could use to get someone's attention. They also decided that when staff members came to chat with her, they would talk by using her book rather than by speaking. Tashia is now using both systems to communicate.

With Tashia, not only was it important to communicate with other people, but also to have conversations that were equitable. If we do not use her form of communication when speaking with her, then we are essentially saying that we do not value her method of communication. And so, our staff began conversing with Tashia and other clients they support by using their systems. This was movement toward a connecting, conversational culture, one in which previously unheard voices could assert their rights and preferences.

Making the Connection Work

Our purpose evolved from teaching clients how to communicate toward taking their just place in society. The broader intent is to maximize their existing communicative capabilities so these clients can more effectively control the direction of their lives.

Such an outcome was achieved in the example of Lisa. Lisa was in a car accident when she was fifteen years old. The accident left her in a coma for more than ten years. For the past five years, Lisa has lived in a skilled nursing facility. Although she has significant physical care needs, Lisa has minimal cognitive brain damage and is quite aware of her world. At some point, Lisa was given a device called a Liberator, which allows one to say hundreds of words and sentences by pressing buttons. A social worker called us to help because Lisa was not using her Liberator. When we arrived to visit her for the first time, we saw that she used two hand signals to indicate yes and no. We readily determined why she did not use her fancy device. First, it was placed on her dresser across the room, so Lisa could not access it. Second, the machine was not programmed. Third, no one had shown her how to use it! After a couple months of training and other accessibility adaptations, Lisa was able to talk for the first time in fifteen years. She was able to call her mom and her sister on the phone and talk with them using her device. She could finally tell her story of the accident and how it made her feel. She tells lousy jokes on the device and laughs at the even lousier ones we throw back at her. The last thing we added to her device was the statement, "Shut off that damn bell! " Lisa's room was right next to the nurse's station. Each time someone at the nursing facility needed assistance, the station bell would ring repeatedly. For all those years, Lisa had no way to tell the nursing staff that it drove her nuts. Now, she had a voice. The first time the nursing staff heard her message, they realized how annoying it must have been for her. They now turn it off quickly when it rings as they respond to the person in need.

We had raised the communication bar for everyone by creating a culture of listening. Staff members asked for more information and skills to meet new communication challenges. We felt an increasing need for more technical information on creating augmentative communication systems. Staff members were asking difficult questions about values and prioritization. We were beginning to think differently about clients and treatment. Yet we were also realizing the truth of William White's (1997) assertion that, although these new ways of thinking "create more humane and effective responses to clients, these philosophies require greater knowledge and skill and greater levels of adaptational energy on the part of a staff" (p. 237). How could we allot sufficient time to help the staff delve into these issues and gain more expertise? It was at this point that we turned to our Training Department for help.

Skill Blocks

As a human service organization, we count among our greatest assets the employees providing direct support to the clients we serve. Therefore, one of our highest agency priorities is the training, development, and retention of qualified employees. The clients we support receive appropriate and cutting-edge services when we promote lifelong learning throughout the organization. If our training becomes stagnant, so will our organizational development. In our agency, new employees receive more than 120 hours of classroom and on-the-job training within their first six months of employment. During this time, employees gain comfort with their job duties and familiarity with agency philosophy and values. This traditional training method is similar to the expert model mentioned earlier. It tends to be rather prescriptive, oriented toward state regulations, organizational procedures, and program operations. Employees generally require from six months to one year to master all the basic tools required to do their job.

Compounding the intensity of new employee training is a high staff turnover rate, especially for employees in their first year. This significantly impacts our ability to move from the prescriptive level of basic training to the more innovative stage that refreshes and enriches our senior staff. Although we hold staff inservices several times each year and offer opportunities to attend conferences as most agencies do, we have spent relatively little time developing the skills of our veteran staff. Ironically, it is those veteran staff members who control the success of our program. It is they who have the greatest impact on our clients' lives. We recognize a need for more intensive training for these employees.

The Training Approach to System Change

Given an agency need for advanced training for veteran staff and individual programs requesting more technical knowledge, it was increasingly apparent that something needed to be done. Rosen (1996) says, "credentialing will be part of the key to the survival of service delivery in the years ahead. As we become more and more decentralized in service delivery, no one will be more important than a well educated direct service worker" (p. 81). Everyone was looking to our Training Department to address this need. If you have any involvement with staff development and training, you are aware of the mushrooming effect that can occur when addressing the diverse training needs of a large organization. Managers often look first to training to solve a wide variety of gaps in staff's performance, when training may not actually be the best solution. Staff training has its drawbacks. It is costly in terms of time and agency resources. It also snowballs; it is very uncommon to eliminate training once it has begun. Consequently, ARC's Training Director Carolyn looks cautiously at new initiatives to assure that there is a true need behind the effort before taking on a new training endeavor. Performance gaps occur for a variety of reasons, including lack of motivation, personal problems, poor job match, incongruent job expectations, environmental stressors, or a lack of knowledge. Training may address a lack of knowledge, but supervisors must address other causes.

Having established that new training is needed, Carolyn partners with other managers and direct care employees to

- identify experts from within the organization or from outside
- determine whether the training should be delivered in-house or externally
- outline the content
- identify the best process or approach for delivering the training

We use this process to develop or revise our training curriculum. However, the knowledge gaps we faced here were different than in the past. We needed a more creative training approach. The existing curriculum emphasized basic skills and generic techniques. It could not address each client's needs; we hoped to assist the direct support staff to do that. We sought to place into our employees' hands the tools and expertise they need to make sound decisions for and with the clients they serve. We would work with the staff to identify specific knowledge gaps and find innovative ways to develop their expertise. We knew this would be a bigger undertaking than previous training initiatives. It would require extensive research, more classroom time, and new systems to measure outcomes. The Skill Block model was born.

What Is a Skill Block?

A Skill Block is a training opportunity for direct service persons to become certified in specialized areas of expertise. These training opportunities are beyond our core curriculum. Rather than being assigned, participants apply for enrollment and must meet all eligibility requirements, including a minimum of eighteen months of employment in good standing, a statement of support from their supervisor, and a commitment to apply their learning to meet organizational needs. Each Skill Block includes a combination of classroom training, apprenticeship, and independent study lasting from six to twelve months. To obtain certification, participants must demonstrate specific competencies as defined by each Skill Block. The organization awards a cash bonus upon certification. Certified employees are eligible for annual recertification through a negotiated contract requiring continuing education and application of skills. Certified employees must share their knowledge and expertise throughout the agency each year.

The Skill Block model affords direct service employees opportunities to develop new skills and to take on new challenges without leaving direct service. The employee gains new experiences and challenges within their position while the agency gains a more competent workforce. The clients gain better services from all of us.

Developing Skill Blocks

As we developed the new Skill Block initiative, we reviewed various state and national training curricula and found none that addressed the training needs of direct support persons beyond the basic core skills. We had to design our own. To begin, Carolyn pulled together managers and direct service persons to identify skill areas in need of enhancement. They brought in information from the clients we serve through satisfaction surveys and client service plans. Once we had identified focus areas, we then prioritized ten Skill Blocks to develop over the next few years. These competency areas include

- advocacy
- assistive technology and communication
- personal living
- community and service networking
- consumer empowerment

- positive learning/crisis management
- education, training, and professional development
- production processes
- service facilitation
- vocational, educational, and career development

Woven through each of these competency areas are the common threads of our agency's core values and philosophy as related to serving clients with developmental disabilities. The agency's associate executive director provided clear direction to guide the development of each block.

> It is vital in every skill block that the trainees experience the topic all the way through—start to finish (assessment, action plan, direct intervention, evaluation, reports). The fundamental purpose for this whole project is empowerment of the direct care staff—the goal is to get the direct staff involved in arenas where they have typically been excluded (i.e., agency-wide committees, Board committees, interagency task forces). In other words, we need to *make it real!* To the greatest extent possible, we want actual outcomes, not theoretical constructs or simulated experiences. (J. O'Melia, personal communication, November 20, 1997)

A manager was assigned to coordinate the content development for each targeted competency area. The manager assembled a design team that included direct support personnel. The team outlined the specific content areas to address and identified the observable competency measurements that would be required for certification (when the participant completes the Skill Block, they will be able to do X). The team also designed the instructional process and methods of delivery. As the design team completed the instruction plan, the manager presented the topic before a peer review panel and incorporated their feedback into the plan.

From Mission to Outcome—Skill Blocks

Although the design teams completed substantial research and planning, we have found that much of the curriculum must be written and revised as it is presented. The staff members enrolled in the initial Skill Blocks uncover areas that need more attention, and they have asked for information on specific items not yet addressed. These staff members are increasing their skills and knowledge in a particular area, and they are helping to improve the training for the next group that comes along.

The Communication Skill Block

The Communication Skill Block offers an example of the outcome of this process. As shared with each participant of the Communication Skill Block

> Our focus within this skill block will not only be to share ways for consumers to communicate more effectively to us, but to also look at ways we can more effectively share

with our consumers. . . . By supporting staff to use a diverse range of approaches which encourage and enable our consumers to communicate, we believe the quality of life for all of us will be improved. (Weiman & Miller, 1999, p. iii)

To attain certification, participants in this block must demonstrate their ability to

- gather complete information for our assessment tool
- use active listening skills to gain and share information
- use sign language to converse over a meal
- make a no- or low-technology augmentative communication system for someone
- program a high-technology, voice-output system for someone
- make communication recommendations that are consistent with a client's existing communication skills, interests, and comfort level
- converse with three clients using various communication systems
- develop augmentative systems to assist clients to design their own training plan

Although some of the skills developed in this curriculum are concrete applications (make a low-tech system), others require applications of judgment (make recommendations). We have seen many proud faces on staff who have successfully developed a system or carried on a conversation in sign language. Yet, it is in the successful judgment calls that we see the real impact. Although participants were initially intimidated by the responsibility of making recommendations, they are thrilled to discover they really can do it. They create conversation with clients with a variety of communicative capabilities. They have also gained an understanding of when to access more tools or expertise.

One staff person expressed at the beginning of the Skill Block that she was only interested in the sign language portion of the training, feeling uncomfortable working with clients with severe communicative limitations. After learning, practicing, and creating communication via multiple means, this same staff member excelled at creating a low-tech system. She stated, "I never thought I could do that stuff. Now, I'm seeing all kinds of possibilities everywhere I go."

Keeping in mind the importance of dialogue over one-way communication, this Skill Block was designed to provide information and to allow for hands-on practice and feedback in the development of functional communication systems. One assignment of the Communication Skill Block is to spend twelve hours in one day using an augmentative communication system that the participants design for themselves. They are not allowed to talk with other people through speech; they are only allowed to use the system they have designed. One participant shared her experience.

I felt isolated. After people realized I couldn't talk, they stopped talking with me. When I went to the store, I felt as if everyone was staring at me when I used this voice-output device. I found myself avoiding communication with everyone. Now, I understand why people aren't using the systems we give them sometimes.

It is important in this Skill Block not only to gain comfort with the various communication tools, but also to assure that the clients served create their own voice. The client's perspective is fundamental to any system design. Each time a participant creates a new communication method, we must consider the values, ethics, and culture of the client. This balance is an important component of empowerment.

Reciprocity in Empowering Relationships—An Example

Each Skill Block requires a substantial investment in time in order to delve deeply into the topic. Although it takes relatively little time to show someone how to do a simple task, it takes much longer to teach others to make judgments, critically evaluate current program practices, and set future direction. We agreed to devote the time in order to promote meaningful, functional outcomes for the clients we serve. We are seeing an immediate return on our investment. We now see empowered staff members enhancing the lives of our clients and empowered clients reciprocating.

> Three dominant themes emerging . . . are *respect, empowerment,* and *collaboration.* Changing the culture of the developmental disabilities field to embrace these concepts is important because the way support staff are treated is a reflection of our attitudes toward people with disabilities. (Ebenstein & Jaskulski, 1996, p. 143)

Take the example of Carrie and Eric. Carrie is enrolled in the Communication block. She had reprogrammed a fairly complex communication system for Eric, a client she supported. Through trial and error, she and Eric began conversing with a variety of people in a variety of places. At one point, Eric indicated that he wanted to be a journalist. Carrie began working with Eric to practice typing on the office computer, and they looked for a journalism class to take. Within a couple of months, Carrie and Eric were both signed up for Journalism at the local community college, and together they completed the class. Eric now writes articles for our agency newsletter and is working on some short stories for a book. Carrie attributes the success of this experience to the Skill Block training she received. Her training enabled her to successfully reprogram and update Eric's device to adapt to the needs of the journalism class. Our new Connecting culture prompted her to share an exciting opportunity with Eric. The magical part of the Skill Block experience is that, although this investment in our employees significantly benefits the clients they serve, the organization and others benefit as well.

Consumer Empowerment Skill Block

> *"Consumers must possess not only a greater voice in the kinds of services they receive, but even regarding the people who deliver these services."*
>
> —Beers, 1996, p. 140

The Communication Skill Block was created to give a voice to the clients we serve. The Empowerment Skill Block was created to give power to that voice. Empowerment of agency clients has always been a goal of the ARC. Prior to offering this training block, the agency had contracted with a private consultant to provide Leadership

Mentoring services for our clients. The consultant facilitated meetings of our consumer councils and mentored client representatives on the agency's governing board. The Leadership Mentoring project served to raise clients' expectations. Over time, the consumer councils expanded their focus from issues of immediate concern to individual members, such as what kinds of snacks to have in the vending machine, to broader issues impacting clients throughout the agency, such as the variety of paid work opportunities.

Empowering within the Skill Block Model

Ultimately, the agency elected to promote client empowerment via the Skill Block model. We chose to certify direct service employees to serve as mentors for our clients. The purpose of the Empowerment block is to "support and assist ARC consumers to participate fully in the planning and implementation of agency services and operations" (O'Melia, 2000, p. 1). In short, we hope to give our consumers a stronger voice in agency governance and service delivery.

Before launching the Empowerment Skill Block, Associate Executive Director Jane met with Executive Director Art to address the potential conflicts of interest arising from employees mentoring client board representatives. There are a couple of concerns in this regard. First, members of the ARC board of directors are responsible to guide staff efforts by setting policy. If employees mentor client members of the board, are staff members trying to tell the board what to do? Second, there is a risk of employees promoting their own agendas instead of fostering the client's perspective. The agency's bylaws prohibit agency employees from serving on the board, and employee members of the association have no voting rights (ARC/RIC, 1995). These checks and balances could be undermined if employees unduly influence client members of the governing body. Supporting the plan, Art concluded that Jane should encourage the mentors to meet with their client mentees outside of board and committee meetings, and that the mentors should direct any questions to staff representatives on the committees, rather than communicating directly with board members. In addition, Jane would devote considerable time in the classroom sessions to values clarification and ways to avoid undue influence on the part of the mentors.

As we worked to develop the content for the Empowerment Skill Block, we reviewed our agency's collection of published curricula intended to teach clients with developmental disabilities about self-determination, self-advocacy, and person-centered planning. We found that most of these programs address similar content areas, including training methods for decision-making, goal-setting, and assertiveness (Human Services Research Institute, 1999; Arc of the United States, 1999). These topics are essentially cognitive processes; to put these skills into practice, one must apply logic and judgment to the situation at hand. The manuals incorporated teaching aides for nonreading learners, such as overheads with picture cues and simplified language. However, these teaching approaches are primarily verbal and therefore are effective for only some of the clients we serve. Moreover, our purpose was to teach staff how to facilitate empowerment in others, rather than teaching clients directly. Ultimately, it was the Skill Block participants themselves who collaborated on the overall structure and design of the experience, resulting in the objectives and measurements for this Skill Block described in Table 10.1.

Maintaining an Informed Perspective

Executive Director Art offered additional support to this project by authorizing us to hire a coinstructor. Enter Linda. Linda has worked for the agency for six years as a receptionist clerk. As both a former client and current employee of the agency, Linda has a unique perspective on what it takes to become "empowered." Linda was hired, and she and Jane are learning together how to teach staff about client empowerment.

TABLE 10.1   *The Empowerment Skill Block*

Objective #1:	Participants will facilitate site consumer council meetings and serve as liaison between councils, program staff, and site managers.
Competency measures:	Monthly meeting minutes completed according to sample
	Observation checklist for facilitating meetings
Objective #2:	Participants will formalize the consumer advisory council structure.
Competency measures:	Quarterly meeting minutes completed according to sample
	Observation checklist for facilitating meetings
Objective #3:	Participants will train and assist consumers to identify, prioritize, and address significant issues.
Competency measures:	Issue analysis according to decision tree
	Journal descriptions of process/outcome
Objective #4:	Participants will provide mentoring and support to consumer board members and consumer members of board committees as needed.
Competency measures:	Consumer satisfaction survey
	Survey of Mentor Effectiveness
	Journal description of contacts
Objective #5:	Participants will train and assist consumers enrolled in the We Can Speak Out project to research and produce a formal presentation on a topical issue.
Competency measures:	Journal description of process/outcome
	Successful public presentation assessed by coordinator.

Source: Used with permission of the author from "Consumer Empowerment: Skill Block Training," p. 1, Jane O'Melia, 2000. All rights reserved.

Linda and Jane collaborate on each aspect of this project. Together they review applications from staff members, check references, and select the participants. They meet between classroom sessions to debrief, plan, and organize materials. Each month they get together to read the participants' journals and prepare feedback. Linda and Jane each keep personal journals of this experience.

> Jane and I are teaching a Skill Block Class on Consumer Empowerment. We are teaching the staff so that they can teach the clients to become more assertive. We focus on different topics each month . . . I think the Skill Block class is going well and am looking forward to many more teachings. We have made progress over the past few months. . . . I have been with the agency a long time and have made progress. I really enjoy teaching the class and teaching the staff so they can help teach the consumers. (L. D. Rowell, personal communication, June 30, 2000)

Piloting the Empowerment Skill Block

The initial implementation of the Empowerment Skill Block involved six participants; one is a supervisor, the others hold direct service positions. In the first session, after discussing general performance expectations, Jane asked the group what they hoped to gain from this experience. They mentioned wanting to better themselves and increase their knowledge base, wanting to empower themselves in order to empower clients, and wanting to learn more about our agency. As they looked ahead, one member questioned whether they might "step on some toes," and all agreed that they might. Jane's executive position and alliance with the executive director gave her the freedom to reassure the group: So long as they acted in good faith on client issues, followed the guidelines that they developed, and brought controversial issues to the table for analysis, we would support them and take whatever heat they might generate. With that in mind, each participant submitted preferences for one special project and for one board committee. The group was clearly enthusiastic about their projects, but some members also admitted feeling confused about what they would actually do. At the end of the session, one member described the class as being "like the first day of kindergarten."

Over the next several sessions, the training group compared current agency processes for obtaining client input with their view of an ideal system. First they discussed the existing consumer-council structure. Through brainstorming exercises, the group outlined responsibilities for facilitating effective meetings and listed the elements to include in meeting minutes. From these brainstormed lists, Linda and Jane devised new checklists to use later as competency measures for assessing each participant's effectiveness as a facilitator with the consumer council.

Following a similar process, the group devised additional competency measures, including two satisfaction surveys to assess mentor effectiveness. The first is a client survey to assess the client's comfort in working with his or her mentor, and the second surveys each staff representative to board committees regarding the extent of participation from client members. Finally, the group designed an issue-analysis model that the mentors and client mentees will follow to devise action plans as issues arise.

Each class included some lecture and discussion. The instructors devoted one session to background information about the agency and how it is governed, including structure and function of the board of directors, agency policies and procedures and the distinction between the two, rules related to board–staff communications, and the various avenues for clients to influence agency operations. Later sessions devoted time to mentoring, interpersonal communication skills, and methods for encouraging participation from others. In our final sessions, we addressed the political system and current legal and legislative issues of significance to the clients we serve.

Raising Their Voices

Currently, each participant is working to complete a special project, in addition to serving as mentor to clients involved in agency governance. Three Skill Block participants are serving as staff representatives to the consumer councils at each of our agency's major sites. These employees support the councils by facilitating monthly meetings and serving as liaisons to site managers. The councils have discussed issues such as staffing patterns, accessibility, and housing shortages. They are researching these topics and applying the issue-analysis model as they formulate corrective action plans. A fourth Skill Block participant is organizing a consumer advisory council; this group consists of elected representatives from each site council. They will meet quarterly to address issues impacting clients across the agency and to make policy recommendations directly to the governing body.

The remaining participants provide staff support to a group of clients who are learning the fine art of public speaking. Under the guidance of the Director of Team Services, Marcia Unwin, the We Can . . . Speak Out! project sponsored a community conference in which the group taught others with disabilities to speak out effectively, modeling both good oratory techniques and mistakes to avoid, as well as demonstrating the use of assistive technology for those without speech. The group believes that the ability to express oneself clearly is an important advocacy skill, and the conference allowed them to share this skill with others. One group member summed up the purpose behind this conference, stating to the media that "people should have to speak out for themselves and not have to have guardians or parents do it for them all the time." After the conference, several attendees asked to join the Speak Out group. The group is continuing to meet and plan future community speaking engagements.

The most recent initiative of the Speak Out group may have significant implications for all of us connected with the ARC. The group has presented a formal proposal to management and will ultimately address the board, seeking to change their designation from "consumers" to "individuals." Their plea is eloquent and deceptively simple; they intend to stop the "them and us." They are challenging our organization to abandon the Fixing model for good, to renounce our sense of separateness, and to cultivate ourselves as one community built on shared experiences, collaborative learning, and mutual respect.

Continuing the Conversation

As we look back on this journey, it is apparent that we began with an open system and a cohesive culture that valued the contributions of its members and resolved issues in a respectful, collaborative fashion. Would another agency providing similar services go the same direction we did? Probably not. Because of the diversity of participants, each organizational system is unique. The construction of an empowering organization is not simply a strategy of borrowing another agency's model, but rather it involves the creation of a learning community in which all members have voice and privilege. Our experience is reflected in the words of Kofman and Senge (1995), who describe such efforts as "building communities of commitment. Without commitment the hard work required will never be done. People will just keep asking for examples of learning organizations rather than seeking what they can do to build such organizations" (p. 16).

We can only share our journey in the context of our organization and leave it to you to glean what might be useful. We urge you to examine your own organizational contexts. In what way do the processes we have applied at ARC fit your setting? Do you find yourself caught in a culture of fixing instead of listening and connecting? Whose voices are heard in your organization, and how might you amplify the voices of those less audible? What would be the impact of redistributing power to include all of the organization's stakeholders? Are you, yourself, ready to acknowledge the essential interdependence within an organization of clients, direct support staff, and management?

An organization that fosters empowerment does so because it is a value, spoken or unspoken. We feel strongly that, given a culture willing to shift power to the clients receiving services, fantastic things can happen. From our journey we learned that anyone, regardless of ability, job title, or societal status, can make a difference when given a voice to do so. Empowering means creating a dialogue with others; it means moving from a hierarchical model of fixing to a connecting model of sharing together.

References

Agosta, J., Melda, K., & Terrill, C. F. (1999). *My voice, my choice: A manual for self-advocates.* Salem, OR: Human Services Research Institute.

ARC of Rock Island County. (1995). *ARC/RIC Bylaws,* Article I, Section 1.4. Author.

Arc of the United States. (1999). *It's my future! Planning for what I want in my life: A self-directed planning process.* Silver Springs, MD: Arc of the United States.

Beers, T. (1996). Concluding perspectives: Sound. In T. Jaskulski & W. Ebenstein (Eds.), *Opportunities for excellence: Supporting the frontline workforce* (pp. 139–141). Washington, DC: President's Committee on Mental Retardation.

Ebenstein, W., & Jaskulski, T. (1996). Conclusion. In T. Jaskulski & W. Ebenstein (Eds.), *Opportunities for excellence: Supporting the frontline workforce* (pp. 142–143). Washington, DC: President's Committee on Mental Retardation.

Hingsburger, D. (1990). *i to I: Self concept and people with developmental disabilities.* Mountville, PA: VIDA Publishing.

Kofman, F., & Senge, P. (1995). Communities of commitment: The heart of learning organizations. In S. Chawla & J. Renesch (Eds.), *Learning organizations* (pp. 15–43). Portland, OR: Productivity Press.

O'Melia, J. (2000). *Consumer empowerment: Skill block training.* Unpublished manuscript.

Rosen, D. (1996). Agency perspectives on the direct support workforce. In T. Jaskulski & W. Ebenstein (Eds.), *Opportunities for excellence: Supporting the frontline workforce* (pp. 77–82). Washington, DC: President's Committee on Mental Retardation.

Ryan, S. (1995). Learning communities: An alternative to the "expert" model. In S. Chawla & J. Renesch (Eds.), *Learning organizations* (pp. 279–291). Portland, OR: Productivity Press.

Sands, D. J., & Wehmeyer, M. L. (1996). *Self-determination across the life span: Independence and choice*

for people with disabilities. Baltimore, MD: Paul H. Brookes Publishing.

Weiman, K., & Miller, L. (1999). *Communication: Skill block training.* Unpublished manuscript.

White, W. (1997). *The incestuous workplace: Stress and distress in the organizational family* (2nd ed.). Center City, MN: Hazelden.

11

The Social Construction of Empowerment

Gilbert J. Greene and Mo-Yee Lee

We find the title of this book *Pathways to Power* to be very relevant to the basic tenets underlying the notion of the *social construction of reality*. From a social constructivist perspective, "one's life is like a path we create as we walk it" (Varela, as cited by White, 1993). We have taken our own unique paths to social constructivism and its application to cross-cultural social work practice.

I (GG) am a White male who was born in Nashville, Tennessee, in 1947, where I grew up and went to elementary school, high school, college (bachelors and masters degrees). I was 16 years old when the Civil Rights Act was passed. I saw a lot of racial segregation and discrimination firsthand before and after 1963. Though I did not directly see or participate in the protests of the Civil Rights movement, I was very aware of them from the news media and conversations with others. None of the course work in my undergraduate (1965–1972) and MSW (1973–1974) programs covered cultural sensitivity, cultural competence, and how to do cross-cultural social work practice. Later, when courses and workshops did become available that dealt with these issues, it seemed that they told us about cultural differences but not how to be competent in constructively talking with people who are culturally different from ourselves. I have found social constructivism as the most helpful framework for helping me to more competently talk with people culturally different from me and also in teaching students how to do so as well.

As a social worker, it took me a while to find social constructivism along the path of professional development. I found that most of what I learned in my MSW program was not very effective in actual practice with most clients. From 1976 to 1978, I obtained considerable advanced training in transactional analysis (TA) and gestalt therapy. This training helped me become a little more effective with a few more clients, but not much more. For the most part, I found that what I learned in my MSW program and in the TA/Gestalt training was primarily designed for people like me: verbal, insightful, psychologically minded, and mainstream culturally and socially. That description did not fit many of the clients with whom I was working at the Mental Health and Behavioral Sciences Service (aka Department of Psychiatry) at the Veterans Administration Hospital in Nashville, Tennessee. However, one thing that I did learn in the TA/Gestalt training is the importance of language in interpersonal communication and change.

During this time I also was exposed to the work of Gregory Bateson (1972), Jay Haley (1963), and the Mental Research Institute of Palo Alto, California (Watzlawick, 1978; Watzlawick, Beavin, & Jackson, 1967; Watzlawick & Weakland, 1977; Watzlawick, Weakland, & Fisch, 1974). The work of these scholars and clinicians put together language, communication, and reality construction in creative and innovative ways. In addition, I found their emphasis on the pragmatics of clinical work especially appealing: (1) If clients are not responding to our interventions, then we should change our interventions rather than blame the client for being unmotivated; (2) all clients possess strengths and resources, and our job is to find ways to help clients discover or rediscover and use them; (3) we should learn and use the client's language and perspectives rather than expect clients to learn the language of our preferred formal theoretical perspective; and (4) we tend to find data to support our theories and assumptions about clients, which can result in self-fulfilling prophecies, positive or negative.

In my PhD program in social work at the University of Illinois at Champaign-Urbana, I continued pursuing my interest in language and communication by studying with Palassana "Bal" Balgopal in the School of Social Work and Norman Denzin in the Department of Sociology. From them I learned, among other things, about symbolic interaction, language and linguistics, interpersonal communication, the social construction of reality, and the importance of culture.

During my professional career I have been very interested in finding and developing clinical approaches and interventions that are effective with and empowering to clients of all kinds, not just those who are "like me." I found that integrating the information mentioned above was invaluable in this endeavor. However, in recent years I have found the newer approaches of solution-focused therapy and narrative therapy also to be helpful in operationalizing the interventive process with clients so that they are more effective and empowered in their lives.

My (MYL) personal and professional experiences that contributed to my interest in social constructivism and its role in culturally competent, empowerment-oriented practice can be summarized as: (a) my personal background as a foreign-born Asian woman who had received social work education in Hong Kong, the United States, and Canada; (b) my clinical social work practice experience in the field of mental health in Hong Kong, Los Angeles, Toronto, and Columbus, Ohio; (c) clinical training in a solution-focused/strengths perspective; and (d) my personal beliefs and values in the strengths, resources, and self-determination of people.

Growing up in Hong Kong but receiving education and practicing clinical social work in North America provides me with an invaluable opportunity to personally experience how people, as cultural beings, develop diverse ways to perceive, experience, and resolve various problems of living. I was drawn to social constructivism as a viable theoretical orientation to work with culturally diverse populations because it explicitly acknowledges the reality construction process in which each specific cultural group develops its own implicit, unwritten rules and norms regarding behaviors and lives as a result of its unique sociocultural-historical backgrounds. My interest in social constructivism is further strengthened by my clinical training in solution-focused brief therapy, both at the Hincks Institute, Toronto, where I received my postgraduate clinical fellowship, and at the Brief Family Therapy Center in Milwaukee, Wisconsin, with Insoo K. Berg and Steve de Shazer. My exposure to Chaos theory, as well as the work of H. R. Maturana and F. J. Varela, during my doctoral study further helps me to revisit my thinking regarding human understanding.

To me, because social work practice is primarily concerned with improving the quality of life through solving problems of living and facilitating positive changes in human behaviors and/or environments, its practices and goals are, therefore, culturally embedded in the socially constructed norms, ideals, and standards regarding what is appropriate, desirable, and healthy, and consequently, inseparable from the communities in which it is being practiced. Building on such a theoretical position, social work practice based on social constructivism strives to respect the diversity and the uniqueness of each cultural group in perceiving, experiencing, and resolving problems. In doing so, it also implies a careful utilization of the strengths and resources offered by a specific cultural group in finding solutions to problems. Such a practice orientation is consistent with the empowerment-based practice that involves the creative use of one's personal resources to gain control over one's life circumstances, achieve personal goals, and improve relational and communal goods. Similarly, it echoes the axiom of a solution-focused approach that focuses on utilizing clients' resources and strengths in the solution-building process. Although social constructivism does not offer clear operational guidelines regarding social work practice, it provides a useful framework for me to rethink and evaluate my practice with culturally diverse populations in order to emphasize empowerment and respect.

The Social Construction of Reality

Humans need to make some coherent sense out of the world in which they live. In making the world seem coherent, humans create and render the world and their lives meaningful. Thus, it has been said that humans are "meaning-making creatures" (Rosen, 1996, p. 3). People come to "know" the world, to "know reality" by interacting with it—the people, the organizations, and the institutions within society—one's knowledge of reality is constructed through such social interactions (Berger & Luckman, 1966). This epistemological perspective is referred to as being *constructivist* (Lyddon, 1995; Rosen, 1996).

The idea that a person's view of reality is socially constructed is not new; consequently, much has been written on this topic. Our discussion of the social construction of reality in this chapter is, in essence, our "construction" of this literature. There are numerous perspectives on the social construction of reality, and we distill these into three major categories: *constructivism*, *social constructionism*, and *social constructivism*.

Constructivism

According to Gergen (1999), constructivism posits that "the mind constructs reality but within a systematic relationship to the external world" (p. 60). To most constructivists, there is an external world, but one can never have direct access to it. The knowledge of the world and the meaning we give to it is a construction of a person's mind (Rosen, 1996). Our knowledge of the world is not an exact one-to-one replication of what is "out there." Human beings and social systems are autopoietic in that they are self-organizing and self-producing (Efran & Greene, 1996; Efran, Lukens, & Lukens, 1990). From this perspective, the meaning people give to the external world as they interact with it is structure-determined; the structure of the individual human organism and human mind, rather than that of the environment, is the best determinant of the meaning people give to their world as they interact with it.

Constructivism, therefore, tends to emphasize how one's interpretation of "reality" is constrained by aspects of individuals such as biology, language, and cognitions. According to Hayes and Oppenheim (1997), "[c]ognitions represent internally organized systems of relations, which comprise a set of rules for processing information or connecting events in personal experience" (p. 23). Consequently, cognitive schema theory is often included in discussions of constructivism (Berlin, 1996).

As people interact with the world, they tend to assimilate experiences into their existing cognitive schemas (assumptions). As long as assimilation is possible, people tend to stay in their "comfort zones"; their lives are stable, but they are not growing and developing. As people go about their lives, they tend to look for the "facts" that are consistent with and will affirm their schemas. When people encounter novel experiences that cannot be assimilated, they must adapt by accommodating them into their cognitive schemas. Such accommodation produces more complexity in the schemas, thus an increase in growth and development (change). However, it is not the novelty by itself that causes the change but the response of a person's unique internal structure and organization (Lee & Greene, 1999). Accommodation is a process that involves people being out of their "comfort zones" temporarily, resulting in new, broader, more flexible comfort zones (Greenberg & Pascual-Leon, 1995; Watson & Greenberg, 1996).

Social Constructionism

Social constructionism emphasizes "discourse as the vehicle through which self and world are articulated, and the way in which such discourse functions within social relationships" (Gergen, 1999, p. 60). From the perspective of social constructionism, one's sense of reality is a result of the use of language within social interactions in interpersonal relationships, group interactions, and community contexts (Becvar, Canfield, & Becvar, 1997). Influencing reality construction within these contexts are cultural, historical, political, and economic factors in society and one's community (Gergen, 1999). Language provides words and categories for making sense of our experience in the world. However, the words and categories of language are full of ambiguities and nuances. Consequently, social constructionists do not see language as providing a one-to-one mirrored representation of experience, but rather it is part of one's life experience and, thus, helps to shape one's interpretation of experience and the meaning given to it.

From the words and categories used in language and discourse, people develop "taken-for-granted" assumptions about reality (Gergen, 1999). As people go about the business of their everyday lives, their assumptive categories guide them in paying attention to certain aspects of their experience and ignoring others. In this process, people tend to notice only those aspects of their experience that are consistent with and validate their view of reality (Gergen, 1999). Thus, a self-fulfilling prophecy is consistently operating in that we human beings tend to find "evidence" that confirms our existing taken-for-granted assumptions about reality and ignore that which does not.

Social Constructivism

Despite the common view that there is not a separate, true reality waiting to be discovered, both constructivism and social constructionism seem to be making truth statements about reality. For constructivism, it is that individual minds play the primary role in reality construction, and for social constructionism, that social processes play the primary role in reality construction. From the perspective of constructivism, then, the self is viewed as being a unified and stable entity, regardless of context. Social constructionism, however, sees the self as being more fluid and responsive to changes in relationships and contexts (Gergen, 1999).

As clinical social workers, we (the authors) are pragmatic in that we are primarily interested in what works in effecting the changes clients are seeking. Therefore, we take a social constructivist approach that considers both individual and social factors in client empowerment. According to Gergen (1999), social constructivism posits "that while the mind constructs reality in its relationship to the world, this mental process is significantly informed by influences from social relationships" (p. 60). Social constructivism takes a view that both individual and social processes are involved in the social construction of reality; it is not a matter of "either/or" but rather "both/and." Consequently, we view social constructivism as fitting well with an ecological perspective in social work practice. The essence of the ecological perspective is the *person-in-environment/person-in-context* configuration (Germain & Gitterman, 1996). With its emphasis on the individual mind in constructing reality, constructivism relates to the "person" side of the ecological situation. As for social constructionism, its emphasis on interpersonal, cultural, historical, political, and economic influences on reality construction relates more to the environmental side of ecology. As social workers, we know that there are reciprocal processes between a person and the environment such that a change in one can bring about a change in the other (Greif & Lynch, 1983). From an ecological perspective, the primary focus for social work intervention is the interface between the qualities of the impinging environment and the attributes of the individual (Germain & Gitterman, 1996). We view social constructivism as encompassing this interface and thus the primary focus of social work practice.

Despite some different views on the social construction of reality, these three perspectives have some common beliefs (Lee & Greene, 1999). People are active participants in developing their knowledge of the world, rather than passive recipients of stimulus-response interaction with their environment. There is not an objective reality standing outside individuals; thus, reality is not discovered but created by human observers. There is no such thing as an objective observer because the very act of observing changes that which is being observed. Language and dialogical interaction are integral to the social construction of reality.

Reality Construction and the Self

One thing that is constructed in this dialogical process is a person's self. A person's definition of self is socially constructed within the contexts of different relationships (Gergen, 1999; Mead, 1934). People tend to define themselves as they believe other people are defining them; this has been referred to as *taking the attitude of the other* (Mead, 1934). Taking the attitude of the other involves people becoming objects to themselves as they are objects of others' observations and evaluations of them. This process of defining a self involves taking the attitude of other people and the larger community, which Mead (1934) referred to as the *generalized other.* Thus, people construct a definition of self out of the many interactions and social relationships they have with other people and with the larger community. The social construction of the self involves people incorporating the opinions they think other people and the larger community have of them. Consequently, the social construction of a self can be problematic for peoples whose members are culturally different from those in the majority in a community or society (Lee & Greene, 1999).

Culture and the Construction of Self

In North America, society is quite multicultural. According to Matsumoto (1997), culture is "the set of attitudes, values, beliefs, and behaviors shared by a group of people, communicated from generation to the next via language or some other means of communication . . . a sociopsychological construct, a sharing across people of psychological phenomena such as values, attitudes, beliefs, and behaviors" (pp. 4–5). These life experiences contribute to the development of the taken-for-granted assumptions a person has about the world (Schein, 1999).

In our multicultural society, there are many cultures with their different languages, uses of language, assumptions about reality, different values, practices, and rituals. In taking a person-in-environment perspective in working with clients, social workers need to consider culture, because, according to Steier (1991), an individual's definition of self is socially constructed as a "person-in-culture" (p. 4).

In a multicultural society, the discourse of the cultural group in the majority is dominant (Baumann, 1996; Robinson, 1999). This "dominant discourse" becomes the standard for setting and judging what is real, desirable, and normal (Baumann, 1996). Those in the privileged majority have cultural, historical, political, and economic factors on their side, and thus the power in deciding what is real, true, desirable, and normal (Gergen, 1999). Consequently, the beliefs, values, practices, and rituals of people from minority cultural groups are subjugated and marginalized by the dominant discourse of the majority; that is, they are seen as less than, deficient, or abnormal as compared with those of the majority (Gonzalez, Biever, & Gardner, 1994; Greene, Jensen, & Jones, 1996).

The beliefs of those in the majority can be too easily construed as the "one true reality" by both majority and minority members. A consequence, therefore, is for those in the minority to develop a sense of self that incorporates the majority's view of them as being deficient, incompetent, or abnormal—in other words, to feel disempowered. Therefore, to make change at any level in society—individual, interpersonal, group, organization, community, or society—power and power relations need to be addressed at some point. Clients in minority cultural groups can be helped by directly or indirectly challenging the power that the views of those in the majority have over them and/or the power that the views of the majority have in a community in general.

Power and Empowerment

Power "is the ability to get what one wants" (Boulding, 1990, p. 15). According to Hopps, Pinderhuges, and Shankar (1995), power "involves the capacity to influence for one's own benefit the forces that affect one's life space . . . (p. 44). Power has relevance at personal, interpersonal, and contextual (organizational/community) levels (Gutiérrez & Lewis, 1999; Gutiérrez, Parsons, & Cox, 1998). According to Miley and DuBois (1999), "[p]ersonal power refers to individuals' abilities to control their destiny and influence their surroundings" (p. 3). People who feel that they do not have sufficient power may have a sense of low self-esteem (Hirayama & Cetingok, 1988), learned helplessness (Hasenfeld, 1989; Nystrom, 1989; Rappaport, 1984), external locus of control (Hasenfeld, 1987; Nystrom, 1989; Rappaport, 1981), low sense of self-efficacy (Gutiérrez & Lewis, 1999; Ozer & Bandura, 1990), or a low sense of personal agency and competence (Zimmerman, Israel, Schulz, & Checkoway, 1992). At the interpersonal level, people who have a sense of power believe that they are able to get people to do what they want them to do (Gutiérrez & Lewis, 1999). At the contextual level, people have a sense of power when the environments in which they live provide resources and options for decision-making, and they know how to obtain and use them (Lee, 2001).

As mentioned, members of a cultural minority group in society tend to be devalued by those in the majority. This negative devaluation can be stigmatizing to minority group members (Gutiérrez & Lewis, 1999). Minority group members are at risk for internalizing this deficit view of themselves, and thus, they construct a sense of self in which they feel personally incompetent and powerless—they devalue themselves (Gutiérrez & Lewis, 1999; Hopps et al., 1995). According to Gutiérrez & Lewis (1999), a result of powerlessness is "a denial of valued identities, social roles, and social resources that limits self-determination and engenders a sense of dependency" (p. 5). Powerlessness that is consistent and pervasive can have a major detrimental effect on a person's mental health, sense of well-being, and, thus, their construction of self (Hopps et al., 1995). Working to empower clients in general and culturally diverse clients in particular has been advocated in the social work literature (Gutiérrez & Lewis, 1999; Lee, 2001; Solomon, 1976).

Empowerment-based social work practice involves both a process and an outcome (Gutiérrez et al., 1998; Lee, 2001). It involves intervening with clients to develop a greater sense of power over their lives. Empowerment-based practice has many dimensions and interventions (Gutiérrez & Lewis, 1999; Gutiérrez et al., 1998; Hopps et al., 1995; Lee, 2001), including:

- developing a collaborative, mutually participatory relationship with clients

- engaging in mutual problem-solving and decision-making with the client

- working with problems and goals as defined by clients

- supporting clients' self-determination

- de-emphasizing the social worker's role as a professional expert

- engaging clients in consciousness raising about the impact of the dominant discourse on their current constructions of reality (Consciousness raising can be done through educational activities or discussion and helps reduce client self-blame.)

- identifying and building on client strengths (This may help clients recognize and validate skills and competencies that have gone unrecognized; clients can also build on strengths to develop new skills.) (Gutiérrez & Lewis, 1999)

This latter point has been a consistent theme throughout the literature on empowerment-based practice. With the exception of Miley, O'Melia, and DuBois (2001), the empowerment-based practice literature has not provided a systematic way of operationalizing ways to work with client strengths. In addition to the literature on empowerment-based practice, there is also considerable literature on strengths-based practice.

Strengths

Strength involves "the capacity to cope with difficulties, to maintain functioning in the face of stress, to bounce back in the face of significant trauma, to use external challenges as a stimulus for growth, and to use social supports as a source of resilience" (McQuaide & Ehrenreich, 1997, p. 203). The strengths perspective is based on the assumptions that: (1) even when problems are severe, all people and environments have abilities and resources that are not being used, are underused, or perhaps have been forgotten; and (2) all people are capable of continued growth and change (Early & GlenMaye, 2000; Rapp, 1998; Saleebey, 1997a).

Like empowerment-based practice, the strengths approach emphasizes taking a collaborative approach in working with clients. A collaborative approach involves keeping the work focused on the problems and goals as defined by clients, as well as eliciting ideas from clients on how to successfully intervene (Early & GlenMaye, 2000). In addition, a social worker implements the strengths perspective by

- doing a strengths assessment with the client
- consistently keeping the focus on client strengths rather than pathology and deficits
- fostering client self-determination so clients can increase their sense of personal agency and control (Kisthardt, 1992; Rapp, 1998).

The strengths perspective has been applied to a wide range of client problems and populations in general and culturally diverse clients in particular (Chazin, Kaplan, & Terio, 2000; Leung, Cheung, & Stevenson, 1994). Central to providing strengths-based social work is the worker routinely interacting with clients in a way that is more characteristic of an egalitarian relationship, rather than one between an expert professional and a nonexpert client (Saleebey, 1997a, 1997b).

Language and Dialogue

Both the empowerment-based and strengths-based practice literature emphasize dialogue as a way of working with clients collaboratively and nonhierarchically (Lee, 2001; Rees, 1998; Saleebey, 1997a, 1997b). According to Gutiérrez and Lewis (1999), empowerment-based practice is based on the belief "that power can be generated in the process of social interaction" (p. 5). Consequently, the social worker and client mutually engaging in dialogue is critical (Gutiérrez & Lewis, 1999; Lee, 2001; Miley et al., 2001; Parsons, Gutiérrez, & Cox, 1998). The strengths perspective advises us to avoid using the language of "pathology and deficit" (Saleebey, 1992, p. 3), and the empowerment approach tells us to use the "language of empowerment" in dialoguing with clients (Rappaport, 1985, p. 16; Rees, 1998, p. 140). In addition, both approaches emphasize using questions in such dialogues and interactions with clients (Miley et al., 2001; Rapp, 1998). Beyond this general guidance, the literature provides few specifics on how to operationalize this type of dialogue in actual practice.

Not until 1997 were specific questions presented for identifying and amplifying client strengths (Saleebey, 1997b). These questions appear to be very much like those identified in the 1980s by solution-focused therapy, which will be discussed below. Both empowerment and strengths perspectives also mention that they help clients socially construct a new reality in which they feel more power and strengths; however, this notion has not been systematically discussed and developed (Gutiérrez & Lewis, 1999; Goldstein, 1997). How, then, might social workers dialogue and interact with clients in a way that socially constructs an increase in their sense of empowerment?

A Social Constructivist Approach to Empowering Clients

Social constructivism is not a separate approach to social work practice but rather is a metaframework for organizing how we work with clients (Lee, 1996). However, some general guidelines that are consistent with social constructivism have evolved for working with clients.

Develop Collaborative Relationships with Clients

From a social constructivist perspective, there are many possible ways of viewing and interpreting a specific phenomenon. No one view is more correct, truthful, and real than any others; in other words, multiple realities exist simultaneously. Therefore, it is very important to discover the client's view of reality, rather than trying to get the client to learn the worker's view as informed by expert professional knowledge and formal theories. When the worker's view of reality is seen as being no more correct than the client's, then they are likely to develop a relationship that is egalitarian. When a relationship is egalitarian, it is also likely to be collaborative.

Consistent with the empowerment-based and strengths-based approaches, a social constructivist perspective emphasizes the importance of developing a collaborative relationship with clients. In using a social constructivist perspective, we also want to focus on the client's defined problems and goals and to solicit and utilize their input on intervening successfully. Problem and goal definitions are determined by clients, rather than predetermined by expert knowledge reflected in a theoretical perspective.

Theoretical perspectives shape our assumptions about our work with clients. We tend to look for "facts" that fit our assumptions and theories. If we assume that all clients have strengths and resources that can be tapped for change, then we are likely to find such strengths and resources. O'Hanlon (1998) believes that clients are much more likely to be cooperative and collaborative when they are treated as if they have strengths and resources.

It is also helpful to assume that clients want to collaborate with us, even when it seems like they do not (Tohn & Oshlag, 1996). On the other hand, we are much more likely to encounter client "resistance," rather than collaboration, if we are expecting the client to be resistant (de Shazer, 1984). Our job is to figure out how to identify and connect with that part of the client that wants to collaborate and wants to change. Such an approach can create a positive, self-fulfilling prophecy that leads not only to client collaboration, but also to client change (Weiner-Davis, 1993).

Take a Position of Curiosity

Because there are equally valid, multiple versions of reality, it is important for the worker to be very curious about how clients view reality. Demonstrating this curiosity in dialoguing with clients is very helpful in developing a collaborative relationship. By showing curiosity about the client's view of reality, we also show that we are truly interested in the client. According to Gergen (1999), "to be curious is a signal of affirmation" (p. 159). Clients want to know that we are truly interested in them as persons and not just cases. It is easier to be curious about clients and to show curiosity when we understand that we can never know "true" reality, that there are many possible valid explanations for the phenomena being discussed (Cecchin, 1987, 1992). The client's view of reality is socially constructed and is as valid as anyone else's. To try to understand clients' realities, we have to listen very closely to their problems and their stories. From listening to and discussing the client's story, an explanation will be discovered that will fit the situation (Lee & Greene, 1999).

Take a "Not-Knowing, Nonexpert" Position

In appreciating that reality is socially constructed, we cannot assume we know and understand the client's assumptions about reality. According to Anderson (1997), this position is operating when the therapist has an attitude or belief that she or he "does not have access to privileged information, can never fully understand another person, always needs to be in a state of being informed by the other, and always needs to learn more about what has been said or may not have been said" (p. 134). From this position, clients are seen as experts on themselves, on their problems, solutions, resources, and competencies; they are to teach us. Taking this position means "relinquishing the grasp of professional realities, and remaining curious and open to the client's vocabularies of meaning" (Gergen, 1999, p. 170). However, workers should have expertise in asking questions from this not-knowing, nonexpert, curious position (Anderson & Goolishian, 1993).

Taking the not-knowing, nonexpert position does not mean that the worker is passive. If the client asks a question or for an opinion, it may be perfectly all right for the worker to give an honest answer, as long as the worker's position is presented as one of many possible ideas (Anderson & Levin, 1998; Greene, Jones, Frappier, Klein, & Culton, 1996). The worker should keep in mind that giving advice or information in the form of "truth statements" is not the purpose of the work, nor is it seen as the mechanism for client change. Taking this not-knowing, nonexpert position can also be helpful in developing and maintaining a collaborative relationship with clients because many people often do not respond positively to experts in positions of authority.

Learn and Use the Client's Language

Because reality is socially constructed, the same could be said for theoretical concepts used for explaining a client's situation and how to therapeutically intervene to bring about client change. Concepts are socially constructed metaphors for describing and talking about reality, not reality itself (the map is not the territory). Consequently, from a social constructivist perspective, it is more useful to learn the client's language and concepts and the meanings the client gives to them. According to Duncan, Hubble, Miller, and Coleman (1998), "meeting clients within their idiosyncratic meaning systems and privileging their experiences, perceptions, and interpretations, will best serve the therapeutic process" (p. 297). This is in contrast to expecting the client to learn the clinician's professional language and theoretical perspective.

Learning the client's language and meanings informs the clinician about the client's explanatory framework (theory) for the situation and how to go about making positive changes. The worker's use of some key client words and metaphors conveys the importance of the client's existing ideas, which reinforces the notion of the clients as experts (Duncan et al., 1998). In addition, using a client's language is one way to build on the client's existing strengths, and it "prevents the client from being trapped in and influenced by a particular theoretical view and increases the chances that any change will generalize outside therapy" (Duncan et al., 1998, p. 302).

Reality Is Co-Constructed through Dialogue

Using the client's language is helpful in learning the client's current view of reality; however, social workers are in the business of facilitating client change. How then do we effectively intervene when clients have constructed a disempowered and devalued sense of self? The social worker's job is to work with clients in a way that results in clients having a more expanded view of reality—a change in their story (personal narrative) in which they view themselves as worthwhile, competent, and with a greater sense of power and personal agency. If it is through language and discourse that we discover clients' reality, then it is through language use and dialogue that clients can experience desired changes in their reality. In clinical practice, the clinician cannot unilaterally change a client's reality (Fruggeri, 1993; Maturana & Varela, 1992). From a constructivist perspective, the worker and client cocreate (co-construct) a more expanded sense of reality for the client in which the presenting problem no longer is present or is appreciably lessened.

In working with clients, it is important to learn and use the client's language, but it is also necessary for the worker to introduce *novelty* into the dialogue and, thus, into the client's story (Anderson & Goolishian, 1993; Fruggeri, 1993). According to Anderson and Goolishian, the interaction between worker and client involves a conversation between them that "is a mutual search and exploration through dialogue, a two-way exchange, a crisscrossing of ideas in which new meanings are continually evolving" (p. 27). In regard to using this approach in therapy, Lax (1993) states:

> Therapy is a process of continuing to engage in a conversation with the *intention* of facilitating/co-creating/co-authoring a new narrative with the clients without imposing a story on them. The starting point is always the client's story about his or her understanding of the world in the context of telling us. . . . It cannot be our story on top of theirs. The therapist is no longer seen as an expert, with a privileged story or view, but as a facilitator of this therapeutic conversation, a master or mistress of the art of conversation. (p. 74)

Given the autopoietic tendencies of people and the importance of the coconstruction of change, *instructional interaction* that occurs in an educational or psychoeducational approach to working with clients will not necessarily be effective

(Maturana & Varela, 1992). As mentioned, this does not mean that the worker does not provide suggestions, ideas, and information to clients. When suggestions, ideas, and information are given to clients, they are not presented as factual truths about reality but rather are put "on the table" for discussion (Lax, 1993, p. 81). Consequently, instead of instructional interaction, social workers should use *dialogical interaction* in working with clients to achieve clients' desired goals and change (Lee & Greene, 1999). In dialogical interaction, novelty is introduced to clients, and then all the worker can do is step back and see how the client responds and adjusts to this novelty (Lee & Greene, 1999).

It is through dialogical interaction that a person's "horizon of understanding" is expanded (Gergen, 1999, p. 144), that meaning and one's sense of self is created and changed. For change to occur, dialogue must be transformative. In dialogue, the opportunity for transformation is always present. Dialogues, according to Gergen, are not just conversations in general but "special kinds of relationships in which change, growth, and new understanding are fostered" (p. 148). The questions we ask can direct the conversation with the client in a way that can maintain the status quo or lead to transformation and change. For dialogues to be transformative, the interactants should not attempt to assign blame to anyone, to focus on the past, or to focus on problems and pathology; instead, they should focus on cooperation rather than conflict, search for solutions and new narratives, and envision a desired future. To have such transformative dialogues with clients in clinical practice, Gergen recommends using questions from solution-focused therapy and narrative therapy. However, he does not relate using these approaches to working with clients' strengths and working toward client empowerment.

If a client's current reality contains problems and a sense of powerlessness, how might a social worker dialogue with a client in a way that co-constructs a new, more expanded reality that contains a sense of empowerment, strengths, and solutions, instead of problems, especially with ethnically diverse clients? Two of the best ways to facilitate this co-constructing process are through using solution-focused therapy (Berg & De Jong, 1996) and narrative therapy (Freedman & Combs, 1996).

Solution-Focused Therapy

Solution-focused therapy was developed at the Brief Family Therapy Center, Milwaukee, Wisconsin. The primary creators of solution-focused therapy were social workers Steve de Shazer and Insoo Kim Berg, and their associates (de Shazer, 1984; de Shazer et al., 1986). Solution-focused therapy is atheoretical, and its use is not restricted to any specific group of clients. The evolved practice techniques and the basic premises, however, are quite consistent with the perspectives of social constructivism, empowerment, and strengths-based practice—ingredients that are conducive to a responsive and respectful social work practice approach, especially in a cross-cultural context. A very fundamental assumption of solution-focused therapy is that all people, regardless of their level of functioning, have strengths, resources, and competencies, although they may not be using them, may be underusing them, or may have forgotten they have them. Solution-focused therapy emphasizes the pragmatic utilization of client strengths, resources, and personal constructions to develop solutions and promote client empowerment (Greene, Lee, Trask, & Rheinscheld, 2000).

Influenced by social constructivism, solution-focused therapy views language as the medium through which personal meanings are expressed and constructed. Furthermore, both language and individuals' construction of their realities are relational in nature. Solution-focused therapy is a specific type of conversation in which the clinician talks "with" the client to codevelop new meanings and new realities through a dialogue of "solutions" (de Shazer, 1994). A solution-focused dialogue consistently emphasizes "solution-talk" over "problem-talk" (De Jong & Berg, 1998; Walter & Peller, 1992).

Solution-talk invites clients to be experts on their situations. Workers essentially consult with clients to discover strengths, competencies, and resources within clients and their cultures (Corcoran, 2000). The worker is the expert in solution-talk, knowing how to keep the dialogue going in a co-constructive way by building the next therapeutic question from the client's previous answer (Berg & DeJong, 1996). The therapeutic process, as such, is collaborative and egalitarian, rather than hierarchical, with the worker in the role of expert (Goolishian & Anderson, 1991). By assuming a not-knowing position, the solution-focused clinician fully honors a client's cultural knowledge, strengths, and resources from within cultural practices and beliefs, as interpreted by the client.

Because reality is socially constructed, social constructivism posits that what people talk about, they create. If the dialogue between worker and client almost exclusively details the client's problems, dysfunctional family history, and deficits, then the client's sense of being deficient, defective, incompetent, and powerless is reinforced. Therefore, to co-construct with a client a greater sense of strength, competency, and empowerment, it is important to consistently keep the dialogue focused on the client's strengths, competencies, resources, successes, and so on. Solution-focused therapy provides a number of specific questions and interventions useful for consistently conducting such dialogues with clients.

Solution-Focused Interventions

The major task of the clinician is to engage clients in a therapeutic conversation that is conducive to a solution-building process (Berg & De Jong, 1996). By listening and exploring the meaning of the clients' perceptions of their situations, the clinician invites clients to be the "experts." The clinician then uses exception questions, outcome questions, coping questions, scaling questions, and relationship questions in assisting clients in constructing a reality that does not contain the problem.

Exception questions inquire about times when the problem is either absent, less intense, or dealt with in a manner that is acceptable to the client (de Shazer, 1985). For example:

> When was the last time you wanted to give up, but instead you hung in there and kept going?

When are there times when you are feeling just a little less depressed than usual?

Outcome questions help clients to construct a future vision of life without the presenting complaint. A widely used format is the *miracle question:*

> Suppose that after our meeting today you go home and go to bed. While you are sleeping, a miracle happens and the problem that brought you here is suddenly solved, like magic. The problem is gone. Because you were sleeping, you don't know that a miracle happened, but when you wake up tomorrow morning, you will be different. How will you know a miracle happened? What will be the first small sign that tells you that the problem is resolved? (Berg & Miller, 1992, p. 359)

A version of the miracle question is the *dream question* (Greene, Lee, Mentzer, Pinnell, & Niles, 1998), which might be more culturally appropriate and relevant than the miracle question for some clients. The miracle question and the dream question can help clients envision a future without the problem or with acceptable improvements in the problem. They can also identify small, observable, and concrete behaviors that will indicate small changes that make a difference in their situation (de Shazer, 1985).

Coping questions ask clients to talk about how they manage to cope with and endure their problems, especially when the client is not able to identify exceptions or times when their life circumstances are overwhelming. Coping questions help clients notice times when they are coping with their problems and what it is they are doing at those times they are successfully coping:

> How have you been able to keep going despite all the discrimination you've encountered?
>
> How are you able to get around and do the things you have to do despite the language differences?

The *scaling question* asks clients to rank their situation or goal on a 1 to 10 scale (Berg, 1994). Usually, 1 represents the worst the client's problem or situation could possibly be, and 10 is the most desirable outcome as defined by the client. Scaling questions provide a simple tool for clients to quantify and evaluate their situation and progress so that they establish clear indicators of progress for themselves (Berg, 1994).

Relationship questions ask clients to imagine how significant others in their environment might react to their problem or situation and changes they make (Berg, 1994). Relationship questions not only contextualize problem definition but also the client's desired goals and changes. The establishment of multiple indicators of change helps clients to develop a clearer vision of a desired future appropriate to their real-life context. Examples are:

> What would your wife (or child, friend, etc.) first notice that would indicate to them that a miracle happened last night and that you are now feeling and thinking more positively about yourself?
>
> How would your wife (or other significant others) rank your motivation to change on a 1 to 10 scale?

The solution-focused approach also uses tasks or homework assignments as interventions (de Shazer & Molnar, 1984; Kral & Kowalski, 1989). If clients are able to identify exception behaviors to the problem, clients are asked to "do more of what works." For clients who focus on the perceived stability of their problematic pattern and fail to identify any exceptions, an observation task, the *formula first-session task*, is given instead: "Between now and next time we meet, we (I) want you to observe, so that you can tell us (me) next time, what happens in your (life, marriage, family, or relationship) that you want to continue to have happen" (Molnar & de Shazer, 1987). Another observation task directs clients' attention to *current successes* in their lives: "Notice what is different about those times when you are able to overcome the temptation or urge to (engage in the problem behavior)." Other tasks that can assist clients in interrupting their problem patterns and discovering new solutions are:

- *Do something different:* "Between now and next time we meet, do something different and tell me what happened."
- The *prediction task*, which asks clients to predict the likelihood of their involuntary problematic behavior occurring. (Berg, 1994)

The purpose of solution-focused questions and tasks is to assist clients in discovering what works for them in their sociocultural context. The clinician cautiously refrains from providing or suggesting any predetermined solutions.

The clinician is responsible for creating a therapeutic dialogical context in which clients experience a solution-building process that is initiated from within and grounded in clients' strengths, as well as a personal construction of the solution reality (Lee, Greene, & Rheinscheld, 1999). In this way, the techniques and interventions of solution-focused therapy operationalize social work practice according to the concepts of social constructivism, empowerment, and the strengths perspective.

Narrative Therapy

We humans make sense out of the world by narrating our experiences through telling each other stories (McLeod, 1997). It is by telling these stories that we socially construct our reality. For many people who become our clients, it can be said that their stories are "problem-saturated" (White & Epston, 1990). The narratives of their lives present their sense of reality, which contains problems. People tell and retell stories about themselves, their families, and other people. Though each retelling might be slightly different, the basic plot lines are unchanged. The more a story is told and retold, the more it becomes a person's reality. For members of culturally diverse groups, the stories told about them by members of those in the majority contain plot lines of being different, deficient, incompetent, and even abnormal. Members of culturally diverse groups may buy into the "reality" of these stories and reinforce them by retelling them to each other. Narrative therapy provides specific questions and interventions that are useful for clients to restory their lives, thus constructing a broader view of reality in ways that are no longer problem saturated and, instead are empowering (Carr, 1998).

Narrative therapy was developed by Michael White in Australia and David Epston in New Zealand (White & Epston, 1990). The development of narrative therapy was influenced by Bateson's (1972) notion that only a "difference that makes a difference" leads to change, Foucault's (1980) critique of the power of social institutions, the deconstruction practices of literary criticism (Derrida, 1978), the anthropology of Myerhoff (1980, 1986), the social constructionism of Gergen (1985), and the narrative theory of Bruner (1986, 1987). Like solution-focused therapy, narrative therapy emphasizes using questioning techniques that operationalize social work practice in a way that is consistent with the ideas of social constructivism and empowerment.

People who are different in society are subjugated to society's dominant narratives. Those narratives are elaborated through normalizing "truths" that shape our lives and relationships. Dominant narratives can be about gender, race, class, and so on. They are created, maintained, and supported by the larger society, culture, social institutions, and family. These "truths" usually take the form of knowledges, norms, or traditions. By internalizing these "truths," people become "docile bodies" who follow activities that support the proliferation of those knowledges (White & Epston, 1990). Language plays an important part in creating and sustaining those knowledges (Goolishian & Anderson, 1987).

From a narrative perspective, problems or suffering occur when clients' narratives of their lives do not completely represent all of their lived experience. This is so because significant aspects of their lived experiences do not fit the dominant narratives and, therefore, are neglected. Equally problematic are the narratives of significant others that do not sufficiently represent an individual's complete lived experience (Parry & Doan, 1994). Often what gets forgotten and left out of clients' narratives are stories of strengths, competencies, and resources, not only of themselves, but also of their culture.

Because dominant narratives are mostly socially constructed in the service of those in power, they may not describe or validate the lived experience of an individual. For instance, a working mother may find herself being torn between her career and family responsibilities in response to her internalization of the dominant narrative regarding traditional female roles as a wife and a mother. Similarly, a lesbian couple may find themselves in psychological pain because of the dominant narrative about normative heterosexual relationships. In other words, the socially constructed dominant narratives oftentimes do not validate personal experience, especially the lived experiences of those who are situated at the margins of society.

Dominant narratives about what is healthy, good, and bad are socially constructed. The way individuals narrate and ascribe meaning to experience is also influenced by personal interpretation of such experience within their specific sociocultural milieu. Building on the notions of power, dominance, social construction, and language, narrative therapy proposes a process that focuses on creating and sustaining dialogues in which clients find the semantic space to rewrite their own story—stories that represent more satisfying and empowering interpretations of clients' lives. The preferred dialogues are characterized by localized language and knowledge, multiple perspectives, and collaborative language.

Problem Deconstruction

The first therapeutic challenge is to assist clients to deconstruct their problem construction by contextualizing the problem (Kelley, 1996). According to White (1993),

> Deconstruction has to do with procedures that subvert taken-for-granted realities and practices: those so-called "truths" that are split off from the conditions and the context of their production; those disembodied ways of speaking that hide their biases and prejudices; and those familiar practices of self and of relationship that are subjugating of persons' lives. Many methods of deconstruction render strange these familiar and everyday taken-for-granted realities and practices by objectifying them. (p. 34)

A narrative approach to working with clients begins like any other approach. The worker asks clients to talk about their problems, to tell their stories. In this process of developing a collaborative relationship and hearing the clients' stories, the worker asks open-ended questions—who, what, when, where, how, how often—to have the clients describe the problem-saturated stories further and the meanings attached to different aspects of them (Kelley, 1996).

- What does he or she define as the presenting problem?
- How does the client experience it?
- What meaning is ascribed to it, and how is it viewed in light of historical events?
- Who else is involved in this problem?
- What events in the past have contributed to its development?
- How did this problem evolve over time?
- What has been tried to fight the effects of the problem?
- How has this problem affected other aspects of the client's life? (p. 466)

Important aspects of the process of problem deconstruction include "separating" the person from the problem, contextualizing the influence of the problem on the person, and questioning or challenging the validity of personal assumptions or dominant narratives underlying the particular problem definition. Critical to this process is *externalizing the problem* (White, 1993). Externalizing the problem involves the worker asking questions and dialoguing with clients in ways that objectify and personify the problem (White, 1988). In conducting externalizing dialogues with clients, the worker begins talking about problems as if they are something outside the clients, unless clients first refer to the problems that way themselves. For example, it is not unusual for a client to externalize a substance abuse problem by saying something like "Cocaine just has control of my life and won't let go."

One way to begin externalizing dialogues is to ask clients to discuss the effects and influence the problem has on their lives (White, 1993). *Effect (relative influence) questions* explore how a problem affects different aspects of the client's life and vice versa. Also, for example, with a client who is presenting with problems of feeling depressed, it is better for the worker to ask "How is depression oppressing you?" rather than "How is 'your' depression oppressing you?"

Conducting such externalizing dialogues with clients makes the problem the target of change, rather than the client (Kelley, 1996). In this way, "the client does not need to defend himself or herself to the clinician, but can join with the clinician to find ways to defend against this problem which is interfering with his or her life" (p. 468). If client resistance does exist, then externalizing the problem redirects it away from the worker and toward the problem.

Examples of some of these questions are:

- What would you call the problem that is most affecting you (or your family)?
- What's your main experience when this "worry" is in charge of your life?
- What effect does "worry" have on others in the family?
- How does "anger" invite trouble into your relationship with your wife (teachers, boss)?
- How does "anorexia" recruit you into its practices of not eating?

Restorying

Deconstructing the problem by using effects questions and externalizing it helps to thin the problem-saturated plot line and to open up semantic space to start co-constructing a new story with a new plot line. Deconstructing the problem narratives of clients' lives paves the way for them to reauthor alternative, beneficial, localized stories that enable them to (re)discover new meanings—possibilities that are more congruent with their lived experiences (White, 1995; Freedman & Combs, 1996). In other words, externalizing the problem helps clients to internalize a sense of personal agency, something they may have lost or not developed due to the dominant narratives in their families, communities, or society (Tomm, 1989).

Central to restoring is identifying with clients' *unique outcomes*. According to Carr (1998), unique outcomes are "experiences or events that would not be predicted by the problem-saturated plot or narrative that has governed the client's life and identity. Unique outcomes include exceptions to the routine pattern within which some aspect of the problem normally occurs" (p. 493). Unique outcomes are neglected but vital aspects of lived experience that are different from the dominant or problem-saturated story (Roth & Epston, 1996; White & Epston, 1990). Unique outcomes, also referred to as *sparkling moments* (White & Epston, 1990), are very similar to exceptions identified in solution-focused therapy.

In the restorying process, the worker also uses *landscape of action questions* and *landscape of consciousness questions* (White, 1993). According to Monk, Winslade, Crocket, and Epston (1997), landscape of action involves "[t]he realm of human experience in which events occur and out of which we fashion the stories with which we make sense of our lives" (p. 303). Landscape of action questions focus on helping clients to discover and describe the details of alternative, beneficial stories. "What will your life look like if you get back your 'old self'?" "Six months from now, what steps do you think you will have taken to let yourself partly get over the divorce?" Because our reality is socially constructed within a "community of others," it is important to include other significant persons in generating alternative, preferred stories in the process of restorying.

Landscape of consciousness involves "[t]he realm of human experience in which we make meaning of the events that happen to us and develop understandings of the connections between events by reference to culturally learned discourse" (Monk et al., 1997, p. 303). Landscape of consciousness questions focus on the meaning-making aspect of the therapeutic dialogue. These questions encourage individuals to review developments as they unfolded through the alternative landscapes of action and to determine what these might reveal about their meaning, intentions, desires, preferences, personal and relationship qualities, values, beliefs, and commitments. Such articulation culminates in a "re-vision" of personal commitment in life. "What does this new change (or behavior) say about you as a person?" "What do these discoveries tell you about what you want for your life?"

Experience-of-experience questions are also used in restorying (White, 1993). These questions invite clients to provide an account of what they believe to be another person's experience of them, thereby generating reflections from different perspectives. "If I had a videotape of your family at the dinner table, what might I have seen that would tell me things are different now than before?" Experience-of-experience questions are similar to solution-focused therapy's use of relationship questions.

The questions used in restorying are not necessarily used in any sequence. The worker integrates them in the therapeutic dialogue as needed in the reauthoring dialogue with the client. Using these questions helps to "thicken the counterplot" that contains previously forgotten or ignored strengths, competencies, and resources of the client, significant others, the environment, and the client's culture.

Reauthoring Context and Re-Membering

The dialogues of restorying aim to consolidate the new identities or stories that clients have generated for themselves based on localized knowledge and narratives. It is important, however, for the new stories to be circulated, heard, and validated by a "community of concern," which Freeman and Lobovits (1993) define as having "the power to appreciate alternative stories in the making, and to offer locally based knowledge and techniques for changing dominant, problem-saturated stories that equate a person with a problem" (p. 222). This has also been referred to as "creating an audience" (Monk et al., 1997) and "spreading the news" (Freedman & Combs, 1996). Narrative therapy suggests rituals of inclusion, appreciation, and celebration to help circulate the new stories to clients' significant others (White, 1988, 1995). These rituals can be "graduation" or appreciation parties in which significant others are invited to come and share. In creating a community of concern or an audience, clinicians can also send "reference letters" or "certificates" to community members who interact with a client (e.g., teachers, probation officers, and parents).

Using a *reflecting team* is another technique utilized by narrative therapists. Team members observe the interview and then dialogue about their personal reactions to the interview with the client, who in turn observes the process (See Friedman, 1995, for reflecting team guidelines). Such a process facilitates the development of multiple perspectives in clients, as well as creating a "community of others" for the client (Zimmerman & Dickerson, 1996). Narrative therapists also utilize various forms of written narratives by therapists or clients in therapy to further facilitate the process of restorying (White & Epston, 1990).

By creating space for clients to give voice to their experiences and to restory their lives in ways that validate their lived experiences, narrative therapy facilitates a therapeutic process that emphasizes clients' local construction of their experiences in an empowering manner.

Social Constructivism and the Environment

To enhance the development of an empowered sense of self, one needs a supportive environment. A supportive environment should meet clients' concrete needs, such as adequate food, housing, safety, opportunities for education and employment, and so on. Inadequately met concrete needs can marginalize people, subject them to the dominant discourse in a community, and contribute to the development of a disempowered sense of self. However, even when these concrete needs are adequately met, people can still be marginalized and feel disempowered if those in the majority see them as being very different.

Worker–client dialogues occur within a larger context in which the client's dominant, problem-saturated story may continue to be repeated and reinforced, thus negating whatever progress that has been made in the clinical work. This larger context may include the client's significant others, other professionals, and organizations and institutions (the larger community) with whom the client interacts. How those in the client's environment talk with and about the client influences the social construction of reality about the client (Berlin, 1996).

As mentioned previously, people who are different and marginalized by those in the dominant group in society are frequently seen as deficient and abnormal. Persons of minority cultural and ethnic groups are at risk of having those in the majority focus only on those aspects of their story that are seen and experienced as negative—deficits, problems, shortcomings, and failures. Often, to be eligible for receiving professional services, people must first be given a formal diagnosis, usually according to the *Diagnostic and Statistical Manual of Mental Disorders-IV-TR*. To qualify for a formal diagnosis (and thereby receive service), a client needs to have numerous identifiable problems, pathologies, and deficits. This emphasis on diagnosis can increase the likelihood of service providers interacting with the client and retelling the client's story among themselves in ways that discount or ignore the client's strengths, resources, competencies, and successes. Such problem-saturated conversations can set up a negative, self-fulfilling prophecy, the social construction of pathology, and a disempowered sense of self. There are numerous discussions in the literature about the involvement of social construction processes in the development of various problems and diagnoses, such as multiple personality disorder (Hartocollis, 1998), codependency (Harkness & Cotrell, 1997), eating disorders (Duran, Cashion, Gerber, & Mendez-Ybanez, 2000), and agoraphobia and panic disorder (Capps & Ochs, 1995). In addition, minority clients are disproportionately much more likely to receive more serious psychiatric diagnoses than those in the majority (Iwamasa, Larrabee, & Merritt, 2000; Neighbors, Jackson, Campbell, & Williams, 1989). Thus, people who are culturally different and also have a formal psychiatric diagnosis have great difficulty escaping stories that are problem-saturated and disempowering.

To make changes so clients can become more empowered, the discourse of those in the clients' environments needs to be conducted in ways that challenge the dominant, problem-saturated story that they repeatedly retell about the clients. The challenging of old stories and the co-construction of new stories about clients that will be retold and circulated in the environment can be addressed within the context of the worker–client relationship, in the clients' interpersonal relationships with significant others, and in the larger organizational and institutional environment.

Social workers working from the perspectives discussed in this chapter (social constructivist, narrative, strengths, and solution-oriented) can become easily frustrated when they encounter professionals involved with some of the same clients who focus only on clients' problems, deficits, pathologies, failures, and so on. The requirement of funding sources for a formal psychiatric diagnosis and detailed client histories that focus on identifying client and family deficits and dysfunction reinforces a problem-saturated orientation and the client's lack of power. When discussing a client's situation with workers involved in the same case, whether from another agency or a member of the treatment team from the same agency, one can use some of the same interviewing and questioning skills that are used with clients for identifying and amplifying the client's strengths, resources, coping skills, and competencies (see Madsen, 1999; Selekman, 1993, for specifics and examples).

This emphasis on problems and deficits, and the resultant problem-saturated dialogues and narratives, is a product of the larger organizational and community environment. We clearly view the clients' environments as integral parts of developing pathways to empowerment for clients. A constructivist approach that emphasizes dialogue, strengths, and narratives has also been applied to addressing organizational and community change (Gutiérrez & Lord, 1996; Saleebey, 1996; Shera, 1996).

Continuing the Conversation

To end this current discussion while setting the stage for continuing the conversation, we raise several questions regarding empowerment. The first question pertains to the helpfulness of using formal psychiatric diagnosis in social work treatment. The language of diagnosis permeates the mental health field and has made important contributions in the realm of assessment. On the other hand, such a language presupposes a person's problem as stable, unchanging, and residing within the individual. The language of diagnosis also focuses on pathology, and we perceive pathology or problem talk as unhelpful because such narratives can sustain a problem-saturated sense of reality and distract our attention from constructing desired solutions. In other words, the language of diagnosis may serve to further disempower the person by repeatedly retelling and circulating the problem-saturated story. From a social constructivist perspective, practitioners should revisit the role and helpfulness of diagnosis in empowerment-based social work practice.

Another question is about the evaluation of empowerment-based social work practice that is influenced by social constructivism. The assumptions of social constructivism are quite different from the assumptions of a positivistic approach of inquiry that underlie many models of empirically based social work research. In this age of accountability, however, social work practitioners are called to responsibly demonstrate the effectiveness of their practice. A search for viable ways to evaluate outcome effectiveness that are consistent with the assumptions of a social constructivist approach constitutes yet another challenge for social work professionals.

A social constructivist approach to an empowerment-based social work practice adopts a holistic view of human existence that emphasizes the importance of connectedness and collaboration across boundaries—between individuals, families, organizations, and the surrounding community. One fundamental question is how to facilitate an open dialogue at the interfaces between and among different levels so that a person is not isolated in his or her search for pathways to empowerment. Clearly, these questions are not raised here to bid for answers but rather for a dialogue that will encourage continuous creative inquiry.

References

Anderson, H. (1997). *Conversation, language, and possibilities.* New York: Basic Books.

Anderson, H., & Goolishian, H. (1993). The client is the expert: A not-knowing approach to therapy. In S. McNamee & K. J. Gergen (Eds.), *Therapy as social construction* (pp. 25–39). Newbury Park, CA: Sage Publications.

Anderson, H., & Levin, S. B. (1998). Generative conversations: A postmodern approach to conceptualizing and working with human systems. In M. F. Hoyt (Ed.), *The handbook of constructive therapies: Innovative approaches from leading practitioners* (pp. 46–67). San Francisco: Jossey-Bass.

Bateson, G. (1972). *Steps to an ecology of mind.* New York: Ballentine.

Baumann, G. (1996). *Contesting culture: Discourses of identity in multi-ethnic London.* Cambridge, UK: Cambridge University Press.

Becvar, R. J., Canfield, B. S., & Becvar, D. S. (1997). *Group work: Cybernetic, constructivist, and social constructionist perspectives.* Denver, CO: Love Publishing.

Berg, I. K. (1994). *Family-based services: A solution-focused approach.* New York: W. W. Norton.

Berg, I. K., & De Jong, P. (1996). Solution-building conversations: Co-constructing a sense of competence. *Families in Society, 77,* 376–391.

Berg, I. K., & Miller, S. D. (1992). Working with Asian American clients: One person at a time. *Families in Society, 73,* 376–391.

Berger, P. L., & Luckman, T. (1966). *The social construction of reality.* Garden City, NJ: Doubleday & Co.

Berlin, S. B. (1996). Constructivsm and the environment: A cognitive-integrative perspective for social work practice. *Families in Society, 77,* 326–335.

Boulding, K. E. (1990). *Three faces of power.* Newbury Park, CA: Sage Publications.

Bruner, J. (1986). *Actual minds, possible worlds.* Cambridge, MA: Harvard University Press.

Bruner, J. (1987). Life as narrative. *Social Research, 54*(1), 11–32.

Capps, L., & Ochs, E. (1995). *Constructing panic: The discourse of agoraphobia.* Cambridge, MA: Harvard University Press.

Carr, A. (1998). Michael White's narrative therapy. *Contemporary Family Therapy, 20,* 485–503.

Cecchin, G. (1987). Hypothesizing, circularity and neutrality revisited: An invitation to curiosity. *Family Process, 26,* 405–14.

Cecchin, G. (1992). Constructing therapeutic possibilities. In S. McNamee & K. J. Gergen (Eds.), *Therapy as social construction* (pp. 86–95). Newbury Park, CA: Sage Publications.

Chazin, R., Kaplan, S., & Terio, S. (2000). The strengths perspective in brief treatment with culturally diverse clients. *Crisis Intervention and Time-Limited Treatment, 6,* 41–50.

Corcoran, J. (2000). Solution-focused family therapy with ethnic minority clients. *Crisis Intervention and Time-Limited Treatment, 6,* 5–12.

De Jong, P., & Berg, I. K. (1998). *Interviewing for solutions.* Pacific Grove, CA: Brooks/Cole Publishing.

Derrida, J. (1978). *Writing and difference.* Chicago: University of Chicago Press.

de Shazer, S. (1984). The death of resistance. *Family Process, 23,* 11–17.

de Shazer, S. (1985). *Keys to solutions in brief therapy.* New York: W. W. Norton.

de Shazer, S. (1994). *Words were originally magic.* New York: W. W. Norton.

de Shazer, S., Berg, I. K., Lipchik, E., Nunnally, E., Molnar, A., Gingerich, W., & Weiner-Davis, M. (1986). Brief therapy: Focused solution development. *Family Process, 25,* 207–221.

de Shazer, S., & Molnar, A. (1984). Four useful interventions in brief family therapy. *Journal of Marital and Family Therapy, 10,* 297–304.

Duncan, B., Hubble, M., Miller, S., & Coleman, S. (1998). Escaping the lost world of impossibility: Honoring clients' language, motivation, and theories of change. In M. F. Hoyt (Ed.), *The handbook of constructive therapies: Innovative approaches from leading practitioners* (pp. 293–313). San Francisco: Jossey-Bass Publishers.

Duran, T. L., Cashion, L. B., Gerber, T. A., & Mendez-Ybanez, G. J. (2000). Social constructionism and eating disorders: Relinquishing labels and embracing personal stories. *Journal of Systemic Therapies, 19,* 23–42.

Early, T., & GlenMaye, L. F. (2000). Valuing families: Social work practice with families from a strengths perspective. *Social Work, 45,* 118–130.

Efran, J. S., & Greene, M. A. (1996). Psychotherapeutic theory and practice: Contributions from Maturana's structure determinism. In H. Rosen & K. T. Kuehlwein (Eds.), *Constructing realities: Meaning-making perspectives for psychotherapists* (pp. 71–113). San Francisco: Jossey-Bass.

Efran, J. S., Lukens, M. D., & Lukens, R. J. (1990). *Language structure and change: Frameworks of meaning in psychotherapy.* New York: W. W. Norton.

Foucault, M. (1980). *Power/knowledge: Selected interviews and other writings.* New York: Pantheon Books.

Freedman, J., & Combs, G. (1996). *Narrative therapy: The social construction of preferred realities.* New York: Norton.

Freeman, J. C., & Lobovits, D. H. (1993). The turtle with wings. In S. Friedman (Ed.), *The new language of change: Constructive collaboration in psychotherapy* (pp. 188–225). New York: Guilford Press.

Friedman, S. (Ed.). (1995). *The reflecting team in action: Collaborative practice in family therapy.* New York: Guilford Press.

Fruggeri, L. (1993). Therapeutic process as the social construction of change. In S. McNamee & K. J. Gergen (Eds.), *Therapy as social construction* (pp. 40–53). Newbury Park, CA: Sage Publications.

Gergen, K. J. (1985). The social constructionist movement in modern psychology. *American Psychologist, 40,* 266–275.

Gergen, K. J. (1999). *An invitation to social construction.* Thousand Oaks, CA: Sage Publications.

Germain, C. B., & Gitterman, A. (1996). *The life model of social work practice: Advances in theory and practice.* New York: Columbia University Press.

Goldstein, H. (1997). Victors or victims? In D. Saleebey (Ed.), *The strengths perspective in social work practice* (pp. 21–35). New York: Longman.

Gonzalez, R. C., Biever, J. L., & Gardner, G. T. (1994). The multicultural perspective in therapy: A social constructionist approach. *Psychotherapy, 31,* 515–524.

Goolishian, H., & Anderson, H. (1987). Language systems and therapy: An evolving idea. *Psychotherapy, 24,* 529–538.

Goolishian, H. A., & Anderson, H. (1991). An essay on changing theory and changing ethics: Some historical and post structural view. *American Family Therapy Association Newsletter, 46*, 6–10.

Greenberg, L., & Pascual-Leon, J. (1995). A dialectical constructivist approach to experiential change. In R. A. Neimeyer & M. J. Mahoney (Eds.), *Constructivism in psychotherapy* (pp. 169–191). Washington, DC: American Psychological Association.

Greene, G. J., Jensen, C., & Jones, D. H. (1996). A constructivist perspective on clinical social work practice with ethnically diverse clients. *Social Work, 41*, 172–180.

Greene, G. J., Jones, D. H., Frappier, C., Klein, M., & Culton, B. (1996). School social workers as family therapists: A dialectical-systemic-constructivist model. *Social Work in Education, 18*, 222–236.

Greene, G. J., Lee, M. Y., Mentzer, R. A., Pinnell, S. R., & Niles, D. (1998). Miracles, dreams, and empowerment: A brief therapy practice note. *Families in Society, 79*, 395–399.

Greene, G. J., Lee, M. Y., Trask, R., & Rheinscheld, J. (2000). How to work with clients' strengths in crisis intervention: A solution-focused approach. In A. R. Roberts (Ed.), *Crisis intervention handbook* (2nd ed., pp. 31–55). New York: Oxford University Press.

Greif, G. L., & Lynch, A. A. (1983). The eco-systems perspective. In C. H. Meyer (Ed.), *Clinical social work in the eco-systems perspective* (pp. 35–71). New York: Columbia University Press.

Gutiérrez, L. M., & Lewis, E. A. (1999). *Empowering women of color*. New York: Columbia University Press.

Gutierrez, L. M., & Lord, C. (1996). Toward a social constructionist method for community practice. In C. Franklin & P. S. Nurius (Eds.), *Constructivism in practice* (pp. 279–290). Milwaukee, WI: Families International.

Gutiérrez, L. M., Parsons, R. J., & Cox, E. O. (Eds.). (1998). *Empowerment in social work practice: A sourcebook*. Pacific Grove, CA: Brooks/Cole.

Haley, J. (1963). *Strategies of psychotherapy*. New York: Grune & Statton.

Harkness, D., & Cotrell, G. (1997). The social construction of co-dependency in the treatment of substance abuse. *Journal of Substance Abuse Treatment, 14*, 473–479.

Hartocollis, L. (1998). The making of multiple personality disorder: A social constructionist view. *Clinical Social Work Journal, 26*, 159–176.

Hasenfeld, Y. (1987). Power in social work practice. *Social Service Review, 61*, 469–483.

Hayes, R. L., & Oppenheim, R. (1997). Constructivism: Reality is what you make it. In T. L. Sexton & B. L. Griffin (Eds.), *Constructivist thinking in counseling practice, research, and training* (pp. 19–40). New York: Teachers College Press.

Hirayama, H., & Cetingok, K. (1988). Empowerment: A social work approach for Asian immigrants. *Social Casework, 69*(1), 41–47.

Hopps, J. G., Pinderhuges, E., & Shankar, R. (1995). *The power to care: Clinical practice effectiveness with overwhelmed clients*. New York: Free Press.

Iwamasa, G. Y., Larrabee, A. L., & Merritt, R. D. (2000). Cultural diversity and ethnic minority. *Psychology, 6*, 284–296.

Kelley, P. (1996). Narrative theory and social work treatment. In F. J. Turner (Ed.), *Social work treatment: Interlocking theoretical approaches* (pp. 461–479). New York: Free Press.

Kisthardt, W. E. (1992). A strengths model of case management: The principles and functions of a helping partnership with persons with persistent mental illness. In D. Saleebey (Ed.), *The strengths perspective in social work practice*. New York: Longman.

Kral, R., & Kowalski, K. (1989). After the miracle: The second stage in solution-focused brief therapy. *Journal of Strategic and Systemic Therapies, 8*, 73–76.

Lax, W. D. (1993). Postmodern thinking in a clinical practice. In S. McNamee & K. J. Gergen (Eds.), *Therapy as social construction* (pp. 69–85). Newbury Park, CA: Sage Publications.

Lee, J. A. B. (2001). *The empowerment approach to social work practice* (2nd ed.). New York: Columbia University Press.

Lee, M. Y. (1996). A constructivist approach to the help-seeking process of clients: A response to cultural diversity. *Clinical Social Work Journal, 24*(2), 187–202.

Lee, M. Y., & Greene, G. J. (1999). A social constructivist framework for integrating cross-cultural issues in teaching clinical social work. *Journal of Social Work Education, 35*, 21–37.

Lee, M. Y., Greene, G. J., & Rheinscheld, J. (1999). A model for short-term solution-focused group treatment of male domestic violence offenders. *Journal of Family Social Work, 3*, 39–57.

Leung, P., Cheung, K. M., & Stevenson, K. M. (1994). A strengths approach to ethnically sensitive practice for child protective service workers. *Child Welfare, LXXIII*, 707–721.

Lyddon, W. J. (1995). Forms and facets of constructivist psychology. In R. A. Neimeyer & M. J. Mahoney (Eds.), *Constructivist in psychotherapy* (pp. 69–92). Washington, DC: American Psychological Association.

Madsen, W. C. (1999). *Collaborative therapy with multistressed families: From old problems to new futures.* New York: Guilford Press.

Matsumoto, D. (1997). *Culture and modern life.* Pacific Grove, CA: Brooks/Cole Publishing.

Maturana, H. R., & Varela, F. J. (1992). *The tree of knowledge: The biological roots of human understanding* (Rev. ed.). Boston: Shambala.

McLeod, J. (1997). *Narrative and psychotherapy.* Thousand Oaks, CA: Sage Publications.

McQuaide, S., & Ehrenreich, J. (1997). Assessing for client strengths. *Families in Society, 78,* 201–212.

Mead, G. H. (1934). *Mind, self, and society.* Chicago: University of Chicago Press.

Miley, K., & DuBois, B. (1999). Empowering processes for social work practice. In W. Shera & L. M. Wells (Eds.), *Empowerment practice in social work: Developing richer conceptual foundations* (pp. 2–12). Toronto, Canada: Canadian Scholars' Press.

Miley, K. K., O'Melia, M., & DuBois, B. L. (2001). *Generalist social work practice: An empowering approach* (3rd ed.). Boston: Allyn & Bacon.

Molnar, A., & de Shazer, S. (1987). Solution focused therapy: Toward the identification of therapeutic tasks. *Journal of Marital and Family Therapy, 13,* 349–358.

Monk, G., Winslade, J., Crocket, K., & Epston, D. (Eds.). (1997). *Narrative therapy in practice: The archaeology of hope.* San Francisco: Jossey-Bass Publishers.

Myeroff, B. (1980). *Number out days.* New York: Simon and Schuster.

Myeroff, B. (1986). "Life not death in Venice": Its second life. In V. W. Turner & E. M. Bruner (Eds.), *The anthropology of experience* (pp. 261–286). Urbana, IL: University of Illinois Press.

Neighbors, H., Jackson, J. S., Campbell, L., & Williams, D. (1989). The influence of racial factors on psychiatric diagnosis: A review and suggestions for research. *Community Mental Health Journal, 25,* 301–311.

Nystrom, J. F. (1989). Empowerment model for delivery of social work services in public schools. *Social Work in Education, 11,* 160–170.

O'Hanlon, W. (1998). Possibility therapy: An inclusive, collaborative, solution-based model of psychotherapy. In M. F. Hoyt (Ed.), *The handbook of constructive therapies: Innovative approaches from leading practitioners* (pp. 137–158). San Francisco: Jossey-Bass Publishers.

Ozer, E. M., & Bandura, A. (1990). Mechanisms governing empowerment effects: A self-efficacy analysis. *Journal of Personality and Social Psychology, 58,* 472–486.

Parry, A., & Doan, R. E. (1994). *Story re-visions: Narrative therapy in the postmodern world.* New York: Guilford Press.

Parsons, R. J., Gutiérrez, L. M., & Cox, E. O. (1998). A model for empowerment practice. In L. M. Gutiérrez, R. J. Parsons, & E. O. Cox (Eds.), *Empowerment in social work practice: A sourcebook* (pp. 3–23). Pacific Grove, CA: Brooks/Cole Publishing.

Rapp, C. A. (1998). *The strengths model: Case management with people suffering from severe and persistent mental illness.* New York: Oxford University Press.

Rappaport, J. (1981). In praise of paradox: A social policy of empowerment over prevention. *American Journal of Community Psychology, 9,* 1–25.

Rappaport, J. (1984). Studies in empowerment: Introduction to the issue. *Prevention in Human Services, 3,* 1–7.

Rappaport, J. (1985). The power of empowerment language. *Social Policy, 17,* 15–21.

Rees, S. (1998). Empowerment of youth. In L. M. Gutierrez, R. J. Parsons, & E. O. Cox (Eds.), *Empowerment in social work practice: A sourcebook* (pp. 130–145). Pacific Grove, CA: Brooks/Cole Publishing.

Robinson, T. L. (1999). The intersections of dominant discourses across race, gender, and other identities. *Journal of Counseling and Development, 77,* 73–79.

Rosen, H. (1996). Meaning-making narratives: Foundations for constructivist and social constructionist psychotherapies. In H. Rosen & K. T. Kuehlwein (Eds.), *Constructing realities: Meaning-making perspectives for psychotherapies* (pp. 3–51). San Francisco: Jossey-Bass Publishers.

Roth, S., & Epston, D. (1996). Consulting the problem about the problematic relationship: An exercise for experiencing a relationship with an externalized problem. In M. F. Hoyt (Ed.), *Constructive therapies* (pp. 148–162). New York: Guilford Press.

Saleebey, D. (1996). Constructing the community: The emergent uses of social constructionism in economically distressed communities. In C. Franklin & P. S. Nurius (Eds.), *Constructivism in practice* (pp. 291–310). Milwaukee, WI: Families International.

Saleebey, D. (1997a). Introduction: Power in the people. In D. Saleebey (Ed.), *The strengths perspective in social work practice* (2nd ed.) (pp. 3–19). New York: Longman.

Saleebey, D. (1997b). The strengths approach to practice. In D. Saleebey (Ed.), *The strengths approach in social work practice* (2nd ed.) (pp. 49–67). New York: Longman.

Schein, E. H. (1999). *The corporate culture survival guide: Sense and nonsense about culture change.* San Francisco: Jossey-Bass Publishers.

Selekman, M. D. (1993). *Pathways to change: Brief therapy solutions with difficult adolescents.* New York: Guilford Press.

Shera, W. (1996). Constructing and deconstructing organizations: An empowerment perspective. In C. Franklin & P. S. Nurius (Eds.), *Constructivism in practice* (pp. 311–322). Milwaukee, WI: Families International.

Solomon, B. (1976). *Black empowerment: Social work in oppressed communities.* New York: Columbia University Press.

Steier, F. (1991). Introduction: Research as self-reflexivity, self-reflexivity as social process. In F. Steier (Ed.), *Research and reflexivity* (pp. 1–11). Newbury Park, CA: Sage.

Tohn, S. L., & Oshlag, J. A. (1996). Solution-focused therapy with mandated clients: Cooperating with the uncooperative. In S. D. Miller, M. A. Hubble, & B. L. Duncan (Eds.), *Handbook of solution-focused brief therapy* (pp. 152–183). San Francisco: Jossey-Bass Publishers.

Tomm, K. (1989). Externalizing the problem and internalizing personal agency. *Journal of Strategic and Systemic Therapies, 8,* 54–59.

Walter, J., & Peller, J. (1992). *Becoming solution-focused in brief therapy.* New York: Brunner/Mazel.

Watson, J. C., & Greenberg, L. S. (1996). Emotion and cognition in experiential therapy: A dialectical constructivist perspective. In H. Rosen & K. T. Kuehlwein (Eds.), *Constructing realities: Meaning-making perspectives for psychotherapists* (pp. 253–274). San Francisco: Jossey-Bass Publishers.

Watzlawick, P. (1978). *The language of change.* New York: Basic Books.

Watzlawick, P., Beavin, J. H., & Jackson, D. D. (1967). *Pragmatics of human communication: Study of interactional patterns, pathologies and paradoxes.* New York: W. W. Norton.

Watzlawick, P., & Weakland, J. H. (1977). *The interactional view: Studies at the Mental Research Institute Palo Alto, 1965–1974.* New York: W. W. Norton.

Watzlawick, P., Weakland, J., & Fisch, R. (1974). *Change: Principles of problem formation and problem resolution.* New York: W. W. Norton.

Weiner-Davis, M. (1993). Pro-constructed realities. In S. Gilligan & R. Price (Eds.), *Therapeutic conversations* (pp. 149–160). New York: W. W. Norton.

White, M. (1988, Summer a). The externalizing of the problem and the reauthoring of lives and relationships. *Dulwich Centre Newsletter.*

White, M. (1993). Deconstruction and therapy. In S. Gilligan & R. Price (Eds.), *Therapeutic conversations* (pp. 22–61). New York: W. W. Norton.

White, M. (1995). *Re-authoring lives.* Adelaide, Australia: Dulwich Centre Publications.

White, M., & Epston, D. (1990). *Narrative means to therapeutic ends.* New York: W. W. Norton.

Zimmerman, J. L., & Dickerson, V. C. (1996). *If problem talked: Narrative therapy in action.* New York: Guilford Press.

Zimmerman, M. A., Israel, B. A., Schulz, A., & Checkoway, B. (1992). Further explorations in empowerment theory: An empirical analysis of psychological empowerment. *American Journal of Community Psychology, 20,* 707–727.

12

Empowering Multicultural Clients by Using Cultural Values and Biculturalization of Interventions

Rowena Fong

My first experience with empowerment (or more accurately, disempowerment) was when I was ten years old and people from the Massachusetts Urban Renewal Office wanted to buy out my Chinese-speaking, immigrant father's wet wash laundry in Cambridge in order to expand Harvard University. Being the first-born child and the interpreter for the family, I remember feeling frightened, very angry, frustrated, and helpless. This experience and others that have happened either to my own family or to my relatives, who were immigrants from Hong Kong and Guangzhou, People's Republic of China, have affected me personally to the point that I am committed to stopping disempowering attitudes and practices. I have found that as an educator and scholar I can do prevention work by informing those who do not know or understand the situations or trials of immigrant or ethnic minority people.

This chapter allows me to explain empowerment from a perspective of the strengths of ethnic cultures, and to operationalize the process of empowerment in assessments and interventions. I approach this task by analyzing cultural values and beliefs of people of color, applying them to culturally appropriate interventions, and offering examples to illustrate points of discussion. This chapter briefly discusses a

The author wishes to thank her co-primary investigator, Dr. Paula Morelli; the staff of the Na Wahine Makalapua Project; the State of Hawaii, Department of Health-Alcohol, Drug Abuse Division; and the Center for Substance Abuse Prevention for their support of the study.

model of biculturalization of interventions as an empowerment tool (Fong, Boyd, & Browne, 1999) and ends with challenges to social work educators and practitioners on how to empower multicultural clients and avoid the continuation of disempowering practices.

Empowerment and Culturally Competent Practice

Empowerment has become a basic tenet to social work practice analyzed by many scholars in the past two decades. Browne's (1995) analysis defines empowerment as an intervention and a product, a process, and "a skill benefiting diverse populations" (p. 358). Empowerment defined by Staples (1990) adds the dimension of power, including to increase power, to wield power, and to share power with others. However defined, empowerment has to consider cultural components and the differences of meaning in terminology. Empowerment to people of color is a multisystemic process involving culturally competent skills to reach a final product of strengths-based functioning. Ethnic minority people continue to struggle to maintain control over their destiny, especially immigrants and refugees, and more advocacy work is needed on their behalf.

Multicultural Application of Empowerment Principles

Empowerment practice involves advocacy and other skills to enable clients to reach their full functioning. Gutiérrez, Parsons, & Cox (1998) suggest five central principles of empowerment practice:

- to provide a safe and supportive environment for a working relationship that fosters a sense of community
- to seek to understand the client in context of his or her environment
- to encourage a relationship that promotes self-confidence and self-direction
- to value the client's strengths
- to model multiple social work roles in the helping relationship

For multicultural ethnic clients, the interpretation of these practice principles may differ between the White and non-White ethnic groups, among the different ethnic groups themselves, and within an ethnic group among the different members. For example, with respect to the first principle, to "provide a safe and supportive environment for a working relationship," what would be defined as a "safe environment" to a multicultural person? This might be answered in several ways, depending on the ethnicity of the client, age, gender, and level of acculturation. To an Issei—or first-generation Japanese elder—a safe environment might mean not only to be respected but also to be allowed to remain silent. This would be safe because Japanese traditional values support nonverbal communication more than verbal exchanges. This cultural value makes cross-cultural social work practice more challenging, balancing respect for the culture with help for the client (Fugita, Ito, Abe, & Takeuchi, 1991; Takamura, 1991).

Another example of the principle to provide a safe environment might mean for a Native American or First Nations person that it is more comfortable to be around a social worker who is accepting of the First Nations person's tendency to bring up historical trauma (Brave Heart, 2001) or to give up personal possessions in "give away" or "potlatch" ceremonies because of the cultural values of sharing and generosity (Yellow Bird, 2001). Certainly, safety does not confine itself to physical safety; it must also include the mental, emotional, cultural, and social dimensions of security and well-being.

The second principle, to seek to understand the client in the context of environment, is so important because of the differing environments influencing any specific ethnic group. For example, in the Asian population, there is an increasing variety within a single ethnic group. Chinese people can originate from very different political environments (United States, Hong Kong, and People's Republic of China), resulting in divergent worldviews that overlap traditional Chinese values. As a result, the social worker's understanding must go beyond merely acknowledging generalized cultural attributes. Ethnic roots of origin affect the cultural values the ethnic minority person uses to shape his or her worldview and way of behaving.

Behaving in a manner to promote the helping relationship for self-direction and self-confidence, as stated as the third empowerment principle, may be difficult for social workers in some situations in working with people of color because of the frequent lack of focus on self in ethnic groups. This is true of most Asian and Pacific Islander families, in which the focus on self is frowned on and instead the cultural value of the family unit is the main system to effect change (Fong, 1994; Mokuau, 1991).

Valuing the client's strengths, the fourth empowerment principle, has become an accepted social work principle, with Saleebey's work (1997) emphasizing the strengths perspective in social work practice. The strengths of clients include, but are not limited to, biological, psychological, emotional, social, spiritual, and environmental dynamics. However, little work has been done beyond identifying and recognizing cultural strengths (Devore & Schlesinger, 1999; Lum, 1999, 2000; Miley, O'Melia, & DuBois, 2001). Fong (1997) writes of using cultural strengths in assessments, and Fong and colleagues (1999) operationalize and describe how to implement cultural strengths in interventions to create a biculturalization of treatment modalities. Indigenous interventions based on cultural values need to be integrated on a more consistent basis into treatment planning and implementation.

To be sensitive to indigenous practices, customs, and values, social workers need to be careful in how they handle themselves in words and behaviors. The fifth empowerment principle calls for social workers to be models for multiple roles in the helping relationship. This may be challenging because role modeling is representative of the personal values and beliefs of the social worker. The social worker's behavior will be very subjective, incorporating values and norms that may be conflicting, if not contradictory, to some of the client's cultural values and beliefs. For example, often a young Laotian girl may struggle with her traditional cultural norm of arranged marriage and may develop conflict with her family and relatives who want her to "marry well." It may seem to a social worker outside the Southeast Asian culture that the girl should be advised to assert herself and to seek other help and female role models outside her culture or even within her culture. Although on the surface this may seem like the advice needed to solve the problem, in fact, the girl is put into a bind of being forced to choose between conflicting cultural norms. What seems to solve the problem in the short run may indeed turn out to be a long-term disadvantage for the girl if she develops an alienation from her indigenous culture, values, norms, and beliefs. Although the social worker is advocating and role modeling assertive behaviors, this action may be detrimental to the adolescent girl who is dependent on other Laotian women as role models for cultural practices.

Four components of the empowerment process, according to Gutiérrez, Parsons, & Cox (1998), include: "attitudes, values, and beliefs"; "validation through collective experience"; "knowledge and skills for critical thinking and action"; and "action" (pp. 4–5). Empowerment practice involves a "value base, sanctions for intervention, theory base to guide practice, guidelines for client–worker relationship, and framework to organize helping activities" (p. 5). Among these elements, the key concepts of attitudes, values, and beliefs have been underdeveloped in the literature with respect to the ethnic minority populations. This chapter will fill a part of that gap in its discussion on cultural values, establishing for them a stronger role in the empowerment process and using them more consistently as empowerment tools.

Cultural Values and Their Role in Empowerment Practice

Culture is all around us and a major part of our lives. People embrace culture in different ways, some more than others. What is culture? Williams (cited in Parillo, 1994) defines culture as "values, attitudes, customs, beliefs, habits, and physical or material objects that are shared by members of a society and are transmitted to the next generation" (p. 30). Basic American values include: (1) "achievement and success," (2) "activity and work," (3) "moral orientation," (4) "humanitarian mores," (5) "efficiency and practicality," (6) "progress," (7) "material comfort," (8) "equality," (9) "freedom," (10) "external conformity," (11) "science and rationality," (12) "nationalism," (13) "democracy," (14) "individualism," and (15) "racism and group superiority themes" (p. 31).

Culture and Value Differences

The basic American attitude of racism and group superiority means "we place higher value on some racial, religious, or ethnic groups than on others through our attitudes and actions" (Parillo, 1994, p. 31). In America, the higher value is often placed on the status of the White, Ivy League–educated, Bible-believing, married, professional male. Ethnic minority people, male or female, struggle to have power, largely, in part, due to cultural values that either directly challenge basic American values or indirectly cause double-bind situations through loyalty dilemmas.

In the United States, the values of selected racial and ethnic groups dominate. People of color who are either born or raised in the United States bring another set of values based on cultural and ethnic heritages. Writing about differences in cultural values between East and West, Chung (1992) cites a group of Vietnamese who suffer from culture shock and compares cultural differences in the following summary of "An Asian View of Cultural Differences":

East	*West*
We live in time	We live in space
We are always at rest	We are always on the move
We are passive	We are aggressive
We accept the world as it is	We try to change it according to our blueprint
We like to contemplate	We like to act
We live in peace with nature	We try to impose our will upon nature
Religion is our first love	Technology is our passion
We delight to think about the meaning of life	We delight in physics
We believe in freedom of silence	We believe in freedom of speech
We lapse in meditation	We strive for articulation
We marry first, then love	We love first, then marry
Our marriage is the beginning of a love affair	Our marriage is the happy end of a romance
Love is an indissoluble bond	Love is a contract
Our love is mute	Our love is vocal
We try to conceal it from the world	We delight in showing it to others
Self-denial is a secret to our survival	Self-assertiveness is the key to our success
We are taught from the cradle to want less and less	We are urged every day to want more and more
We glorify austerity and renunciation and enjoyment	We emphasize gracious living
Poverty is to us a badge of spiritual elevation	Poverty is to us a sign of degradation
In the sunset years of life we renounce the world and prepare for the hereafter. (p. 41)	We retire to enjoy the fruits of our labor

Cultural Values as Strengths

Cultural values to ethnic minorities who uphold traditional norms and beliefs are perceived as strengths. When these cultural values are ignored, power is taken away from their being. Cultural values should be identified and used as strengths and tools for power building. People of color can acquire power through familiarity with cultural values and beliefs. Each ethnic group has such traditional values, which are upheld to various degrees depending upon levels of acculturation, age, gender, region, and sexual orientation. For example, characteristic values among most of the Latino population, according to Gutiérrez, Yeakley, and Ortega (2000), are:

- Allocentrism: A sense of identity and commitment to collectives and groups, rather than the individual;
- A focus on intergroup and intragroup harmony, with an avoidance of conflict and confrontation;
- Familism: A loyalty and attachment to one's nuclear and extended family;
- A preference for closeness in interpersonal space;
- A flexible time orientation, with an emphasis on the "here and now" rather than on the future; and
- Traditional male/female gender role expectations. (pp. 542–543)

Zuniga (2001) also writes that the Latino family will favor the parent–child relationship over the marital relationship. To understand and uphold these values in assessments and treatment planning in social work practice is to empower the client and allow the client to continue to draw strength through the cultural resources available.

Most ethnic groups use cultural values as strengths. Miley and colleagues (2001) assert the importance of recognizing cultural strengths and building a cultural knowledge base. In several of the Asian and Southeast Asian cultures that have original roots in Confucianism, such as the Chinese, Korean, and Vietnamese groups, traditional values that may function as strengths will include respecting and deferring to elders, being a part of the extended family, performing family roles according to sibling birth order and gender, and maintaining harmonious relationships for the sake of not losing face or bringing shame to the family system. The strengths perspective applied to empowering people of color, especially immigrants and refugees, means to identify the critical traditional values and to assess how they might manifest themselves as strengths in the client's life. In order to do that, the culturally competent social worker must have a sense of what the different groups value and determine as important components in their daily functioning. Because they live in America, a group's ethnic cultural values may not be as pure but may have become integrated into American values. However, it is still important to know the traditional preferences among the various ethnic groups.

Arguments are often raised that ethnicity does not exclude White people. This is true. A social worker would also want to find the strengths, for example, in the traditional cultures of the Serbian and Croatian refugees who migrate to the United States when assessing the resources available to these newcomer clients. Another argument raised is that some cultural values may not be perceived as strengths, especially when these attitudes and beliefs come from a country with a political orientation that is diametrically opposed to American values. An example might be the Chinese families from the People's Republic of China, whose population explosion forced the Communist government to mandate birth-control measures at the national level. The 1979 single-child policy (Fong, 1990) was passed to limit the number of children each Chinese family could have (except those in the minority groups of China). However, the backlash became evident when the Confucian ideal of having sons to maintain the family name and to care for the elders outweighed the socialists' attempts to convince the Chinese society that "women upheld half the sky" and to have a female child was acceptable. The United States and China clashed on human rights issues when, for example, reports from China indicated that women were being forced to abort female fetuses involuntarily.

The values of the People's Republic of China toward female babies do not seem to indicate a strengths perspective, and they need to be recognized for what they are. However, to confuse the Chinese values in the People's Republic of China with those from other geographical locations would be incorrect. Chinese values need to be differentiated by time and place, and more importantly, the values need to be distinguished within the Chinese culture itself. Fong and Wu (1994) speak of the differences in values of Chinese groups; it is critically important to differentiate them and to use them as empowerment tools.

Using Cultural Values as Empowerment Tools

A new pathway to empowerment for people of color is to better use the identified cultural values as empowerment tools to guide assessments and the intervention selection process. Empowerment practice shapes interventions to "enhance mental, spiritual, and physical wellness, as well as social justice" (Cox & Joseph, 1998, p. 169). According to Pinderhughes (1983), empowerment strategies also teach about power dynamics to individuals and families and the systems in which they live. People of color create power by upholding their values and insisting on indigenous interventions. Their values enhance their well-being in the emotional, social, physical, mental, and spiritual domains. However, because empowerment has different meanings for different ethnic groups, the selection of empowerment strategies needs to be carefully self-identified by each ethnic group.

The empowerment strategy of using cultural values in prevention and treatment services has been noted with the Pacific Islander population. Mokuau and Natividad (1998) write that "common among proponents of culturally competent programming is that services to minority populations can be enhanced by infusing programs with cultural worldviews and values" (p. 145). In describing substance abuse prevention and treatment services in Guam, Mokuau and Natividad say that "prevention professionals should strive for program content that integrates cultural esteem and cultural values, such as spirituality and the importance of family, with health promotion activities" and "guidance from members of the Chamorro community regarding how to integrate cultural values and practices effectively" (p. 146). They advocate involvement and recommend that "Chamorros must be involved in the design and delivery of prevention and treatment services to assure a fit between those services and the cultural values" (p. 147). This involvement "taps their pride in cultural heritage" (p. 147) and develops an "ownership of the services" (p. 147), a "form of empowerment and a means of self-determination within the community" (p. 147).

The example of the Chamorro community is a good illustration of identifying and implementing cultural values into an established treatment modality, yet more work needs to be done to add indigenous interventions onto the mainstream treatment services. Fong, Boyd, and Browne (1999) propose the integration of culturally indigenous and Western interventions in their work on a biculturalization of interventions model. They describe the use of cultural values in selecting interventions that are culturally competent. This process is the first such model "to identify the important values in the ethnic culture which can be used to reinforce the therapeutic interventions" (p. 105).

Biculturalization of Interventions

The biculturalization of interventions (Fong et al., 1999) is a process, an empowerment tool whereby social workers combine an indigenous intervention with a Western one, integrating cultural values and beliefs with modified therapeutic techniques to successfully achieve acceptable levels of client functioning. The five steps in this process are as follows:

1. Identify the important values in the ethnic culture to be used to reinforce the selection and implementation of both the indigenous and Western intervention.
2. Choose a Western intervention whose theoretical framework and values are compatible to the ethnic cultural values of the family client system.
3. Select an indigenous intervention familiar to the ethnic client system and analyze what techniques can be reinforced and integrated into or alongside the Western intervention.
4. Develop a framework and approach that integrates the values and techniques of the ethnic culture and both the Western and indigenous intervention.
5. Apply the Western intervention by explaining the techniques and reiterating to the family client system how the techniques reinforce cultural values and support indigenous interventions. (p. 105)

The biculturalization of interventions can be used as an empowerment tool for several reasons. As a tool, it is a step-by-step process to be used to help solve a problem. As a means toward empowerment, it gives ethnic minority clients an opportunity to enhance their mental, emotional, social, physical, and spiritual well-being because it is grounded in using cultural values as the foundation building blocks. Finally, as a social work practice method, it is working toward treating the problem in a culturally competent manner, building on the cultural values and strengths of the client.

Biculturalization of Interventions:
A Substance Abuse Treatment Example

The case example that follows illustrates how to use cultural strengths and apply them to a biculturalization of interventions process to produce an empowerment treatment of services in a substance abuse program. The project, Na Wahine Makalapua (translation is "to blossom forth the women"), a residential treatment program for substance abusing Hawaiian women, operated from 1992 to 1996. Designed to support forty-nine pregnant and postpartum women and their infants, the Na Wahine Makalapua (NWM) project was a residential program with substance abuse counselors who worked with the Hawaiian kupuna (elders) to support and empower the women as they regained custody of their children. The services in the program were offered by a Hawaiian agency named Ho'omau Ke Ola, a substance abuse treatment agency that uses non-Western methods of healing and diagnosing in its treatment program (De-Cambra, Marshall, & Ono, 1998). The Hawaiian program included kupuna (elders), Ho'oponopono, and Deep Culture therapy. In all three areas, the value of family (o'hana) is important. Ho'omau Ke Ola used cultural strengths in its program planning and implementation.

> Through client, family, and staff feedback, it became increasingly apparent that interventions which reflected Hawaiian cultural values and worldview were believed to have a greater efficacy on substance abuse treatment in terms of personal growth and change. Consequently Ho'omau Ke Ola began a process of incorporating some of the Hawaiian values and viewpoints that had been historically suppressed by the hegemony of Western science and medicine. (p. 74)

Fong (1994) contends that to empower Asian and Pacific Island families one should start with the family as the unit of focus and change. The critical value of family, or o'hana, in Hawaiian culture must be incorporated into practice methods to ensure cultural competence. The Hawaiian cultural value of family, or family-centered practice (Ho'oponopono), is core to several substance abuse treatment centers in Hawaii (De-Cambra et al., 1998; Fong & Morelli, 1998). In using the family in problem solving, respecting authority and elders, and promoting Deep Culture therapy, social workers are able to empower their Native Hawaiian clients to go back to their roots and identity. The family problem-solving method of Ho'oponopono is used to solve conflicts within the Hawaiian family. It includes a multistage process of praying, stating the problem, confessing wrongdoing, making restitution, offering forgiveness, releasing the negative entanglements, and summarizing the family strengths (Mokuau, 1990; Pukui, Haetig, & Lee, 1972).

Deep Culture therapy is storytelling, role-playing, and "peeling away hurt and pain" (Fong & Morelli, 1998, p. 45). For six hours twice a month, a Hawaiian elder would facilitate therapy groups in which the Hawaiian participants would listen to traditions, values, and legends in the Hawaiian culture, role-play and enact these stories, then discuss their feelings and makiki, or "peel away the hurt and pain the client is feeling" (Fong & Morelli, p. 45). As the client role-played the struggles, the reenactment became both healing and cathartic. Common themes discovered with substance abusing women in Deep Culture therapy were lack of self-appreciation and internalized oppression. The sessions opened and closed with prayer. A restriction placed on the process was for the client not to leave when the pain became unbearable but to use the kupuna, the Hawaiian elder, as a "spiritual and cultural instrument" (p. 46).

These indigenous interventions of Ho'oponopono and Deep Culture therapy were used jointly and in a bicultural manner with the substance abuse treatment services required of the women. The Hawaiian cultural values of roots and heritage, as well as a positive identity with the Hawaiian ideas and beliefs, complemented the treatment services for substance abuse and built on the cultural values and strengths of involving family members in the service delivery system.

Biculturalization of Interventions: A Child Welfare Example

Another example of biculturalization of interventions would be to use the Hawaiian family problem-solving method of Ho'oponopono with structural family therapy, when both interventions share the common values of including the family members in treatment services, specifically translating the problem of an individual family member into a family undertaking (Fong et al., 1999, p. 161). A case example is a fifteen-year-old Hawaiian boy with a truancy problem who is also using drugs. The school authorities notify the parents, who have marital and financial problems, with the mother suffering from severe depression that causes her to neglect the children. Structural family therapy is recommended for the family because of the unclear roles in the home between the parents and the lack of structure in family functioning.

Because of the strong value of family (o'hana) in Hawaiian culture, Ho'oponopono is also recommended so extended family members can come and make peace within this family in order for additional support to occur. The theoretical underpinnings of structural family therapy and Ho'oponopono both emphasize family structure and support, conforming to strong cultural values within the Hawaiian culture. By identifying important cultural values and using them as a basis to select indigenous and Western interventions, a biculturalization of interventions occurs that assures more cultural competency and compatibility with ethnic minority families, thus enhancing empowerment.

Empowerment in Political and Cultural Contexts

People of color are disempowered when values dissonant to their culture are imposed on them. They are forced to adapt to ways that are either unnatural to them, are guilt-producing, or are double-bind formulating. People of color are disempowered when assessments erroneously mislabel them or misconstrue their values and belief systems. They are disempowered when spirituality is misunderstood and labeled. People of color are disempowered when professional interventions supercede their own natural ways of handling matters, undermining the power of indigenous healers. For example, in the Tongan culture, the matai, a well-respected community leader, plays an important role in problem-solving. In the Hawaiian culture, the elder kapuna plays a very important role in role modeling and educating about Hawaiian culture. They and other natural healers and leaders need to be a regular part of treatment services.

Continuing the Conversation

Key points in determining culturally competent and empowering practices with ethnic minority clients are: (1) the use of cultural values as strengths in the assessment and intervention determining processes, (2) the implementation of bicultural interventions that combine appropriate indigenous treatments with Western interventions, and (3) the avoidance of disempowerment practices by adopting and integrating cultural practices that are meaningful to the ethnic clients served.

To implement an empowerment approach, social workers can ask the following questions to evaluate their empowerment practices with clients of color. Do I really know what kind of environments my ethnic clients come from and what matters to them in their culture? Can I see what they value in their culture? Can I really accept these values as strengths? How can I use these values as strengths? Do I know what meaningful practices clients have in their own cultures to solve their problems? How can I use these practices with orientation to practice? Do these two treatment modalities fit? If not, how can I make them fit, or how can I choose another treatment that would complement their indigenous practice better?

Disempowerment practices will continue if social workers insist on ignoring the strengths present in cultural values. Cultural resources need to be more than simply identified. They need to be integrated into mainstream social work practices. Empowerment practices useful for people of color need to include processes, products, skills, and interventions that are created by the ethnic clients, rather than imposed on them by others.

References

Brave Heart, M. (2001). Culturally and historically congruent clinical social work assessment with Native clients. In R. Fong & S. Furuto (Eds.), *Culturally competent social work practice: Skills, interventions, and evaluations* (pp. 163–177). Boston: Allyn & Bacon.

Browne, C. (1995). Empowerment in social work practice with older women. *Social Work, 40*, 358–364.

Chung, D. (1992). Asian cultural commonalities: A comparison with mainstream American culture. In S. Furuto, R. Biswas, D. Chung, K. Murase, & F. Ross-Sheriff (Eds.), *Social work practice with Asian Americans* (pp. 27–44). Newbury Park, CA: Sage.

Cox, E. O., & Joseph, B. H. R. (1998). Social service delivery and empowerment. In L. M. Gutiérrez, R. J. Parsons, & E. O. Cox (Eds.), *Empowerment in social work practice* (pp. 167–186). Pacific Grove, CA: Brooks/Cole.

DeCambra, H., Marshall, W., & Ono, M. (1998). Ho'omau Ke Ola: To perpetuate life as it was meant to be. In N. Mokuau (Ed.), *Responding to Pacific Islanders: Culturally competent perspectives for substance abuse prevention, Cultural Competence Series 8* (pp. 73–96). Washington, DC: U.S. Department of Health and Human Services, Center for Substance Abuse Prevention.

Devore, W., & Schlesinger, E. G. (1999). *Ethnic-sensitive social work practice* (5th ed.). Boston: Allyn & Bacon.

Fong, R. (1990). *China's single-child policy*. Unpublished manuscript. Cambridge, MA: Harvard University.

Fong, R. (1994). Family preservation: Making it work for Asians. *Child Welfare, 73*, 331–341.

Fong, R. (1997). Child welfare practice with Chinese families: Assessment issues for immigrants from the People's Republic of China. *Journal of Family Social Work, 2*, 33–48.

Fong, R., Boyd, T., & Browne, C. (1999). The Gandhi technique: A biculturalization approach for Asian and Pacific Islander families. *Journal of Multicultural Social Work, 7*(2), 95–110.

Fong, R., & Morelli, P. (1998). *Fifth-year evaluation of the Na Wahine Makalapua: Pregnant and postpartum women and their infants in Hawaii.* Demonstration grant from the state Department of Health, Alcohol and Drug Abuse Division. Honolulu: University of Hawaii.

Fong, R., & Wu, D. (1996). Socialization issues for Chinese American children. *Social Work in Education, 18*(2), 71–78.

Fugita, S., Ito, K., Abe, J., & Takeuchi, D. (1991). Japanese Americans. In N. Mokuau (Ed.), *Handbook of social services for Asians and Pacific Islanders* (pp. 61–78). New York: Greenwood Press.

Gutiérrez, L. M., Parsons, R. J., & Cox, E. O. (1998). A model for empowerment practice. In L. M. Gutiérrez, R. J. Parsons, & E. O. Cox (Eds.), *Empowerment in social work practice: A sourcebook* (pp. 3–23). Pacific Grove, CA: Brooks/Cole.

Gutiérrez, L., Yeakley, A., & Ortega, R. (2000). Educating students for social work with Latinos: Issues for the new millenium. *Journal of Social Work Education, 36*(3), 541–557.

Lum, D. (1999). *Culturally competent practice*. Pacific Grove, CA: Brooks/Cole.

Lum, D. (2000). *Social work practice and people of color* (3rd ed.). Pacific Grove, CA: Brooks/Cole.

Miley, K., O'Melia, M., & DuBois, B. (2001). *Generalist social work practice: An empowering approach* (3rd ed.). Boston: Allyn & Bacon.

Mokuau, N. (1990). A family-centered approach in Native Hawaiian culture. *Families in Society, 71*(10), 607–613.

Mokuau, N. (1991). *Handbook of social services for Asian and Pacific Islanders.* New York: Greenwood Press.

Mokuau, N., & Natividad, L. (1998). Chamorros: Recognizing a people and their issues with substance abuse. In N. Mokuau (Ed.), *Responding to Pacific Islanders: Culturally competent perspectives for substance abuse prevention, Cultural Competence Series 8* (pp. 137–150). Washington, DC: U.S. Department of Health and Human Services, Center for Substance Abuse Prevention.

Parrillo, V. (1994). *Strangers to these shores: Race and ethnic relations in the United States.* Boston: Allyn & Bacon.

Pinderhughes, E. (1983). Empowerment for our clients and for ourselves. *Social Casework, 31*, 214–219.

Pukui, M., Haetig, C., & Lee, C. (1972). *Nana I Ke Kumu: Vol. 1*, Honolulu, HA: Hui Hanai.

Saleebey, D. (1997). *The strengths perspective in social work practice* (2nd ed.). New York: Longman.

Staples, L. H. (1990). Powerful ideas about empowerment. *Administration in Social Work, 14*(2), 29–42.

Takamura, J. (1991). Asian and Pacific Island elderly. In N. Mokuau (Ed.), *Handbook of social services for Asians and Pacific Islanders* (pp. 185–202). New York: Greenwood Press.

Yellow Bird, M. (2001). Critical values and First Nations peoples. In R. Fong & S. Furuto (Eds.), *Culturally competent social work practice: Skills, interventions, and evaluations* (pp. 61–74). Boston: Allyn & Bacon.

Zuniga, M. (2001). Latinos: Cultural competence and ethics. In R. Fong & S. Furuto (Eds.), *Culturally competent social work practice: Skills, interventions, and evaluations* (pp. 47–60). Boston: Allyn & Bacon.

Empowering Mental Health Consumers: Assessing the Efficacy of a Partnership Model of Case Management

Wes Shera

My interest and commitment to the area of mental health is longstanding. As a young man, I had an intense interest in psychology. I completed an honors degree in psychology and took my first human services job in a psychiatric hospital. In this position, I learned the traditional medical model approach to working with persons with psychiatric disabilities. Subsequent training in social work broadened my perspective and helped me to develop a more holistic perspective of mental health.

Some of the most pivotal learning experiences for me involved the mental illness of significant people in my life. As a supportive person, I witnessed the personal angst of obsessive-compulsive and manic-depressive disorders. I was also stunned at the narrow focus of most psychiatrists. The expert model focusing primarily on psychotropic solutions fell far short of dealing with the day-to-day realities of struggling with mental illness. This experience led me to understand the importance of the "lived experience" of those who endure a psychiatric disability.

There is growing literature on illness narratives, with a particular focus on the self, self-esteem, self-efficacy, and social competence of the mentally ill (Bednar, Wells, & VandenBos, 1991; Estroff, 1989; Estroff, Lachicotte, Illingworth, & Johnston, 1991; Leete, 1989; Liberman et al., 1986; Robson, 1988). Strauss (1992) suggests that the success of our interventions with the severely mentally ill depends significantly on the degree to which we connect with the "person" behind the disorder. This literature and longitudinal investigations, such as that by Harding, Zubin, and Strauss (1987), indicate that both our professional attitudes (Shera & Delva-Tauili'ili, 1996) and our

214

provider-driven approaches to the delivery of mental health care may not be meeting the needs of clients, many of whom do return over time to acceptable levels of social functioning.

Another important development that has had a major impact on my thinking has been the work of Charles Rapp and his colleagues at the University of Kansas. They have been instrumental in developing a strengths approach to practice with persons experiencing a mental illness (Rapp, 1998). It validates the historical and current strengths of individuals and recognizes that recovery occurs within a broad range of individual, family, and community resources.

The second area of practice and writing that has had a major impact on my work is empowerment practice. The literature on empowerment (Coyne, 1987; Swift & Levin, 1987; Zimmerman, 1990b, 1990c) describes interventions that actively involve consumers and their significant others in determining what will work. Rather than viewing the client as a passive receptacle for intervention, the professional can work collaboratively with the client and share responsibility for the design, implementation, monitoring, and evaluation of treatment plans (Boker, 1992; Corrigan, Liberman, & Engel, 1990; Coyne, 1987). Esso Leete (1992), a consumer advocate who has schizophrenia, claims that the behaviors of professionals are frequently disempowering and reinforce stigma toward the mentally ill:

> There is a lack of client choice in our treatment plans, our medication management, and our disposition after discharge. There is an insistence by the system that we do not know what is best for us and therefore need guardians and parents to make choices for us, even when we are not legally certified as incompetent. Clearly, mental health systems do not perceive that one of their duties should be the empowerment of the client, not enslavement. (p. 23)

Empowerment has been described as a multilevel construct that emphasizes health promotion, self and mutual help, and multiple definitions of competence (Fairweather & Fergus, 1993; Zimmerman, 1990a). Gutiérrez (1990) defines empowerment as a process of increasing personal, interpersonal, or political power so that individuals can take action to improve their life situations.

Some of the central features of the emerging empowerment paradigm in the field of mental health include: Clients are treated as subjects rather than objects; the focus is on clients' strengths rather than pathology; clients actively participate throughout the helping process; resources are seen as the total community rather than just formal services; emphasis is placed on the rejuvenation or creation of informal social networks; and monitoring, evaluation, and advocacy are done in a collaborative fashion.

Case Management

Deinstitutionalization of severely mentally ill adults began several decades ago in an effort to be more humane and to curb the high cost of caring for these individuals in institutions.

Community support programs were initiated by community mental health centers to link clients with needed resources. A critical component of these programs is case management services, which perform the linking function in the support program. A wide variety of models of case management have emerged (Robinson & Bergman, 1989), and guidelines for planning and implementing case management systems have been developed (National Institute of Mental Health, 1989).

Although in principle there is acceptance and support for case management services, we are only beginning to move toward determining their efficacy. Reviews of research on case management (Chamberlain & Rapp, 1991; Korr & Cloninger, 1991; Rubin, 1992; Solomon, 1992) have identified a number of directions for research and have emphasized the need for randomized, controlled trials to determine the efficacy of alternative approaches to delivering case management services. The National Institute of Mental Health (NIMH) has funded a number of case management research projects across the country (NIMH, 1990).

The literature in this area (Harris & Bergman, 1993; Raiff & Shore, 1993; Rose, 1992; Wilson, 1992) identifies a paradigm shift in both case management services and outcome research related to case management. This shift is described as moving from viewing people with psychiatric disabilities principally as service recipients to seeing them as having the potential for full community membership. Mirin and Namerow (1991) suggest that patients, as consumers of mental health care, are, and should be, playing a more active role in treatment design. An underlying assumption of this approach is that clients' perceptions regarding treatment efficacy and their satisfaction with the type and method of delivery will significantly influence which treatments and intended outcomes they will accept. Two models of case management that are illustrative of this emerging paradigm are the Strengths Model (Rapp, 1998) and the Advocacy/Empowerment Model (Rose, 1991, 1992). The Partnership Model employed in this study integrates and builds on the foundation work of these two models.

The Partnership Model

After extensive consultation and an exhaustive review of the appropriate literature, a six-module training manual on the Partnership Model of case management was developed for an experimental group of case managers. The modules that make up the Partnership Model detail such topics as values and attitudes for client-driven case management and strategies related to engagement, assessment and planning, partnership, monitoring and evaluation, and long-term support and disengagement.

Client-Driven Case Management: Values and Attitudes. This module specifically addresses the issue of stigma and uses a wide variety of materials to help case managers appreciate the importance of understanding the persons with whom they are working. This includes not only recognizing their value but also their history, their struggle, and their desire to regain personhood. Optimism and hopefulness are critical attitudes needed by workers to promote the empowerment of consumers who must also change their view of themselves from hopeless and self-doubting to hopeful and positive (Manning, 1998).

Engagement Strategies.   This module discusses the critical first contacts between consumers and the case manager. The module focuses on validating consumers' dignity and recognizing their willingness to work with the case manager. Effective practitioners begin immediately to promote clients' hopes and active participation by using a range of interpersonal skills and continually reinforcing the idea that clients are experts in their lives and full partners in the helping process (Miley, O'Melia, & DuBois, 2001). This module discusses a number of empowerment-based strategies needed to develop these collaborative working relationships.

Assessment and Planning Strategies.   In partnership assessment and planning, the service provider's task is to work collaboratively with the consumer to develop a plan to achieve consumer goals. This process includes a strengths assessment, a resources assessment, and a planning process in which the consumer is a full partner. Focusing and building on consumer strengths is a refreshing alternative to the deficit model and is congruent with social work values (Saleebey, 1997). Resources assessment recognizes that the client is embedded in family and community contexts that can provide a variety of supports. This module provides case managers with a variety of strategies to engage and maintain full consumer participation in this process of assessment and planning.

Partnership Intervention Strategies.   A central principle of this model is that interventions are the result of a collaborative process of planning and that both parties have equal obligations to ensure their implementation. It is critical that the consumer identifies goals, objectives, and the pace; however, it is equally important that the case manager provide honest feedback about the feasibility of what is being undertaken. The range of possible interventions is very broad, from individual supportive psychotherapy to building social networks in the community. The worker, in response to consumer goals, can provide valuable advice on feasible alternatives, including best-practice information (Shera, 2001). The consumer can suggest other alternatives or assess the situational and contextual appropriateness of what is being considered.

Partnership Monitoring and Evaluation.   This module speaks to the importance of continuous monitoring and evaluation in assessing the implementation and outcomes of intervention plans. Consumers are encouraged to develop self-monitoring to assess their own symptoms and service plans, and case managers monitor the quality of their work and that of other providers in working to meet the needs of consumers. A comprehensive evaluation identifies what works, clarifies the methods and strategies that a consumer uses most effectively, and empowers the consumer with information that might be useful in the future (Miley et al., 2001).

Long-Term Support and Disengagement.   This module helps case managers to recognize the need to initiate disengagement or to increase support during periods of high need. The consumer and case manager are encouraged to create ongoing communication strategies to ensure the appropriate level of involvement. Over time, consumers become more embedded in community-based services and networks and have less need for formal professional services. The quality of the relationship developed during the work together should encourage an honest dialogue about the resource limits of the worker and the changing nature of the consumer's need both for support and for independence.

The Partnership Model training package was the key resource for training the case managers involved in the experimental intervention. The initial training was conducted over a six-week period and then reinforced through ongoing individual and team supervision.

The Partnership Study

This study was a randomized clinical trial to compare the effectiveness of two models of case management for severely mentally ill adults. The first approach to case management, reflecting the current mode of service, was designated as the control condition in the study. This approach, essentially a Broker Model, emphasized provider-driven case management services. Case managers were trained to conduct diagnostic evaluations and to carry out treatment plans prescribed by the professional community. The second approach, the Partnership Model, used client-driven case management services. Case managers were trained to assess client strengths and capacities and to work collaboratively with clients to develop and implement personal plans.

The specific aims of the study were:

- to compare the level of psychological empowerment of severely mentally ill clients participating in the Partnership Model with clients participating in the Broker Model

- to compare the level of behavioral empowerment of severely mentally ill clients participating in the Partnership Model with clients participating in the Broker Model

Study Design

The design for this study was a two-group (treatment/control), pre/post test design. Participants were randomly selected from the service populations at the two study sites and randomly assigned to either the experimental or control condition. The designated sites were two community mental health centers, one urban and one rural.

Sample

Statistical power calculations indicated that at least 80 persons per condition were required to detect significant differences between the two groups. To account for attrition, an initial sample 25 percent larger than needed was selected. A total of 219 individuals with severe mental illness completed pretests. An analysis of the demographic data obtained in the pretests found that the study population did not statistically differ from those persons receiving services from the state's Adult Division of Mental Health.

Measures

The pre/post measures of psychological and behavioral empowerment were selected after a thorough review of available instruments and pilot testing of several instruments with the service population. The instruments that were selected assess changes in the individuals' perceptions of themselves, their own capabilities, and the degree to which individuals become socially integrated into the larger community.

To measure psychological empowerment, the study used instruments validated by others studying the concept (Zimmerman & Rappaport, 1988) or by researchers studying similar concepts with the severely mentally ill. Three instruments were selected because they were believed to measure individual aspects of psychological empowerment: (a) self-esteem, (b) self-efficacy, and (c) mastery.

The Index of Self Esteem (ISE) (Hudson, 1982) was developed during the late 1970s with the severely mentally ill and was subsequently revalidated (Abell, Jones, & Hudson, 1984). The scales for Self Efficacy (SEF) (Tipton & Worthington, 1985) and Mastery (MGML) (Pearlin, Meaghan, Lieberman, & Mullan, 1981) have been used in studies to measure individual dimensions of psychological empowerment (Zimmerman & Rappaport, 1988).

We expected the study subjects' perceptions of self-esteem, self-efficacy, and mastery to significantly improve as a result of working with case managers who systematically implemented the Partnership Model of case management, as opposed to those case managers who used the Broker Model.

As the psychological empowerment of experimental subjects changed, we also anticipated that they would exhibit changes in behavioral empowerment. Changes in behavior and increasing empowerment of study participants were to be exhibited by greater integration into the larger community, improved self-care, and increased proactivity in the working relationship with their case manager. These behavioral changes were measured with a second set of pre/post measures. The Role Functioning Scale (RFS) (McPheeters, 1984) consists of five subscales:

- working productivity
- extended social networks
- global personal distress
- independent living/self-care
- immediate social network relationships

The scale has been validated in various studies and has been found particularly useful in studies of the severely mentally ill (Green & Gracely, 1987). One subscale, Personal Care, of the Community Living Skills Scale (CLS) (Hill House, 1983) was also selected as a measure of behavioral empowerment. Respondents judge the degree to which they engage in nineteen personal-care behaviors (e.g., takes medication, does own shopping). This subscale was developed by a consumer group and proved reliable in comparative studies with more established measures such as the Global Assessment Scale (Smith & Ford, 1990). This instrument was administered both to study subjects and significant others (e.g., spouse or family member).

Finally, the Relationship with Case Manager Scale (RCM) assesses the interaction of the case manager and the study subject during the provision of case management services. This instrument was developed by the research project staff and the test-retest correlation with similar clientele at another community mental health center was .93.

The pretest data were analyzed to determine the reliability of each of the scales used in the study. Using the reliability procedure of SPSS-PC+, the reliability coefficients (Cronbach's alpha) were found to range from .71 to .92.

The scale means for each site were calculated and compared. There were no statistically significant differences for scale means between the two sites or between the treatment and control groups. These results indicate the equivalence, at the time of the pretest, of the study populations both by condition and site.

Monitoring Instruments

In addition to the outcome measures, a set of monitoring instruments was developed by the research team to facilitate the implementation of the intervention and to observe the operational differences in the two models of case management during the study period. Client monitoring instruments were used to track subject rates of hospitalization, changes in personal living status, changes in vocational/educational status, and the nature and extent of social networks available to the individual. Quarterly records also tracked the number of client goals established and achieved.

Results

A total of 219 clients completed all seven of the empowerment scales on the pretest. A total of 148 clients completed all seven scales on the posttest. Attrition analysis of the pretest data indicated no statistical difference between the 148 completers and the 71 noncompleters. A demographic profile of the 148 clients who completed the study is provided in Table 13.1.

A correlation matrix of the change scores of the seven empowerment scales indicated that the change scores of the three psychological empowerment scales (PES) were weakly intercorrelated and were also weakly correlated with the change scores of the four behavioral empowerment scales (BES). The change scores of the four BES were highly intercorrelated. The results of the correlation analysis supported the separateness of the two constructs (psychological and behavioral empowerment). Unfortunately, no statistically significant overall treatment effect was found on the changes of the three PES as well as the four BES.

t Tests were completed to determine if there were significant differences from pretest to posttest for control and treatment groups on any of the scales. Table 13.2 reveals that the control group had improved scores on community living skills, as rated

TABLE 13.1 *Demographic Characteristics of the 148 Subjects*

	N	%
Gender		
Female	65	43.9
Male	83	56.1
Ethnicity		
Hawaiian/Part Hawaiian	29	19.6
Caucasian	43	29.1
Japanese	47	31.8
Other	29	19.6
Education		
Postsecondary	31	21.1
Secondary	82	55.8
Presecondary	34	23.1
Age		
20–29	18	12.2
30–39	52	35.1
40–49	39	26.4
50–59	21	14.2
60 and older	18	12.2
Diagnosis		
Schizophrenic Disorders	95	64.2
Affective Disorders	29	19.6
Other Disorders	24	16.2

by assessor ($t = 3.06$, $df = 61$, $p < .002$), and role functioning ($t = 1.68$, $df = 61$, $p < .049$), whereas the treatment group had improved scores on community living skills, as rated by assessor ($t = 4.02$, $df = 85$, $p < .000$), role functioning ($t = 3.03$, $df = 85$, $p < .002$), and relationship with case manager ($t = 3.38$, $df = 85$, $p < .001$).

A stratified analysis using demographic variables such as gender, diagnosis, education, and ethnicity as the stratifying variables was performed to check if the demographic variables were confounding variables. The stratified analysis indicated that the overall results were the same for each level of diagnosis, education, and ethnicity.

The analysis on gender, however, indicated that the results were different for males and females. A statistically significant treatment effect for mastery was found for females ($F = 4.77$, $df = 1,61$, $p < .033$). Given the interesting and unanticipated gender effects in the study, we conducted a gender-specific stepwise backward deletion regression analysis for each scale with the remaining empowerment scales and demographic (DEMO) variables as possible predictors. The results are presented in Table 13.3.

TABLE 13.2   *Paired t Tests on Outcome Measures for Clients in Control and Treatment Groups*

Scale	Control Group (N = 62)				Treatment Group (N = 86)			
	Pre	Post	t	p ≤	Pre	Post	t	p ≤
Self-esteem[1]	41.13	40.03	−0.56	0.288	40.49	41.10	0.33	0.370
Self-efficacy	45.23	44.10	−0.76	0.226	45.43	43.91	−1.35	0.091
Mastery	30.40	31.77	1.31	0.97	29.86	31.14	1.29	0.100
Community[2] Living Skills[1]	61.53	62.92	0.98	0.166	62.55	62.60	0.06	0.478
Community[3] Living Skills[1]	56.98	61.25	3.06**	0.002	59.44	63.94	4.20***	0.000
Role Functioning	20.55	21.97	1.68*	0.049	20.98	23.44	3.03**	0.002
Relationship with Case Manager	8.16	8.57	1.23	0.112	8.60	9.86	3.38**	0.001

[1]Lower scores indicate higher level of self-esteem.
[2]Rated by service user.
[3]Rated by assessor.
*$p < .05$
**$p < .01$
***$p < .001$

For males, variables in all three sets (PES, BES, DEMO) were significant predictors for only community living skills, as rated by assessor. None of the PES variables significantly predicted role functioning or relationship with case manager. None of the BES variables predicted self-esteem, mastery, or community living skills (as rated by assessor). The demographic variables predicted only self-esteem, mastery, community living skills (as rated by assessor), and relationship with case manager.

For females, variables in all three sets (PES, BES, DEMO) were significant predictors only for self-esteem, self-efficacy, and community living skills (as rated by service user). At least one of the BES predicted all of the PES variables as well as the other two BES scales. The demographic variables predicted only self-esteem, self-efficacy, and community living skills.

As a final procedure to determine overall gender-specific treatment effect, we performed a gender-specific MANCOVA (Table 13.4). The only statistically significant finding was an overall treatment effect for males, specifically, an improvement in their relationship with their case managers ($F = 6.93$, $df = 1, 65$, $p < .011$).

Discussion and Implications

Although we did not find overall treatment effects for the Partnership Model of case management, we did find some robust and interesting gender–specific effects. Using ANOVA, treatment females showed significant gains in mastery, whereas treatment

TABLE 13.3 *Standardized Regression Scores by Gender and Dependent Variables*

	ISE		SEF		MGM		CLS		RFS	
SEX	F	M	F	M	F	M	F	M	F	M
ISLAND		.218*								
TRTGRP						.206*				
DIAG 1			−.323**							
DIAG 2	.350**									
RACE 1	−.229**						.335**			
RACE 2										
RACE 3										
EDUC 1										
EDUC 2										
ISE			−.512**	−.300**						
SEF	−.440**	−.399**			.272*	.474**		.388**		
MGM			.329**				.377**			
CLS			.227*	.307*						
RFS										
SCL	−.464**		−.510**		−.286*		.379**		.343**	.327**
RCM	.298*		.288*						.520**	.491**
ADJ R2	.442	.201								

*p <.05
**p <.01

males improved their working relationships with case managers. The finding for males was confirmed by a more detailed analysis (MANCOVA).

A number of limitations impeded a more complete test of this model of case management. The study was limited to 14 months, which is typically too short to demonstrate the type of significant outcomes desired with this population. The lack of intensity of treatment because of constantly increasing caseloads and some possibility of contamination across teams because of physical proximity may have also been relevant factors. Lastly, the balancing dynamics of gender may have played a role. On a number of the measures, a positive change or lack of change by the females was balanced by either a negative change or lack of change by the males, so no overall statistically significant change was found.

TABLE 13.4 *Multivariate Analysis of Covariance by Gender-Dependent Variable*

	DISE		DSEF		DMGM		DCLS		DRFS	
	F	M	F	M	F	M	F	M	F	M
TREAT	0.643	0.002	0.003	0.462	0.217	0.444	0.088	1.585	0.088	1.882
	0.427	0.961	0.957	0.499	0.643	0.507	0.768	0.213	0.929	0.175
ISLE	0.233	2.931	1.614	0.024	0.079	0.194	0.029	1.888	0.079	0.254
	0.631	0.092	0.211	0.878	0.780	0.661	0.866	0.174	0.780	0.616
T*1	0.886	0.103	0.391	0.257	0.053	0.339	0.458	0.477	0.807	2.640
	0.352	0.749	0.535	0.614	0.819	0.562	0.502	0.492	0.374	0.109
DIAG 1										
DIAG 2	2.64									
	.001***									
RACE 1					−2.36		2.02			
					.023*		.049*			
RACE 2										
RACE 3					−2.86					
					.006**					
EDUC 1									−2.10	
									0.41*	
EDUC 2			−2.03			−.254				
			.023*			.214				
DISE							−2.34			
							.024*			
DSEF								2.59		
								0.12*		
DMGM										
DCLS	−2.69		2.67		3.54	2.04				
	.010**		.009**		.001*	.046*				
DRFS										
DSCL			2.06		−3.79					
			.043*		.000***					
DRCM										

*p <.05
**p <.01
***p <.001

224

Although we do know that there are different patterns of onset, course, and symptomology between males and females with severe mental illnesses (Childers & Harding, 1990; Mowbray, Herman, & Hazel, 1992), some authors suggest that we have neglected gender effects in research on severe mental illness (Wahl & Hunter, 1992). There are only a limited number of studies in the area of severe mental illness that have specifically addressed gender-related differentials in treatment response (Dail & Koshes, 1992; Goering, Wasylenki, Stonge, Paduchak, & Lancee, 1992; Hass, Glick, Clarkin, Spencer, & Lewis, 1990).

A preliminary identification of factors that contribute to this differential includes: different social and occupational role demands, greater dependency of females on families, pre-morbid and inter-morbid functioning of clients, and differences in symptomology at time of admission (Hass et al., 1990). A major implication, both from previous research and from the current study on case management, is that we need to enhance our understanding of gender differences in the need for and response to treatment, so we can develop more gender-appropriate programs for the severely mentally ill.

From an empowerment perspective, the issue of gender differences is critical. Feminist theorists have underscored power as a central concept (Yoder & Kahn, 1992) in their work. They offer the perspective that power differences frequently underlie what appear to be gender differences in behavior: As society is currently configured, power and gender are never independent. Current constructs of empowerment, particularly as they are applied to working with the severely mentally ill, have not drawn on this perspective.

The case managers using the Partnership Model convinced us that the process of empowerment must be individualized, personalized, and contextualized. It must recognize each individual as unique and validate this by connecting with the "person behind the disorder" (Strauss, 1992). Readiness of consumers to engage in empowerment is also a critical concern. The study also underscored the importance of understanding empowerment as a multilevel construct. The agency, family, and community contexts within which people function provide both opportunities for and limitations on the empowerment of the severely mentally ill.

The Organizational Context of Empowerment

The case managers who were involved in the study believed that the Partnership Model had the potential to be very effective. The biggest barrier they identified was the caseload size. Many case managers wanted to work in partnership with consumers but felt disempowered within their organizational settings.

Empowerment at the organizational level is defined as a process of enhancing self-efficacy among organizational members by identifying conditions that foster powerlessness and removing them, both formally through organizational practices and informally by means of techniques that provide efficacy information (Conger &

Kanungo, 1988). Because of the bureaucratic, top-down nature of most organizations, employees have a greater tendency to become vulnerable as a result of lack of communication, to lose control in a patriarchal organizational culture, and to become helpless, a situation in which employees subscribe to the bureaucratic norms in order to survive. Vulnerability, loss of control, and a sense of helplessness, similar to conditions faced by clients, foster powerlessness. The task of removing these and other conditions, then, becomes a major focus in the process of developing a more empowered organization.

My subsequent work in this area has identified some of the lessons learned in reviewing the literature on organizational empowerment (Shera, 1998) and has identified a range of strategies for creating more effective organizations through strategies of empowerment (Shera & Page, 1995). Maximizing consumer voice in the design and delivery of services is a major responsibility of social workers in the field of mental health (Shera, 2001). An example of such a service is the Village in Long Beach, California. Strategies used in this system of care include assisting members in their homes, neighborhoods, and work settings; placing high priority on prevention of relapse; teaching consumers to advocate for themselves; focusing on work as a normalizing activity; and emphasizing quality in the delivery of services (Goodrick, 1995). Although these developments have significantly improved our understanding of how empowerment practice is operationalized in the field of mental health, further work is needed to deepen this understanding.

Continuing the Conversation

This study of a Partnership Model of case management served to enhance my understanding of the complexities and levels of empowerment practice with persons who are experiencing a severe mental illness. Although most writers agree that the construct of empowerment is multilevel, we are also only beginning to understand the interdependencies that connect the various levels. We are also beginning to appreciate how feminist, postmodern, and constructivist perspectives are infusing this approach with new vitality by addressing the social, structural, and systemic issues that act as impediments to the empowerment process (Shera & Wells, 1999).

In reviewing our experience with the Partnership Model, several critical questions emerge:

- How do we modify educational programs to shift the attitudes and practice skills of professionals to be more congruent with empowerment practice?
- What organizational conditions are most conducive to empowerment practice?
- Is it feasible to implement approaches such as the Partnership Model in the context of deficit-oriented, medically driven, managed behavioral health care systems?
- How can consumer groups contribute to the enhancement of empowerment practice in the field of mental health?

- Are the core concepts of the Partnership Model transferable to practice with families, service systems, and communities?
- Given the need to individualize and contextualize interventions, how do we develop research strategies to document their effectiveness?

A major impediment to the further development of empowerment practice has been the relative paucity of research on this approach. Recent efforts to develop, with the assistance of consumers, appropriate instruments for measuring both the processes and outcomes of empowerment are encouraging. The area also lends itself to a wide variety of studies employing a diversity of research methods, from tests of interventions to narrative studies. An emerging theme of this research is the importance of modeling the process of empowerment in the conduct of the research. This development is congruent with increasing experience and scholarship in the area of participatory research and empowerment evaluation (Whitmore, 1998).

Empowerment practice provides us with a dynamic, value-focused framework that is inclusive and consumer-focused and that addresses the structural inequities so prevalent in our society today. I have committed my future research and scholarship to the development of this important approach to practice in the hope that I can make a meaningful contribution.

References

Abell, N., Jones, B. L., & Hudson, W. (1984). Revalidation of the index of self esteem. *Social Work Research and Abstracts, 20*, 11–16.

Bednar, R. L., Wells, M. G., & VandenBos, G. R. (1991). Self-esteem: A concept of renewed clinical relevance. *Hospital and Community Psychiatry, 42*, 123–125.

Boker, W. (1992). A call for partnership between schizophrenic patients, relatives and professionals. *British Journal of Psychiatry, 161* (Suppl. 18), 10–12.

Chamberlain, R., & Rapp, C. A. (1991). A decade of case management: A methodological review of outcome research. *Community Mental Health Journal, 27*, 171–188.

Childers, S. E., & Harding, C. M. (1990). Gender, premorbid social functioning, and long-term outcome in DSM-III schizophrenia. *Schizophrenia Bulletin, 16*, 309–318.

Conger, J. A., & Kanungo, R. N. (1988). The empowerment process: Integrating theory and practice. *Academy of Management Review, 13*, 471–482.

Corrigan, P. W., Liberman, R. P., & Engel, J. D. (1990). From noncompliance to collaboration in the treatment of schizophrenia. *Hospital and Community Psychiatry, 41*, 1203–1211.

Coyne, J. C. (1987). The concept of empowerment in strategic therapy. *Psychotherapy, 24*, 539–545.

Dail, P. W., & Koshes, R. J. (1992). Treatment issues and treatment configurations for mentally ill homeless women. *Social Work in Health Care, 17*, 27–44.

Estroff, S. E. (1989). Self, identity, and subjective experiences of schizophrenia: In search of the subject. *Schizophrenia Bulletin, 15*, 189–196.

Estroff, S. E., Lachicotte, W. S., Illingworth, L. C., & Johnston, A. (1991). Everybody's got a little mental illness: Accounts of illness and self among people with severe, persistent mental illnesses. *Medical Anthropology Quarterly, 5*, 331–369.

Fairweather, G. W., & Fergus, O. F. (1993). *Empowering the mentally ill.* Austin, TX: Fairweather Publishing.

Goering, P., Wasylenki, D., Stonge, M., Paduchak, D., & Lancee, W. (1992). Gender differences among clients of a case management program for the homeless. *Hospital and Community Psychiatry, 43*, 160–165.

Goodrick, D. (1995). Integrating values, resources, and strategies to achieve outcomes. *California Alliance for the Mentally Ill, 4*(2), 61–65.

Green, R. S., & Gracely, E. J. (1987). Selecting a rating scale for evaluating services to the chronically mentally ill. *Community Mental Health Journal, 23,* 91–102.

Gutiérrez, L. M. (1990). Working with women of color: An empowerment perspective. *Social Work, 35,* 149–153.

Harding, C. M., Zubin, J., & Strauss, J. S. (1987). Chronicity in schizophrenia: Fact, partial fact, or artifact. *Hospital and Community Psychiatry, 38,* 477–486.

Harris, M., & Bergman, H. C. (1993). *Case management for mentally ill patients: Theory and practice.* Langhorne, PA: Harwood Academic Publishers.

Hass, G. L., Glick, I. D., Clarkin, J. F., Spencer, J. H., & Lewis, A. B. (1990). Gender and schizophrenia outcome: A clinical trial of an inpatient family intervention. *Hospital and Community Psychiatry, 16,* 277–292.

Hill House. (1983). *The Client Oriented Program Evaluation (COPE); the Community Living Skills Scale.* Columbus, OH: Ohio Department of Mental Health.

Hudson, W. W. (1982). *The clinical measurement package: A field manual.* Homewood, IL: Dorsey Press.

Korr, W. S., & Cloninger, L. (1991). Assessing models of case management: An empirical approach. *Journal of Social Service Research, 14,* 129–147.

Leete, E. (1989). How I perceive and manage my illness. *Schizophrenia Bulletin, 15,* 197–200.

Leete, E. (1992). The stigmatized patient. In P. J. Fink & A. Tasman (Eds.), *Stigma and Mental Illness* (pp. 17–25). Washington, DC: American Psychiatric Press.

Liberman, R. P., Mueser, K. T., Wallace, C. J., Jacobs, H. E., Eckman, T., & Massel, H. K. (1986). Training skills in the psychiatrically disabled: Learning coping and competence. *Schizophrenia Bulletin, 12,* 631–647.

Manning, S. (1998). Empowerment in mental health programs: Listening to the voices. In L. Gutierrez, R. Parsons, & E. Cox (Eds.), *Empowerment in social work practice: A sourcebook* (pp. 89–109). Pacific Grove, CA: Brooks/Cole Publishing.

McPheeters, H. L. (1984). Statewide mental health outcome evaluation: A perspective of two southern states. *Community Mental Health Journal, 20,* 44–55.

Miley, K., O'Melia, M., & DuBois, B. (2001). *Generalist social work practice: An empowering approach* (3rd ed.). Boston: Allyn & Bacon.

Mirin, S. M., & Namerow, M. J. (1991). Why study treatment outcome? *Hospital and Community Psychiatry, 42,* 1007–1013.

Mowbray, C. T., Herman, S. E., & Hazel, K. L. (1992). Gender and serious mental illness: A feminist perspective. *Psychology of Women Quarterly, 16,* 107–126.

National Institute of Mental Health. (1989). *Guidelines for planning and implementing case management systems, P.L. 99-660, Title V* (DHHS Publication). Washington, DC: U.S. Government Printing Office.

National Institute of Mental Health. (1990, April). Community research program: Research demonstration projects. Rockville, MD: Author.

Pearlin, L. I., Meaghan, E. G., Lieberman, M. A., & Mullan, J. T. (1981). The stress process. *Journal of Health and Social Behavior, 22,* 347–348.

Raiff, N. R., & Shore, B. K. (1993). *Advanced case management: New strategies for the nineties.* Newbury Park, CA: Sage Publications.

Rapp, C. (1998). *The strengths model: Case management with people suffering from severe and persistent mental illness.* New York: Oxford University Press.

Robinson, G. K., & Bergman, G. T. (1989). *Choices in case management: A review of current knowledge and practice for mental health programs* (Contract No. 278–87–0026). Washington, DC: National Institute of Mental Health.

Robson, P. J. (1988). Self-esteem: A psychiatric view. *British Journal of Psychiatry, 153,* 6–15.

Rose, S. M. (1991). Strategies of mental health programming: A client-driven model of case management. In C. Hudson & A. Cox (Eds.), *Dimensions of state mental health* (pp. 139–154). New York: Praeger.

Rose, S. M. (1992). *Case management and social work practice.* New York: Longman.

Rubin, A. (1992). Is case management effective for people with serious mental illness? A research review. *Health and Social Work, 17,* 138–150.

Saleebey, D. (1997). *The strengths perspective in social work practice* (2nd ed.). New York: Longman.

Shera, W. (1998). Constructing and deconstructing organizations: An empowerment perspective. In C. Franklin & P. S. Narvis (Eds.), *Constructivism in practice* (pp. 311–322). Milwaukee, WI: Families International.

Shera, W. (2001). Managed care and the severely mentally ill: Current issues and future challenges. In N. Veeder & W. Peebles-Wilkins (Eds.), *Managed care services: Policy, programs, and research* (pp. 230–242). New York: Oxford University Press.

Shera, W., & Delva-Tauili'ili, J., (1996). Changing MSW students' attitudes towards the severely mentally ill. *Community Mental Health Journal*, *32*, 159–169.

Shera, W., & Page, J. (1995). Creating more effective human service organizations through strategies of empowerment. *Administration in Social Work*, *19*, 1–15.

Shera, W., & Wells, L. (Eds.). (1999). *Empowerment practice in social work: Developing richer conceptual foundations*. Toronto, Canada: Canadian Scholars' Press.

Smith, M. K., & Ford, J. (1990). A client-developed functional level scale: The Community Living Skills Scale. *Journal of Social Service Research*, *13*, 61–85.

Solomon, P. (1992). The efficacy of case management services for severely mentally disabled clients. *Community Mental Health Journal*, *28*, 163–180.

Strauss, J. S. (1992). The person—Key to understanding mental illness: Towards a new dynamic psychiatry, III. *British Journal of Psychiatry*, *161*(Suppl. 18), 19–26.

Swift, C., & Levin, G. (1987). Empowerment: An emerging mental health technology. *Journal of Primary Prevention*, *8*, 71–95.

Tipton, R. M., & Worthington, E. L. (1985). The measurement of generalized self efficacy: A study of construct validity. *Journal of Personality Assessment*, *48*, 345–348.

Wahl, O. T., & Hunter J. (1992). Are gender effects being neglected in schizophrenia research? *Schizophrenia Bulletin*, *18*, 313–317.

Wilson, S. F. (1992). Community support and community integration: New directions for client outcome research. In S. M. Rose (Ed.), *Case management and social work practice* (pp. 245–257). New York: Longman.

Whitmore, E. (1998). *Understanding and practicing participatory evaluation. New directions for evaluation, No. 80*. San Francisco: Jossey-Bass Publishers.

Yoder, J. D., & Kahn, A. S. (1992). Toward a feminist understanding of women and power. *Psychology of Women Quarterly*, *16*, 381–388.

Zimmerman, M. A. (1990a). Taking aim on empowerment research: On the distinction between individual and psychological conceptions. *American Journal of Community Psychology*, *18*, 169–177.

Zimmerman, M. A. (1990b). Toward a theory of learned hopefulness: A structural model of analysis of participation and empowerment. *Journal of Research in Personality*, *24*, 71–86.

Zimmerman, M. A. (1990c). Empowerment; Forging new perspectives in mental health. In J. Rappaport & E. Seldman (Eds.), *Handbook of community psychology*. New York: Plenum Press.

Zimmerman, M. A., & Rappaport, J. (1988). Citizen participation, perceived control, and psychological empowerment. *American Journal of Community Psychology*, *16*, 729–737.

14

Unacknowledged Resources of Aging: Empowerment for Older Adults

Karla Krogsrud Miley

I never expected to work in the field of aging services. My experiences in graduate school focused on children, and my first job as a school social worker in suburban Chicago further solidified my interest in working with children and their families. Several years later, my husband, our two young children, and I were living in a small, relatively isolated farming community in south central Illinois. I was enjoying being a stay-at-home mom until an unexpected call from the local nursing home administrator led to a job in aging services. This launched a change in the direction in my career as a social worker and a journey of learning about aging from the best possible teachers—the older adults with whom I was privileged to work.

When I was a young adult in my thirties, I didn't foresee the relevance of my experiences in aging services to our family, and I didn't realize that I would learn from another master teacher—my mother, who chose to move from Minneapolis to Illinois when she could no longer live independently. "Little Mother," as she was affectionately called by our friends, was short in stature, but not in wisdom, although she would be the last to describe herself as wise. As the disease process of Alzheimer's progressed, my mother sometimes drifted into metaphors to communicate her thoughts and feelings. I learned to listen to the power of her word images rather than to get bogged down in grief over her limitations. For example, she insisted that the Adult Day Center was a school. She was intent on getting up "in time" for the bus (sometimes the middle of the night), and she thought her "teachers" were remiss in not assigning homework! Over time she revealed that her hope was to relearn the basics. "After all," she said, "I'm not so smart anymore, and I want to be able to read again." To her, the day center had become her ray of hope, as indeed it was for many older adults in our community. My mother modeled trust in others in the midst of a world she couldn't remember and often didn't understand, courage in spite of her fears, and resilience in the face of the many changes in her life. In the face of degenerating bodily functions and even when she could no longer speak, she taught dignity, the meaning of commitment to others, and, above all, patience and peace in waiting for death. My mother taught me important lessons throughout her life; however, in many ways, her instruction on the roles of aging mother and adult daughter was as powerful as anything I learned as a child.

Finally, as a middle-aged woman, I am beginning to process my own aging. Ten years ago, I couldn't imagine being retired. Although I'm not quite ready to relinquish the role of college professor, I now dream about the possibilities, and among those possibilities is changing our views of aging. When I talk with my developmental psychology students about issues in older adulthood, I tell them that there are two good reasons to realign their view of aging to one of success and resilience. One reason is self-preservation: They themselves are aging, so a positive view will contribute to their own successful aging process. The second is also self-preservation, although from a different angle: I remind them that members of my age cohort were initiated into adulthood through participating in marches, sit-ins, and protests, and through developing coalitions to promote social change. As older adults, we are likely to apply those skills with renewed energy to ensure opportunities for our own successful aging by confronting ageist attitudes and confining policies, programs, and services.

These three intertwining paths of learning have led me on my journey toward an empowerment perspective for older adults—the pathways of learning from my clients, my personal experiences with my mother, and my own experiences with aging. As a whole, my experiences suggest that several elements of empowerment—telling life stories, promoting expertise, and honoring self-determination—are particularly important in discovering the heretofore-unacknowledged resources of aging. I have incorporated a series of vignettes, drawn from my professional and personal experiences with older adults, into a conceptual framework that highlights these facets of empowerment.

Telling Life Stories

Life stories provide patterns of connection and form the basis of human identity. According to Saleebey (1997a), "cultural and personal stories and lore are often profound sources of strength, guidance, stability, comfort, or transformation and are often overlooked, minimized or distorted" (p. 51). The stories that are important to people represent the reservoir of their strengths. Reminiscences reveal the storyteller's abilities, characteristics, past accomplishments, networks of support, and survivorship skills. To recognize strengths in older adults, particularly those whose health is frail, we need a vision of their resourcefulness unobstructed by ageism. To access the power of life stories, we need to understand the processes of reminiscence and life review. Finally, to understand the significance of life stories, we draw on the narrative perspective.

Obscuring Our Views of Strengths

Shortly after I began working at the nursing home, someone asked me how I could stand to work in a place where decrepit old people, who had no purpose left in life, lined up in wheelchairs, waiting to die. I was stunned both by the question and my response to it. I said something like, "What do you mean decrepit and worthless! You're talking about real people with hopes, desires, and purposes. You have to look beyond appearances to understand who they really are!" The question reflects the pervasive force of ageism and negative stereotyping. It reflects the barrage of negative images of decline and disease that we often associate with aging. I found that as I got to know the residents as people, my images of aging changed. Listening to life stories, and seeing them as sources of strength and potential, requires hearing that is unobstructed by ageism.

Understanding more clearly the actualities of aging helps us to place aging processes in perspective, differentiating aging from disease, thereby confronting the ingrained ageism present in our society. Misconceptions about aging, such as believing most older adults have significant health issues, are forgetful and incapable of learning, and live unproductive lives (Rowe & Kahn, 1998), suggest that the norm for older adults is physical and cognitive decline and withdrawal from activities and social interactions. In fact, studies suggest that "many of the physical and mental problems of older Americans—once inaccurately blamed on aging—are, in fact, due to disease" (Pryor, 1994, p. 12). Ageism persists even though the lives of most aging adults, even many of those older adults whose health is frail, contradict this view of aging. By maintaining an ageist bias, we are likely to overlook the valuable capacities, contributions, and resources of older adults (Grant, 1996; Woolf, n.d.).

Discovering Strengths through Reminiscence

Reminiscing is the process of recollecting experiences and telling (and retelling) stories that capture the storyteller's perceptions and interpretations of life past. Of reminiscing, Schlarch (1994) says, "we remember; and through our memories, we create ourselves, both for ourselves and in relationship to other people. Through that self-construction, we add consistency to our lives and to our sense of self. And through that consistency, a sense of emotional protection" (p. 22). As such, reminiscing provides meaning and continuity to our lives. Even if not factually accurate, reminiscing and the narration of memoir provide powerful metaphors for what we believe is significant in our life experiences.

Clearly, reminiscence has face value; however, studies suggest additional benefits. Webster (1999) reports on the results of several studies that use the Reminiscence Functions Scale to identify the roles and functions of reminiscing. Among the dimensions these studies identify are problem-solving, or tapping recollections of past problem-solving activities; social bonding, or using stories as ways to connect and reconnect with others; intimacy maintenance, or using recollected images of persons to remember the warmth of emotional bonds in their absence; and teaching and informing, or sharing life stories as ways to communicate morality messages. In one large-scale (N = 710) age comparison study, no age differences were identified in how the respondents, ages 17 to 91, utilized reminiscence. This study demonstrates that reminiscing is not an activity reserved for older adults, nor is reminiscence universal. For example, Webster describes another study based on a sample of centenarians that found that nearly 50 percent of the respondents reported no life-review activities. Interestingly, reminiscence for those who no longer remember words seems to involve powerful images of context and emotion (Woodward, 1994).

Martha's Story: Drawing on Survival Strengths

I remember Martha's stories about living through the Dust Bowl years in Kansas. How she loved to tell about the ingenious ways she and her first husband managed to provide for their children: how they built a sod hut, battled the blowing dust, and nurtured a small garden in impossible conditions. She talked about the visual illusions created by the ever-blowing prairie grass and swirling dust. The only distinguishable landmark near their home was a lone tree on the southwest horizon. Martha always worried that they would lose their way to and from the trading post, located several miles away. In the summer, tall grass grew higher than the roof of their hut; in the winter, blowing snow made travel even riskier. She and her husband created an ingenious system of ropes marking paths so they could do chores and find the privy without danger of getting lost. When they eventually came back to Illinois, they returned, not as defeated farmers, but as survivors of difficult times. Martha's stories took on renewed significance in their retelling. I believe she was drawing on the courage, ingenuity, and survival skills of her youth to deal with the difficulties she faced as she grew older.

Pat's Story: Finding Sources of Hope

One of the things that has always fascinated me about my husband's Southern family is their accumulation of stories dating back to the Revolutionary War. My father-in-law, Pat, was a remarkable storyteller. He would often hold us spellbound with his tales of low-country swamps and alligators, fascinating adventures of years past, and family memories passed down through the generations. The summer he died he told stories over and over again about his parents, how they met, where they got married, and what it was like for him to grow up as a Miley in the low country of South Carolina. When we visited, he had us searching for wedding presents he knew had been given to his parents, for pictures of his boyhood home, for books that had been annotated, and for letters that had been carefully stored away on the upper shelves of closets. He kept a plat book by his chair so he could show us the exact locations of his stories. He was particularly interested in reminiscing about South Island, where his parents were married and he was probably conceived. When he died a few weeks later, my mother-in-law told us that his death was peaceful: "It was like Pat had packed his suitcase and traveled joyfully to his beloved South Island." We all knew reminiscing was meaningful to Pat; however, it was this comment that provides insight into the deeper meaning of the stories that were integral to the end of Pat's own life story. He was drawing on his recollections of his beginnings (his genesis) as he prepared for his last journey with a sense of optimism and hope. Eric Erikson (1963) suggests that the ultimate foundation for hopefulness is the legacy of our infancy and trusting relationships with our parents. In his last book, *Vital Involvement in Old Age* (Erikson, Erikson, & Kivnick, 1994), he and his colleagues make clear the significance of life stories as a way to realize a sense of integration in the whole perspective of the cycle of life.

Understanding the Significance of Life Stories

There is an intricate relationship among life stories, reminiscing, and narrative. According to Webster (1999):

> The stories we tell about ourselves, of necessity, invoke certain types of memories. When those retrieved memories take the form of personally experienced episodes from our past, we are reminiscing. When reminiscences are logically cojoined and sequentially patterned we have a form of simple narrative.

Rosen (1996), indicates that "knowledge, and the meaning we imbue it with, is a construction of the human mind. The way we represent what we know to ourselves does not bear a one-to-one correspondence with a given external reality existing independently of our knowledge of it" (p. 5). As Rosen says, "we are born into stories: the stories of our parents, our families, and our culture. These made meanings, which predate us and envelop us upon our arrival into the world, can be constraining, even imprisoning, or they can be freeing and liberating" (p. 23). Rosen further explains:

> Everyone has a story to tell. Most stories are a mixture of pain, suffering, frustration, and shame on the one hand and pleasure, joy, satisfaction, and pride on the other hand. . . . Yet often, people who risk revealing their stories to others find relief and, sometimes, even release. They have been trapped in their respective stories and the simple act of telling these stories to others brings new meaning and perspective to people's lives. (p. 29)

As we learned in Chapter 11, Gergen (1999) emphasizes the influence of sociocultural contexts on knowledge and meaning. This social construction of reality applies to our present state of knowledge as well as our legacy of meaning. The very process of telling stories is embedded in our contexts of family and culture. Through telling and retelling of stories, we make meaning and restory our lives, refining the foundation of identity that forms our future (Dean, 1993; Freedman & Combs, 1996; White & Epston, 1990).

Promoting Expertise

There are many ways to characterize expertise—capacities, competence, acumen, and inventiveness, to name a few. Sometimes expertise is obvious; other times it is hidden or undiscovered. Even when people run into difficulties, they still have expertise, the expertise of being the most qualified expert about their own situations. For social workers, fostering client expertise can have a profound effect on our work with others. As a tenet of empowerment, it necessitates a new balance of power, elevating clients to the status of collaborative partners. Strategies to promote the expertise of older adults include drawing on strengths-oriented conversations and maintaining their active participation in plans that evolve. Perspectives on successful aging and resiliency add further dimensions to our understanding of expertise.

Enhancing Active Participation through Strengths-Focused Conversations

Orienting conversations toward strengths is a foundational strategy for empowerment-based social work practice (Miley, O'Melia, & DuBois, 2001). This approach to conversations honors the inherent potential of those involved. According to Saleebey (1997a), identifying strengths is a conduit for discovering the stories, narratives, and cultural perspectives that form the core of one's identity. "Personal and familial parables of falls from grace and redemption, of failure and resurrection, of struggle and resilience may also provide the diction, the metaphors from which one may construct a more vibrant vision of the self and world" (p. 51). Strengths-oriented conversations provide resources for coping with current concerns.

Working collaboratively with clients is a second avenue for promoting expertise. A key element in maintaining clients' active participation is ensuring that they have access to information, the power base of decision-making. With respect to working with older adults, the kinds of information they might need includes such details of their current situations as the implications and requirements of their health conditions, the differences between aging and disease, their options for programs and services and the extent to which they qualify, and the availability of support within their network of family members and friends. As advocates, we ensure the rights of clients to exercise their power of choice. Given the effects of Alzheimer's disease or other degenerative disorders, promoting expertise takes a different form. It requires a creative imagination and flexibility to see beyond the disabilities and imitations to locate possibilities and strengths.

Mack's Story: Uncovering Hidden Strengths

When I think of Mack, I always smile, remembering his delightful sense of humor and the dramatic changes he experienced when we discovered his hidden talents. A massive stroke had resulted in incontinence, little strength on the right side of his body, and an inability to speak. Mack transferred to the nursing home after a lengthy hospitalization and relatively unsuccessful experience in a rehabilitation center. There was little joy in Mack's life except on those Fridays when his buddies took him uptown to the tavern to have a few beers.

Coincidentally, I was working the Saturday he had a major falling out with his family over his Friday night adventures. Mack happened to be in one of the lounges when his daughter came storming in. She was obviously distraught when she accused her dad of loving his drinking buddies and ignoring his family. "You can talk, Dad; I heard you with my own ears, singing and having a good time at the bar. What have I ever done to you that you should be so mean to me? If you really loved me, Dad, you'd talk to me, too." Mack just sat in his wheelchair with tears welling up in his eyes, looking bewildered. His daughter was grabbing her coat to leave when I walked into the lounge. She told me the full story when I asked if there was some way I could be helpful. Basic information about the brain—the left-brain location of language and the right-brain location of music and singing and the impact of Mack's stroke on his ability to speak, but not on his ability to sing—helped resolve the misunderstanding. After that, Mack typically treated me to a song when he saw me in his corridor.

Solving his problem with incontinence was more challenging. The nursing staff had exhausted the possibilities, but Mack's serenades gave me an idea. If communication was the issue, why not use his talent for singing? He was enthusiastic, but thought of an even better plan himself: whistling. He developed quite an intricate system for signaling staff. They loved it, and he was a proud man. That exercise of control made a significant difference to his level of life satisfaction and sense of personal well-being.

Marge's Story: Breaking Out of Limitations and Exercising Choice

Consider the example of Marge, a woman who had a long history of revolving-door admissions and discharges from one of the state mental hospitals. Her bouts with depression began in her forties and plagued her much of her adult life. She came to the nursing home after living in several other facilities that had accepted large numbers of individuals who were discharged from the state hospital as a result of deinstitutionalization. She was a pleasant woman, with a gait that revealed her struggle with Parkinson's disease, a gentle spirit, and eyes that communicated with others even though she hadn't spoken for several years. Her family had requested placement in the local nursing home because the staff had a reputation for personalized care and because they wanted to "have Mom living closer to home."

At the first meeting to discuss Marge's care plan, the staff doctor agreed that Marge might be reacting adversely to the Parkinson's medication and prescribed withdrawal from the medication. The results were amazing. The involuntary movements characteristic of Parkinson's disease returned, but Marge regained control of her tongue and began to talk! One of her first questions was, "Where's my husband? Why doesn't he visit?" She didn't know her husband had died several years earlier because her adult children had decided not to tell her of his death, reasoning that their mother no longer connected enough to reality to understand.

I remember the family members' struggle in deciding how best to approach their mother, and their worry that she would turn away from them in anger. I suggested that they tell the truth—that they were concerned about her well-being and had no idea that she was aware of her circumstances. United in their decision to confess their secret, they decided to hold a private family meeting the next evening, including as many family members as possible.

I spent time with Marge the day after she learned of her husband's death. I shall always remember her reaction because it so powerfully reflected her ability to forgive and reconcile with her family. She said, "I'm so relieved. I thought I had been abandoned! Of course, I'm sad, but I now understand why he stopped coming to see me.

I've missed him so." When we spoke of her children's keeping the death secret, Marge grabbed my hand and said, "I do wish my children had told me, but I know they love me and thought they were taking care of me. Now they've shown how much they love me by their courage in coming to me with the truth."

After she began to come to terms with her grief, Marge was an active participant on the residents' council, and a regular at various social events and activities. Well-liked by residents and staff, she played a key role in helping others understand the plight of those who for one reason or another had lost their ability to speak. People might not expect that someone with such a long history of mental illness and institutionalization would have within her the ability to achieve such a satisfactory resolution to her life story. Clearly, focusing on strengths has the power to uncover innumerable resources for change.

A year or so later, the staff doctor told Marge about a different medication that was available to treat Parkinson's disease. After obtaining the doctor's solemn promise to abide by her instruction to withdraw the medication if she became disoriented, she agreed to a trial run. Unfortunately, the dreaded side effects appeared within a few days. I spoke with her after the new medication had washed out of her system. "That's okay," she said, "I had hoped I wouldn't have to endure the shaking the rest of my life, but I have a choice. I'd rather tremble than not be able to communicate. I was lost for so long in silence. I'm just glad that I was found; I cherish the gift of being able to speak and know myself again."

Dorothy's Story: Adapting to Her Strengths

During the earlier stages of my mother's disease, it was evident that Dorothy needed support. She had difficulty making decisions, thinking things through, and planning ahead, but she could still, as she said, "do her part" by helping out with day-to-day household tasks. As her disease progressed, I faced the challenge of figuring out how to structure tasks so that we could continue to work side-by-side. For example, she couldn't follow a recipe, but she could mix ingredients; she was unable to decide which silverware to select from the drawer, but she could set the table if I put everything out; and she took seriously her nightly role as "cat guard," ensuring that Quick Silver, our sneaky cat, didn't assume that the meal on the dining room table was for him.

As I reflect on my mother's reactions to the ravages of advanced Alzheimer's disease, I think she grieved deeply about her inability to do things as she had in the past. One afternoon when I was rushing around, she spoke with remarkable lucidity when she opened her eyes from a power nap. "Karla, Karla, Karla," she said. "Sit down to be *with* me. That's more important than doing, doing, doing. Learn from me how to patiently wait." Looking back, I realize I was listening to an existential expert instructing me on an ultimate value, valuing ourselves for who we are.

Considering the Meaning of Success and Resiliency in Aging

A new emphasis marks the advent of the new century, differentiating aging per se from disease processes. To mark the shift in the formal study of aging, researchers use different labels, including healthy aging (Bellos, 1992), productive aging (Holstein, 1992; Morrow-Howell, 2000), resourceful aging (Heil & Marks, 1991), successful aging (Baltes & Baltes, 1990; Freund & Baltes, 1998; Kivnick & Jernstedt, 1996; Rowe & Kahn, 1997, 1998; Schulz & Heckhausen, 1996), and, borrowing from a long tradition in the literature on responses to stress, resiliency in aging (Gutheil & Congress, 2000). These views give rise to hope among those of us who are approaching older adulthood. For example, based on the results of the MacArthur Foundation study of aging, Rowe and Kahn (1998) conclude that three elements underlie successful aging: "avoiding disease and disability, continuing engagement with life, including both social relationships and productive activity, [and] maintaining mental and physical functioning" (p. 49). These results suggest that aging successfully involves preventing decline and creatively adapting to any changes that occur, such as in sensory capacities or mobility, to minimize their potentially negative impact.

Another example, a qualitative study by Fisher and Specht (1999), explores other characteristics of successful aging, including such factors as having positive interactions with others, opportunities for growth, sense of purpose, and independence. They also identified a relationship between creativity and successful aging. As one sixty-nine-year-old respondent remarked, "If you're going to age successfully, you're coping. Creativity involves everything you do—an emotional or mental coping. Life itself is a matter of creativity, especially when you're older, because you have the time to think about the challenges and come up with solutions." Or, according to another respondent, "It [creativity] gives you an interest, something to look forward to, something to fill your mind and days. I think you have to have an interest. There's nothing more exciting than having a new project."

Rowe and Kahn (1998) predict that "gerontologists of the new millennium will increasingly focus on how to promote successful aging, or how older adults can retain the ability to function in their environments as they age" (p. xiii). Clearly, social workers will need to expand their roles in aging services to include leadership in prevention initiatives and community education for aging adults.

However, a question lingers: If older adults experience declines in health and mobility, does this mean they've failed to age successfully? If our emphasis is on linkages between health and success, are we in danger of judging harshly older adults whose health is poor? Some claim we are (Scheidt & Humpherys, 1999; Gutheil & Congress, 2000). If our definition of success is limited to health, then it's logical to assume that those older adults with physical disabilities or cognitive frailties have somehow failed the test of success. However, as we have discovered through the examples in this chapter, many older adults, even those whose health is marked by substantial decline demonstrate considerable strength and resilience, most certainly indicators of authentic success.

According to Gutheil and Congress (2000), "resilience in old age may be best thought of as the ability to survive and overcome numerous major stressors, including disease, disability, and a range of other major losses" (p. 42). Contributing factors include the ability to reframe the meaning of stress, maintain a sense of mastery, demonstrate flexibility, and draw on the resources of social support. Longstanding research suggests that one's sense of personal control contributes to psychological well-being (Smith et al., 2000; Taylor, Kemeny, Reed, Bower, & Gruenewald, 2000). "Resilience is fostered by interdependence with others and grounded in the ability to adapt to changing demands" (p. 44). Finally, "resilience is not the cheerful disregard of one's difficult and traumatic life experiences; neither is it the naïve discounting of life's pains. It is, rather, the ability to bear up in spite of these ordeals" (Saleebey, 1997b, p. 9).

An empowerment orientation to social work presses us to search for and enhance resilience. Only then can we identify many varieties of "success." Even for those older adults who seem to have given up, fostering resiliency is a catalyst for hope.

Honoring Self-Determination

Self-determination presupposes having options and then having opportunities to make decisions about those options freely rather than by coercion (DuBois & Miley, 2002). Being able to exercise choice is fundamental to empowerment and plays a significant role in one's sense of well-being. For example, a Swedish study of the daily life of the "oldest old" living independently with the assistance of community-based supports, points to the importance of directly involving clients in decision-making (Carlsson-Ågren, Berg, & Wenestam, 1992). The researchers found that respondents who exercised more control over their own lives were better adjusted. In contrast, those who were not as well-adjusted were more likely controlled by external forces than by their own choices. The study concluded that plans for caregiving interventions should be driven by the personal preferences of the participants. The following sections explore facets of self-determination, including details related to promoting involvement, the significance of accepting individuals' choices, and inherent dilemmas.

Promoting Involvement

Promoting involvement takes on different forms depending on the circumstances. In some instances, clients fully expect to be involved, and we define our roles as simply ones that support their assertiveness. In other instances, particularly when older adults are frail or expect us to be experts who will tell them what to do, we must apply more sophisticated skills to encourage their active involvement. When abilities to communicate are limited, we must be flexible and innovative in creating dialogue that fosters involvement.

Dorothy's Story: Finding Her Voice in Her World of Silence

One of the tragedies of Alzheimer's disease is that, over time, it strips people of their abilities to communicate their cherished life stories, and thus, creates barriers to those resources from the past they can draw on to make meaning of their lives. I recognized the importance of life stories in my work with older adults who were experiencing dementia, but the significance of family members and the difficulties they faced became clearer to me as I journeyed with my mother. I can remember initially wondering about what to say when my mother lost her ability to speak. I had to recall my advice to others in similar circumstances—listen to their eyes and carry on—simple advice for an extraordinarily difficult task. Often, I would ask, "What do you want to talk about tonight, mother?" and then offer some possibilities until her eyes told me I'd hit the jackpot! Often, favored topics were the stories that she had told me over and over in the past. One of the nurses commented to me that she noticed that I always spoke with my mother as if she were a real part of the conversation. I don't know if my mother actually understood my words, or if understanding really mattered. I do know she responded to my presence, my touch, my smell, and the sound of my voice. I honestly believe she took part in the conversation in her own way. The style of conversation simply had to change to accommodate her disability; the process of respect for her as a person remained the same.

Looking back on my mother's experience with Alzheimer's disease, I have a greater appreciation for the tenacity required of family members to ensure that their loved ones continue to have a voice in decision-making. I was bombarded by advice from many medical professionals and some well-meaning friends about decisions that I should make for my mother. I braced myself for their responses to my assertion that I would need to talk this over with Dorothy, because, after all, she needed to have her say in any decisions.

I found that even when she could no longer speak, my mother continued to express her views. For example, after my mother took up residence in a nursing home, I visited with her almost every evening at dinnertime. One day, when I arrived a little late, an aide indicated that Dorothy was being very uncooperative. She had spit out the sauerkraut the aide had sneaked into her mouth, sealed her mouth tightly, and then batted the plate away. "What do you suppose Dorothy's saying to you?" I asked (knowing that my mother hated even the smell of sauerkraut). With a look of sudden insight and eagerness to please, the aide said, "She doesn't like this food! I'll get her the substitute meal!" As I replied, "I know Dorothy thanks you for listening and understanding," I saw my mother's eyes brighten and she gave us her best smile, as if to say, "I like to eat what I like to eat and nothing else!" My mother was not particularly assertive in her younger years, but as an older woman, even with the degeneration of Alzheimer's disease, she held her own.

Accepting Individual Choices

Choices are unique, as are the ways people inform us of their decisions. Influenced by numerous contingencies, choices reflect the unique perspectives of decision-makers, including their perceptions and beliefs, experiences of the past and expectations for the future, and the influences of their social network. People don't always make choices that others think are the "right" decisions, or the ones they, themselves, would have made in those circumstances. Some people are straightforward in communicating their priorities; others may behave in ways that mask the actual meaning of their response. We must look beyond the apparent to understand the underlying dimensions of the choices that people make and the significance to them of making those choices.

Harry's Story: Asserting His Views

A number of years ago I discovered an interesting article called "The Good Die Younger" (Wacker, 1985). Essentially, Wacker reported research that indicated that people identified by nursing home staff as cooperative and compliant often died sooner than those who were judged as cantankerous and difficult. When I read this article, I thought of Harry, who often spit on the floor and rapped his cane to make his point. He absolutely refused to participate in any planned activities at the nursing home. I did notice that he hung around the lounge before meals, although not to socialize. He liked to position himself to dart to his table when dinner was served—to protect his dessert!

Residents had been making plans for their garden, talking about their gardens of the past, nurturing seedlings, and, generally, getting ready for the big event for several weeks. We were amazed when Harry showed up for the official planting event and commanded the seat with the best view. When an aide asked Harry if he'd like to do some planting, he retreated quickly, rapping his cane and hollering, "If I want to plant, I'll go out to my own farm to plant in the real country dirt!" I managed to get to the patio door to hold it for him as he left, thanked him for coming, and suggested that we could really use the advice of a farmer who knew about real country dirt to make the project a success. He mumbled an obscenity, but I took the fact that he didn't threaten me with his cane as a good sign. Harry never formally worked on the garden project, but he did check on the plants when he didn't think anyone was looking. Harry was a man who knew how to protect his turf and assert his own decisions. He has helped me remember that behavior that appears uncooperative is often, in its own way, a strategy to self-protect and ensure independence.

Beatrice's Story: Maintaining Her Independence

Then there was Beatrice, a retired teacher, who carefully selected and arranged her treasures for her room. Recovery from a broken hip was long and arduous, and Beatrice, herself, concluded that she would be ill-advised to return to her cherished Victorian-style home with its treacherous stairs and second-floor bathroom. Her daughters and daughters-in-law spent several weeks sorting and packing under Beatrice's supervision, getting the house ready to be sold. From Beatrice's perspective, they were encouraging her to consider moving to the Chicago area, rather than staying in the nursing home in her hometown. She struggled with her decision, torn between following her children's advice or her own inclinations.

She described her decision to me in this way, "Don't get me wrong, I love my children and grandchildren, and I know that it would be more convenient if I moved. They wouldn't have to travel so far to see me. But I worry that I would be an inconvenience in their lives—and totally dependent on them for a social connection at that. My friends and my independent life mean the world to me. That's why I've decided to stay here in this town where I've lived all of my life. I can count on visits from my friends and entertaining my book club right here in the party room." During the three years she lived in the nursing home, she was quite the social butterfly, and her family managed "trips home" to see her regularly. I can't help but think that she would have been the first to install a computer with e-mail options had she lived long enough to welcome in the Information Age.

Beatrice was the kind of person who reflected on life, analyzed situations, and then told you exactly what she thought. She had a way of getting to the heart of the matter. One day when she was particularly angry with a staff member who had been offering some unwanted and inappropriate advice, she said, "Sometimes other people presume they know what I want, but they've got it all confused. They're too busy listening to their own thoughts and seem to have forgotten to listen to me. They're old enough to know better, too. As a matter of fact, they're quick to complain when their own kids turn the tables on them." I asked her how she managed people like these. She chuckled as she confided that she used a direct, school-teacher approach to "put them in their place." Some days Beatrice was more pensive in her comments on growing older, and she said things like, "Let me tell you what it's really like to be old. People tend to ignore you, act like what you have to say doesn't matter any more." After I shared that I noticed she continued to speak up, Beatrice's eyes twinkled, and she reported that she'd never been one to give up. She'd always liked a good debate.

Dorothy's Story: Creating Family Dilemmas

Before we had any idea that Alzheimer's disease was lurking in my mother's future, Dorothy experienced a crisis with her diabetes and nearly died when she was visiting with us. My mother concluded on her own that she could no longer stay in the home where she had lived for more than forty years, but she was unclear about how she wanted to proceed. My husband and I urged her to consider moving to Illinois, and she was holding that open as an option. She decided on her plan one day when we were sitting together in my garden. I think the quiet of the garden and the warmth of the sunshine had inspired her. We had just returned from taking a tour of various apartment-style options available in my community, and she was clearly torn between moving to Illinois or locating an option in Minneapolis that would have a built-in system of community-based support. Quite decisively, she directed me, "Go call the Augustana Apartments in Minneapolis. If they have an apartment available, I'll move there. I've always said that's where I'd like to live if I couldn't stay in my own home. I still belong in Minneapolis." And so she made the first in a series of difficult decisions. At that point, my mother had a number of options. As time passed, her options became more and more limited, both by the nature of her physical illness and by her ability to understand. However, with careful planning even within these boundaries, she still was able to lead the way.

I have sometimes wondered if the course of my mother's illness would have been different had I insisted that she move to Illinois at that point in her life. If I had insisted, I believe she would have moved to please me, her only child. I've thought, perhaps we could have avoided the ups and downs of the diabetes she found difficult to control by herself. Perhaps we could have forestalled the onset of cognitive frailty. Then I come to my senses, realize that this outcome is a fantasy, and, put in perspective, I recall the potential deleterious effects of imposing decisions on others, even when we think we have the good of the other person in mind. Keeping a balance in decision-making is difficult for family members—at least it was for me—and I was clearly committed to ensuring that my mother, in so far as possible, remain in charge of the decisions about her life.

Responding to Inherent Challenges

Dilemmas are implicit in honoring self-determination, particularly because of the challenges inherent in complex decision-making. Factors that may influence our role include such things as the legal status of the individual's competence to make decisions, considerations of safety, and limitations imposed by bureaucratic rules and funding shortfalls. We may have to factor in family members—partners, siblings, children, or grandchildren, to name a few—who identify themselves as stakeholders, and who may or may not support their loved one's full participation in decision-making. Mediating differences requires us to balance numerous contingencies, involving others, yet ensuring that the client's voice is heard.

Several modes of interaction may undermine empowerment. One pitfall is acting paternalistically, deciding for others as if we know what is best for them in their situations. Another is maternalism, an approach in which caring behaviors disguise control—not maliciously or intentionally undermining empowerment, rather overpowering the vulnerable individual with resourcefulness (Collopy, 1992). Collopy warns that precisely when "care is beneficent, intrusions upon autonomy can go unchecked, unscrutinized, even unobserved behind the curtain of good intentions" (p. 56). Finally, risks are also inherent in "over respecting" autonomy as those "who 'overrespect' an individual's autonomy run the risk of engaging in benign neglect and underserving the client" (Austin, 1996, p. 93). Somehow we must "strike a balance between the press for autonomous decision making and the imperative of providing a 'safety net' of services" (DuBois & Miley, 2002, p. 435).

Continuing the Conversation

Voices continue to echo in my mind—those stories I've shared and those I have yet to tell. Each time I hear their messages and open myself to their lessons, I learn more about processes of empowerment for older adults—listening to life stories, promoting expertise, and honoring self-determination. At the time I interacted with those people whose stories I have shared in this chapter, I believe our conversations were meaningful to them. Reciprocally, they have given me, and now you, much in return: the wisdom of their perspectives on life and direction about applying an empowerment method to our work with older adults.

Their instruction is timely, as the field of aging services is increasingly prominent by virtue of extraordinary demographic trends. Projections indicate that the proportion of people in the United States sixty-five years of age or older will grow from 13 percent in 2000 to 20 percent of the population by 2030 (Federal Interagency, 2000). The fastest growing segment of the population older than sixty-five are those over eighty-five. Projections predict that 18.2 million people will be eighty-five years or older by 2050, representing an increase of more than 400 percent. In addition, the number of centenarians (people 100 years of age and older) has nearly doubled in the last decade. The worldwide implications of aging cannot be ignored when we consider the population projections for 2150, when approximately one-third of all people will be age sixty and older and one-tenth will be age eighty and older (Mirkin & Weinberger, 2000). Without a doubt, "changes in age distribution have complex social and economic implications at the societal and individual levels" (p. 4).

The intensity of the stories, the increasing numbers of aging adults, and the implications of demographic trends for social and economic change challenge us to explore issues that relate to our perspectives, the older adults with whom we may work, and sociocultural responses to aging. With respect to our own practice as professional social workers, we need to ask questions such as: How do our own perspectives on aging, including remnants of ageism, issues with our own parents or grandparents, unresolved grief, and biases for or against particular options, all influence our ability to work effectively with older adults? What supports do we need to maintain a sense of balance in our perspective, to avoid the pitfalls of paternalism, maternalism, and client abandonment? We must recognize that, in relation to older adults, our work is often embedded in their family relationships, which influence dramatically courses of action. Keeping this in mind, how do we determine the identity of the client, and what does this imply for our interactions with other family members? What is mental competence, and how do the legal nuances of competence impact our work with older adults who are cognitively frail? How do boundaries of decision-making change as decline occurs? What steps ensure that individuals can continue to have voices even in the face of cognitive decline? Finally, with respect to the sociopolitical implications of empowerment, what changes are likely to occur as more older adults are in positions to influence programs and policies? What social justice issues might underlie a narrow focus on "successful" aging? And what are the social and economic implications of changing demographics for individuals and for societies?

Empowerment for older adults provides a means for discovering and utilizing those resources of aging that have heretofore remained hidden and untapped. It underscores the significance of telling and listening to life stories, promoting expertise, and honoring self-determination. Placed in a sociopolitical context, when aging adults join together to speak, the power of their collective voices will be heard as more influential, actions will be taken, and little by little, change will occur, creating a climate that acknowledges and promotes the resources of aging.

References

Austin, C. D. (1996). Aging and long term care. In C. D. Austin & R. W. McClelland (Eds.), *Perspectives on case management practice* (pp. 1–16). Milwaukee, WI: Families International.

Baltes, P. B., & Baltes, M. M. (Eds.). (1990). *Successful aging*. New York: Cambridge University Press.

Bellos, N. (1992). Healthy aging: A new perspective for public policy. *Educational Gerontology, 18,* 111–122.

Carlsson-Ågren, M., Berg, S., & Wenestam, C. G. (1992). Daily life of the oldest old. *Journal of Sociology and Social Welfare, 19*(2), 109–124.

Collopy, B. J. (1992). Autonomy in long term care: Some critical distinctions. In S. M. Rose (Ed.), *Case management and social work practice* (pp. 56–76). New York: Longman.

Dean, R. G. (1993). Constructivism: An approach to clinical practice. *Smith College Studies in Social Work, 63*(2), 127–146.

DuBois, B., & Miley, K. K. (2002). *Social work: An empowering profession* (4th ed.). Boston: Allyn & Bacon.

Erikson, E. (1963). *Childhood and society* (2nd ed.). New York: W. W. Norton.

Erikson, E. H., Erikson, J. M., & Kivnick, H. Q. (1994). *Vital involvement in old age.* New York: W. W. Norton.

Federal Interagency Forum on Age-Related Statistics. (2000). *Older Americans 2000: Key indicators of well-being—Population.* Retrieved September 3, 2000, from the World Wide Web: http://www.agingstats.gov/chartbookw000/population.html

Fisher, B. J., & Specht, D. K. (1999). Successful aging and creativity in later life. *Journal of Aging Studies, 13*(4), 457+. Retrieved September 30, 2000, from InfoTrac database (Expanded Academic ASAP) on the World Wide Web: www.infotrac.galegroup.com

Freedman, J., & Combs, G. (1996). *Narrative therapy: The social construction of preferred realities.* New York: W. W. Norton.

Freund, A. M., & Baltes, P. B. (1998). Selection, optimization, and compensation as strategies of life management: Correlations with subjective indicators of successful aging. *Psychology and Aging, 13*(4), 531–543.

Gergen, K. J. (1999). *An invitation to social construction.* Thousand Oaks, CA: Sage Publications.

Grant, L. D. (1996). Effects of ageism on individual and health care providers' responses to healthy aging. *Health and Social Work, 21*(1), 9–15.

Gutheil, I. A., & Congress, E. (2000). Resiliency in older people: A paradigm for practice. In E. Norman (Ed.), *Resiliency enhancement: Putting the strengths perspective into social work practice* (pp. 40–52). New York: Columbia University Press.

Heil, W. A., & Marks, L. N. (1991). Resourceful aging: Today and tomorrow. *Ageing International, 18*(1), 17–34.

Holstein, M. (1992). Productive aging: A feminist perspective. *Journal of Aging and Social Policy, 4*(3/4), 17–34.

Kivnick, H. Q., & Jernstedt, H. L. (1996). Mama still sparkles: An elder role model in long-term care. *Marriage & Family Review, 24*(1/2), 123–164.

Miley, K. K., O'Melia, M., & DuBois, B. (2001). *Generalist social work practice: An empowering approach* (3rd ed.). Boston: Allyn & Bacon.

Mirkin, B., & Weinberger, M. B. (2000). *The demography of population ageing.* Retrieved October 16, 2000, from the World Wide Web: http://www.org/popin/popdiv/untech/pdf/untech1.pdf

Morrow-Howell, N. (2000). *Productive engagement of older adults: Effects on well-being.* Washington University, Center for Social Development. Retrieved November 19, 2000, from the World Wide Web: http://www.gwb.wustl.edu/users/csd/workingpapers/reportmhowell.pdf

Pryor, H. (1994, August). Theory into practice: Gerontologist Robert Butler shows how research into aging can work. *AARP Bulletin, 35*(9), 12.

Rosen, H. (1996). Meaning-making narratives: Foundations for constructivist and social constructionist psychotherapies. In H. Rosen & K. T. Kuehlwein (Eds.), *Constructing realities: Meaning-making perspectives for psychotherapists* (pp. 3–51). San Francisco: Jossey-Bass Publishers.

Rowe, J. W., & Kahn, R. L. (1997). Successful aging. *The Gerontologist, 37*(4), 433–440.

Rowe, J. W., & Kahn, R. L. (1998). *Successful aging.* New York: Panthenon Books.

Saleebey, D. (1997a). The strengths approach to practice. In D. Saleebey (Ed.), *The strengths perspective in social work practice* (2nd ed., pp. 49–57). New York: Longman.

Saleebey, D. (1997b). Introduction: Power in the people. In D. Saleebey (Ed.), *The strengths perspective in social work practice* (2nd ed., pp. 3–19). New York: Longman.

Scheidt, R. J., & Humpherys, D. R. (1999). Successful aging: What's not to like? *Journal of Applied Gerontology, 18*(3), 277–282. Retrieved January 8, 2001, from EBSCO database (Academic Search Elite) on the World Wide Web: http://www.ehost.com

Schlarch, A. (1994). *Response to Kathleen Woodward's "Telling Stories."* University of California, Berkeley, Center on Aging. Retrieved January 8, 2001, from the World Wide Web: http://socrates.berkeley.edu/~aging/publications.html

Schulz, R., & Heckhausen, J. (1996). A life span model of successful aging. *American Psychologist, 51*(7), 702–714.

Smith, G. C., Kohn, S. J., Savage-Stevens, S. E., Finch, J. F., Ingate, R., & Lim, Y.-O. (2000). The effects of interpersonal and personal agency on perceived control and psychological well-being in adulthood. *The Gerontolgist, 40*(4), 458–469.

Taylor, S. E., Kemeny, M. E., Reed, G. M., Bower, J. E., & Gruenewald, T. L. (2000). Psychological resources, positive illusions, and health. *The American Psychologist, 55*(1), 99–109.

Wacker, R. (1985, December). The good die younger. *Science, 85,* 64, 66, 68.

Webster, J. D. (1999). World views and narrative gerontology: Situation reminiscence behavior within a lifespan perspective. *Journal of Aging Studies, 13*(1), 29–42. Retrieved January 8, 2001, from EBSCO database (Academic Search Elite) on the World Wide Web: http://www.ebscohost.com

White, M., & Epston, D. (1990). *Narrative means to therapeutic ends.* New York: W. W. Norton.

Woodward, K. (1994). *Telling stories: Aging, reminiscence, and the life review.* University of California, Berkeley, Center on Aging. Retrieved January 8, 2001, from the World Wide Web: http://socrates.berkeley.edu/~aging/publications.html

Woolf, L. M. (n. d.). *Effects of age and gender on perceptions of younger and older adults.* Retrieved November 19, 2000, from the World Wide Web: http://www.webster.edu/~woolflm/ageismwoolf.html

Name Index

Subject Index